VOLUME MEASURES

1 tsp	**90ml** (3fl oz)	**300ml** (10fl oz)	**900ml** (1½ pints)
2 tsp	**100ml** (3½fl oz)	**360ml** (12fl oz)	**1 litre** (1¾ pints)
1 tbsp (=3 tsp)	**120ml** (4fl oz)	**400ml** (14fl oz)	**1.2 litres** (2 pints)
2 tbsp	**150ml** (5fl oz)	**450ml** (15fl oz)	**1.4 litres** (2½ pints)
3 tbsp	**200ml** (7fl oz)	**500ml** (16fl oz)	**1.5 litres** (2¾ pints)
4 tbsp = **60ml** (2fl oz)	**240ml** (8fl oz)	**600ml** (1 pint)	**1.7 litres** (3 pints)
75ml (2½fl oz)	**250ml** (8fl oz)	**750ml** (1¼ pints)	**2 litres** (3½ pints)

LIQUID VOLUME MEASURES

½ cup	120ml (4fl oz)
⅔ cup	150ml (5fl oz)
1 cup	250ml (8fl oz)
2 cups	450ml (15fl oz)
2½ cups	600ml (1 pint)
4¼ cups	1 litre (1¾ pints)

DRY MEASURES

1 CUP FRESH BREADCRUMBS	60g	2oz
1 CUP BULGUR WHEAT	115g	4oz
1 CUP FLOUR	115g	4oz
1 CUP COUSCOUS	175g	6oz
1 CUP ICING SUGAR	175g	6oz
1 CUP PEARL BARLEY	200g	7oz
1 CUP BUTTER	225g	8oz
1 CUP UNCOOKED RICE	225g	8oz
1 CUP WHITE/BROWN SUGAR	225g	8oz

MasterChef
KITCHEN
BIBLE

MasterChef
KITCHEN
BIBLE

Top Tips from
John Torode and Gregg Wallace 6

MODERN CLASSIC RECIPES 8

SOUPS 10

EGG AND CHEESE DISHES 20

FISH DISHES 28

MEAT DISHES 38
All About Roast Beef 38
All About Roast Lamb 50
All About Roast Pork 64

POULTRY AND GAME DISHES 70
All About Roast Poultry 70
All About Roast Game Birds 90

PASTA AND RICE DISHES 98

SIDE DISHES 114

DESSERTS 130

CAKES AND BAKES 160

MASTERCHEF RECIPES 180

STARTERS 182

MAIN COURSES 194

DESSERTS 212

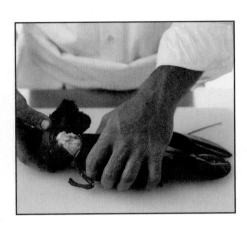

MASTERCHEF KNOW-HOW 242

EQUIPMENT 244

FISH 250

SHELLFISH 276

POULTRY AND GAME BIRDS 288

MEAT 304
Other Meats Cooking Chart 312

VEGETABLES 324
Vegetables Cooking Chart 336

HERBS, SPICES, AND FLAVOURINGS 376

FRUITS AND NUTS 394

EGGS AND DAIRY PRODUCTS 424

RICE, GRAINS, AND PULSES 438

DOUGH, PASTRY, AND CAKE 450

PASTA, NOODLES, AND GNOCCHI 464

SAVOURY SAUCES AND STOCKS 476

Flavour Pairings 492

Index 504

Acknowledgements 512

CONTENTS

JOHN TORODE

To be a better cook, the odd shortcut, tip, or helpful hint is essential. The best tip I can give anyone is that you have to practise – pick a few recipes, and cook them over and over again. Like a piece of music, the more you practise, the better it will be. Soon you will be showing off with your best dish – and that's what exciting and innovative cooking is all about – showing off. Good luck, and as a great golfer once said, "The more I practise the luckier I get!".

Learn the basics, and from there the options are endless. I believe that you should learn to cook 5 things well, and then you will have the ability to refine, redesign, and perfect the basis of a good (soon-to-be) repertoire:

A great roast. Start with chicken, roast potatoes, gravy, stuffing, and vegetables. Learn every time you cook it, season, and taste. That humble roast, with a little work, can be a beautiful thing.

A great steamed sponge pudding and custard. That pudding starts as a basic thing, but add passion fruit to the bottom of the mould or something else – now you know how to make a pudding. Large or small, individual or to share, you choose. And proper custard: hot – delicious, flavoured – more delicious, cold – very delicious, frozen – amazing ice cream.

The best stew you can find a recipe for. It takes time, it's slow cooking, and it's not expensive. A stew is one thing, but with some dumplings it's another, with great mash it's amazing, with a pastry top it's a pie, cooked a bit longer and ripped apart with a fork it's a filling for cannelloni or ravioli.

A great tomato-based pasta sauce, with olive oil and a little garlic, a few shallots, fresh tomatoes, left to melt. Serve with deli-bought ravioli, add some anchovies and olives – yum. Cook some chorizo or spicy sausage and add a handful of clams – a real beauty. Just serve with spaghetti and grated Parmesan or pecorino – simplistic and elegant. Oh and it works beautifully as a pizza topping.

Basic bread dough, one rich in olive oil and quick rising. Great for focaccia, served hot from the oven, sliced and grilled for sandwiches, a simple pizza dough, or top with a scraping of crème fraîche and a sprinkling of smoked bacon and shaved shallots for a French tart.

So – now you are in business!

GREGG WALLACE

The most expensive commodity I know of is knowledge. You either pay somebody clever for it or you learn expensive lessons through your own mistakes. Here are some things I wish someone had told me years ago:

Know your oils. Most of us who cook know we use olive oil for cooking and virgin olive oil for salad dressings. Even though millions of bottles are sold I rarely find anybody who knows what extra virgin and virgin olive oils are. Both are the first press, only oil with less than 1% acidity can be called extra virgin.

Know your spuds. If you want quality potato results you have to find the spud to fit the job. For chips you need starchy, for mash you want floury, for a gratin you need waxy. Two decent all-rounders are the Maris Piper and my favourite, the King Edward. Secondly, a new potato is only new if you can rub the skin off with your thumb; if you can't, it's just a salad potato.

King veg. Asparagus is the undisputed luxury item of the vegetable world, but the stems are far sturdier than the heads. Tie the spears into a bunch with string and boil standing up with the heads out of the water. As the stems boil, the heads steam.

The right kit. Please, please, please use a sharp knife. It is blunt knives that slip – all of my bad cuts come from blunt knives, not sharp ones.

Chocs away. Yes – the correct way to melt chocolate is in a glass bowl on top of a pan of boiling water. This is creating a bain marie, ensuring the delicate chocolate isn't subjected to fierce heat. But I know for a fact you can get the same effect putting chocolate in a microwave on low for a couple of minutes.

Get fruity. The way to use soft fruit out of season is to preserve it in season. For perfect freezing, place each berry on a tray – don't let them touch. Once they are frozen solid you can put them all in a bag together. I promise you that if you do it this way you'll have no mush when you thaw.

Travel with salad. Picnics are wonderful things, but how do you keep your food fresh? (I'm thinking fruits or, particularly, salad leaves.) You can make your own fridge. Take two plastic containers – a big one for your salad and a smaller one that will fit in the bottom of the big one. Fill the smaller one with water, seal it and freeze it, then put it back in the big bowl – you've got a fridge.

Well dressed. A salad is not a salad without dressing. A couple of things to remember: don't put anything acidic (lemon or vinegar for example) onto delicate leaves before combining the acid with oil, otherwise it will cook the leaves. Season the dressing – never season the salad after you've dressed it as the salt and pepper will just stick to the first bit of dressing it finds.

I scream. A completely naughty cheat this, I know, but if you need custard very quickly, melt then heat up vanilla ice cream. It's OK – it's eggs, cream, sugar, and vanilla.

You may not be able to use all these tips straight away, so make space for them in that big brain of yours for use at a later date. One day I promise you, they will come in handy.

Gregg

MODERN
CLASSIC
RECIPES

100 WELL-LOVED MODERN CLASSIC RECIPES THAT GOOD HOME COOKS SHOULD KNOW.

BOUILLABAISSE

ORIGINALLY NOTHING MORE THAN A HUMBLE FISHERMAN'S SOUP USING THE REMAINS OF THE DAY'S CATCH, NOW AN ACCLAIMED DISH. USE THE FISH BONES AND HEADS, AND THE PRAWN SHELLS TO MAKE THE STOCK IF YOU HAVE TIME.

4 tbsp OLIVE OIL

1 ONION, thinly sliced

2 LEEKS, thinly sliced

1 small FENNEL BULB, thinly sliced

2–3 GARLIC CLOVES, finely chopped

4 TOMATOES, skinned, deseeded, and chopped

1 tbsp TOMATO PURÉE

250ml (8fl oz) DRY WHITE WINE

1.5 litres (2¾ pints) FISH STOCK or CHICKEN STOCK

pinch of SAFFRON THREADS

strip of ORANGE ZEST

1 BOUQUET GARNI

SALT and freshly ground BLACK PEPPER

1.35kg (3lb) mixed WHITE AND OILY FISH and SHELLFISH, such as red gurnard, John Dory, monkfish, red mullet, heads and bones removed, peeled raw prawns, and cleaned mussels

2 tbsp PERNOD

8 thin slices of day-old FRENCH BREAD, toasted, to serve

FOR THE ROUILLE

125g (4½oz) MAYONNAISE

1 BIRD'S-EYE CHILLI, deseeded and roughly chopped

4 GARLIC CLOVES, roughly chopped

1 tbsp TOMATO PURÉE

½ tsp SALT

PREPARATION TIME
20 minutes

COOKING TIME
45 minutes

SERVES 4

1 Heat the oil in a large saucepan over a medium heat. Add the onion, leeks, fennel, and garlic and fry gently, stirring frequently, for 5 minutes, or until the vegetables are softened but not coloured. Add the tomatoes, tomato purée, and wine and stir until blended.

2 Add the stock, saffron, orange zest, and bouquet garni. Season to taste with salt and pepper, and bring to the boil. Reduce the heat, partially cover the pan, and simmer for 30 minutes, or until the soup is reduced slightly, stirring occasionally.

3 To make the rouille, place all ingredients into a blender or food processor and process until smooth. Transfer to a bowl, cover with cling film, and chill until required.

4 Just before the liquid finishes simmering, cut the fish into chunks. Remove the orange zest and bouquet garni from the soup and add the fish (but not the shellfish). Reduce the heat to low and let the soup simmer for 5 minutes, then add the shellfish and simmer for further 2–3 minutes, or until all the fish is cooked through, the prawns are pink and the mussels have opened. Stir in the Pernod and season to taste with salt and pepper.

5 To serve, spread each piece of toast with rouille and put 2 slices in the bottom of each bowl. Ladle the soup on top and serve.

MASTERCHEF **FISH** KNOW-HOW: See **Bone a Round Fish through the Stomach** 266

MASTERCHEF **FISH** KNOW-HOW: See **Bone a Round Fish from the Back** 267

MASTERCHEF **SHELLFISH** KNOW-HOW: See **Clean Mussels** 284

MASTERCHEF **SAVOURY SAUCES AND STOCKS** KNOW-HOW: See **Make Fish Stock** 484

GAZPACHO

FOR A REFRESHING, LIGHT TWIST, TRY USING FRESHLY SQUEEZED ORANGE JUICE INSTEAD OF HALF THE OLIVE OIL.

2cm (¾in) thick slice stale BREAD, crusts removed

1kg (2¼lb) TOMATOES, skinned, deseeded, and chopped

1 small CUCUMBER, peeled and chopped,
   plus extra to serve

1 small RED PEPPER, deseeded and chopped,
   plus extra to serve

2 GARLIC CLOVES, crushed

4 tbsp SHERRY VINEGAR

120ml (4fl oz) EXTRA VIRGIN OLIVE OIL,
   plus extra to serve

SALT and freshly ground BLACK PEPPER

1 HARD-BOILED EGG, yolk and white chopped separately

PREPARATION TIME
15 minutes, plus chilling

SERVES 4

1 Soak the bread in cold water for 2 minutes. Drain off excess water, then put the bread in a food processor or blender with the tomato flesh, cucumber, red pepper, garlic, and sherry vinegar. Process until smooth. Pour in the olive oil and process again. Dilute with a little water if too thick. Season to taste with salt and pepper.

2 Transfer the soup to a serving bowl, cover with cling film, and chill for at least 1 hour.

3 When ready to serve, finely chop the extra cucumber and red pepper. Place the cucumber, pepper, and egg yolk and white in individual bowls, and arrange on the table, along with a bottle of olive oil. Ladle the soup into bowls and serve, letting each diner add their own garnish.

LOBSTER BISQUE

YOU CAN RESERVE THE LOBSTER TAIL MEAT, MIX IT WITH DICED AVOCADO, ROCKET, SOME CHILLI, AND LIME JUICE AND SERVE IT ON RYE BREAD AFTER THE SOUP.

1 LOBSTER, cooked,
   about 1kg (2¼lb) in weight
50g (1¾oz) BUTTER
1 ONION, finely chopped
1 CARROT, finely chopped
2 CELERY STICKS, finely chopped
1 LEEK, finely chopped
½ FENNEL BULB, finely chopped
1 BAY LEAF
1 sprig of TARRAGON
2 GARLIC CLOVES, crushed
75g (2½oz) TOMATO PURÉE
4 TOMATOES, roughly chopped
120ml (4fl oz) COGNAC or BRANDY
100ml (3½fl oz) DRY WHITE WINE
   or VERMOUTH
1.7 litres (3 pints) FISH STOCK
120ml (4fl oz) DOUBLE CREAM
SALT and freshly ground BLACK PEPPER
pinch of CAYENNE PEPPER
juice of ½ LEMON
snipped CHIVES, to garnish

PREPARATION TIME
45 minutes

COOKING TIME
1hour 10 minutes

SERVES 4

1 Split the lobster in half, remove the meat from the body, and chop the meat into small pieces. Twist off the claws and legs, break the claws at the joints, and crack the shells with the back of a knife. Chop the shell into rough pieces.

2 Melt the butter in a large saucepan over a medium heat, add the vegetables, herbs, and garlic, and cook gently for 10 minutes, or until softened, stirring occasionally.

3 Add the chopped lobster shells. Stir in the tomato purée, chopped tomatoes, Cognac, white wine, and fish stock. Bring to the boil and simmer for 1 hour.

4 Leave to cool slightly, then ladle into a food processor. Process the soup in short bursts until the shell breaks into very small pieces.

5 Strain the soup through a coarse sieve, pushing as much liquid through as you can. Then pass the soup again through a fine mesh sieve before returning to the heat.

6 Bring to the boil, add the reserved lobster meat and the cream, then season to taste with salt and pepper and add cayenne pepper and lemon juice to taste. Serve in warm bowls, garnished with chives.

MINESTRONE

THIS SUBSTANTIAL SOUP MAKES A GREAT LUNCH OR SUPPER DISH, AND YOU CAN
ADD WHATEVER VEGETABLES ARE IN SEASON.

100g (3½oz) DRIED WHITE
   CANNELLINI BEANS
2 tbsp OLIVE OIL
2 CELERY STICKS, finely chopped
2 CARROTS, finely chopped
1 ONION, finely chopped
400g (14oz) can CHOPPED TOMATOES
750ml (1¼ pints) CHICKEN STOCK
   or VEGETABLE STOCK
SALT and freshly ground BLACK PEPPER
60g (2oz) small SHORT-CUT PASTA
4 tbsp chopped FLAT-LEAF PARSLEY
40g (1½oz) PARMESAN or GRANA PADANO CHEESE,
   finely grated

PREPARATION TIME
20 minutes, plus soaking

COOKING TIME
1 hour 45 minutes

SERVES 4–6

1 Put the cannellini beans in a large bowl, cover with cold water, and leave to soak for at least 6 hours or overnight.

2 Drain the beans, place in a large saucepan, cover with cold water, and bring to the boil over a high heat, skimming the surface as necessary. Boil for 10 minutes, then reduce the heat to low, partially cover the pan, and leave the beans to simmer for 1 hour, or until just tender. Drain well and set aside.

3 Heat the oil in the rinsed-out pan over a medium heat. Add the celery, carrots, and onion and fry, stirring occasionally, for 5 minutes or until softened but not browned. Stir in the beans, the tomatoes with their juice, the stock, and season to taste with salt and pepper. Bring to the boil, stirring, then cover and leave to simmer for 20 minutes.

4 Add the pasta and simmer for a further 10–15 minutes or until cooked but still firm to the bite. Stir in the parsley and half the cheese, then adjust the seasoning. Serve hot, sprinkled with the remaining cheese.

ROAST TOMATO SOUP

TRY ROASTING A RED PEPPER WITH THE TOMATOES, REMOVE THE BLACKENED SKIN AND SEEDS AND PURÉE WITH THE REST. ADD A PINCH OF DRIED CHILLI FLAKES TOO.

8 PLUM TOMATOES, about 675g (1 ½ lb)
  in total, quartered

1 RED ONION, cut into 8 wedges

2 GARLIC CLOVES, unpeeled

3 tbsp OLIVE OIL

SEA SALT and freshly ground
  BLACK PEPPER

1 litre (1 ¾ pints) hot VEGETABLE STOCK

3 tbsp SUN-DRIED TOMATO PASTE

PREPARATION TIME
10 minutes

COOKING TIME
30 minutes

SERVES 4

1 Preheat the oven to 180°C (350°F/Gas 4). Put the tomatoes, onion, and garlic on baking trays covered with baking parchment. Drizzle with the oil, and season well with sea salt and freshly ground black pepper. Roast until they are soft, caramelized, and slightly browned – allow 10–15 minutes for the garlic, 15–20 minutes for the onion, and 25 minutes for the tomatoes. Squeeze the garlic from their skins once they have cooled slightly.

2 Transfer to a blender, add the stock and tomato paste, then whiz until smooth but still slightly chunky. Season with sea salt and freshly ground black pepper, reheat gently, and serve hot.

VICHYSSOISE

DESPITE ITS FRENCH NAME, THIS SILKY, SMOOTH CHILLED SOUP ORIGINATES FROM AMERICA AND CAN BE SERVED HOT. TRY SWEET POTATO WITH THE LEEKS, TOO.

30g (1oz) BUTTER

3 large LEEKS, green ends discarded, finely sliced

2 POTATOES, about 175g (6oz) in total,
   peeled and chopped

1 CELERY STICK, roughly chopped

1.2 litres (2 pints) fresh
   VEGETABLE STOCK

SALT and freshly ground BLACK PEPPER

150ml (5floz) DOUBLE CREAM, plus
   extra for garnish

2 tbsp snipped CHIVES, to serve

PREPARATION TIME
15 minutes

COOKING TIME
45 minutes

SERVES 4

1 Heat the butter in a heavy saucepan over a medium heat and add the leeks. Press a piece of damp greaseproof paper on top, cover, and cook, shaking gently from time to time for 15 minutes, or until the leeks are softened and golden.

2 Add the potatoes, celery, and stock, and season with salt and pepper. Bring to the boil, stirring, then cover and simmer for 30 minutes, or until the vegetables are tender.

3 Remove the pan from the heat and leave to cool slightly, then process in a blender until very smooth, in batches if necessary. Season to taste with salt and pepper, and allow the soup to cool completely before stirring in the cream. Chill for at least 3 hours before serving.

4 To serve, pour into serving bowls. Drizzle a little cream over the top of each, and sprinkle with chives and a grinding of black pepper.

EGGS BENEDICT

TRY PUTTING HAM OR SMOKED SALMON ON THE MUFFINS BEFORE THE EGGS.

8 large EGGS
4 ENGLISH MUFFINS
BUTTER, for spreading
FOR THE HOLLANDAISE
2 tbsp WHITE WINE VINEGAR
4 EGG YOLKS
115g (4oz) BUTTER, melted
SALT and freshly ground BLACK PEPPER
juice of ½ LEMON

PREPARATION TIME
20 minutes

COOKING TIME
20 minutes

SERVES 4

1 First make the Hollandaise sauce. Heat the vinegar in a small pan and allow to bubble until it reduces by half. Remove from the heat, add 2 tbsp water, then whisk in the egg yolks one at a time.

2 Return the pan to a very low heat and whisk continuously until the mixture is thick and light. Remove from the heat and gradually whisk in the melted butter. Season to taste with salt and pepper, and stir in the lemon juice.

3 Fill 2 large saucepans with boiling water to a depth of 5cm (2in). When tiny bubbles appear at the bottom of the pan, carefully crack 4 eggs into each pan.

4 Leave the pans on the heat for 1 minute, then remove and let the eggs sit in the hot water for exactly 6 minutes. Remove the eggs, using a slotted spoon, and drain on kitchen paper.

5 Meanwhile, preheat the grill on its highest setting, split each muffin in half, and toast both sides.

6 Butter each muffin half and place 2 on each serving plate. Top each half with a poached egg and spoon the Hollandaise sauce over the top.

OMELETTE AUX FINES HERBES

TRY ADDING SOME GIROLLES, OR OTHER WILD MUSHROOMS, SAUTÉED IN A LITTLE BUTTER FIRST, TO THE COOKED OMELETTE BEFORE FOLDING.

1½ tbsp each chopped CHIVES, FLAT-LEAF PARSLEY,
    TARRAGON, and CHERVIL
12 EGGS
100g (3½ oz) BUTTER
SALT and freshly ground BLACK PEPPER
a few CHIVE STALKS, to garnish

PREPARATION TIME
5 minutes

COOKING TIME
6 minutes

SERVES 4

1 Mix the herbs together. Heat a good omelette pan and melt a quarter of the butter.

2 For each omelette, break 3 eggs into a small bowl and beat them lightly with a fork (do not whisk them as they will scramble). Add some seasoning and a quarter of the mixed chopped herbs. Pour into the warmed omelette pan. As the omelette starts to set around the outside, draw the set egg into the centre and tilt the pan so that the raw egg fills the space. When almost set, stop stirring, and cook for a further 30 seconds until the omelette is golden brown underneath, but the top is still creamy.

3 Fold the omelette by tilting the pan and shuffling the omelette forward – it should roll up like a large cigar. Roll it onto a warm plate and garnish with a few fresh chive stalks on the side. Repeat for the remaining 3 omelettes, melting fresh butter before cooking each one.

CROQUE MONSIEUR

THIS IS GOOD WITH SOME THINLY SLICED TOMATO AND TORN BASIL ON THE HAM.

400g (14oz) GRUYÈRE CHEESE
60g (2oz) BUTTER, plus extra for spreading
2 tbsp PLAIN FLOUR
2 tsp DIJON MUSTARD
150ml (5fl oz) MILK
8 slices of WHITE SANDWICH BREAD
8 thin slices of HAM

PREPARATION TIME
15 minutes

COOKING TIME
10 minutes

SERVES 4

1 Cut 115g (4oz) of the cheese into thin slices and grate the rest.

2 Melt the butter in a saucepan over a low heat. Remove from the heat and stir in the flour. Return to the hob and cook for 1 minute. Remove from the heat again and stir in the mustard and milk. Return to the hob and cook, stirring until thick and smooth. Stir in the grated cheese, and set aside until ready to use.

3 Toast 4 of the bread slices on 1 side only. Turn over and spread the untoasted sides lightly with butter and top with the ham and cheese slices. Press the remaining 4 slices of bread on top and spread with the cheese mixture.

4 Grill until the cheese is bubbling and golden brown. Serve at once.

CHEESE SOUFFLÉ

THE MOST POPULAR SAVOURY SOUFFLÉ IS A SIMPLE CHEESE ONE. ANY HARD CHEESE CAN BE USED BUT PICK ONE WITH A FAIRLY STRONG FLAVOUR, SUCH AS MATURE CHEDDAR, OR A MIXTURE OF GRUYÈRE AND PARMESAN.

45g (1½oz) BUTTER

45g (1½oz) PLAIN FLOUR

225ml (8fl oz) MILK

SALT and freshly ground PEPPER

125g (4½oz) MATURE CHEDDAR CHEESE, grated

½ tsp FRENCH MUSTARD

5 large EGGS, separated

1 tbsp grated PARMESAN CHEESE

PREPARATION TIME
20 minutes

COOKING TIME
30–35 minutes

SERVES 4

1 Grease a 1.2 litre (2 pint) soufflé dish. Melt the butter in a small saucepan, stir in the flour until smooth, and cook over a medium heat for 1 minute. Whisk in the milk until blended, then bring to the boil, stirring constantly, until thickened and smooth. Remove the pan from the heat, season to taste with salt and pepper, and stir in the cheese and mustard.

2 Gradually stir in 4 of the egg yolks into the cheese. Save the remaining egg yolk for another recipe.

3 Preheat the oven to 190°C (375°F/Gas 5) and put a baking tray in the oven. In a large, clean bowl, whisk all the egg whites, until stiff peaks form. Stir 1 tbsp of the egg whites into the cheese mixture to "loosen" it, then fold in the rest using a large metal spoon.

4 Transfer the mixture to the soufflé dish and sprinkle the Parmesan over the top. Place the dish on the baking tray and bake for 25–30 minutes, or until the soufflé is puffed and golden brown. Serve at once.

QUICHE LORRAINE

GRIDDLED ASPARAGUS OR SAUTÉED MUSHROOMS ARE A GOOD VEGETARIAN
SUBSTITUTE FOR BACON.

FOR THE PASTRY

225g (8oz) PLAIN FLOUR, plus extra
   for dusting
115g (4oz) BUTTER, cubed
1 EGG YOLK

FOR THE FILLING

200g (7oz) LARDONS
1 ONION, finely chopped
75g (2½oz) GRUYÈRE CHEESE, grated
4 large EGGS, lightly beaten
150ml (5fl oz) DOUBLE CREAM
150ml (5fl oz) MILK
freshly ground BLACK PEPPER

PREPARATION TIME
35 minutes, plus chilling

COOKING TIME
35 minutes

SERVES 4–6

1 To make the pastry, place the flour and butter in a food processor and blend until the mixture resembles fine crumbs. Add the egg yolk and 3–4 tbsp of chilled water, enough to make a smooth dough. Turn out on a floured surface and knead briefly. Alternatively, rub the butter into the flour with your fingers until crumbly, then add the egg yolk and water. Cover and chill for at least 30 minutes. Preheat the oven to 190°C (375°F/Gas 5).

2 On a lightly floured surface, roll out the pastry and line a 23cm (9in) deep flan tin, pressing the dough to the sides. Prick the base of the pastry and line with greaseproof paper and baking beans. Bake blind for 12 minutes, then remove the paper and beans, and bake for a further 10 minutes, or until lightly golden.

3 Meanwhile, heat a large frying pan and dry-fry the lardons for 3–4 minutes. Add the onion, fry for a further 2–3 minutes, then spread the onions and bacon over the pastry case. Add the cheese.

4 Whisk together the eggs, cream, milk, and black pepper, and pour into the pastry case. Place the tin on a baking tray and bake for 25–30 minutes, or until golden and just set. Allow to set, then slice and serve while still hot.

MASTERCHEF **DOUGH, PASTRY, AND CAKE** KNOW-HOW: See **Blind Bake** 460

PANCETTA WITH SCALLOPS

THIS IS ALSO GOOD WITH FRESH LIME SQUEEZED OVER TO CUT THROUGH THE RICH SALTINESS OF THE PANCETTA, AND A DUSTING OF DRIED CHILLI FLAKES TO ADD KICK.

a knob of BUTTER

1 tbsp OLIVE OIL, plus extra for drizzling

12 fresh KING or QUEEN SCALLOPS

150g (5½oz) PANCETTA, cubed

PREPARATION TIME
5 minutes

COOKING TIME
10 minutes

SERVES 4

1 Heat a non-stick frying pan over a medium-high heat. Add the butter and 1 tbsp of olive oil.

2 Season the scallops and add to the pan. Sear for 1–2 minutes on one side until golden, then turn over and cook on the other side for 1–2 minutes more, turning the first scallop that went into the pan first and quickly working your way to the last one. Remove from the pan with a slotted spoon, and set aside to keep warm.

3 Add a drizzle of olive oil to the same pan, tip in the pancetta, and cook for 5–8 minutes until crispy. When cooked, tip over the scallops to serve, along with any juices from the pan. Serve immediately.

LOBSTER THERMIDOR

THIS IRRESISTIBLY INDULGENT SEAFOOD DISH IS THOUGHT TO BE NAMED IN HONOUR OF A PLAY CALLED *THERMIDOR* THAT OPENED IN 1894 IN PARIS.

2 cooked LOBSTERS, about 675g (1½lb) each

PAPRIKA, to sprinkle

LEMON wedges, to serve

FOR THE SAUCE

30g (1oz) BUTTER

2 SHALLOTS, finely chopped

120ml (4fl oz) WHITE WINE

120ml (4fl oz) FISH STOCK

150ml (5fl oz) DOUBLE CREAM

½ tsp made ENGLISH MUSTARD

1 tbsp LEMON JUICE

2 tbsp PARSLEY, chopped

2 tsp TARRAGON, chopped

SALT and freshly ground BLACK PEPPER

75g (2½oz) GRUYÈRE CHEESE, grated

PREPARATION TIME
25 minutes

COOKING TIME
20 minutes

SERVES 4

1 Cut the lobsters in half lengthways. Remove the meat from the claws and tail, along with any coral or meat from the head. Cut the meat into bite-sized pieces. Clean out the shells and reserve.

2 To prepare the sauce, melt the butter in a small saucepan, add the shallots, and fry gently until softened but not browned. Add the wine and boil for 2–3 minutes, or until the liquid is reduced by half.

3 Add the stock and cream and boil rapidly, stirring, until reduced and slightly thickened. Stir in the mustard, lemon juice, and herbs, then season to taste with salt and pepper. Stir in half the cheese.

4 Preheat the grill on its highest setting. Add the lobster meat to the sauce, then divide between the lobster shells. Top with the remaining cheese.

5 Place the lobsters on a foil-lined grill pan and grill for 2–3 minutes, or until bubbling and golden. Sprinkle with a little paprika and serve hot with lemon wedges.

MOULES MARINIÈRES

GIVE THIS DISH AN EXTRA TWIST BY ADDING SOME CHOPPED FENNEL, CELERY, OR CARROT WITH THE ONION AND A GOOD SPLASH OF PERNOD WITH THE WINE.

60g (2oz) BUTTER
2 ONIONS, finely chopped
3.6kg (8lb) fresh MUSSELS, cleaned
2 GARLIC CLOVES, crushed
600ml (1 pint) DRY WHITE WINE
4 BAY LEAVES
2 sprigs of THYME
Freshly ground BLACK PEPPER
2–4 tbsp chopped PARSLEY

PREPARATION TIME
20 minutes

COOKING TIME
10 minutes

SERVES 4

1 Melt the butter in a very large heavy saucepan, add the onion, and fry gently until softened but not browned. Add the mussels, garlic, wine, bay leaves, and thyme, and season to taste with salt and pepper. Cover, bring to the boil, and cook for 5–6 minutes, or until the mussels have opened, shaking the pan frequently. If you do not have a large enough saucepan for all the mussels, cook them in 2 pans instead.

2 Remove the open mussels with a slotted spoon, discarding any that remain closed. Transfer the mussels to warmed bowls, cover, and keep warm.

3 Strain the liquid into a pan and bring to the boil. Season to taste with pepper, add the parsley, pour it over the mussels, and serve at once.

MASTERCHEF **SHELLFISH** KNOW-HOW: See **Clean Mussels** 284

SALAD NIÇOISE

TRY USING WELL-DRAINED CANNED TUNA, BROKEN INTO LARGE FLAKES, INSTEAD OF FRESH STEAKS IF TIME IS SHORT.

12 baby NEW POTATOES, halved

150g (5½oz) GREEN BEANS, trimmed

4 x 150g (5½oz) TUNA STEAKS

150ml (5fl oz) EXTRA VIRGIN OLIVE OIL,
    plus extra for brushing

SALT and freshly ground BLACK PEPPER

2 tsp DIJON MUSTARD

1 GARLIC CLOVE, finely chopped

3 tbsp WHITE WINE VINEGAR

juice of ½ LEMON

8 ANCHOVY FILLETS IN OLIVE OIL, drained

1 RED ONION, finely sliced

250g (9oz) PLUM TOMATOES, quartered lengthways

12 BLACK OLIVES

2 ROMAINE LETTUCE HEARTS, trimmed and torn
    into pieces

8–10 BASIL LEAVES

4 EGGS, hard-boiled

PREPARATION TIME
25 minutes

COOKING TIME
10 minutes

SERVES 4

1 Put the potatoes in a saucepan of lightly salted water, bring to the boil and boil for 6 minutes. Add the beans and boil a further 3–4 minutes or until just tender. Drain and quickly place the vegetables into a bowl of ice water.

2 Preheat a ridged griddle pan over a medium-high heat. Brush the tuna steaks with 1–2 tbsp olive oil and season to taste with salt and pepper. Sear the tuna steaks for 2 minutes on each side. The centres will still be slightly pink. Set the tuna aside. Drain the potatoes and beans.

3 Meanwhile, to make the vinaigrette, whisk together the Dijon mustard, garlic, vinegar, olive oil, and lemon juice. Season to taste with salt and pepper.

4 Place the green beans, anchovies, onion, tomatoes, olives, lettuce, and basil in a large bowl. Drizzle with the vinaigrette and gently toss.

5 Divide the salad between 4 plates. Peel and quarter each egg and add them to the plates. Cut each tuna steak in half and arrange both halves on top of the salad.

SALMON FISHCAKES

FOR A DELICIOUS ACCOMPANIMENT, TRY SERVING THESE WITH ROUILLE.

450g (1lb) POTATOES, cubed
900g (2lb) SALMON FILLETS, skinned and boned
1 ONION, halved
2–3 BAY LEAVES
1 tsp BLACK PEPPERCORNS
4 SPRING ONIONS, finely chopped
2 tbsp HORSERADISH CREAM
SALT and freshly ground BLACK PEPPER
juice and zest of 1 LEMON
large handful of DILL, chopped
pinch of CAYENNE PEPPER

FOR THE COATING
225g (8oz) fresh BREADCRUMBS
2 tbsp snipped CHIVES (optional)
2 tbsp chopped PARSLEY (optional)
PLAIN FLOUR, for coating
2 EGGS, beaten
SUNFLOWER OIL, for frying

PREPARATION TIME
30 minutes, plus cooling and chilling

COOKING TIME
30 minutes

SERVES 6

1 Place the potatoes in a saucepan of cold water and boil for 20 minutes, or until very tender. Drain and mash. Set aside.

2 Place the salmon in cold water with the onion, bay leaves, and peppercorns. Bring to the boil, simmer for 2 minutes, then turn off the heat and leave to cool for 20 minutes. Drain well, discarding the cooking liquids, and cool.

3 Flake the salmon into a large bowl. Fold in the cooled mashed potatoes and all the other fishcake ingredients. Mix well and shape into 12 round cakes. Ideally, chill for 1 hour before coating.

4 Thoroughly mix the breadcrumbs with the herbs (if using). Put the flour, eggs, and breadcrumbs on separate plates and roll the salmon cakes in flour, then egg, then breadcrumbs.

5 Heat the sunflower oil in a frying pan and fry the fishcakes for 3–4 minutes on each side, or until crisp and hot through. Drain on kitchen paper and serve while hot.

MASTERCHEF **FISH** KNOW-HOW: See **Bone a Round Fish through the Stomach** 266
MASTERCHEF **FISH** KNOW-HOW: See **Bone a Round Fish from the Back** 267
MASTERCHEF **FISH** KNOW-HOW: See **Skin a Fillet** 271

SEA BASS IN A SALT CRUST

YOU CAN STUFF THE BODY CAVITY WITH FRESH THYME SPRIGS BEFORE BAKING. SERVE WITH AIOLI (GARLIC MAYONNAISE) AND BABY NEW POTATOES.

1 whole SEA BASS, about 1.3–2kg (3–4½lbs),
  trimmed and gutted, but not scaled

1kg (2.2lbs) COARSE SEA SALT

1–2 EGG WHITES

splash of WATER

PREPARATION TIME
5 minutes

COOKING TIME
22–25 minutes

SERVES 4

1 Preheat the oven to 220°C (425°F/Gas 7). Rinse the fish inside and out and pat dry with kitchen paper. Spread a layer of salt onto a large piece of foil on a baking tray. Lay the fish on top. Moisten the remaining salt with the egg whites and a splash of water if necessary. Pack this mixture on the fish to completely encase it.

2 Bake in the oven for 22–25 minutes. Lift the fish onto a serving dish. Take to the table and carefully chip off any remaining salt crust. Using clean utensils, peel away the skin and serve the fish straight from the bone.

FISHERMAN'S PIE

THIS IS DELICIOUS WITH SWEET POTATO MASH INSTEAD OF ORDINARY POTATOES, OR TRY USING COOKED SLICED WAXY POTATOES, SUCH AS NICOLA. BRUSH THEM WITH MELTED BUTTER, THEN SPRINKLE WITH GRATED PARMESAN BEFORE BAKING.

500g (1lb 2oz) FLOURY POTATOES, such as KING EDWARD
  or MARIS PIPER, peeled and cut into chunks
450ml (15fl oz) MILK
100g (3½oz) BUTTER, plus extra for topping
SALT and freshly ground BLACK PEPPER
300g (10oz) raw PRAWNS, shells on
400g (14oz) fresh HADDOCK fillets
200g (7oz) un-dyed SMOKED HADDOCK fillets
4 BLACK PEPPERCORNS, lightly crushed
1 BAY LEAF
several sprigs of FLAT-LEAF PARSLEY
4 tbsp PLAIN FLOUR
squeeze of LEMON juice
2 tbsp DOUBLE CREAM
4 tbsp chopped FLAT-LEAF PARSLEY
pinch of CAYENNE PEPPER

PREPARATION TIME
25 minutes

COOKING TIME
50 minutes–1 hour

SERVES 4

1 Place the potatoes in a large saucepan with cold salted water. Boil for 10–15 minutes, or until the potatoes are tender when pierced with a knife; drain well. Mash until smooth, then beat in 150ml (5fl oz) of the milk and 60g (2oz) of the butter. Season to taste with salt and pepper. Set aside.

2 Meanwhile, remove the prawn heads and shells and reserve the shells. Then de-vein the prawns and set aside.

3 Put the fresh and smoked fish in a frying pan with the remaining milk. Bring to a gentle simmer, and simmer for 10 minutes, or until the flesh flakes easily. Use a slotted spoon to remove the fish from the pan and set aside. Add the prawn shells, peppercorns, bay leaf, and parsley sprigs to the milk and simmer over a very low heat for 10 minutes.

4 Meanwhile, preheat the oven to 220°C (425°F/Gas 7). Melt the remaining butter in a saucepan over a medium heat. Sprinkle in the flour and cook, stirring, for 1 minute. Remove from the heat. Strain the milk and gradually stir into the butter mixture. Return to the heat and simmer until the sauce thickens, stirring all the time. Stir in the lemon juice and cream, and season to taste with salt and pepper. Stir in the chopped parsley, cayenne, and prawns, and flake in the fish, discarding skin and any bones.

5 Spoon the fish mixture into the pie dish, top with the mashed potatoes, and dot with a little extra butter. Place the dish on a baking tray and bake for 20–25 minutes, or until the topping is golden and the filling is hot when you test the centre with a knife. Remove the pie from the oven and serve immediately.

MASTERCHEF **FISH** KNOW-HOW: See **Bone a Round Fish through the Stomach** 266
MASTERCHEF **FISH** KNOW-HOW: See **Bone a Round Fish from the Back** 267
MASTERCHEF **FISH** KNOW-HOW: See **Skin a Fillet** 271
MASTERCHEF **SHELLFISH** KNOW-HOW: See **Prepare Prawns** 284

ALL ABOUT

ROAST
BEEF

RICH, HEARTY, AND, IF COOKED
CORRECTLY, MELT-IN-THE-MOUTH,
ROAST BEEF IS A TRUE CLASSIC.

ROAST RIB OF BEEF

PREPARATION TIME
10 minutes

COOKING TIME
1 hour

**SERVES 4,
PLUS
LEFTOVERS**

2.25kg (5lb) RIB OF BEEF, bone in (use 2 ribs)

OLIVE OIL, to coat

SALT and freshly ground BLACK PEPPER

1–2 tbsp WHOLEGRAIN MUSTARD

1 Preheat the oven to 200°C (400°F/Gas 6). Rub the beef with olive oil and season with salt and black pepper.

2 Sit the beef in a roasting tin with the bones on the underside, and rub the mustard over the fatty area. Roast in the oven for about 15 minutes until it begins to brown, then reduce the oven temperature to 180°C (350°F/Gas 4). Roast for a further 1 hour, or until cooked to your liking.

3 Remove the beef from the oven and leave to rest in a warm place for about 20 minutes. Slice and serve with roast potatoes, Yorkshire pudding, horseradish, and seasonal vegetables of your choice. Remember to save your beef bones for making stock.

BEEF ESSENTIALS

USE THIS CHART TO IDENTIFY THE BEST BEEF CUTS FOR ROASTING, THEN ENSURE
YOU PREPARE YOUR MEAT FOR MAXIMUM FLAVOUR.

BEEF ROASTING CHART

CUT	DESCRIPTION
Rump/popeseye	From the top of the leg, this has a coarser grain than sirloin but nevertheless yields a good roasting joint. Rump steak is preferred by many to sirloin for its fat content.
Topside/top rump	Boneless, less expensive, and leaner than sirloin but still good for roasting and grilling/frying. When sliced very thinly it is called minute steak.
Sirloin	Tender and marbled with fat, this yields one of the most popular steaks and the best roasting joint of beef on the bone, with a covering of fat. Without the bone, this joint cooks a little quicker.
Fillet	Extremely tender, but can be very lean. The whole fillet, the centre portion called Châteaubriand, and the tapering end or tail are usually roasted but can also be braised. Steaks are often cut thicker, so adjust cooking times.
Ribeye	The trimmed main muscle from the forerib yields a good marbled joint and a tender steak (ribeye/entrecôte).
Brisket	The element of fat makes it a good braising joint. Also good for curing. Slices can be fried but must be served pink or they will toughen.
Forerib	From the shoulder end of the sirloin, this is a less expensive, but excellent bone-in joint for roasting and braising.
Silverside	For braising, this lean joint needs moisture to prevent it from drying out. Slices are suitable for quick cooking only if served pink; sometimes sliced thinly into minute steaks.
T-bone steak	A large, tender cut, including the sirloin and fillet on either side of the bone.
Flank/skirt	Has long fibres and connective tissue so needs either slow cooking or quick frying. Cut across the grain. If flash-fried it must be served very pink or it will toughen.
Thick flank and thin flank	These cuts can be rolled into a joint, sliced, or diced for braising and stewing, or minced.
Rib/short rib/runner	Chunks of rib bone with meat and fat attached. Stew to make a hearty, rustic dish.
Chuck/blade	With a variety of marbling and connective tissue, these shoulder cuts are superb for braising, stewing, and mincing.

ROAST

Rump joint: 190°C (375°F/Gas 5). 20 min per 450g (1lb) plus 20 min for rare; 25 min per 450g (1lb) plus 25 min for medium; 30 min per 450g (1lb) plus 30 min for well-done.

Roast topside joint as rump joint.

Sirloin joint bone-in: Preheat oven to 230°C (450°F/Gas 8). Roast for 25 min. Reduce heat to 190°C (375°F/Gas 5) and roast 12–15 min per 450g (1lb) for rare; 20 min per 450g (1lb) for medium; 25 min per 450g (1lb) for well-done. Rest 20–30 min. Boneless sirloin joint: Preheat oven to 190°C (375°F/Gas 5). Roast 20 min per 450g (1lb) plus 20 min for rare; 25 min per 450g (1lb) plus 25 min for medium; 30 min per 450g (1lb) plus 30 min for well-done. Rest 20–30 min.

Whole fillet, Châteaubriand, and fillet tail: Preheat oven to 230°C (450°F/Gas 8). Brown meat in hot oil in a frying pan, then place in oven. Roast for 10–12 min per 450g (1lb) for rare; 12–15 min per 450g (1lb) for medium; 14–16 min per 450g (1lb) for well-done. Rest 10 min.

Roast ribeye joint as rump joint.

Brisket joint: Preheat oven to 180°C (350°F/Gas 4). Pot-roast for 30–40 min per 450g (lb) plus 30–40 min.

Roast forerib joint as bone-in sirloin joint.

Not recommended.

Not recommended.

Not recommended.

Not recommended.

Not recommended.

Not recommended.

MAXIMIZE FLAVOUR

1 When preparing beef for roasting, remove the meat from the refrigerator in advance to allow it to come to room temperature. Preheat the oven. Brush the meat with oil and scatter over fresh herbs, such as thyme or rosemary. Alternatively, you could make multiple cuts into the fat and stick slivers of garlic and herbs inside. Position the meat, rib-side down, in a roasting tin and place in the oven.

2 After 20 minutes, reduce the oven temperature (see chart, left), then continue roasting for the calculated amount of time (approximately 2 hours or more, depending on the size), basting occasionally to keep the meat moist and flavourful.

BEEF ESSENTIALS

IT'S IMPORTANT TO LEAVE YOUR MEAT TO REST – AND YOU CAN USE THE RESTING
TIME TO PERFECT THE CLASSIC ROAST BEEF TRIMMINGS.

TEST AND REST

The most accurate way to test that your roast is
done is by inserting a meat thermometer (50°C/120°F
for medium rare). Before carving, leave the roast to
stand for 15–30 minutes, covered with kitchen foil.
Letting the meat rest for 15–30 minutes after
roasting allows the muscles to relax, so the juices are
retained within the meat and carving is easier. The
meat will not go cold during this time – as long as it is
covered and not cut into, it will stay hot inside. This
leaves plenty of time for you to turn your attention to
the all-important trimmings.

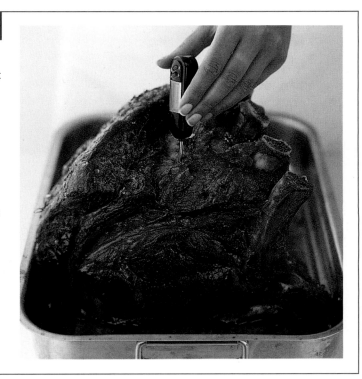

YORKSHIRE PUDDINGS

PREPARATION TIME	COOKING TIME	SERVES 6
20 minutes	30 minutes	

125g (4½oz) PLAIN FLOUR

a pinch of SALT

2 EGGS

300ml (10fl oz) MILK

1–2 tbsp SUNFLOWER OIL or CORN OIL

1 Preheat the oven to 220°C (425°F/Gas 7). Sift the
flour into a bowl and add the salt. Make a well, pour in
the eggs and a little milk. Stir the mixture, adding the
flour gradually, then the remaining milk. Whisk with a
balloon whisk, then refrigerate for 30 minutes.

2 Add a little oil to each hole of the bun tin and put in
the oven for 5 minutes. Remove, then pour in the batter.
Cook for 20–30 minutes, until risen and crisp.

CRISPY ROAST POTATOES

PREPARATION TIME
25 minutes

COOKING TIME
40 minutes

SERVES 4

900g (2lb) FLOURY POTATOES, such as Maris Piper,
   peeled and quartered
SEA SALT
1 tbsp PLAIN FLOUR
4 tsp OLIVE OIL

1 Preheat the oven to 220°C (425F/Gas7). Put the potatoes in a pan of salted water, boil then "nearly" cook over a medium heat for 10–15 minutes. Drain, then return to the pan.

2 Add the flour, put the lid on, and shake the pan. Put the oil in a large roasting tin, and pop it in the oven until hot. Remove from the oven and add the potatoes one by one, turning each in the oil. Add the salt and return to the oven for 30–40 minutes, until golden.

HORSERADISH SAUCE

PREPARATION TIME
10 minutes

**MAKES
250ML
(8FL OZ)**

75g (2½oz) fresh HORSERADISH, grated
1 tsp made ENGLISH MUSTARD
1 tbsp WHITE WINE VINEGAR
1 tsp CASTER SUGAR
juice of ½ LEMON
150ml (5fl oz) DOUBLE CREAM
SALT and freshly ground BLACK PEPPER

1 Put all the ingredients in a large bowl and whisk to a soft peak consistency by hand, or with an electric hand whisk. Season to taste with salt and pepper.

2 Spoon into a serving bowl and chill until you are ready to serve.

BEEF STROGONOFF

SERVE THIS ON A BED OF RICE OR BUTTERED NOODLES WITH A GREEN SALAD.

675g (1½lb) FILLET STEAK, or RUMP, or SIRLOIN, trimmed

3 tbsp PLAIN FLOUR

SALT and freshly ground BLACK PEPPER

1 tbsp PAPRIKA, plus extra for sprinkling

60g (2oz) BUTTER or 4 tbsp OLIVE OIL

1 ONION, thinly sliced

225g (8oz) CHESTNUT MUSHROOMS, sliced

300ml (10fl oz) SOURED CREAM or CRÈME FRAÎCHE

1 tbsp FRENCH MUSTARD

LEMON JUICE

PREPARATION TIME
15 minutes

COOKING TIME
25 minutes

SERVES 4

1 Thinly slice the steak into 5cm (2in) strips. Season the flour with salt, pepper, and paprika, then coat the beef strips in the flour. Heat a deep frying pan, put in half the butter or oil, add the onion, and fry over a low heat for 8–10 minutes, or until soft and golden. Add the mushrooms and fry for a few minutes, or until just soft.

2 Remove the onions and mushrooms and keep warm. Increase the heat and, when the pan is hot, add the remaining butter, put in the beef strips, and fry briskly, stirring, for 3–4 minutes.

3 Return the onions and mushrooms to the pan and season to taste with salt and pepper. Shake the pan over the heat for 1 minute.

4 Lower the heat, stir in the cream and mustard, and cook gently for 1 minute; do not allow the cream to come to the boil.

5 Add lemon juice to taste and serve immediately.

CHÂTEAUBRIAND WITH BÉARNAISE

THIS IS A TRADITIONAL DISH THAT CANNOT BE BETTERED. DO TRY IT WITH VENISON FILLET FOR A DELICIOUS CHANGE.

450g (1lb) CHÂTEAUBRIAND (beef fillet, centre cut)
SALT and freshly ground BLACK PEPPER
50g (1¾ oz) BUTTER
2 tbsp OLIVE OIL

FOR THE BÉARNAISE SAUCE
100ml (3½ fl oz) WHITE WINE
2 tbsp WHITE WINE VINEGAR
1 SHALLOT, finely chopped
1 tbsp chopped TARRAGON
2 EGG YOLKS
100g (3½ oz) BUTTER, cubed

PREPARATION TIME
15 minutes

COOKING TIME
20 minutes

SERVES 2

1 Preheat the oven to 230°C (450°F/Gas 8).

2 First make the sauce. Combine the wine, vinegar, shallot, and half of the tarragon in a small pan and boil until reduced to 2 tbsp. Pour this into a heatproof bowl set over a pan of barely simmering water. Stir in the egg yolks, then gradually add the butter, piece by piece as it melts and the sauce thickens; stir constantly. If the sauce curdles, beat in a few drops of water. As soon as all the butter has been incorporated, remove from the heat and strain the sauce. Add the remaining tarragon, and season with salt and pepper. Keep warm.

3 Season the beef with black pepper. Heat the butter and oil in a heavy frying pan. When the butter stops foaming, add the beef and brown well on all sides.

4 Transfer to the oven and roast for 10–12 minutes. Remove from the oven and allow to rest in a warm place for 8–10 minutes (for medium-rare), or longer, if you wish.

5 Slice the beef into rounds and serve with the warm Béarnaise sauce.

BOEUF BOURGUIGNON

THE SAME COOKING TECHNIQUE WORKS WELL WITH VENISON BUT TRY ADDING GUINNESS INSTEAD OF RED WINE AND ADDING A HANDFUL OF STONED PRUNES.

175g (6oz) STREAKY BACON RASHERS, chopped

1–2 tbsp OLIVE OIL

900g (2lb) lean BRAISING STEAK, cut into
  4cm (1½in) cubes

12 small SHALLOTS

1 tbsp PLAIN FLOUR

300ml (10fl oz) BEAUJOLAIS, or other red wine

300ml (10fl oz) BEEF STOCK

115g (4oz) BUTTON MUSHROOMS

1 BAY LEAF

1 tsp DRIED HERBES DE PROVENCE

SALT and freshly ground BLACK PEPPER

4 tbsp chopped PARSLEY

mashed POTATOES, to serve

PREPARATION TIME
25 minutes

COOKING TIME
2 hours 30 minutes

SERVES 4

1 Preheat the oven to 160°C (325°F/Gas 3). Fry the bacon in a non-stick frying pan until lightly browned. Drain on kitchen paper and transfer to a casserole.

2 Depending on how much fat is left from the bacon, add a little oil to the pan if necessary so that you have about 2–3 tbsp. Fry the beef in batches over a high heat, transferring to the casserole as they brown.

3 Reduce the heat to medium and fry the shallots. Transfer to the casserole with a slotted spoon and stir the flour into the remaining fat in the frying pan. If the pan is quite dry, mix the flour with a little of the wine or stock. Pour the wine and stock into the frying pan and bring to the boil, stirring constantly until smooth.

4 Add the mushrooms, bay leaf, and dried herbs. Season to taste with salt and pepper and pour the contents of the pan over the meat and shallots in the casserole. Cover and cook in the oven for 2 hours, or until the meat is very tender.

5 Garnish with chopped parsley and serve with mashed potatoes.

SHEPHERD'S PIE

TRADITIONALLY A RECIPE TO USE MEAT AND POTATOES LEFT OVER FROM A SUNDAY ROAST, THIS VERSION IS TOPPED WITH FRESH POTATO AND LEEK MASH.

675g (1½lb) MINCED LAMB or LEFTOVER LAMB,
  finely chopped
2 tbsp SUNFLOWER OIL
1 large ONION, chopped
1 GARLIC CLOVE, crushed
2 CARROTS, sliced
90ml (3fl oz) DRY RED WINE
2 tbsp PLAIN FLOUR
250ml (8fl oz) LAMB STOCK or GRAVY
1 tbsp WORCESTERSHIRE SAUCE
2 tbsp chopped FLAT-LEAF PARSLEY
1 tbsp ROSEMARY, finely chopped
SALT and freshly ground BLACK PEPPER

FOR THE POTATO AND LEEK MASH

900g (2lb) FLOURY POTATOES,
  such as KING EDWARD, peeled
2 large LEEKS, cut in half lengthways, sliced
60g (2oz) BUTTER
150ml (5fl oz) MILK, warmed

PREPARATION TIME
30 minutes

COOKING TIME
30 minutes

SERVES 4–6

1 To make the leek mash, cut the potatoes into large chunks and place in a large saucepan. Cover with water and bring to the boil. Boil for 12 minutes, add the leeks, and cook for a further 5 minutes, or until the vegetables are tender, and drain.

2 Mash the potatoes and leeks and return them to a low heat. Stir in the butter and milk and season to taste with salt and pepper. Preheat the oven to 200°C (400°F/Gas 6).

3 To make the filling, if using minced lamb, fry it in a large frying pan over a medium-high heat, stirring, for 5 minutes, or until lightly browned and all the grains are separate. Pour off the fat, remove the meat from the pan, and set aside.

4 In the same pan, heat the oil. Fry the onion and garlic, stirring for 3–5 minutes, or until softened, then add the carrots. Add the cooked mince or chopped lamb to the pan and stir together.

5 Add the wine, increase the heat to high, and cook for 2–3 minutes. Stir in the flour once the wine has evaporated. Stir in the stock, Worcestershire sauce, parsley, and rosemary, and season to taste with salt and pepper. Bring to the boil, then reduce the heat to low, and simmer for 5 minutes.

6 Spoon the filling into a large ovenproof dish and top with the mashed potatoes. Place the dish on a baking tray and bake for 30 minutes, or until the mashed potatoes are golden. Leave to rest for 5 minutes, then serve straight from the dish.

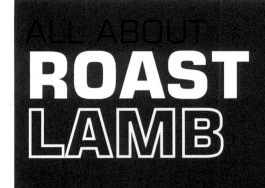

ALL ABOUT
ROAST
LAMB

PERFECTING THIS SUNDAY LUNCH
FAVOURITE IS ALL ABOUT BALANCING
FATTINESS WITH FLAVOUR.

ROAST LEG OF LAMB

PREPARATION TIME
15 minutes

COOKING TIME
1 hour 45 minutes

**SERVES 6,
PLUS
LEFTOVERS**

2kg (4½lb) LEG OF LAMB
4 GARLIC CLOVES, peeled but left whole
handful of fresh ROSEMARY SPRIGS
SALT and freshly ground BLACK PEPPER
600ml (1 pint) hot VEGETABLE STOCK
1 tsp REDCURRANT JELLY

1 Preheat the oven to 200°C (400°F/Gas 6). Spike the lamb leg evenly all over with the point of a sharp knife, then stuff the garlic cloves and small sprigs of rosemary into the holes (see overleaf). Season the lamb all over with salt and black pepper.

2 Sit the leg of lamb in a roasting tin, and roast in the oven for about 15 minutes, until it begins to brown. Reduce the oven temperature to 180°C (350°F/Gas 4), and continue to roast for a further 1 hour (for rare), basting it with its juices halfway through the cooking time; allow 1½ hours for well done. Remove the lamb to a large plate, cover with foil, and leave to rest in a warm place for 15 minutes while you make the gravy.

3 To make the gravy, tilt the roasting tin at a slight angle, and skim off any fat. Sit the tin over a high heat on the hob or stovetop. Add the stock and redcurrant jelly, and bring to the boil, scraping up any bits from the bottom of the tin with a wooden spoon. Reduce the heat slightly, and simmer, stirring all the time, for 5–8 minutes. Taste, and season if needed. Carve at the table, and serve with roast or creamy mashed potato, fresh mint sauce, and seasonal vegetables.

LAMB ESSENTIALS

USE THIS CHART TO IDENTIFY THE BEST LAMB CUTS FOR ROASTING. THEN PERFECT YOUR PREPARATION AND THE CLASSIC LAMB ACCOMPANIMENT – MINT SAUCE.

ROASTING TIMES

CUT	DESCRIPTION	ROAST
Leg	On the bone or boned and rolled, the hind leg is a prime roasting cut. Half leg joints are either fillet (rump) end or shank end. Can be boned and butterflied for barbecuing. Tender steaks and chops (gigot chops) are cut from the leg or chump (rump). Diced boneless leg meat is suitable for kebabs and stews.	Leg steaks and chops (2.5cm/1in thick): Preheat oven to 200°C (400°F/Gas 6). Brush meat with butter or oil and roast for 30–45 min. Leg joint, bone-in or boneless: roast for 25–30 min per 450g (1lb), then rest 5 min per 450g (1lb).
Saddle	A prime bone-in roasting joint from the back of the lamb, consisting of both loins joined together. The fillet/filet mignon is a tiny tender muscle underneath the backbone, cooked whole.	Roast saddle as leg joint.
Loin	The most tender muscle above the backbone. Joints can be left on the bone or boned and rolled. Loin chops include the loin eye; double loin chops include the fillet and sometimes kidney. Barnsley chops, sliced through the whole loin, include the loin eye and fillet on either side of backbone. Butterfly/Valentine steaks are nearly sliced through and opened out to form thin, heart shapes. Noisettes/medallions are small, round loin steaks.	Roast loin and Barnsley chops as leg steaks and chops. Not recommended for butterfly steaks. Loin joint: Preheat oven to 220°C (425°F/Gas 7). Brown joint on all sides, then roast for 8–10 min; rest for 5–10 min.
Best end of neck	From the fore end of the loin, best end gives cutlets when sliced through the bone. The neck fillet makes a good mini-roast. When trimmed of fat, and the chine bone is removed, best end becomes a rack. If the rib ends are exposed it is called a French rack. Two racks leaning together form a guard of honour; two formed into a circle and stuffed make a crown roast.	Roast neck fillet and cutlets as leg steaks and chops. Roast rack of lamb as loin joint. Roast crown roast, guard of honour, and best end joints as leg joint.
Shoulder	May be the whole shoulder, or halved into blade end or knuckle end, and bone-in or boned and rolled, sometimes with stuffing. Cut into chops or steaks, on or off the bone, and into boneless dice, which can be quite fatty.	Shoulder joint, bone-in or boneless: Preheat oven to 200°C (400°F/Gas 6). Roast for 20–30 min per 450g (1lb) plus 30 min. Rest for 30 min.
Shank	A tasty cut from the end of the fore and back legs needing long, slow cooking. Back leg shanks are the plumpest.	Not recommended.
Breast	A cheaper cut from under the ribs. If boned, good for stuffing and rolling.	Not recommended.
Flank	Tougher cut suitable for stuffing and slow cooking, or for mincing.	Not recommended.
Scrag end	Slices of neck on the bone; sometimes boned and diced.	Not recommended.

MAXIMIZE FLAVOUR

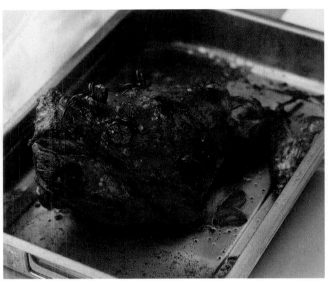

1 Using a sharp knife, make deep slits over the joint 5cm (1in) apart. Press halved garlic cloves deep into the holes with some rosemary tips. Brush the meat with oil or melted butter, season with black pepper and salt.

2 Place the lamb in the roasting tin in the middle of the oven and roast as per instructions (see chart, left). Remove from the hot oven, cover with foil, and let rest for 20–30 minutes.

MINT SAUCE

PREPARATION TIME
10 minutes

SERVES 4

handful of fresh MINT LEAVES,
   finely chopped
1–2 tsp SUGAR
1 tbsp WHITE WINE VINEGAR

1 Put the mint in a serving bowl and add the sugar and vinegar. Set aside to infuse for 10 minutes.

2 Stir well to make sure the sugar has dissolved, then taste and adjust the seasoning, adding more sugar or vinegar, if needed.

RACK OF LAMB WITH FLAGEOLET
BEANS AND HERBS

TRY RUBBING THE LAMB WITH CUT GARLIC FIRST AND ROASTING IT ON SOME DICED
CARROTS AND CELERY, SOFTENED IN BUTTER FIRST. SERVE WITH NEW POTATOES.

1 RACK OF LAMB with 8 cutlets
½ tbsp OLIVE OIL
a few ROSEMARY SPRIGS,
   leaves finely chopped
SALT and freshly ground BLACK PEPPER
150ml (5fl oz) hot VEGETABLE STOCK
1 tsp REDCURRANT JELLY
400g (14oz) can FLAGEOLET BEANS, drained
handful of fresh MINT LEAVES,
   finely chopped

PREPARATION TIME
15 minutes

COOKING TIME
40 minutes

SERVES 4

1 Preheat the oven to 200°C (400°F/Gas 6). Smother the lamb with the oil, sprinkle over the rosemary, and season well with salt and pepper. Sit the rack in a roasting tin and put in the oven to roast for 40 minutes for pink lamb, or longer if you like your meat well done.

2 Remove the lamb from the roasting tin and keep warm (covered with foil) while you prepare the beans. Sit the tin on the hob over a medium to high heat, add the stock, and bring to the boil. Reduce to a simmer, stir in the redcurrant jelly until dissolved, then stir through the flageolet beans and simmer gently for 5 minutes. Remove from the heat and stir through the mint.

3 Slice the rack into 8 cutlets and serve with the beans.

CASSOULET

ALSO GOOD WITH BELLY PORK AND CHICKEN INSTEAD OF PANCETTA AND DUCK.

350g (12oz) DRIED HARICOT BEANS

1 tbsp OLIVE OIL

8 TOULOUSE SAUSAGES

250g (9oz) piece of PANCETTA or
 a whole CHORIZO SAUSAGE, cut into small pieces

2 ONIONS, peeled and finely chopped

1 CARROT, peeled and chopped

4 GARLIC CLOVES, crushed

4 DUCK LEGS

1 sprig of THYME, plus ½ tbsp chopped THYME LEAVES

1 BAY LEAF

SALT and freshly ground BLACK PEPPER

2 tbsp TOMATO PURÉE

400g (14 oz) can chopped TOMATOES

200ml (7fl oz) WHITE WINE

½ day-old BAGUETTE

1 tbsp chopped PARSLEY

PREPARATION TIME
30 minutes, plus soaking

COOKING TIME
3 hours 45 minutes

SERVES 4–6

1 Soak the beans in cold water for several hours or overnight. Drain, place in a saucepan, cover with cold water, bring to the boil and boil rapidly for 10 minutes. Drain.

2 Heat the olive oil in a frying pan and brown the sausages for 7–8 minutes, turning occasionally. Remove from the pan and set aside. Add the pancetta to the pan and cook for 5 minutes. Remove and set aside with the sausages. Add the onions and carrot, and cook gently for 10 minutes, or until soft. Then add three-quarters of the garlic and cook for 1 minute.

3 Preheat the oven to 220°C (425°F/Gas 7). Prick the duck legs all over with a fork and roast for 30 minutes. Remove from the oven. Reserve the duck fat and reduce the oven to 140°C (275°F/Gas 1).

4 In a heavy casserole, layer the ingredients, beginning with half the beans, then onions, carrot, sausages, pancetta, and duck legs, followed by the remaining beans. Push the thyme sprig and bay leaf in among everything and season well with salt and pepper.

5 Mix together 900ml (1½ pints) boiling water with the tomato purée, tomatoes, and wine, then pour into the casserole. Cover and cook in the oven for 3 hours, adding a little extra water if required.

6 Cut the crusts off the baguette, then tear the bread into pieces and place in a food processor with the remaining garlic. Process into coarse crumbs. Heat 2 tbsp of the duck fat in a frying pan and fry the crumbs over a medium heat for 7–8 minutes, or until crisp and golden. Drain on kitchen paper and stir in the herbs. Remove the cassoulet from the oven and stir. Sprinkle the breadcrumb topping over in a thick, even layer and serve.

VEAL MILANESE

SERVE THE CUTLETS AND SAUCE PILED ONTO FRESH EGG TAGLIATELLE, AND ACCOMPANY THE DISH WITH A CRISP, GREEN SALAD.

4 tbsp PLAIN FLOUR

SALT and freshly ground BLACK PEPPER

4 VEAL CUTLETS, about 115g (4oz) each

3 tbsp OLIVE OIL

1 small ONION, finely chopped

60ml (2fl oz) DRY WHITE WINE

200g (7oz) jar marinated ARTICHOKE HEARTS, drained

400g (14oz) can PLUM TOMATOES, drained

a few BASIL LEAVES, torn

PREPARATION TIME
10 minutes

COOKING TIME
20–25 minutes

SERVES 4

1 Combine the flour and ½ tsp each of salt and pepper on a plate. Dip the cutlets in the seasoned flour until lightly coated all over, shaking off any excess.

2 Heat 1 tbsp of the oil in a large frying pan over a medium-high heat. Add 2 of the cutlets and fry, turning once, for 2–3 minutes on each side, or until golden brown and cooked through. Remove from the pan and keep warm. Heat another 1 tbsp of oil and repeat with the remaining 2 cutlets.

3 Add the remaining oil to the pan and fry the onion for 4–5 minutes, or until soft. Add the wine and bring the mixture to the boil, stirring and scraping up any sediment from the bottom of the pan. Stir in the artichokes, tomatoes, and basil, and bring back to the boil, breaking up the tomatoes with a wooden spoon. Season to taste. Serve topped with the cutlets.

BLANQUETTE DE VEAU

THIS DELICATELY FLAVOURED STEW IS ALSO GOOD MADE WITH CHICKEN OR RABBIT.

675g (1½lb) diced VEAL LEG

2 ONIONS, roughly chopped

2 CARROTS, peeled and chopped

squeeze of LEMON juice

1 BOUQUET GARNI (6 PARSLEY STALKS, 1 BAY LEAF,
   1 CELERY STALK, 5 BLACK PEPPERCORNS,
   and 3 fresh THYME SPRIGS, tied in muslin)

SALT and freshly ground BLACK PEPPER

85g (3oz) BUTTER

18 WHITE PEARL ONIONS

225g (8oz) BUTTON MUSHROOMS, quartered

2 tbsp PLAIN FLOUR

1 EGG YOLK

2–3 tbsp SINGLE CREAM

NUTMEG, freshly grated

chopped PARSLEY, to garnish

PREPARATION TIME

15 minutes

COOK TIME

1 hour 15 minutes

SERVES 4

1 Put the veal, onions, carrots, lemon juice, and bouquet garni in the casserole with enough water to just cover. Season with salt and pepper. Simmer over a low heat for 1 hour, or until the meat is tender.

2 Meanwhile, melt 30g (1oz) of the butter in a frying pan over a medium heat. Add the onions and fry, stirring occasionally, until golden. Add another 30g (1oz) of butter and the mushrooms. Fry for 5 minutes, or until soft, stirring occasionally.

3 Strain off the cooking liquid from the veal, reserving 600ml (1 pint). Add the meat and vegetables to the mushrooms and onions, then set aside and keep warm.

4 Melt the remaining butter in a large pan. Add the flour and stir constantly for 1 minute. Remove the pan from the heat and gradually stir in the reserved liquid. Return the pan to the heat and bring the sauce to the boil, stirring, until it thickens. Adjust the seasoning to taste.

5 Remove the pan from the heat, and let it cool slightly. Beat the egg yolk and cream in a small bowl, then slowly stir it into the sauce. Add the meat and vegetables, and grated nutmeg to taste. Reheat, without boiling, for 5 minutes. Garnish with parsley, and serve.

OSSO BUCCO

THIS CLASSIC, RICH VEAL STEW FROM MILAN IS FLAVOURED WITH GARLIC AND SALTY ANCHOVIES, AND IS TRADITIONALLY SERVED WITH RISOTTO ALLA MILANESE.

3 tbsp PLAIN FLOUR

SALT and freshly ground BLACK PEPPER

4 thick VEAL OSSO BUCCO slices (from shank)

60g (2oz) BUTTER

4 tbsp OLIVE OIL

4 GARLIC CLOVES, chopped

½ ONION, chopped

4 tbsp TOMATO PURÉE

about 120ml (4fl oz) BEEF STOCK or WATER

4 tbsp chopped FLAT-LEAF PARSLEY

2 ANCHOVY FILLETS IN OIL, drained and chopped

grated zest of 1 LEMON

PREPARATION TIME
15 minutes

COOKING TIME
1 hour 45 minutes

SERVES 4

1 Season the flour with salt and pepper, then roll the veal in the flour and shake off any excess.

2 Melt the butter with the oil in a large flameproof casserole. Add the veal, fry for 5 minutes, or until browned on all sides. Remove and set aside. Add the garlic and onion to the casserole and fry gently, stirring occasionally, for 5 minutes, or until softened but not browned.

3 Stir in the tomato purée, stock or water, and salt and pepper to taste and bring to the boil. Reduce the heat to low, cover the casserole and simmer for 1½ hours, or until the veal is tender. Check as it cooks and add more liquid, if necessary. The gravy should be thick but not stiff.

4 To serve, combine the parsley, anchovies, and lemon zest in a bowl. Stir the mixture into the casserole and serve immediately.

ALL ABOUT...

ROAST PORK

COOKED PERFECTLY,
ROAST PORK CAN BE A
SUCCULENT SUCCESS.

ROAST PORK

PREPARATION TIME
20 minutes

COOKING TIME
1 hour 45 minutes

**SERVES 6,
PLUS
LEFTOVERS**

2kg (4½lb) BONELESS PORK LOIN, skin scored

4 GARLIC CLOVES, grated or finely chopped

handful of BLACK OLIVES, pitted and finely chopped

pinch of DRIED OREGANO

SEA SALT and freshly ground BLACK PEPPER

OLIVE OIL, to coat

1 Preheat the oven to 220°C (425°F/Gas 7). Lay the pork out skin-side down. Mix the garlic, olives, and oregano in a bowl, and season with salt and black pepper. Rub the mixture in a line down the middle of the pork, then roll the pork up tightly and secure with string. Sit the roll in a large roasting tin, cut-side down. Rub all over with olive oil, then rub sea salt into the cuts.

2 Roast the pork in the oven for about 20 minutes until the skin is really golden and crispy for perfect crackling. Reduce the oven temperature to 190°C (375°F/Gas 4), and continue to roast for a further 1 hour to 1¼ hours until the pork is cooked through. Remove to a large plate, and leave to rest in a warm place for about 15 minutes.

3 Cut the pork into slices, and serve with gravy made with the pan juices, apple sauce, crispy roast potatoes, and seasonal vegetables – and a generous piece of crackling for each portion.

PORK ESSENTIALS

USE THIS CHART TO IDENTIFY THE BEST CUTS OF PORK FOR ROASTING, THEN PERFECT THE ESSENTIAL PORK TRIMMINGS – CRACKLING AND APPLE SAUCE.

PORK ROASTING CHART

CUT	DESCRIPTION	ROAST
Leg	The hind leg is a prime but lean roasting joint, bone-in or boned and rolled. Leg steaks are lean, boneless slices; escalopes (schnitzels) are thinner. Cubed boneless leg is suitable for kebabs and stir-frying.	Leg joint: Preheat oven to 220°C (425°F/Gas 7). Roast for 30 min, then reduce heat to 160°C (325°F/Gas 3) and cook for 23 min per 450g (1lb). Rest for 20–30 min.
Chump	From the rump end of the back, this yields a roasting joint that is usually boned and rolled, as well as the largest of the pork chops.	Roast chump joint as leg joint.
Loin	Tender loin joints are sold on the bone with skin on, and also boned and skinless. Rack is a joint from the fore end of the loin, sometimes with the skin on; two racks tied together and stuffed become a crown roast. Loin is cut into chops, with bone, and into steaks, which are slices with a covering of fat on one side.	Roast loin joint and rack as leg joint.
Belly	A fatty cut, boned and rolled as a joint, or sliced/diced for grilling and frying or marinating and slow-cooking. Spare ribs, trimmed from inside the belly, are a popular cut for marinating and grilling or baking.	Spare ribs and slices: Preheat oven to 180°C (350°F/Gas 4). Roast for 20–30 min, then coat with marinade/sauce and roast for a further 10–15 min until well glazed. Or slow-roast at 160°C (325°F/Gas 3) for 1–1½ hours, basting with liquid or sauce; increase heat to 200°C (400°F/Gas 6) and roast for 20–30 min to brown and glaze. Belly joint: Preheat oven to 220°C (425°F/Gas 7). Score skin and rub with salt. Roast for 20 min, then reduce heat to 150°C (300°F/Gas 2) and cook for 3–4 hours.
Shoulder	Shoulder/hand/blade joint may be on the bone or boned and stuffed; slow-roast for delicious flavour. A steak is a succulent slice of shoulder; a chop includes some bone. Diced, boneless, forequarter meat is suitable for stews.	Shoulder/hand/blade joint: Preheat oven to 220°C (425°F/Gas 7). Score skin and rub with salt. Brown for 30 min, then reduce heat to 150°C (300°F/Gas 2) and continue roasting for 3–3½ hours.
Trotters	Need very slow simmering; then they are cooled, stuffed, and grilled.	After cooking and cooling, halve, brush with butter, and roll in breadcrumbs. Roast at 200°C (400°F/Gas 6) for 15–20 min, or until crisp and brown.
Head and cheek/ jowl	Pig's head is cooked whole for buffets but mostly used to make brawn. Cheek and jowl are fatty cuts from the head that can be used like belly.	Head: Preheat oven to 190°C (375°F/Gas 5). After braising, protect ears with foil and roast for 30–45 min to colour; remove foil for the last 15 min.
Fillet/tenderloin	A slim, tender, tapering muscle from the hind end of the loin that is usually cooked whole. May be sliced into medallions, which when part-sliced and opened out become Valentine steaks.	Not recommended.
Neck/collar	A well-marbled cut that can be sliced, diced, or cooked as a joint.	Not recommended.

MAKE PERFECT CRACKLING

1 Using a very sharp knife, score the rind of a pork shoulder widthways, working from the centre, outwards. Repeat for the other end. Massage the rind liberally with sea salt, then rub the entire shoulder with a little oil.

2 When finished resting, hold the meat with a carving fork and cut just beneath the crackling. Lift away the crackling in one piece. Using kitchen scissors or a sharp knife, cut the crackling crossways in half. Serve alongside the roasted meat.

APPLE SAUCE

PREPARATION TIME
10 minutes

COOKING TIME
10 minutes

SERVES 4

450g (1lb) COOKING APPLES, peeled, cored, and quartered

2–3 tbsp SUGAR (depending on the tartness of the apples)

1 Put the apples in a pan, sprinkle over 1 tbsp of water, then add the sugar. Cover and cook on a low heat for 10 minutes, or until the apples have begun to break down.

2 Stir with a wooden spoon until the sauce reaches your preferred consistency – either a smooth purée or more chunky. Taste and add more sugar, if required. Serve warm or cold with roast pork.

PORK BELLY WITH ONIONS AND POTATOES

FOR ADDED FLAVOUR, ADD SOME THICK WEDGES OF GREEN DESSERT APPLE OR
UNRIPE PEARS, PEELED AND CORED, FOR THE LAST HOUR OF COOKING.

1kg (2¼lb) piece of PORK BELLY

1 tsp SEA SALT

6 tbsp OLIVE OIL

3 large RED ONIONS, cut into eighths

4 large POTATOES, cut into wedges

250g (9oz) CRIMINI MUSHROOMS, halved

300ml (10fl oz) MEDIUM-DRY CIDER

4 GARLIC CLOVES, chopped

1 heaped tbsp fresh THYME

600ml (1 pint) light VEGETABLE STOCK

1 tsp freshly ground BLACK PEPPER

steamed BROCCOLI, to serve

PREPARATION TIME
10 minutes

COOKING TIME
1 hour 50 minutes

SERVES 6

1 Preheat the oven to 220°C (425°F/Gas 7). Score the skin of the pork belly deeply, then rub the salt and
2 tbsp of the oil into it. Transfer to a baking tray and place in the oven for 20 minutes, or until the skin has
crisped up. Remove from the oven and reduce the temperature to 160°C (325°F/Gas 3).

2 While the pork is roasting, heat the remaining oil in a large frying pan, add the onions and potatoes, and cook for
10 minutes, stirring constantly. Add the mushrooms and cook for 5 minutes. Add the cider and cook for 2 minutes.
Transfer the mixture to a large baking dish, add the garlic, thyme, stock, and pepper, and combine well. Nestle the
pork in the mixture, ensuring the crackling is not covered, and roast in the oven for 1½ hours.

3 Allow to rest for 10 minutes, then cut the pork up with kitchen scissors and serve with steamed broccoli.

HONEY-GLAZED GAMMON

TRY SERVING THE HAM WITH BABY ROAST POTATOES AND CAULIFLOWER CHEESE.

1.5kg (3lb 3oz) boneless GAMMON JOINT

1 ONION, quartered

2 BAY LEAVES

6 PEPPERCORNS

handful of CLOVES

grated zest and juice of 1 ORANGE

3 tbsp set HONEY

PREPARATION TIME
15 minutes

COOKING TIME
2 hours

SERVES 8–10

1 Place the joint in a large saucepan with water to cover. Add the onion, bay leaves, and peppercorns. Bring slowly to the boil, then simmer for 1½ hours. Remove from the pan. Allow to cool.

2 Preheat the oven to 200°C (400°F/Gas 6). Using a sharp knife, carefully remove the skin from the ham and discard. Place the ham in a roasting tin, cut a criss-cross pattern in the fat and push a clove into the centre of each diamond. Combine the orange zest, honey, and 2 tbsp of the orange juice, then brush the surface of the ham with the mixture.

3 Bake for 10 minutes, then baste with the remaining glaze. Return to the oven and bake for 20 minutes, or until golden. Allow to rest before carving. Also delicious served cold.

ALL ABOUT
ROAST
POULTRY

BEAUTIFULLY ROASTED POULTRY IS A WONDERFUL THING, AND ONE OF THE SIMPLEST MEALS TO COOK.

ROASTING POULTRY

Use these times as a guide, bearing in mind the size and weight of each bird varies. Be sure to preheat the oven before cooking your bird(s), and always check that the bird is fully cooked before serving.

BIRD	OVEN TEMP	COOKING TIME
Chicken	200°C (400°F/Gas 6)	20 mins per 450g (1lb) plus 20 mins
Turkey 3.5–4.5kg (7–9lb)	190°C (375°F/Gas 5)	2½–3 hrs total cooking
5–6kg (10–12lb)	190°C (375°F/Gas 5)	3½–4 hrs total cooking
6.5–84.5kg (13–17lb)	190°C (375°F/Gas 5)	4½–5 hrs total cooking
Duck	180°C (350°F/Gas 4)	20 mins per 450g (1lb) plus 20 mins
Goose	180°C (350°F/Gas 4)	20 mins per 450g (1lb) plus 20 mins
Poussin	190°C (375°F/Gas 5)	12 mins per 450g (1lb) plus 12 mins

ROAST CHICKEN

PREPARATION TIME
15 minutes

COOKING TIME
1 hour 15 minutes

SERVES 4, PLUS LEFTOVERS

1.3kg (3lb) OVEN-READY CHICKEN

50g (1¾oz) BUTTER

1 LEMON, quartered

SALT and freshly ground BLACK PEPPER

150ml (5fl oz) hot VEGETABLE STOCK or WATER

1 Preheat the oven to 200°C (400°F/Gas 6). Sit the chicken in a roasting tin, then coat evenly all over with the butter – this ensures crisp, evenly golden skin. Stuff the neck end (see overleaf) or push the lemon in the body cavity and season the chicken all over with salt and black pepper.

2 Roast in the oven for about 1 hour 15 minutes until cooked through and golden, basting with the juices 2 or 3 times. To check whether the chicken is cooked, pierce the thickest part of the thighs with a knife. If the juices run clear, it is done; if it is pink or bloody, cook for a little longer. Remove to a large plate, cover with foil, and leave to rest in a warm place for about 15 minutes before carving. Serve with gravy, made with the pan juices, roast potatoes, and seasonal vegetables.

POULTRY ESSENTIALS

A WELL PREPARED BIRD MAKES GOOD EATING. IF IT COMES WITH GIBLETS, USE THEM TO MAKE STOCK FOR THE GRAVY.

1 STUFF THE BIRD

A stuffing to accompany a bird can be cooked in one of two ways – either stuffed into the neck end (as below) or cooked separately in the oven. If stuffing the bird, stuff it under the skin, rather than into the cavity, as this will ensure that it cooks properly. It will also help to protect the breast meat as it roasts and any butter or fat in the mixture will help to keep the meat moist.

WATERCRESS & APRICOT STUFFING

50g (1½oz) DRIED APRICOTS

3 slices WHITE BREAD, processed into crumbs

50g (1½oz) HAZELNUTS, skinned

bunch of WATERCRESS, roughly chopped

Put the apricots in a small pan of water and bring to the boil. Drain and add to the breadcrumbs. Put the hazelnuts into a food processor and process for a few seconds, then add the chopped watercress and breadcrumbs. Process for a few seconds, then season and put into a bowl.

To stuff the bird, lift the flap of skin from around the wishbone area at the neck and draw this back until it exposes as much of the breast as necessary. Push the stuffing in under the skin onto the breast, then pull back the skin to cover it and tuck in under the bird.

2 BASTE & COOK

1 Preheat the oven (see chart on p70). Paint oil, rub on butter, and season the bird. Place in a pan, pour in 150ml stock, and put in the middle of the oven. After 15 minutes, reduce the heat to 190°C/375°F (Gas 5).

3 MAKE GRAVY

1 Using a large spoon skim off most of the fat from the pan juices. Put the pan on the stovetop over a low heat. Mix 1 tbsp plain flour with 1 tbsp of the bird fat and whisk it into the remaining pan juices.

2 Roast for a further 25 minutes, then baste the bird with the juices in the pan. Turn the bird over onto its breast so that the oven heat can focus on the thighs. Baste the bird again, then continue roasting for another 25 minutes.

3 Turn the bird onto its back and test for doneness. Insert a skewer into the thigh or the thick end of the breast. If the juices run clear, the bird is cooked. If there are traces of blood continue cooking and test again after 10 minutes.

2 Add 300ml (10 fl oz) water or stock and 1 tbsp tomato purée, increase the heat, and bring to a boil, whisking constantly to get rid of any lumps.

3 Strain the gravy through a sieve, into a clean container, for maximum smoothness, then pour into a gravy boat, ready to serve piping hot.

ROAST TURKEY

TURKEY HAS PARTICULAR CHALLENGES; IT HAS A TENDENCY TO BECOME DRY IF NOT TREATED WITH UTMOST CARE.

3 ONIONS, 1 finely chopped, 2 peeled and quartered

250g (9oz) BUTTER

125g (4oz) BREADCRUMBS

Handful of fresh FLAT LEAF PARSLEY, finely chopped

SALT and freshly ground BLACK PEPPER

4kg (9lb) TURKEY

PREPARATION TIME
15 minutes

COOKING TIME
3 hours 15 minutes

SERVES 6, PLUS LEFTOVERS

1 First, make the stuffing. Melt half the butter in a pan over a low heat, add the chopped onion, and sweat gently until soft. Remove from the heat, stir through the breadcrumbs and parsley, season, and set aside to cool. Preheat the oven to 200°C (400°F/Gas 6). Sit the turkey in a large roasting tin, and season, inside and out. Spread the remaining butter over the skin. Stuff the onion quarters into the body cavity, and the stuffing into the neck end. Roast for 20 minutes, then reduce the oven temperature to 190°C (375°F/Gas 5).

2 Cover the turkey loosely with foil, and roast for 20 minutes per 450g (1lb) plus 20 minutes. Baste every hour with juices from the tin. Pierce the bird with a skewer. If the juices run clear, it is ready; if not, cook for a little longer. Remove the foil for the last 10–15 minutes.

3 Remove the turkey from the tin, and put on a large warmed plate. Cover with foil, and leave to rest in a warm place for 15 minutes. Serve slices of turkey with gravy, roast potatoes, cranberry sauce, and seasonal vegetables.

CHICKEN CACCIATORE

"HUNTER-STYLE CHICKEN" IS TRADITIONALLY SERVED WITH POLENTA TO SOAK UP THE DELICIOUS JUICES, BUT IS ALSO GOOD WITH RISOTTO ALLA MILANESE.

4 CHICKEN LEG QUARTERS, about 1.5kg (3lb 3oz)
  total weight
SALT and freshly ground BLACK PEPPER
2 tbsp OLIVE OIL
2 GARLIC CLOVES, sliced
1 ONION, chopped
200ml (7fl oz) DRY WHITE WINE
1 CELERY STICK, chopped
200g (7oz) BUTTON MUSHROOMS, sliced
400g (14oz) can CHOPPED TOMATOES
150ml (5fl oz) CHICKEN STOCK
1 tbsp TOMATO PURÉE
2 tsp chopped ROSEMARY
2 tsp chopped SAGE
8 pitted BLACK OLIVES, halved

PREPARATION TIME
20 minutes

COOKING TIME
35–40 minutes

SERVES 4

1 Trim any excess fat from the chicken and season with salt and pepper. Heat half the oil in a large, heavy frying pan and fry the chicken in batches, until brown on all sides. Remove and keep hot. Pour the excess fat out of the pan.

2 Add the remaining oil, garlic, and onion and fry gently for 3–4 minutes to soften, but not brown. Add the wine and boil for 1 minute. Stir in the celery, mushrooms, tomatoes, stock, purée, rosemary, and sage.

3 Return the chicken to the pan, cover and cook over a low heat for 30 minutes, or until the chicken is cooked through.

4 Remove the lid, add the olives, then cover and cook for a further 5–10 minutes. Serve hot.

CHICKEN KIEV

USE OTHER COMBINATIONS FOR A FILLING, SUCH AS CURRY OR TARRAGON BUTTER, A PIECE OF GRUYÈRE CHEESE, OR MOZZARELLA AND PESTO. SERVE WITH RICE.

115g (4oz) BUTTER, softened
2 GARLIC CLOVES, crushed
finely grated zest of 1 LEMON
2 tbsp chopped PARSLEY
SALT and freshly ground BLACK PEPPER
4 skinless boneless CHICKEN BREASTS
3 tbsp PLAIN FLOUR
1 EGG, beaten
150g (5½oz) fresh BREADCRUMBS
SUNFLOWER OIL, for deep-frying

PREPARATION TIME
25 minutes, plus chilling

COOKING TIME
8–10 minutes

SERVES 4

1 Place the butter in a bowl and stir in the garlic, lemon zest, and parsley. Season to taste with salt and pepper. Form into a block, wrap in cling film, then chill until firm.

2 Place each chicken breast between 2 sheets of cling film; pound them flat using a rolling pin.

3 Cut the butter into 4 sticks and place one on each of the breasts. Fold the other side of the chicken up and over the butter, enclosing it completely. Secure each with 2 cocktail sticks. Chill, if time.

4 Season the flour with salt and pepper. Keeping the chicken closed, dip each piece in the seasoned flour, then in beaten egg, and finally into the breadcrumbs to coat evenly.

5 Heat the oil to 180°C (350°F). Fry the chicken for 6–8 minutes depending on size, or until golden brown and cooked through.

6 Remove with a slotted spoon and drain on kitchen paper. Serve hot.

MASTERCHEF **POULTRY** KNOW-HOW: See **Deep Fry Stuffed Chicken** 299
MASTERCHEF **POULTRY** KNOW-HOW: See **Bread and Fry Escalopes** 301

CHICKEN LIVER PÂTÉ

TRY STIRRING IN SOME SAUTÉED, SLICED MUSHROOMS TO THE BLENDED PÂTÉ.
SERVE WITH GHERKINS AND MELBA TOAST.

350g (12oz) CHICKEN LIVERS, thawed if frozen
115g (4oz) BUTTER
150ml (5fl oz) RED WINE
¼ tsp dried THYME
10 CHIVES, snipped, plus extra for garnishing
SALT and freshly ground BLACK PEPPER

PREPARATION TIME
10 minutes, plus cooling and chilling
COOKING TIME
8 minutes
SERVES 4

1 Rinse the chicken livers and pat them dry with kitchen paper. Trim away any white sinew or greenish portions from the livers with small scissors, then cut each in half.

2 Melt half the butter in a large frying pan over a medium heat until it foams. Add the livers and cook, stirring often, for 4 minutes, or until browned.

3 Add the wine, thyme, and chives to the pan. Bring to the boil then reduce the heat and cook, stirring occasionally for 4 minutes, or until the liquid is reduced and the livers are just cooked through when sliced open.

4 Remove the pan from the heat and leave to cool for 10 minutes. Add salt and pepper to taste, then tip the livers and sauce into a blender, and blend until smooth. Adjust the seasoning if necessary. Spoon the pâté into a serving bowl, pressing it down with the back of the spoon so it is firmly packed, then set aside.

5 Melt the remaining butter over a medium heat, then pour it over the top of the pâté. Chill, uncovered, for at least 2 hours. Serve garnished with snipped chives.

COARSE MEAT TERRINE

TRY ADDING A HANDFUL OF WHOLE HAZELNUTS FOR DELICIOUS NUTTINESS.

350g (12oz) rindless STREAKY BACON RASHERS
250g (9oz) CHICKEN LIVERS
300g (10oz) MINCED PORK
450g (1lb) MINCED VEAL
1 ONION, finely chopped
2 GARLIC CLOVES, crushed
1 tsp DRIED OREGANO
½ tsp GROUND ALLSPICE
115g (4oz) BUTTER, melted
120ml (4fl oz) DRY SHERRY
SALT and freshly ground BLACK PEPPER

PREPARATION TIME
30 minutes, plus pressing

COOKING TIME
1 hour 30 minutes

SERVES 8

1 Preheat the oven to 180°C (350°F/Gas 4). Using the back of a knife, stretch the bacon rashers, and use them to line the terrine dish, or other ovenproof bowl or dish, leaving the ends hanging over the sides of the dish.

2 Mince or chop the chicken livers and mix with the minced pork, minced veal, onion, garlic, oregano, allspice, and melted butter. Stir in the sherry and season with salt and pepper.

3 Spoon the mixture into the dish and fold the ends of the bacon over the top. Cover tightly with foil or a lid, and stand the dish in a roasting tin, filled with enough hot water to reach halfway up the sides of the terrine dish.

4 Cook in the oven for 1½ hours, then remove and cover with fresh foil. Place a weight on top and leave to cool, then chill, for up to 24 hours, then turn out and cut into slices. Serve with slices of warm crusty bread or toast, topped with gherkins or cocktail onions.

COQ AU VIN

SERVE THE CHICKEN WITH CREAMY MASHED POTATOES AND STEAMED BROCCOLI.

2 tbsp PLAIN FLOUR

SALT and freshly ground BLACK PEPPER

4 CHICKEN portions

60g (2oz) BUTTER

125g (4½oz) diced PANCETTA

2 GARLIC CLOVES, crushed

1 CARROT, diced

1 CELERY STICK, roughly chopped

4 tbsp BRANDY or COGNAC

750ml (1¼ pints) RED WINE, such
   as BEAUJOLAIS

1 BAY LEAF

4–5 sprigs of THYME

1 tbsp OLIVE OIL

450g (1lb) BUTTON ONIONS

1 tsp SOFT LIGHT BROWN SUGAR

1 tsp RED WINE VINEGAR

225g (8oz) BUTTON MUSHROOMS

PREPARATION TIME
30 minutes

COOKING TIME
1 hour 30 minutes

SERVES 4

1 Season the flour to taste with salt and pepper. Coat the chicken with 1 tbsp of the seasoned flour. Melt half the butter in the casserole, add the chicken, and fry gently until golden brown on all sides.

2 Add the pancetta, garlic, carrot, and celery, and fry until softened. Add the remaining flour and cook for 1–2 minutes. Pour in the brandy and wine, stirring to remove any sediment from the bottom of the casserole. Add the bay leaf and thyme, bring to the boil, cover, and simmer for 1 hour.

3 Meanwhile, melt the rest of the butter with the olive oil in a frying pan. Add the onions and fry until just brown. Stir in the sugar, vinegar, and 1 tbsp water.

4 Add the onions and mushrooms to the chicken, and cook for another 30 minutes, or until the chicken is cooked through and the vegetables are tender.

5 Transfer the chicken and vegetables to a hot serving dish. Discard the bay leaf and thyme. Skim off any excess fat and boil the sauce for 3–5 minutes, or until reduced. Pour over the chicken and serve.

TANDOORI CHICKEN

YOU CAN ADD SOME PLAIN YOGURT TO THE MARINADE AND OMIT THE GHEE OR BUTTER WHEN ROASTING. SERVE IT WITH BASMATI RICE AND A CRISP SALAD.

8 CHICKEN PIECES, such as breasts,
   thighs and legs, skin removed
GROUNDNUT OIL or SUNFLOWER OIL, for brushing
60g (2oz) GHEE or BUTTER, melted
1 RED ONION, thinly sliced, to serve
LEMON WEDGES, to serve

FOR THE TANDOORI MARINADE
1 ONION, coarsely chopped
2 large GARLIC CLOVES
1cm (½in) piece fresh ROOT GINGER,
   peeled and coarsely chopped
3 tbsp fresh LEMON JUICE
¼ tsp SALT
1¼–1½ tsp CHILLI POWDER, to taste
1 tsp GARAM MASALA
pinch of TURMERIC
pinch of KASHMIRI CHILLI POWDER
pinch of SAFFRON POWDER

PREPARATION TIME
10–15 minutes, plus at least 3
hours marinating

COOKING TIME
25–35 minutes

SERVES 4

1 Use a fork to prick the chicken pieces all over, then place them in a non-metallic bowl and set aside.

2 To make the marinade, put the onion, garlic, and ginger in a blender or food processor and blend until a paste forms, scraping down the side of the bowl. Add the lemon juice, salt, and the spices, and process again.

3 Pour the marinade over the chicken and rub in well. Cover the bowl with cling film, and leave to marinate in the refrigerator for at least 3 hours, occasionally turning the chicken pieces in the marinade.

4 Preheat the oven to 220°C (425°F/Gas 7) and remove the chicken from the fridge. Put a rack in a roasting pan lined with kitchen foil, shiny-side up, and grease the rack. Arrange the chicken on the rack then brush with melted ghee. Roast for 20–25 minutes, or until the juices run clear.

5 Preheat the grill on its highest setting. Pour off the juices that have accumulated in the bottom of the pan. Brush the chicken with more ghee and place under the grill for 5–10 minutes, or until the edges are lightly charred. Serve with the onion slices and lemon wedges.

CHICKEN TIKKA MASALA

A BRITISH-INDIAN INVENTION. SERVE WITH RICE, MANGO CHUTNEY, AND RAITA.

8 skinless, boneless CHICKEN THIGHS

2 GARLIC CLOVES, coarsely chopped

2.5cm (1in) piece of fresh ROOT GINGER, peeled and
coarsely chopped

juice of 1 LIME

1 RED CHILLI, deseeded

2 tbsp coarsely chopped CORIANDER LEAVES,
plus extra to garnish

2 tbsp VEGETABLE OIL

1 RED ONION, chopped

1 tsp GROUND TURMERIC

1 tsp GROUND CUMIN

1 tbsp TOMATO PURÉE

300ml (10fl oz) DOUBLE CREAM

1 tbsp LEMON JUICE

SALT and freshly ground BLACK PEPPER

PREPARATION TIME
20 minutes, plus marinating

COOKING TIME
25 minutes

SERVES 4

1 Place the chicken in a single layer in a shallow dish. Put the next 5 ingredients and 1 tbsp of the oil in a food processor, process into a paste, and spread over the chicken. Set aside to marinate for 2 hours.

2 Heat the remaining oil in a frying pan, add the onion, and fry until softened and starting to colour. Add the turmeric and cumin, and fry gently for 2–3 minutes.

3 Preheat the grill on its highest setting. Lift the chicken from the dish, reserving any marinade left behind, and place on a foil-lined grill rack. Grill for 5 minutes, or until almost cooked and slightly scorched at the edges, turning once.

4 Stir the tomato purée and cream into the frying pan with any leftover marinade. Add the lemon and stir over a medium heat until mixed in. Place the chicken into the pan and baste with the sauce. Simmer for 5 minutes or until the chicken is cooked through. Season to taste with salt and pepper and serve, sprinkled with coriander.

SOUTHERN FRIED CHICKEN

SERVE THIS SUCCULENT CHICKEN WITH A BOWL OF CHIPS, SOME GRIDDLED CORN COBS, BACON ROLLS, AND FRIED BANANAS.

225g (8oz) PLAIN FLOUR

SALT and freshly ground BLACK PEPPER

1 tsp DRIED THYME

1 tsp CAJUN SEASONING

1 tsp SUGAR

4 CHICKEN DRUMSTICKS

4 CHICKEN THIGHS

1 EGG, beaten

SUNFLOWER OIL, for deep-frying

FOR THE DIP

200ml (7fl oz) SOURED CREAM

2 tbsp CHIVES, snipped

PREPARATION TIME
20 minutes, plus chilling

COOKING TIME
25 minutes

SERVES 4

1 Put the first 5 ingredients in a freezer bag, hold the top firmly together, and shake well.

2 Add the chicken drumsticks and thighs to the bag one at a time and shake until coated.

3 Dip the pieces into the beaten egg, then repeat step 2. Lay the coated chicken on a plate in a single layer and chill for 30 minutes.

4 Meanwhile, make the dip. Mix the soured cream with the chives and season to taste with salt and pepper. Transfer to a small serving bowl, cover with cling film, and chill until ready to serve.

5 Heat the oil for deep-frying to 170°C (340°F) and fry the chicken for 15–20 minutes, or until golden brown and cooked through, then drain on kitchen paper.

6 Serve the chicken with the dip alongside.

THAI GREEN CHICKEN CURRY

TRY COOKING SOME HALVED GREEN BEANS OR SOME BATONETTES OF COURGETTE AND ADDING TO THE CURRY JUST BEFORE SERVING.

1 tbsp OLIVE OIL

4 tsp shop-bought THAI GREEN CURRY PASTE (use more
   paste for a spicier sauce)

4 skinless, boneless CHICKEN BREASTS,
   about 140g (5oz) each, cut into bite-sized pieces

2 tbsp NAM PLA (Thai fish sauce)

400ml (14oz) can COCONUT MILK

175g (6oz) CUP MUSHROOMS, chopped

6 SPRING ONIONS, trimmed, with the green part cut
   into 5mm (¼in) slices

SALT and freshly ground BLACK PEPPER

chopped CORIANDER, to garnish

PREPARATION TIME
10 minutes

COOKING TIME
10 minutes

SERVES 4

1 Heat the oil in a large frying pan over a medium heat. Add the curry paste and stir. Add the chicken and stir-fry for 2 minutes, or until lightly browned.

2 Pour in the nam pla and coconut milk and bring to the boil, stirring. Lower the heat, stir in the mushrooms and most of the spring onions, and season with salt and pepper to taste, then simmer for about 8 minutes, or until the chicken is tender and cooked through.

3 Serve hot, garnished with coriander and the remaining sliced spring onions.

ALL ABOUT
ROAST
GAME BIRDS

AS A RULE, THE DARKER AND LEANER
THE MEAT OF A GAME BIRD, THE MORE
CAREFULLY IT NEEDS TO BE COOKED.

ROAST QUAIL

PREPARATION TIME
10 minutes

COOKING TIME
20–25 minutes

SERVES 4

8 QUAIL
½ tsp freshly grated NUTMEG
SALT and freshly ground BLACK PEPPER
small bunch of SAGE LEAVES
8 PANCETTA SLICES
2 crisp DESSERT APPLES, cored and sliced
15g (½oz) BUTTER, melted
2 tsp DEMERARA SUGAR
4 tbsp CALVADOS or CIDER BRANDY

1 Preheat the oven to 200°C (400°F/Gas 6). Season the birds inside and out with the nutmeg, and salt and pepper. Tuck a couple of sage leaves into the cavity, and wrap a strip of pancetta around each bird, tucking the ends underneath.

2 Toss the apples in the butter, sprinkle with the sugar, and place in a roasting tin. Arrange the quail on top and roast for 20–25 minutes, turning occasionally, until both the quail and apples are golden brown.

3 Lift the quail and apples on to a warmed serving plate. Stir the calvados into the roasting tin to deglaze, boil for 30 seconds, then spoon over the quail to serve. Accompany with roast potatoes and green beans.

GAME BIRD ESSENTIALS

USE THESE TECHNIQUES TO ENSURE YOUR GAME BIRD ROASTS EVENLY AND THAT THE MEAT REMAINS MOIST AS IT COOKS.

TRUSS

Trussing smaller game birds such as quails and poussins before roasting helps them to keep their shape and ensures that each part of the bird cooks evenly, without overcooking any of the bony parts first. Hold the bird, breast-side down, on a work surface, tuck the neck skin under the bird, and cover with the wings. Turn the bird over and pass a length of string under the tail end of the bird. Tie a secure knot over the leg joints. Bring the strings along the sides of the body, between the breasts and the legs, and loop them around the legs. Turn the bird over, so that it is breast-side down again and tie the strings tightly under the body. Bring both ends of the string down between the sides of the body and the insides of the wings. Tie the wing bones at the neck opening so they are tucked securely under the body.

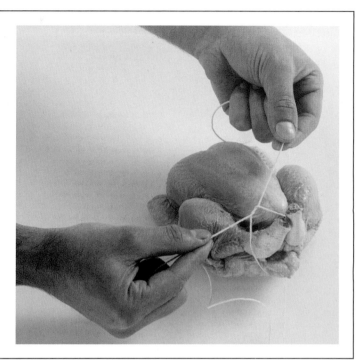

LARD AND BARD

Larding is the technique of inserting fat deep into meat. This is unnecessary when serving game pink; it is only necessary if you want to cook the meat past that stage. To lard, cut the fat into strips and insert the strips deep into the meat with a larding needle or sharp knife. This task is much easier if the fat has been frozen beforehand. Barding means wrapping the meat in fat before cooking it. You can use bacon and pancetta, for example. Here, quails are barded by being wrapped in vine leaves and streaky bacon before they are roasted.

GAME ROASTING CHART

BIRD	DESCRIPTION	ROAST
Quail	Farmed bird, not hung, so mild-flavoured. Sometimes sold boned and stuffed. Allow 1 bird per person (or 2 if large appetites!).	Put a bay leaf or small sprig of rosemary inside to flavour. Truss bird. Season well. Smear all over with butter. Preheat the oven to 200°C (400°F/Gas 6) Roast 20–25 minutes, basting frequently until tender and just cooked through.
Grouse	Plump with dark flesh and unique gamey flavour, renowned world-wide. Allow 1 whole or 2 breasts per person.	Put half an onion or some herbs inside to flavour. Truss bird. Season well. Rub with oil. Bard breast with bacon. Preheat oven to 200°C (400°F/Gas 6) Roast 35–40 minutes.
Mallard	Dark, rich meat, much less fatty than domestic duck. Allow 1 breast each or 1 bird for 2–3 people.	Put some sage and/or half an onion inside to flavour. Truss bird. Season well. Smear well with butter or duck fat. Preheat oven to 220°C (425°F/Gas 7). Roast 30–35 minutes.
Partridge	Young birds have paler flesh and are more tender. Allow 1 bird per person.	Put a sprig of thyme and/or half a small lemon inside to flavour. Truss bird. Season well. Bard breast with bacon or pancetta. Preheat oven to 200°C (400°F/Gas 6). Roast 40 minutes.
Pheasant	One of the most popular game birds with pale flesh. If hung, has a stronger, gamey flavour. Allow 1 breast each or 1 bird for 2–3 people.	Put half an onion and/or apple inside to flavour. Truss bird. Season well. Rub with oil. Bard breast with bacon. Preheat oven to 200°C (400°F/Gas 6). Roast 50 minutes–1 hour.
Teal	Very small duck with a superb flavour. Allow 1 bird per person.	Push some sage leaves and/or orange slices inside for flavour. Truss bird. Season well. Smear with butter. Preheat oven to 230°C (450°F/Gas 8). Roast 15 minutes, basting frequently.
Wood Pigeon	Dark red flesh with a distinctive flavour. Farmed birds (squabs) are fatter and more tender than wild ones. Allow 1 bird or 2–3 breasts per person.	Only roast if farmed. Put a bay leaf inside to flavour. Truss bird. Season well. Smear all over with butter or bard with bacon. Preheat oven to 230°C (450°F/Gas 8). Roast 15 minutes, basting frequently.
Woodcock	Considered one of the finest for flavour, particularly if cooked with entrails intact and head on. Also available drawn. Allow 1 bird per person.	Usually roasted undrawn, but can be drawn first. Season well. Smear all over with butter. Preheat oven to 230°C (450°F/Gas 8). Roast 15 minutes, basting frequently. Serve on toast.

SEARED DUCK WITH FIVE-SPICE AND NOODLES

THIS IS REALLY GOOD SERVED WITH A BEANSPROUT, SPRING ONION, AND ROASTED RED PEPPER SALAD, DRESSED WITH HONEY, RICE VINEGAR, AND SOY SAUCE.

4 DUCK BREASTS, about 150g (5½oz) each,
  skin on, and scored in a criss-cross pattern
2–3 tsp FIVE-SPICE PASTE or POWDER
knob of BUTTER
2 tbsp freshly squeezed ORANGE JUICE
1 tsp PALM SUGAR or SOFT LIGHT BROWN SUGAR
250g fresh CHINESE EGG NOODLES
handful of CORIANDER, finely chopped

PREPARATION TIME
10 minutes

COOKING TIME
20 minutes

SERVES 4

1 Rub the duck breasts in the five-spice paste or powder. Melt the butter in a frying pan over a high heat. Add the duck breasts, skin-side down, and cook for about 8 minutes until the skin is golden and crisp. Carefully pour the fat away from the pan, then turn the breasts over and cook on the other side for a further 6 minutes.

2 Remove the meat from the pan, cut into slices, and arrange on a warm plate. Pour away any remaining fat, then add the orange juice to the pan along with the sugar. Let it simmer for a minute or two, scraping up any sediment from the bottom of the pan with a wooden spoon.

3 Add the noodles and toss them in the sauce for a couple of minutes. Remove from the heat and stir through the coriander. Serve immediately with the warm duck breasts.

CRISPY ROAST DUCK

TRY SHREDDING THE ROASTED DUCK AND WRAPPING IT IN CHINESE PANCAKES WITH HOISIN SAUCE, SPRING ONION, AND CUCUMBER JULIENNE.

1 DUCK, about 1.8kg (4lb)
1 tsp FIVE-SPICE POWDER
3 tbsp OYSTER SAUCE
1 tsp SALT
FOR THE GLAZE
3 tbsp HONEY
1 tbsp DARK SOY SAUCE
2 tbsp RICE WINE or DRY SHERRY

PREPARATION TIME
1 hour 15 minutes, plus
drying and resting

COOKING TIME
1 hour 35 minutes

SERVES 4

1 Rinse the duck inside and out and pat dry with absorbent kitchen paper. Mix the five-spice powder, oyster sauce, and salt, and spread over and inside the bird.

2 Insert a meat hook through the neck end, or tie string around the neck to hang the duck. Place the duck in a colander in the sink, pour a kettle of boiling water over it, then pat dry with kitchen paper. Repeat this pouring and drying 5 times.

3 To make the glaze, put the honey, soy sauce, rice wine, and 150ml (5fl oz) water in a saucepan, and bring to the boil. Reduce the heat, simmer for 10 minutes, or until sticky, then brush the glaze over the duck until thoroughly coated.

4 Hang the duck over a roasting tin or shallow tray in a well-ventilated place and leave for 4–5 hours, or until the skin is dry.

5 Preheat the oven to 230°C (450°F/Gas 8). Place the duck in a roasting tin, breast-side up, and pour 150ml (5fl oz) cold water into the tin. Roast for 20 minutes, reduce the oven to 180°C (350°F/Gas 4), and roast for 1¼ hours, or until the skin is crisp and golden.

6 Leave the duck to stand for 10 minutes, then joint and arrange the duck on a serving platter. Serve at once.

SMOKED HADDOCK RISOTTO

A MODERN TAKE ON KEDGEREE, THIS IS GOOD WITH A DASH OF CURRY POWDER
FRIED WITH THE ONION. TRY TOPPING WITH HALVED HARD-BOILED QUAIL'S EGGS.

1 tbsp OLIVE OIL

60g (2oz) UNSALTED BUTTER

1 ONION, finely chopped

1 CELERY STICK, finely chopped

200g (7oz) ARBORIO RICE

150ml (5fl oz) DRY CIDER

1 litre (1¾ pints) CHICKEN STOCK

150g (5½oz) fillet of UNDYED
   SMOKED HADDOCK, skinned and chopped

50g (1¾oz) BABY LEAF SPINACH

grated zest and juice of 1 LEMON

60g (2oz) PARMESAN CHEESE,
   freshly grated

SALT and freshly ground
   BLACK PEPPER

4 tbsp DOUBLE CREAM

PREPARATION TIME
10 minutes

COOKING TIME
30 minutes

SERVES 4

1 Heat the oil and half the butter in a large saucepan. Add the onion and celery and fry on a medium heat for 5 minutes until softened but not browned. Add the rice, cook for a few minutes, stirring until glistening. Add the cider and leave to bubble until it has been absorbed. Start adding the stock, a ladleful at a time, allowing the rice to absorb all the liquid before adding more.

2 When the rice is nearly cooked and you have only 1 more ladleful of stock to go, after about 15 minutes, add the haddock, and the last of the stock. Cook until the stock is absorbed, then stir in the spinach, and lemon zest. As soon as the spinach is wilted, stir in the lemon juice, Parmesan cheese, the rest of the butter, cut in small flakes, and the cream. Taste and adjust the seasoning.

3 Spoon the risotto on to warm plates and serve straight away.

MASTERCHEF **FISH** KNOW-HOW: See **Skin a Fillet** 271

MASTERCHEF **RICE, GRAINS, AND PULSES** KNOW-HOW: See **Make Risotto** 447

LASAGNE AL FORNO

TRY VEAL MINCE INSTEAD OF BEEF, AND ADD A SLUG OF PORT TO THE RAGÙ.

1 tbsp OLIVE OIL

1 large ONION, chopped

2 CELERY STICKS, chopped

2 small CARROTS, chopped

50g (2oz) PANCETTA, diced

500g (1lb 2oz) lean MINCED STEAK

400g (14oz) can CHOPPED TOMATOES

1 tsp DRIED OREGANO

60g (2oz) BUTTER

60g (2oz) PLAIN FLOUR

600ml (1 pint) MILK

SALT and freshly ground BLACK PEPPER

150g (5½oz) RICOTTA CHEESE

12 pre-cooked LASAGNE SHEETS

50g (1¾oz) PARMESAN CHEESE, grated

PREPARATION TIME
25 minutes

COOKING TIME
1 hour 35 minutes

SERVES 4

1 To make the ragù sauce, heat the oil in a saucepan and sauté the onion, celery, carrots, and pancetta for 5 minutes, or until beginning to brown. Add the beef and cook until browned, breaking up with the side of a spoon, until all the grains are separate. Add the tomatoes, oregano, and 150ml (5fl oz) water. Bring to the boil, then reduce the heat and simmer for 40 minutes.

2 Meanwhile, to make the béchamel sauce, melt the butter in a small saucepan and stir in the flour. Cook over a low heat, stirring, for 1 minute. Remove the pan from the heat and gradually beat in the milk. Return to the heat and cook, stirring constantly, until the sauce thickens. Season to taste with salt and pepper, then stir in the ricotta.

3 Preheat the oven to 190°C (375°F/Gas 5). Spread a little béchamel sauce over the base of the ovenproof dish. Arrange a layer of lasagne sheets on top, then add a third of the ragù sauce in an even layer. Drizzle 1 or 2 spoonfuls of the béchamel over the meat sauce and top with another layer of lasagne.

4 Repeat until all the lasagne and sauce has been used, finishing with a thick layer of béchamel sauce. Sprinkle Parmesan on top and bake for 45 minutes, or until piping hot and the sauce bubbles around the edge.

MACARONI CHEESE
GOOD SERVED WITH SOME ROASTED VINE TOMATOES AND CRISPY PANCETTA.

400g (14oz) DRIED MACARONI

85g (3oz) BUTTER

100g (3½oz) fresh BREADCRUMBS

4 tbsp PLAIN FLOUR

1 tsp MUSTARD POWDER

pinch of GROUND NUTMEG

400ml (14fl oz) MILK, warmed

175g (6oz) CHEDDAR CHEESE, coarsely grated

100g (3½oz) MOZZARELLA CHEESE,
   drained and finely diced

60g (2oz) PARMESAN CHEESE, coarsely grated

PREPARATION TIME
20 mins

COOKING TIME
35 mins

SERVES 6

1 Bring a large pan of lightly salted water to the boil over a high heat. Add the macaroni and boil for 2 minutes less than specified on the packet. Drain well and set aside, shaking off any excess water.

2 Meanwhile, preheat the oven to 200°C (400°F/Gas 6) and grease a large ovenproof serving dish. Melt 30g (1oz) of the butter in a small pan. Add the breadcrumbs, stir, then remove the pan from the heat and set aside.

3 Melt the remaining butter in a large saucepan over a medium heat. Sprinkle over the flour, then stir for 30 seconds. Stir in the mustard powder and nutmeg, then remove the pan from the heat and slowly whisk in the milk. Return the pan to the heat and bring the mixture to the boil, whisking, for 2–3 minutes, or until the sauce thickens. Remove from the heat. Stir in the Cheddar cheese until melted and smooth, then add the macaroni and mozzarella and stir together.

4 Transfer the mixture to the prepared dish and smooth the surface. Toss the breadcrumbs with the Parmesan cheese and sprinkle over the top. Place the dish on a baking tray and bake for 25 minutes, or until heated through and golden brown on top. Leave to stand for 2 minutes, then serve straight from the dish.

LINGUINE ALLE VONGOLE

USE THE SAME TOMATO AND GARLIC SAUCE WITH RAW PEELED PRAWNS OR WITH SQUID RINGS. SIMMER JUST UNTIL THE PRAWNS ARE PINK OR THE SQUID TENDER.

2 tbsp OLIVE OIL

1 ONION, finely chopped

2 GARLIC CLOVES, finely chopped

400g (14oz) can CHOPPED TOMATOES

2 tbsp SUN-DRIED TOMATO PURÉE

120ml (4fl oz) DRY WHITE WINE

2 x 140g (5oz) jars CLAMS IN NATURAL JUICE, strained,
    with the juice reserved

SALT and freshly ground BLACK PEPPER

350g (12oz) DRIED LINGUINE

4 tbsp finely chopped FLAT-LEAF PARSLEY,
    plus extra to garnish

PREPARATION TIME
5 minutes

COOKING TIME
20 minutes

SERVES 4

1 Heat the oil in a large saucepan over medium heat. Add the onion and garlic, and fry, stirring frequently, for 5 minutes or until softened. Add the tomatoes with the juices, tomato paste, wine, and reserved clam juice, and season to taste with salt and pepper, then bring to the boil, stirring. Reduce the heat to low, partially cover the pan and leave to simmer for 10–15 minutes, stirring occasionally.

2 Meanwhile, bring a large pan of salted water to the boil over a high heat. Add the linguine, stir, and boil for 10 minutes, or according to the packet instructions, until the pasta is tender but still with some bite. Drain the pasta into a large colander and shake to remove any excess water.

3 Add the clams and chopped parsley to the sauce and continue to simmer for 1–2 minutes to heat through. Season with salt and pepper to taste.

4 Add the linguine to the sauce and use 2 forks to toss and combine all the ingredients so the pasta is well coated and the clams evenly distributed. Sprinkle with extra parsley and serve at once.

PAD THAI

THIS IS A SIMPLE VERSION OF ONE OF THAILAND'S NATIONAL DISHES, WHERE IT IS OFTEN SERVED ROLLED UP IN A THIN OMELETTE.

2 tbsp chopped CORIANDER

1 RED THAI CHILLI, deseeded and finely chopped

4 tbsp SUNFLOWER OIL

250g (9oz) raw TIGER PRAWNS, peeled

4 SHALLOTS, finely chopped

1 tbsp PALM or LIGHT BROWN SUGAR

4 large EGGS, beaten

2 tbsp OYSTER SAUCE

1 tbsp NAM PLA (Thai fish sauce)

juice of 1 LIME

350g (12oz) FLAT RICE NOODLES,
   cooked according to packet instructions

250g (9oz) BEANSPROUTS

4 SPRING ONIONS, sliced

115g (4oz) UNSALTED ROASTED PEANUTS,
   coarsely chopped

1 LIME, cut into 4 wedges, to serve

PREPARATION TIME
20 minutes

COOKING TIME
10 minutes

SERVES 4

1 Mix together the coriander, chilli, and sunflower oil. Heat half the mixture in a wok, add the prawns, and stir-fry for 1 minute. Remove and set aside.

2 Add the remaining flavoured oil to the wok and stir-fry the shallots for 1 minute. Add the sugar and the eggs, and cook for 1 minute, stirring frequently to scramble the eggs as they begin to set.

3 Stir in the oyster sauce, nam pla, lime juice, noodles, and beansprouts, and return the prawns to the wok. Stir-fry for 2 minutes, then add the spring onions and half the peanuts. Toss everything together for 1–2 minutes, or until piping hot.

4 To serve, divide between 4 individual bowls, scatter the remaining peanuts on top, and add a lime wedge.

PAELLA

THIS IS A SEAFOOD VERSION; FOR A MIXED PAELLA, OMIT THE LANGOUSTINES, AND ADD SOME PIECES OF CHICKEN AND DICED CHORIZO WITH THE ONIONS.

1.2 litres (2 pints) hot FISH STOCK

large pinch of SAFFRON THREADS

2 tbsp OLIVE OIL

1 ONION, finely chopped

2 GARLIC CLOVES, crushed

2 large TOMATOES, skinned and diced

12 peeled, raw KING PRAWNS

225g (8oz) SQUID, sliced into rings

400g (14oz) PAELLA RICE

85g (3oz) PETIT POIS

4 LANGOUSTINES or DUBLIN BAY PRAWNS

12–16 MUSSELS, cleaned

1 tbsp chopped PARSLEY, to garnish

PREPARATION TIME
10 minutes

COOKING TIME
30 minutes

SERVES 4

1 Pour a little of the hot fish stock into a cup or jug, add the saffron threads, and set aside to infuse. Heat the oil in a paella pan or large frying pan, and fry the onion and garlic until softened. Add the tomatoes and cook for 2 minutes, then add the prawns and squid, and fry for 1–2 minutes, or until the prawns turn pink.

2 Stir in the rice, then stir in the saffron liquid, peas, and 900ml (1½ pints) of stock. Simmer, uncovered, without stirring, over a low heat for 12–14 minutes, or until the stock has evaporated and the rice is just tender, adding a little extra stock if necessary.

3 Meanwhile, cook the langoustines in 150ml (5fl oz) simmering stock for 3–4 minutes, or until cooked through. Transfer to a warm plate with a slotted spoon. Add the mussels to the stock, cover, and cook over a high heat for 2–3 minutes, or until open. Remove from the pan with a slotted spoon, discarding any that have not opened.

4 Reserve 8 mussels for garnish. Remove the rest from their shells and stir into the paella. Arrange the reserved mussels and langoustines on top, and garnish with parsley.

MASTERCHEF **SHELLFISH** KNOW-HOW: See **Clean Mussels** 284

RISOTTO ALLA MILANESE

SOME SAY IT SHOULD HAVE WHITE WINE IN, SOME SAY NOT, BUT IT ENHANCES THE FLAVOUR EXQUISITELY. SERVE AS AN ACCOMPANIMENT OR A STARTER.

2 good pinches SAFFRON STRANDS

1.2 litres (2 pints) boiling CHICKEN STOCK

85g (3oz) UNSALTED BUTTER

2 tbsp OLIVE OIL

1 BANANA SHALLOT, very finely chopped

400g (14oz) RISOTTO RICE

150ml (5fl oz) DRY WHITE WINE

85g (3oz) GRANA PADANO or PARMESAN CHEESE,
   freshly grated, plus a few shavings for garnish (optional)

SALT and freshly ground BLACK PEPPER

PREPARATION TIME
5 minutes

COOKING TIME
25 minutes

SERVES 4–6

1 Put the saffron in a cup with 3 tbsp of the boiling stock and set aside to infuse.

2 Melt half the butter with the oil in a large saucepan. Add the shallot and fry very gently, stirring, for 3 minutes until softened but not browned.

3 Stir in the rice until glistening and translucent.

4 Stir in the wine and simmer gently until completely absorbed.

5 Stir in a ladleful of the stock and cook over a gentle heat until it has been absorbed. Continue cooking, stirring in a ladleful of the stock at a time until the liquid is used and the rice is creamy, but still with some bite, about 20 minutes.

6 Strain the saffron liquid into the rice. Stir in with the remaining butter, in small flakes, and the grated cheese. Taste and season, if necessary. Serve straight away, garnished with a few Parmesan shavings, if using.

MASTERCHEF **RICE, GRAINS, AND PULSES** KNOW-HOW: See **Make Risotto** 447

PAPPARDELLE ALLA BOLOGNESE

THE RICH, MEATY, SLOW-SIMMERED SAUCE GOES WELL WITH MOST PASTA SHAPES.
USE LAMB OR VEAL MINCE FOR A CHANGE AND ADD SOME CHOPPED ROSEMARY.

2 tbsp OLIVE OIL

100g (3½ oz) SMOKED LARDONS

1 ONION, finely chopped

2 GARLIC CLOVES, crushed

400g (14oz) lean MINCED STEAK

115g (4oz) BUTTON MUSHROOMS, sliced

120ml (4fl oz) RED WINE

2 tbsp TOMATO PURÉE

400g (14oz) can CHOPPED TOMATOES

1 tsp DRIED OREGANO

good pinch of SUGAR

SALT and freshly ground BLACK PEPPER

90ml (3fl oz) DOUBLE CREAM

450g (1lb) DRIED PAPPARDELLE PASTA

freshly grated PARMESAN CHEESE, to serve

PREPARATION TIME
15 minutes

COOKING TIME
2 hours

SERVES 4

1 Heat the oil in a deep, heavy saucepan and fry the lardons for 1–2 minutes. Add the onion and garlic, and continue to fry, stirring occasionally, for 5 minutes, or until softened but not browned.

2 Stir in the meat, breaking up any lumps, then cook for a further 10 minutes, or until it is evenly coloured, stirring frequently until all the grains are separate. Stir in the mushrooms and fry, stirring for 1 minute. Add the wine, tomato purée, tomatoes, and sugar. Season to taste with salt and pepper, then bring to the boil.

3 Reduce the heat to very low, cover the pan, and simmer very gently for 1½ hours. Stir occasionally to prevent sticking. Stir the cream into the ragù, cover, and simmer for a further 30 minutes.

4 Bring a large pan of lightly salted water to the boil. Add the pappardelle and simmer for 8–10 minutes, or until cooked but still with some bite. Drain well, spoon the ragù over, and serve with freshly grated Parmesan.

SPAGHETTI PUTTANESCA

TRY ADDING SOME RAW PEELED PRAWNS TO THE SAUCE FOR THE LAST 5 MINUTES.

4 tbsp OLIVE OIL

2 GARLIC CLOVES, finely chopped

½ fresh RED CHILLI, deseeded and finely chopped

6 canned ANCHOVIES, drained and finely chopped

115g (4oz) BLACK OLIVES, pitted and chopped

1–2 tbsp CAPERS, rinsed and drained

450g (1lb) TOMATOES, skinned, deseeded, and chopped

450g (1lb) DRIED SPAGHETTI

chopped PARSLEY, to serve

freshly grated PARMESAN CHEESE, to serve

PREPARATION TIME
15 minutes

COOKING TIME
25 minutes

SERVES 4

1 Heat the oil in a saucepan, add the garlic and chilli, and cook gently for 2 minutes, or until the garlic is slightly coloured. Add the anchovies, olives, capers, and tomatoes and stir, breaking down the anchovies to a paste.

2 Reduce the heat and let the sauce simmer, uncovered, for 10–15 minutes, or until the sauce has thickened, stirring frequently.

3 Cook the spaghetti in plenty of lightly salted boiling water for 10 minutes, or as directed on the packet. Drain.

4 Toss the spaghetti with the sauce and serve sprinkled with parsley and Parmesan cheese.

MASTERCHEF **VEGETABLES** KNOW-HOW: See **Deseed and Cut Chillies** 371

MASTERCHEF **PASTA, NOODLES, AND GNOCCHI** KNOW-HOW: See **Cook Dried Pasta** 468

PASTA ALLA CARBONARA

GOOD WITH COOKED BABY BROAD BEANS, POPPED OUT OF THEIR SKINS, STIRRED IN.

450g (1lb) DRIED PASTA, such as TAGLIATELLE,
SPAGHETTI, or LINGUINE

4 tbsp OLIVE OIL

175g (6oz) PANCETTA or CURED UNSMOKED BACON
RASHERS, rind removed, and finely chopped

2 GARLIC CLOVES, crushed

5 large EGGS

75g (2½oz) PARMESAN CHEESE, grated,
plus extra to serve

75g (2½oz) PECORINO CHEESE, grated,
plus extra to serve

SALT and freshly ground BLACK PEPPER

1 sprig of THYME, leaves only, chopped (optional)

PREPARATION TIME
10 minutes

COOKING TIME
10 minutes

SERVES 4–6

1 Bring a large saucepan of salted water to the boil. Add the pasta, and bring to the boil for 10 minutes, or according to the packet instructions, until the pasta is *al dente*.

2 Meanwhile, heat half the oil in a large frying pan over a medium heat. Add the pancetta and garlic and fry, stirring, for 5–8 minutes, or until the pancetta is crispy.

3 Beat the eggs and cheeses together, add pepper to taste, and the thyme, if using. Drain the pasta well and return to the pan. Add the eggs, pancetta, and the remaining oil, and stir until the pasta is coated. Serve while still hot, sprinkled with the extra cheese.

CELERIAC REMOULADE

THIS IS THE PERFECT WAY OF SERVING CELERIAC AS A STARTER OR SIDE DISH BUT IT WORKS EQUALLY WELL WITH FENNEL.

1 SHALLOT, peeled and finely chopped

1 tsp CAPERS, rinsed

½ tbsp GHERKINS, chopped

2 tbsp DOUBLE CREAM

2 tsp DIJON MUSTARD

3 tbsp MAYONNAISE

juice of ½ LEMON

1 small CELERIAC

SALT and freshly ground BLACK PEPPER

PREPARATION TIME
15 minutes

SERVES 6

1 Mix together all the ingredients, except the celeriac and seasoning, in a large bowl.

2 Peel, quarter, and shred the celeriac finely in a food processor or with a sharp knife. Quickly add to the sauce (to prevent discolouration) and mix thoroughly. Season to taste with salt and pepper. Chill in the refrigerator until ready to serve.

MASTERCHEF **SAVOURY SAUCES AND STOCKS** KNOW-HOW: See **Make Mayonnaise** 490

COLESLAW

EQUALLY GOOD MADE WITH RED CABBAGE, WITH SOME CHOPPED WALNUTS AND
A HANDFUL OF RAISINS ADDED.

250g (9oz) WHITE CABBAGE
2 large CARROTS, coarsely grated
2 CELERY STICKS, finely sliced
2 SPRING ONIONS, finely sliced
120ml (4fl oz) MAYONNAISE
4 tsp MILK
juice of 1 small LEMON
2 tbsp chopped FLAT-LEAF PARSLEY
1 tbsp snipped CHIVES
SALT and freshly ground BLACK PEPPER

PREPARATION TIME
15 minutes

SERVES 4

1 Slice the cabbage as finely as possible, discarding the stalk, and place the shreds in a large bowl. Add the prepared carrots, celery, and spring onions, and mix together.

2 In a small bowl, mix together the mayonnaise and milk, then the lemon juice, parsley, and chives, and season to taste with salt and pepper. Add this dressing to the vegetables and stir until well mixed. Cover and set aside for a couple of hours to allow the flavours to develop.

MASTERCHEF **VEGETABLES** KNOW-HOW: See **Core and Shred Cabbage** 367

GRATIN DAUPHINOIS

A GRATIN RICH WITH CREAM AND FRAGRANT WITH GARLIC AND NUTMEG. TRY LAYERING THE POTATOES WITH SOME GRATED GRUYÈRE CHEESE, TOO.

900g (2lb) even-sized WAXY POTATOES, such as NICOLA

SALT and freshly ground BLACK PEPPER

600ml (1 pint) DOUBLE CREAM

1 GARLIC CLOVE, cut in half

freshly grated NUTMEG

45g (1½oz) BUTTER, at room temperature

PREPARATION TIME
20 minutes

COOKING TIME
1 hour 30 minutes

SERVES 4–6

1 Preheat the oven to 180°C (350°F/Gas 4). Butter a gratin dish.

2 Peel the potatoes and slice them into even rounds 3mm (⅛in) thick – use a mandolin or a food processor fitted with a fine slicing blade, if you have one. Rinse the potato slices in cold water, drain, and pat dry with kitchen paper or a tea towel.

3 Arrange the potato slices in layers in the prepared dish, seasoning each layer well with salt and pepper.

4 Pour the cream into a saucepan, add the garlic and a good grating of nutmeg, and bring just to the boil. Pour the cream over the potatoes and dot the top with small knobs of butter.

5 Cover with foil and bake for 1 hour. Remove the foil and continue baking for 30 minutes, or until the potatoes are tender when pierced with a knife and the top is golden. Serve hot, straight from the oven.

TABBOULEH

ALTHOUGH NOT TRADITIONAL, THIS IS DELICIOUS WITH SOME TOASTED PINE NUTS AND CRUMBLED FETA CHEESE, ADDED BEFORE SPOONING INTO THE SALAD LEAVES.

115g (4oz) BULGUR WHEAT

juice of 2 LEMONS

75ml (2½fl oz) OLIVE OIL

SALT and freshly ground BLACK PEPPER

1 bunch of FLAT-LEAF PARSLEY

1 small bunch of MINT LEAVES

4 SPRING ONIONS, finely chopped

2 large TOMATOES, deseeded and diced

1 head of LITTLE GEM LETTUCE

PREPARATION TIME
20 minutes, plus standing

SERVES 4

1 Put the bulgur wheat in a large bowl, pour over cold water to cover, and leave to stand for 15 minutes, or until the wheat has absorbed all the water and the grains have swollen.

2 Add the lemon juice and olive oil to the wheat, season to taste with salt and pepper, and stir to mix.

3 Just before serving, finely chop the parsley and mint, discarding any coarse stalks. Mix the parsley, mint, and spring onions into the wheat.

4 Arrange the lettuce leaves on a serving plate and spoon the salad into the leaves.

ROASTED VEGETABLES

ROOTS SUCH AS CELERIAC AND BEETROOT, ROASTED IN THEIR SKINS AND PEELED BEFORE SERVING, AS WELL AS FENNEL, ALSO WORK WONDERFULLY.

900g (2lb) FLOURY POTATOES,
   such as MARIS PIPER, peeled and quartered

4 CARROTS, peeled and quartered

4 PARSNIPS, peeled and quartered

4 tbsp OLIVE OIL

4 BANANA SHALLOTS, peeled and quartered

1 bulb of GARLIC, separated into cloves but left unpeeled

2 sprigs of ROSEMARY, torn into leaves

SEA SALT

PREPARATION TIME
25 minutes

COOKING TIME
1 hour

SERVES 4–6

1 Preheat the oven to 200°C (400°F/Gas 6). Put the potatoes and carrots in a pan of salted water, bring to the boil, then boil for 5 minutes. Add the parsnips and cook a further 3 minutes. Drain well, then return to the pan.

2 Put the lid back on the pan and give the pan a good shake to rough up the edges of the vegetables.

3 Put the oil in a large roasting tin and place it in the oven until really hot. Remove from the oven and carefully add the part-cooked vegetables, the shallots, and garlic cloves, turning each piece over in the hot oil. Sprinkle with the rosemary and season with sea salt. Return to the oven to roast for about 1 hour, or until the vegetables are golden and tender. Turn them over halfway through cooking.

CHIPS

USE CELERIAC FOR A CHANGE FROM POTATOES, BUT SOAK IN WATER WITH A
SPLASH OF LEMON JUICE OR VINEGAR.

900g (1kg) MARIS PIPER POTATOES,
  peeled and cut into thick chips
GROUNDNUT OIL, for deep-frying
coarse SEA SALT

PREPARATION TIME
10 minutes, plus soaking

COOKING TIME
20 minutes

SERVES 4

1 Soak the potatoes in cold water for 10 minutes, drain, and dry thoroughly. Heat the oil to 160°C (325°F) and cook the potatoes, a batch at time, for a few minutes in the oil until soft, but do not brown. Drain on kitchen paper.

2 Increase the heat of the fryer to 180°C (350°F). Give the chips a second frying to allow them to brown and crisp. This will take about 2–3 minutes. Using a slotted spoon, lift the chips onto clean kitchen paper, to drain, and then transfer to a serving bowl. Sprinkle with coarse sea salt and serve hot.

GUACAMOLE

THIS CAN BE SIMPLY CRUSHED AVOCADO AND LIME TO SERVE IN FAJITAS.

3 large, ripe AVOCADOS

juice of ½ LIME

½ small ONION, finely chopped

1 ripe TOMATO, deseeded and chopped

1 RED CHILLI, deseeded and finely chopped

10 sprigs of CORIANDER, chopped,
  plus extra to garnish

SALT

TORTILLA CHIPS, to serve

PREPARATION TIME
20 minutes

SERVES 6

1 Prepare the avocados by removing and discarding the skins and stones. Place the avocados into a mixing bowl and mash with a fork to create a chunky mixture.

2 Add the lime juice, followed by the onion, tomato, and chilli. Mix well, stir in the chopped coriander, and season with salt to taste.

3 Pile the guacamole into a serving bowl, garnish with coriander, and serve immediately with tortilla chips.

MASTERCHEF **VEGETABLES** KNOW-HOW: See **Stone and Remove Avocado Flesh** 368

MASTERCHEF **VEGETABLES** KNOW-HOW: See **Deseed and Cut Chillies** 371

APPLE PIE

YOU CAN FLAVOUR THE PIE WITH CINNAMON OR GROUND CLOVES INSTEAD OF MIXED SPICE, AND TRY ADDING A HANDFUL OF RAISINS TO THE APPLES AS WELL.

350g (12oz) SHORTCRUST PASTRY

finely grated zest of 1 LEMON

2 tbsp fresh LEMON JUICE

100g (3½oz) CASTER SUGAR

4 tbsp PLAIN FLOUR

1 tsp ground MIXED SPICE

1kg (2¼lb) BRAMLEY APPLES, peeled and thinly sliced

2 tbsp MILK, to glaze

PREPARATION TIME
25 minutes, plus chilling

COOKING TIME
50 minutes

MAKES 8 SLICES

1 Divide the dough into 2 pieces: one piece should be two-thirds of the dough, the other about one-third. On a lightly floured work surface, roll the larger piece into a 30cm (12in) circle and use it to line a 23cm (9in) deep pie plate, leaving any excess to overhang. Cover with cling film and chill for at least 15 minutes. Roll out the remaining dough into a 25cm (10in) circle, place on a plate, cover, and refrigerate.

2 Meanwhile, preheat the oven to 200°C (400°F/Gas 6) with a baking tray inside. Mix the lemon zest and juice, sugar, flour, and mixed spice in a large bowl. Gently toss with the apple slices.

3 Tip the filling into the pie plate. Lightly brush the pastry on the rim of the pie plate with water and place the smaller dough circle on top. Crimp the edges together and cut off the excess pastry. Carefully brush the top of the pastry with milk and cut a few slits.

4 Put the pie on the hot baking tray in the oven. Reduce the temperature to 190°C (375°F/Gas 5) and bake for 50–55 minutes, or until the pastry is golden brown. Leave to stand for 5 minutes, then slice and serve hot.

BREAD AND BUTTER PUDDING

CAREFUL COOKING IN A LOW OVEN WILL PRODUCE A PUDDING WITH A SMOOTH, VELVETY TEXTURE.

30g (1oz) BUTTER, plus extra to grease

5–6 slices of day-old BREAD, crusts removed, about 175g (6oz) in total

60g (2oz) RAISINS

3 EGGS

300ml (10fl oz) FULL-FAT MILK

200ml (7fl oz) SINGLE CREAM

60g (2oz) CASTER SUGAR

1 tsp PURE VANILLA EXTRACT

4 tbsp APRICOT JAM

2–3 tsp LEMON JUICE

PREPARATION TIME
15 minutes, plus soaking

COOKING TIME
40 minutes

SERVES 4

1 Lightly grease an ovenproof dish with a little butter. Spread the remaining butter on the slices of bread. Cut each slice in half diagonally, then in half again to form 4 triangles.

2 Place the raisins in the bottom of the dish and arrange overlapping slices of bread on the top. Beat together the eggs, milk, cream, sugar, and vanilla extract. Carefully pour the mixture over the bread and leave to soak for at least 30 minutes.

3 Preheat the oven to 180°C (350°F/Gas 4). Place the dish in a deep roasting tin and pour boiling water into the tin to a depth of 2.5cm (1in). Bake in the oven for 30–40 minutes, until still slightly moist in the centre, but not runny.

4 Meanwhile, put the jam in a small pan with the lemon juice and 1 tbsp water. Bring to the boil, then push through a sieve. Carefully brush or spoon the sieved jam over the surface of the hot pudding.

TRADITIONAL CHRISTMAS PUDDING

FOR A MODERN FESTIVE FEEL, SUBSTITUTE SOME DRIED CRANBERRIES FOR SOME OF THE MIXED DRIED FRUIT AND SERVE IT WITH AMARETTO-FLAVOURED CREAM.

700g (1½lb) MIXED DRIED FRUIT

55g (2oz) chopped ALMONDS

2 EATING APPLES, coarsely grated (including skin)

1 large CARROT, grated

175g (6oz) shredded SUET

115g (4oz) dark MUSCOVADO SUGAR

225g (8oz) fresh BREADCRUMBS

115g (4oz) PLAIN FLOUR

1 tsp MIXED SPICE

½ tsp grated NUTMEG

½ tsp GROUND CINNAMON

¼ tsp GROUND GINGER

200ml (7fl oz) GUINNESS or BROWN ALE

2 EGGS, beaten

TO DECORATE

CASTER SUGAR

small SPRIG OF HOLLY

1 ladleful BRANDY

PREPARATION TIME
15 minutes, plus standing

COOKING TIME
7 hours (initially), plus 3 hours
(to serve)

**MAKES 2 X 1 LITRE
(1¾ PINT) PUDDINGS**

1 Put all the ingredients in a large mixing bowl. Mix thoroughly with a wooden spoon to combine – at this point get everyone in the house to stir the pudding and make a wish! If time, cover and leave overnight to mature.

2 Grease two 1-litre (1¾ pint) pudding basins. Line the bases with a circle of baking parchment.

3 Spoon the mixture into the basins and smooth the surfaces. Cover each pudding with a circle of baking parchment then a saucer or small plate that fits inside the top of the basins. Cover with a double thickness of foil, twisting and folding under the rims to secure.

4 Steam for 7 hours until really dark, topping up the saucepan with boiling water as necessary.

5 Cool then cover with clean foil and store in a cool, dark place (for several months, if necessary, and can also be frozen one year for the next). When ready to serve, steam for a further 3 hours.

6 Turn out onto a serving dish. Remove the base paper, if necessary.

7 Put a little foil round the base of the sprig of holly and push into the top of the pudding. Dust the pudding with caster sugar. Warm a ladleful of brandy, ignite, pour around the pudding and bring to the table, immediately, while still flaming. Serve with cream and brandy sauce (a sweet white sauce, flavoured to taste with brandy).

CHOCOLATE FONDANTS

YOU CAN MAKE WHITE CHOCOLATE FONDANTS IN THE SAME WAY. TURN OUT ONTO A POOL OF RASPBERRY COULIS.

150g (5½oz) UNSALTED BUTTER,
  cubed, plus extra for greasing
1 heaped tbsp PLAIN FLOUR, sifted,
  plus extra for dusting
150g (5½oz) DARK CHOCOLATE (70% cocoa)
  broken into pieces
3 large EGGS
75g (2½oz) CASTER SUGAR
COCOA POWDER or ICING SUGAR,
  for dusting (optional)
CREAM or ICE CREAM, to serve (optional)

PREPARATION TIME
20 minutes

COOKING TIME
12–15 minutes

SERVES 4

1 Preheat the oven to 200°C (400°F/Gas 6). Thoroughly grease the sides and base of 4 x 150ml (5fl oz) dariole moulds or ramekin dishes. Sprinkle the insides with a little flour, then turn the flour around in the dish until all the butter is covered with a thin layer of flour. Tip out the excess flour. Line the bases of the ramekins with small discs of baking parchment.

2 Gently melt together the chocolate and butter in a heatproof bowl over simmering water, stirring occasionally. Make sure the base of the bowl does not touch the water. Cool slightly.

3 In a separate bowl, whisk together the eggs and sugar. Once the chocolate mixture has cooled slightly, beat it into the eggs and sugar until thoroughly combined. Sprinkle the flour over the top of the mixture and gently fold it in.

4 Divide the mixture between the moulds or ramekins, making sure that the mixture does not come right up to the top. At this stage the fondants can be refrigerated for several hours or overnight, as long as they are brought back to room temperature before cooking.

5 Cook the fondants in the middle of the oven for 5–6 minutes if using moulds, 12–15 minutes for ramekins. The sides should be firm, but the middles soft to the touch. Run a sharp knife around the edge of the moulds or ramekins. Turn the fondants out onto individual serving plates by putting a plate on top and inverting the whole thing. Gently remove the mould or ramekin and peel off the parchment.

6 Dust with cocoa powder or icing sugar if desired, and serve immediately with cream or ice cream.

CHOCOLATE AND WALNUT ROULADE

FOR A CHANGE FROM WALNUT CREAM, FOLD IN SOME APPLE PURÉE AND FLAVOUR WITH CINNAMON. MAKE A BLACKBERRY COULIS INSTEAD OF RASPBERRY.

5 EGGS

125g (4½oz) CASTER SUGAR, plus extra for dusting

200g (7oz) DARK CHOCOLATE (70% cocoa)

60g (2oz) WALNUTS, finely chopped

300ml (10fl oz) DOUBLE CREAM

1 tbsp ICING SUGAR

a few drops of VANILLA EXTRACT

FOR THE RASPBERRY COULIS

450g (1lb) RASPBERRIES

2 tbsp ICING SUGAR, sifted

2 tsp LEMON JUICE

6 TINY MINT SPRIGS, to decorate

PREPARATION TIME
40 minutes

COOKING TIME
12–14 minutes

SERVES 6

1 Preheat the oven to 220°C (425°F/Gas 7). For the roulade sponge, line a 20 x 30cm (8 x 12in) Swiss roll tin with baking parchment. Snip the corners to fit the paper neatly into the tin. Separate the eggs and beat the yolks with the sugar until pale and foamy.

2 Melt the chocolate in a bain marie or a bowl set over a pan of simmering water. Leave to cool for about 10 minutes before adding to the egg yolk mixture – if the chocolate is hot it will cook the eggs and make the mixture too stiff to incorporate the whites.

3 Whisk the egg whites until stiff but still moist. Gently cut and fold them into the egg yolk and chocolate, taking care not to lose too much air from the whites. Spoon gently into the prepared tin. Place in the oven and bake for 12–14 minutes until just cooked – the top should spring back when gently pressed.

4 Lay another sheet of baking parchment on a clean tea towel on the work surface. Dust with caster sugar. Carefully turn out the roulade on to the sugared paper. Gently lift off the baking paper, using a knife to ease the roulade from it, then leave it resting on top of the roulade. Cover with another clean tea towel and allow to cool.

5 To make the walnut cream, whip the cream in a bowl with the 1 tbsp icing sugar until softly peaking. Flavour to taste with vanilla extract and gently fold in the walnuts. Cover the bowl with cling film and chill until needed.

6 To make the coulis, purée the raspberries with the icing sugar in a food processor, then pass through a sieve set over a bowl. Sharpen to taste with lemon juice. Cover the bowl with cling film and chill until required.

7 When the roulade is cold, trim the edges with a sharp knife. Spread with the cream and gently roll up from one short edge, using the parchment underneath to help. Wrap in the parchment and chill until ready to serve.

8 To serve, cut a thick slice of roulade per person. Place on serving plates and surround with a swirl of raspberry coulis. Put a cluster of raspberries to one side and add a small sprig of mint to each.

MASTERCHEF **FLAVOURINGS** KNOW-HOW: See **Prepare Chocolate** 393

MASTERCHEF **DOUGH, PASTRY, AND CAKE** KNOW-HOW: See **Roll a Sponge Roulade** 463

MASTERCHEF **EGGS AND DARY PRODUCTS** KNOW-HOW: See **Whip Cream** 436

CHERRY CLAFOUTIS

THIS FRENCH FAVOURITE CAN BE ENJOYED WARM OR AT ROOM TEMPERATURE.

750g (1lb 10oz) CHERRIES

3 tbsp KIRSCH

75g (2½oz) CASTER SUGAR

BUTTER, for greasing

4 large EGGS

1 VANILLA POD, split

100g (3½oz) PLAIN FLOUR, sifted

300ml (10fl oz) MILK

pinch of SALT

PREPARATION TIME
15 minutes, plus standing

COOKING TIME
35–45 minutes

SERVES 6

1 Toss the cherries with the kirsch and 2 tbsp of the sugar in a medium-sized bowl, and leave to stand for 30 minutes.

2 Meanwhile, preheat the oven to 200°C (400°F/Gas 6). Butter a 25cm (10in) flan tin, and set aside.

3 Strain the liquid from the cherries and beat it with the eggs, the seeds from the vanilla pod, and the remaining sugar. Slowly beat in the flour, then add the milk and salt and mix to make a smooth batter.

4 Arrange the cherries in the dish, then pour over the batter. Place in the oven and bake for 35–45 minutes, or until the top is browned and the centre is firm to the touch.

5 Dust with sifted icing sugar and allow to cool on a wire rack. Serve with plenty of thick cream or crème fraîche, or with vanilla ice cream.

CRÈME BRÛLÉE

TRY REPLACING A LITTLE OF THE CREAM WITH IRISH CREAM OR COFFEE LIQUEUR.

500ml (16fl oz) DOUBLE CREAM
1 VANILLA POD, split in half lengthways
5 EGG YOLKS
50g (1¾oz) CASTER SUGAR
4 tbsp GRANULATED SUGAR

PREPARATION TIME
20 minutes, plus standing

COOKING TIME
45 minutes

SERVES 6

1 Preheat the oven to 140°C (275°F/Gas 1). Place the cream in a saucepan and add the vanilla pod. Heat the cream over a low heat until just simmering, then remove from the heat, and set aside to infuse for 1 hour.

2 Whisk the egg yolks and caster sugar together in a bowl until well combined. Remove the vanilla pod halves from the cream, and use the tip of a sharp knife to scrape the seeds into the cream.

3 Whisk the cream into the egg mixture, then strain through a sieve into a jug. Pour the mixture evenly into 6 ramekins, and place them in a roasting tin half filled with boiling water. Bake for 40 minutes, or until just set. Remove from the tin, cool, and chill.

4 To serve, preheat the grill to its highest setting. Sprinkle 2 tsp sugar evenly over the top of each pudding and grill until the sugar caramelizes. Alternatively use a blow torch. Chill until required.

MASTERCHEF **FLAVOURINGS** KNOW-HOW: See **Extract Vanilla Seeds** 390
MASTERCHEF **EGGS AND DAIRY PRODUCTS** KNOW-HOW: See **Separate Yolks and Whites** 428

CRÈME CARAMEL

FOR A CHOCOLATE VERSION, MELT SOME GRATED DARK CHOCOLATE IN THE MILK.

175g (6oz) SUGAR
1 VANILLA POD
600ml (1pint) FULL-FAT MILK
4 EGGS
4 EGG YOLKS
60g (2oz) CASTER SUGAR

PREPARATION TIME
20 minutes, plus chilling

COOKING TIME
35–40 minutes

SERVES 4

1 Preheat the oven to 160°C (325°F/Gas 3). Pour boiling water into the individual ramekins and set aside. Fill a large bowl with cold water. Tip the sugar into a heavy saucepan and place over a low heat, until the sugar has just dissolved. Dip a pastry brush in water and brush the sides of the pan where any sugar crystals form. Increase the heat and boil rapidly, gently swirling the pan until the caramel is golden brown. Place the base of the pan in the bowl of cold water to rapidly cool to prevent it cooking any further.

2 Working quickly, empty the ramekins and divide the hot caramel between them. Gently swirl the dishes so that the caramel comes halfway up the sides of each ramekin. Set aside to cool.

3 Using a sharp knife, split the vanilla pod and scrape out the seeds; place both the seeds and pod in a saucepan with the milk, and heat until almost boiling. Remove from the heat and discard the pod.

4 Meanwhile, whisk the eggs, egg yolks, and caster sugar together in a large bowl. Pour the warm milk mixture over, whisking to combine, then pour into the ramekins. Place the ramekins in a roasting tin and pour boiling water into the tin to come halfway up the sides of the dishes. Bake for 25–30 minutes, or until just set in the centre. Remove from the tin, allow to cool, then chill until ready to serve.

5 Gently pull the edges of the custard away from the sides of the ramekin using a fingertip. Place a serving plate over the top of the ramekin and invert on to the plate.

MASTERCHEF **FLAVOURINGS** KNOW-HOW: See **Extract Vanilla Seeds** 390

MASTERCHEF **EGGS AND DAIRY PRODUCTS** KNOW-HOW: See **Separate Yolks and Whites** 428

RICE PUDDING

LOVELY WITH SOME CHOPPED DRIED APRICOTS AND FLAKED ALMONDS ADDED.

15g (½oz) BUTTER, plus extra
   for buttering
60g (2oz) SHORT-GRAIN RICE,
   such as ARBORIO (or use a basic one)
600ml (1 pint) FULL-FAT MILK
30g (1oz) CASTER SUGAR
pinch of ground CINNAMON
   or grated NUTMEG

PREPARATION TIME
15 minutes

COOKING TIME
2–2½ hours

SERVES 4

1 Lightly butter a 900ml (2 pint) ovenproof serving dish. Rinse the rice under cold running water, then drain well. Pour the rice and the milk into the dish and leave to rest for 30 minutes.

2 Preheat the oven to 150°C (300°F/Gas 2). Add the sugar, stir, then sprinkle the top with cinnamon or nutmeg, and dot with the butter. Bake for 2–2½ hours, or until the skin of the rice is golden.

CHOCOLATE MOUSSE

AN ELEGANT WAY OF SERVING THE MOUSSE IS IN A DEMITASSE WITH A CHOCOLATE TEASPOON OR MINT STICK LAID ON THE SAUCERS.

115g (4oz) DARK CHOCOLATE (70% cocoa), broken up,
    plus extra grated or curled to serve
1 tbsp BRANDY or COGNAC
2 EGGS, separated
35g (1¼oz) CASTER SUGAR
150ml (5fl oz) DOUBLE CREAM

PREPARATION TIME
20 minutes, plus chilling

COOKING TIME
20 minutes

SERVES 4

1 Place the chocolate and brandy or cognac in a heatproof bowl over a pan of simmering water. When the chocolate has melted, stir until combined, remove from the heat, and allow to cool slightly.

2 Place the egg yolks and sugar in a large bowl and whisk until thick and creamy. Then whisk in the chocolate mixture.

3 Whip the cream in a bowl until stiff. Gently fold in the chocolate mixture until combined, taking care not to over mix. Whisk the egg whites until stiff, and gently fold into the chocolate mixture.

4 Spoon into individual dishes and refrigerate for at least 2 hours. If you like the mousse soft, take it out of the refrigerator and let it warm to room temperature before serving. Decorate with grated chocolate or chocolate curls before serving.

MASTERCHEF **FLAVOURINGS** KNOW-HOW: See **Prepare Chocolate** 393

MASTERCHEF **EGGS AND DAIRY PRODUCTS** KNOW-HOW: See **Whisk Egg Whites** 429

MASTERCHEF **EGGS AND DAIRY PRODUCTS** KNOW-HOW: See **Whip Cream** 436

LEMON TART

TRY THIS WITH CHOCOLATE PASTRY. SIMPLY SUBSTITUTE 3 TBSP FLOUR WITH COCOA.

FOR THE PASTRY

175g (6oz) PLAIN FLOUR,
   plus extra for dusting
85g (3oz) BUTTER, chilled
45g (1½oz) CASTER SUGAR
1 EGG

FOR THE FILLING

5 EGGS
200g (7oz) CASTER SUGAR
zest and juice of 4 LEMONS
250ml (8fl oz) DOUBLE CREAM
ICING SUGAR and LEMON ZEST, to serve

PREPARATION TIME
35 minutes, plus chilling

COOKING TIME
45 minutes

MAKES 8 SLICES

1 To make the pastry, place the flour, butter, and sugar into a food processor and pulse until it resembles breadcrumbs. Add the egg and process until the pastry draws together into a ball.

2 Roll out the pastry on a lightly floured surface into a large circle and use to line a 23cm (9in) loose-bottomed flan tin. Chill for at least 30 minutes.

3 Beat the eggs and sugar together until combined. Beat in the lemon zest and juice, then whisk in the cream. Chill.

4 Preheat the oven to 190°C (375°F/Gas 5). Line the pastry case with greaseproof paper, fill with baking beans, and bake blind for 10 minutes. Remove the paper and beans, and bake for 5 minutes, or until the base is crisp.

5 Reduce the oven to 140°C (275°F/Gas 1). Place the tart tin on a baking tray. Pour in the lemon filling, being careful not to allow the filling to spill over the edges. Bake for 30 minutes, or until just set. Remove from the oven and cool. Serve dusted with icing sugar and sprinkled with lemon zest over the top.

MASTERCHEF **DOUGH, PASTRY, AND CAKE** KNOW-HOW: See **Sweet Shortcrust Pastry** 455
MASTERCHEF **DOUGH, PASTRY, AND CAKE** KNOW-HOW: See **Blind Bake** 460

PAVLOVA

THIS PAVLOVA IS TOPPED WITH SWEET SUMMER BERRIES, BUT IT IS EQUALLY
DELICIOUS TOPPED WITH ANYTHING FROM SLICED KIWI FRUIT TO POACHED PEAR
SLICES, DRIZZLED WITH CHOCOLATE SAUCE.

6 EGG WHITES, at room temperature
pinch of SALT
350g (12oz) CASTER SUGAR
2 tsp CORNFLOUR
1 tsp VINEGAR
300ml (10fl oz) DOUBLE CREAM
STRAWBERRIES, RASPBERRIES, and
   BLUEBERRIES, to decorate

PREPARATION TIME
15 minutes, plus cooling

COOKING TIME
1 hour 15 minutes

MAKES 6 SLICES

1 Preheat the oven to 180°C (350°F/Gas 4). Line a baking tray with greaseproof paper. Put the egg whites in a large, clean, grease-free bowl with a pinch of salt. Whisk until stiff, then start whisking in the sugar 1 tbsp at a time, whisking well after each addition. Continue whisking until the egg whites are stiff and glossy, then whisk in the cornflour and vinegar.

2 Spoon the meringue onto the baking tray and spread to form a 20cm (8in) circle. Bake for 5 minutes, then reduce the oven to 140°C (275°F/Gas 1) and cook for a further 1¼ hours, or until the outside is crisp. Allow it to cool completely before transferring to a serving plate.

3 Whip the cream until it holds its shape, then spoon it onto the meringue base. Decorate with the fruit and serve.

MASTERCHEF **EGGS AND DAIRY PRODUCTS** KNOW-HOW: See **Whisk Egg Whites** 429
MASTERCHEF **EGGS AND DAIRY PRODUCTS** KNOW-HOW: See **Whip Cream** 436

BLUEBERRY CRUMBLE

FOR ADDED FLAVOUR, SUBSTITUTE HALF THE FLOUR WITH GROUND ALMONDS.

450g (1lb) BLUEBERRIES
2 large PEACHES or 2 EATING APPLES, sliced
grated zest of ½ LEMON
2 tbsp CASTER SUGAR

FOR THE CRUMBLE TOPPING
115g (4oz) PLAIN FLOUR
75g (2½oz) BUTTER, cut in small pieces
60g (2oz) ROLLED OATS
100g (3½oz) DEMERARA SUGAR

PREPARATION TIME
15 minutes

COOKING TIME
30 minutes

SERVES 4

1 Preheat the oven to 190°C (375°F/Gas 5). Spread the blueberries and peaches over the base of a shallow ovenproof dish and sprinkle with the lemon zest and caster sugar.

2 Sift the flour into a bowl. Add the butter and rub in with your fingertips until the mixture resembles breadcrumbs. Stir in the oats and sugar. Spoon over the fruit to cover completely and press down gently with the back of a spoon.

3 Place the dish on a baking tray and bake in the oven for 30 minutes, or until golden. Leave the dish to cool briefly before serving.

PECAN PIE

AS A VARIATION ON THE ORIGINAL, TRY STIRRING HALF WALNUTS AND HALF CHOPPED DRIED DATES INTO THE SYRUP MIXTURE INSTEAD OF THE PECANS.

200g (7oz) SWEET SHORTCRUST PASTRY

PLAIN FLOUR, for dusting

150ml (5fl oz) MAPLE SYRUP

60g (2oz) BUTTER

175g (6oz) LIGHT SOFT BROWN SUGAR

a few drops of pure VANILLA EXTRACT

pinch of SALT

3 EGGS

200g (7oz) SHELLED PECAN NUTS

PREPARATION TIME
15 minutes, plus chilling

COOKING TIME
1 hour 30 minutes

MAKES 8 SLICES

1 Roll the pastry out on a lightly floured surface, then use it to line a 23cm (9in) loose-bottomed flan tin. Trim around the top edge of the tin, and prick the base all over with a fork. Chill for at least 30 minutes.

2 Preheat the oven to 200°C (400°F/Gas 6). Line the pastry case with greaseproof paper, and fill with baking beans. Bake for 10 minutes, then remove the paper and beans, and bake for another 10 minutes, or until pale golden. Remove the pastry case from the oven and reduce the temperature to 180°C (350°F/Gas 4).

3 Pour the maple syrup into a saucepan, and add the butter, sugar, vanilla extract, and salt. Place the pan over a low heat, and stir constantly until the butter has melted, and the sugar dissolved. Remove the pan from the heat, and leave the mixture to cool until it feels just tepid, then beat in the eggs, one at a time. Stir in the pecan nuts, then pour the mixture into the pastry case.

4 Bake for 40–50 minutes, or until just set. Cover with a sheet of foil if it is browning too quickly.

5 Remove the pie from the oven, transfer it to a wire rack and leave to cool for 15–20 minutes. Remove from the tin and either serve it warm or leave it on the wire rack to cool completely.

MASTERCHEF **DOUGH, PASTRY, AND CAKE** KNOW-HOW: See **Sweet Shortcrust Pastry** 455

MASTERCHEF **DOUGH, PASTRY, AND CAKE** KNOW-HOW: See **Blind Bake** 460

BANOFFEE PIE

IT'S WORTH BOILING TWO CANS OF CONDENSED MILK AT THE SAME TIME, THEN KEEPING ONE CHILLED IN THE FRIDGE FOR READY-MADE DULCE DE LECHE.

350g (12oz) can SWEETENED CONDENSED MILK

200g (7oz) DIGESTIVE BISCUITS, crushed

1 tbsp LIGHT SOFT BROWN SUGAR

60g (2oz) BUTTER, melted

3 BANANAS

2 tsp LEMON JUICE

300ml (10fl oz) WHIPPING CREAM or DOUBLE CREAM

1 shot of ESPRESSO COFFEE, cooled

a little grated DARK CHOCOLATE

a few toasted chopped NUTS (optional)

PREPARATION TIME
20 minutes, plus milk boiling and chilling

MAKES 8 SLICES

1 To make the dulce de leche, remove any label on the condensed milk. Put the unopened can in a saucepan of water. Bring to the boil, reduce the heat, part-cover with a lid and simmer gently for 3 hours, topping up with water as it evaporates. Remove from the pan and leave to cool.

2 Mix the biscuit crumbs with the brown sugar and melted butter in a bowl. Press into the base and up the sides of a 20cm (8in) flan dish. Chill in the refrigerator until firm.

3 Slice the bananas and toss them in the lemon juice. Spread them over the biscuit base.

4 Open the can of dulce de leche and spread it over the bananas.

5 Whip the cream with the cold espresso until softly peaking, then spread over the dulce de leche. Sprinkle with a little grated chocolate and some chopped nuts, if using. Chill for at least 1 hour before serving.

MASTERCHEF **EGGS AND DAIRY PRODUCTS** KNOW-HOW: See **Whip Cream** 436

MASTERCHEF **DOUGH, PASTRY, AND CAKE** KNOW-HOW: See **Shortcrust Pastry** 454

SUMMER PUDDING

MAKE THIS ALL YEAR WITH OTHER FRUITS, SUCH AS STEWED APPLES AND BLACKBERRRIES IN AUTUMN, OR EVEN RHUBARB AND GINGER IN LATE SPRING.

12 slices WHITE BREAD, crusts removed
125g (4½oz) BLACKCURRANTS
125g (4½oz) REDCURRANTS
150g (5½oz) CASTER SUGAR
250g (9oz) MIXED BERRIES, such as STRAWBERRIES,
  RASPBERRIES, MULBERRIES, and BLUEBERRIES

PREPARATION TIME
20–25 minutes, plus chilling

COOKING TIME
5 minutes

SERVES 6

1 Line a 900ml (1½ pint) pudding basin with bread slices, beginning with a circle cut to fit the base, then overlapping slices evenly around the side.

2 Lightly cook the currants with the sugar until soft and the juices have run. Stir in the berries and cook for 1 minute, or until just softening.

3 Spoon some of the juices over the bread, then fill the basin with the fruit. Make sure the fruit is packed well into the basin. Cover the fruit with bread, ensuring it is completely covered with an even layer.

4 If there is any juice remaining, spoon this over the top layer of bread. Stand the basin in a dish to catch any overspill of juice. Cover with cling film and place a small plate on top. Put a weight on the plate and chill overnight.

5 Turn out onto a serving plate to serve.

PROFITEROLES

THE WHIPPED CREAM CAN BE FLAVOURED WITH A LITTLE INSTANT COFFEE POWDER AND SWEETENED SLIGHTLY WITH ICING SUGAR.

FOR THE CHOUX BUNS

60g (2oz) PLAIN FLOUR

50g (1¾oz) BUTTER

2 EGGS, beaten

FOR THE FILLING AND TOPPING

400ml (14fl oz) DOUBLE CREAM

200g (7oz) DARK CHOCOLATE, broken into pieces

25g (scant 1oz) BUTTER

2 tbsp GOLDEN SYRUP

PREPARATION TIME
30 minutes, plus chilling

COOKING TIME
30 minutes

SERVES 4

1 Preheat the oven to 220°C (425°F/Gas 7). Line 2 large baking trays with baking parchment. Sift the flour onto a separate piece of baking parchment.

2 Put the butter and 150ml (5fl oz) water into a small saucepan and heat gently until melted. Bring to the boil, remove from the heat, and tip in the flour. Beat quickly with a wooden spoon until the mixture is thick, smooth, and forms a ball in the centre of the saucepan. Cool for 10 minutes.

3 Gradually add the eggs, beating well after each addition. Use enough egg to form a stiff, smooth, and shiny paste. Spoon the mixture into a piping bag fitted with a 1cm (½in) plain nozzle.

4 Pipe walnut-sized rounds, set well apart, on the prepared baking trays. Bake for 20 minutes, or until risen, golden, and crisp. Remove from the oven and make a small slit in the side of each bun to allow the steam to escape. Return to the oven for a further 2 minutes, allow them to crisp, then transfer to a wire rack to cool completely.

5 When ready to serve, pour 100ml (3½fl oz) cream into a saucepan and whip the remainder until just peaking. Pile into a piping bag fitted with a 5mm (¼in) plain nozzle.

6 Add the chocolate, butter, and golden syrup to the saucepan with the cream and heat very gently until melted, stirring frequently. Meanwhile, pipe cream into each choux bun and pile onto a serving plate or cake stand.

7 When the sauce has melted, mix well, and pour over the choux buns. Serve immediately.

MASTERCHEF **EGGS AND DAIRY PRODUCTS** KNOW-HOW: See **Whip Cream** 436

MASTERCHEF **DOUGH, PASTRY, AND CAKE** KNOW-HOW: See **Choux Pastry** 455

TIRAMISU

THIS LUSCIOUS PUDDING MEANS "PICK-ME-UP" IN ITALIAN. FOR A SPECIAL
OCCASION, SERVE IT WITH ICED AMARETTO TO SIP ALONGSIDE.

120ml (4fl oz) cold ESPRESSO COFFEE
75ml (2½fl oz) COFFEE-FLAVOURED LIQUEUR
350g (12oz) MASCARPONE CHEESE
3 tbsp CASTER SUGAR
360ml (12fl oz) DOUBLE CREAM
14 SPONGE FINGERS
COCOA POWDER, to decorate
coarsely grated DARK CHOCOLATE,
  to decorate

PREPARATION TIME
20 minutes, plus cooling and
at least 4 hours chilling
SERVES 4

1 Mix the coffee and liqueur together in a shallow, wide serving bowl and set aside.

2 Put the mascarpone cheese and sugar in a bowl, and beat for a minute or two, until the sugar dissolves. Whip the cream in another bowl until it holds its shape, then fold it into the mascarpone mixture. Put a couple of spoonfuls of the mascarpone mixture in the bottom of a serving dish.

3 Dip and turn 1 sponge finger in the coffee mixture until just soaked, then place it on top of the mascarpone in the dish; repeat with 6 more sponge fingers, placing them side by side in the dish. Cover with half the remaining mascarpone mixture, then soak and layer the remaining sponge fingers. Top with the remaining mascarpone and smooth the surface. Cover the dish with cling film and chill for at least 4 hours.

4 Sprinkle the top with cocoa powder and grated chocolate just before serving.

MASTERCHEF **FLAVOURINGS** KNOW-HOW: See **Prepare Chocolate** 393
MASTERCHEF **EGGS AND DAIRY PRODUCTS** KNOW-HOW: See **Whip Cream** 436

RED VELVET CUPCAKES

FOR BLUE VELVET CUPCAKES MAKE PLAIN VANILLA CUPCAKES, COLOUR THE
MIXTURE BLUE, AND DECORATE THE FROSTING WITH FRESH OR DRIED BLUEBERRIES.

100g (3½oz) SELF-RAISING FLOUR

15g (½oz) COCOA POWDER

½ tsp BAKING POWDER

115g (4oz) softened BUTTER

115g (4oz) CASTER SUGAR

2 EGGS

1 tsp RED FOOD COLOURING

FOR THE FROSTING

200ml (7fl oz) DOUBLE CREAM

200g (7oz) CREAM CHEESE

6 tbsp ICING SUGAR

CAKE CRUMBS, crumbled, to decorate

PREPARATION TIME
15 minutes

COOKING TIME
15 minutes

MAKES 12

1 Preheat the oven to 180°C (350°F/Gas 4). Line a bun tray with 12 cupcake cases.

2 Sift the flour, cocoa powder, and baking powder together into a large mixing bowl. Add the softened butter, caster sugar, eggs, and food colouring. Beat with a wooden spoon, electric hand whisk, or mixer until well combined. Spoon the mixture into the cupcake cases, and bake for 15 minutes, or until well risen and the centres spring back when lightly pressed. Transfer to a wire rack to cool.

3 To make the frosting, place the cream cheese in a bowl and lightly whip with the icing sugar. Then whisk in the cream cheese until softly peaking. Swirl on the cup cakes and sprinkle with crumbled cake crumbs.

BLACK FOREST GÂTEAU

THIS IS A CLASSIC CAKE THAT CANNOT BE IMPROVED. HOWEVER, DON'T WASTE THE REMAINING CHERRY JUICE – USE IT AS A BASIS FOR A BERRY FRUIT SALAD.

6 EGGS
175g (6oz) CASTER SUGAR
125g (4½oz) PLAIN FLOUR
50g (1¾oz) COCOA POWDER
1 tsp VANILLA EXTRACT
85g (3oz) BUTTER, melted
600ml (1 pint) DOUBLE CREAM
2 x 425g (15oz) can pitted BLACK CHERRIES
4 tbsp KIRSCH
150g (5½oz) DARK CHOCOLATE, grated

PREPARATION TIME
55 minutes

COOKING TIME
40 minutes

SERVES 8

1 Preheat the oven to 180°C (350°F/Gas 4). Lightly grease and line the bottom of a 23cm (9in) deep springform cake tin with baking parchment. Put the eggs and sugar into a large heatproof bowl, and place over a saucepan filled with simmering water. Don't let the bowl touch the water. Whisk until the mixture is pale and thick, and will hold a trail. Remove from the heat and whisk for another 5 minutes, or until cooled slightly.

2 Sift the flour and cocoa together and fold into the egg mixture using a large metal spoon or a spatula. Fold in the vanilla and butter. Transfer to the prepared tin and level the surface. Bake in the oven for 40 minutes, or until risen and just shrinking away a little from the sides. Turn it out on to a wire rack, discard the lining paper, and cover with a clean cloth. Allow the cake to cool completely.

3 Carefully cut the cake into 3 layers. Drain 1 can of cherries, placing 6 tbsp of the juice into a bowl with the kirsch. Roughly chop the drained cherries. Drizzle a third of the kirsch and cherry syrup over each layer of sponge.

4 Whip the cream until it just holds its shape. Place 1 layer of the cake onto a serving plate. Spread a thin layer of cream over the top of the sponge, and scatter with half the chopped cherries. Repeat with the second layer and top with the final layer of sponge. Using a palette knife, spread a thin layer of cream around the edges of the cake to cover, and spoon the remaining cream into a piping bag fitted with a star-shaped nozzle.

5 Using a spoon or a palette knife, press the grated chocolate onto the side of the cake. Pipe swirls of cream around the top edge of the cake. Drain the second tin of cherries and use them to fill the centre of the cake. Scatter any remaining chocolate over the piped cream.

MASTERCHEF **FLAVOURINGS** KNOW-HOW: See **Prepare Chocolate** 393

MASTERCHEF **EGGS AND DAIRY PRODUCTS** KNOW-HOW: See **Whip Cream** 436

MASTERCHEF **DOUGH, PASTRY, AND CAKE** KNOW-HOW: See **Prepare and Line a Cake Tin** 463

CARROT CAKE

FOR AN INTERESTING CHANGE FROM CARROT CAKE, TRY MAKING IT WITH GRATED PARSNIPS, AND ADDING CHOPPED DRIED PEARS INSTEAD OF SULTANAS.

215g (7½oz) PLAIN FLOUR

200g (7oz) CASTER SUGAR

1½ tsp BICARBONATE OF SODA

1 tsp BAKING POWDER

1 tsp GROUND CINNAMON

½ tsp each GROUND CLOVES, NUTMEG,
    ALLSPICE, and SALT

150ml (5fl oz) SUNFLOWER or CORN OIL

3 EGGS

165g (5½oz) peeled, grated CARROTS

125g (4½oz) chopped WALNUTS

150g (5½oz) SULTANAS

FOR THE FROSTING

225g (8oz) CREAM CHEESE

75g (2½oz) soft UNSALTED BUTTER

2 tsp pure VANILLA EXTRACT

450g (1lb) ICING SUGAR, sifted

grated zest of 1 ORANGE

PREPARATION TIME
25 minutes

COOKING TIME
30–35 minutes

SERVES 8 OR MORE

1 Preheat the oven to 180°C (350°F/Gas 4). Grease and line a traybake tin about 23 x 30cm (9 x 12in). In a large bowl, combine the flour, sugar, bicarbonate of soda, baking powder, spices, and salt.

2 Beat together the oil and eggs, then stir them into the flour mixture until just combined. Add the carrots, walnuts, and sultanas and mix well.

3 Pour the mixture into the tin and spread evenly. Bake for 30–35 minutes, or until a knife inserted in the centre comes out clean. Cool in the tin.

4 To make the frosting, beat the cheese, butter, and vanilla together with an electric mixer until smooth. Gradually beat in the sugar. Fold in the orange zest with a spatula. Spread the frosting over the top of the cooled cake.

MADELEINES

FOR A MOISTER CAKE, SUBSTITUTE GROUND ALMONDS FOR HALF THE FLOUR.

60g (2oz) BUTTER, melted but not hot,
  plus extra for greasing
60g (2oz) CASTER SUGAR
2 EGGS
1 tsp VANILLA EXTRACT
60g (2oz) PLAIN FLOUR, sifted
ICING SUGAR, to dust

PREPARATION TIME
15–20 minutes

COOKING TIME
10 minutes

MAKES 12

1 Preheat the oven to 180°C (350°F/Gas 4). Carefully brush the moulds with melted butter and dust with flour.

2 Put the sugar, eggs, and vanilla extract into a mixing bowl and whisk until the mixture is pale, thick, and will hold a trail. This should take 5 minutes with an electric whisk, or slightly longer if you are using a hand whisk.

3 Sift the flour over the top and pour the melted butter down the side of the mixture. Using a large metal spoon, fold them in carefully and quickly, being careful not to knock out any air.

4 Fill the moulds with the mixture and bake in the oven for 10 minutes. Remove from the oven and transfer to a wire rack to cool, before dusting with icing sugar.

SCOTCH PANCAKES

THESE PANCAKES ARE ALSO CALLED DROP SCONES BECAUSE THE BATTER IS DROPPED ONTO A FRYING PAN. TRY USING RYE FLOUR INSTEAD OF WHEAT.

225g (8oz) PLAIN WHITE FLOUR
4 tsp BAKING POWDER
1 large EGG
2 tsp GOLDEN SYRUP
200ml (7fl oz) MILK
SUNFLOWER OIL

PREPARATION TIME
10 minutes

COOKING TIME
15 minutes

MAKES 24

1 Sift the flour and baking powder into a bowl; make a well in the centre and add the egg, golden syrup, and milk. Whisk well to make a smooth batter the consistency of thick cream. If the mixture is too thick, beat in a little more milk.

2 Fold a tea towel in half and lay it on a baking tray. Heat a flat griddle pan or large frying pan over a medium heat until hot and lightly grease with oil.

3 Lift out 1 tbsp of batter, cleaning the back of the spoon on the edge of the bowl. Drop the batter from the tip of the spoon onto the hot pan to make a nice round shape. Repeat, leaving enough room between the rounds for the pancakes to rise and spread.

4 Bubbles will appear on the surface of the pancakes. When they begin to burst, ease a palette knife underneath the pancakes and gently flip to cook the other side. To ensure even browning, lightly press the flat blade on the cooked side after you have turned the pancake; place cooked pancakes inside the folded towel to keep them soft while you fry the rest of the batch.

5 Add a little oil to the hot pan after each batch and check that it does not get too hot. If the pancakes are pale and take a long time to cook, turn up the heat. If they brown too quickly on the outside and are still raw in the middle, reduce the heat. They are best eaten freshly baked and warm.

SHORTBREAD

RING THE CHANGES BY ADDING CHOCOLATE CHIPS OR LEMON ZEST TO THE DOUGH.

175g (6oz) UNSALTED BUTTER, softened

75g (2½oz) CASTER SUGAR, plus extra for sprinkling

250g (9oz) PLAIN FLOUR, plus extra
  for dusting

½ tsp SALT

PREPARATION TIME
15 minutes

COOKING TIME
20 minutes

MAKES 10

1 Preheat the oven to 180°C (350°F/Gas 4). In a large bowl, beat the butter and sugar together until soft and creamy. Add the flour and salt, and carefully mix together until well combined and the mixture forms into a firm dough.

2 Turn out onto a lightly floured surface and knead gently until smooth. Roll the dough out to a thickness of 5mm (¼in). Using a 7.5cm (3in) fluted cutter, stamp out 10 rounds.

3 Arrange the shortbread on a large baking tray, spaced slightly apart. Prick the tops with a fork and bake for 20 minutes, or until lightly golden. Sprinkle with sugar and allow them to cool on the baking tray.

TUILE BISCUITS

THESE ARE PARTICULARLY GOOD WITH SOME FLAKED ALMONDS AND A FEW DROPS OF ALMOND EXTRACT ADDED TO THE MIXTURE.

50g (1¾oz) BUTTER, softened

50g (1¾oz) ICING SUGAR

1 EGG

50g (1¾oz) PLAIN FLOUR

PREPARATION TIME
10 minutes

COOKING TIME
30 minutes

MAKES 15

1 Preheat the oven to 200°C (400°F/Gas 6). Place the butter and icing sugar in a bowl, and cream together until light and fluffy. Beat in the egg and gently fold in the flour.

2 Line a baking tray with baking parchment. Place 1–2 tsp of the mixture on the lined baking tray and spread it thinly to make a round 6–8cm (2½–3½in) in diameter. Make another 1 or 2 rounds on the tray. Bake for 5–8 minutes, or until they just start to turn a pale golden colour.

3 Remove the baking tray from the oven and, working quickly, slide a palette knife under the tuiles to release them, then drape them over a rolling pin so that they cool in a curved shape.

4 Repeat the baking and shaping process with the remaining mixture.

VICTORIA SPONGE CAKE

GOOD FOR DESSERT WITH MORE CREAM AND FRESH RASPBERRIES PILED ON TOP.

175g (6oz) BUTTER, softened

175g (6oz) CASTER SUGAR

3 EGGS, lightly beaten

175g (6oz) SELF-RAISING FLOUR

6–8 tbsp RASPBERRY JAM

150ml (5fl oz) DOUBLE CREAM

ICING SUGAR, to dust

PREPARATION TIME
20 minutes

COOKING TIME
20–25 minutes

SERVES 8

1 Preheat the oven to 190°C (375°F/Gas 5). Lightly grease two 20cm (8in) sandwich tins and line the bottom of the tins with baking parchment.

2 Beat the butter and sugar together until pale and fluffy. It is important to beat the mixture well at this stage to incorporate as much air as possible, which helps prevent the eggs from curdling.

3 Add the eggs a little at a time, beating well after each addition. If the mixture begins to curdle, beat in 1–2 tbsp of the flour. Sift the flour, and fold into the egg mixture using a large metal spoon or a spatula.

4 Divide the mixture equally between the prepared tins, and spread evenly to level the tops. Bake for 20–25 minutes, until pale golden and springy to the touch. Allow the cakes to cool in the tins for 5 minutes, before turning out onto a wire rack. Peel off the lining paper, and allow to cool completely.

5 When the cakes are cool, place one upside down on a serving plate, and spread with the raspberry jam. Lightly whip the cream, until just holding its shape, and spread over the jam. Add the remaining cake layer, and dust lightly with icing sugar before serving.

MASTERCHEF **EGGS AND DAIRY PRODUCTS** KNOW-HOW: See **Whip Cream** 436

MASTERCHEF **DOUGH, PASTRY, AND CAKE** KNOW-HOW: See **Prepare and Line a Cake Tin** 463

MASTERCHEF
RECIPES

RECIPES FROM THE MASTERCHEF SERIES TO TAKE YOUR COOKING TO THE NEXT LEVEL.

GOAT'S CHEESE AND RED ONION TART

LISA FAULKNER Celebrity champion 2010

FOR THE PASTRY

small sprig of THYME

100g (3½oz) PLAIN FLOUR

25g (scant 1oz) BUTTER

25g (scant 1oz) LARD

FOR THE RED ONION JAM

25g (scant 1oz) BUTTER

25g (scant 1oz) SOFT BROWN SUGAR

1 tbsp BALSAMIC VINEGAR

1–2 tbsp CASSIS

SALT and freshly ground BLACK PEPPER

2 RED ONIONS, finely sliced

FOR THE GOAT'S CHEESE

175g (6oz) crumbly GOAT'S CHEESE

1 EGG YOLK

1–2 tbsp DOUBLE CREAM

FOR THE SALAD

handful of ROCKET LEAVES

2 tbsp OLIVE OIL

2 tsp LEMON JUICE

PREPARATION TIME
25 minutes, plus chilling

COOKING TIME
55 minutes

SERVES 4

1 To make the pastry, strip the thyme leaves into a blender or a food processor and add the flour, butter, and lard. Mix on the pulse setting to form crumbs. Gradually add enough cold water (about 2–3 tbsp) to form a soft dough. Wrap in cling film and chill for 30 minutes.

2 To make the onion jam, melt the butter in a sauté pan and add the sugar, vinegar, cassis, and some seasoning. Add the onions, bring to the boil and cook, uncovered, over a very low heat for 30 minutes.

3 Heat the oven to 200°C (400°F/Gas 6). Place a sturdy baking sheet in the oven. Divide the pastry into quarters, then roll them out, and use to line four 10cm (4in) loose-bottomed tart tins. Line with greaseproof paper and baking beans. Place on the heated baking sheet and cook for 10 minutes. Remove the beans and lining paper and return to the oven for 5 minutes. Leave to cool for a few minutes.

4 Trim away any rind on the goat's cheese and crumble the cheese into a bowl. Mix with the egg yolk and a splash of cream. Season with salt and pepper.

5 Reserve about a third of the red onion jam to use as garnish, then divide the rest between the tartlets and spoon the goat's cheese mixture on top. Return to the oven for 7–8 minutes, or until the tops are bubbling and tinged with brown.

6 For the salad, rinse the rocket leaves and pat dry. Pour the olive oil and lemon juice into a bowl, and season with plenty of salt and pepper. Add the rocket leaves and toss gently to coat.

7 To serve, place a spoonful of red onion jam on the centre of each plate. Carefully remove the tarts from their tins and sit them on top of the jam. Top with rocket salad and serve.

OPEN LASAGNE OF ROASTED SQUASH AND WILD MUSHROOMS WITH SAGE BUTTER

TIM KINNAIRD Finalist 2010

FOR THE PASTA

good pinch of SAFFRON STRANDS
150g (5½oz) TIPO "00" FLOUR
SALT
1 large EGG
1 EGG YOLK

FOR THE SQUASH

1 small CROWN PRINCE SQUASH,
  peeled and seeded, about 350g
  (12oz) peeled weight, and cut into
  bite-sized pieces
1 tbsp EXTRA VIRGIN OLIVE OIL
SALT and freshly ground
  BLACK PEPPER
¼–½ tsp CHILLI FLAKES

FOR THE MUSHROOMS

knob of BUTTER
200g (7oz) mixed WILD MUSHROOMS,
  such as girolles, porcini, and pied
  blue, wiped and evenly chopped
1 GARLIC CLOVE, finely chopped
3 tbsp MARSALA WINE
2–3 tbsp chopped FLAT-LEAF PARSLEY
100ml (3½fl oz) DOUBLE CREAM

FOR THE SAGE BUTTER

75g (2½oz) UNSALTED BUTTER
small bunch of fresh SAGE, leaves only

PREPARATION TIME
1 hour 15 minutes

COOKING TIME
1 hour

SERVES 4

1 Preheat the oven to 220°C (425°F/Gas 7). Soak the saffron in 2 tsp warm water for 10 minutes. Make the pasta dough, adding the saffron and water to the dough with the eggs.

2 Put the squash on a baking tray, drizzle with the olive oil, and scatter over the salt, pepper, and chilli flakes. Roast for 35 minutes or until soft and tinged with brown. Shake the tin occasionally for even roasting.

3 To cook the mushrooms, melt the butter in a large sauté pan until it foams, add the mushrooms and salt and pepper, and fry over high heat for 4–5 minutes or until just turning golden. Reduce the heat to medium, add the garlic, and fry for 1 minute. Add the Marsala and bubble for a few minutes. Stir in the parsley and cream and set aside.

4 For the sage butter, melt the butter in a heavy pan and cook gently until it turns a warm nutty brown. Take care not to burn it. Set aside.

5 Divide the dough into 2 and roll into sheets.

6 Bring a pan of water to the boil. Brush off the excess flour from the pasta, place in the water, and boil for 4–5 minutes or until *al dente*. Drain in a colander and then cut out twelve 8cm (3in) diameter circles using an oiled round pastry cutter. Brush with olive oil and set aside.

7 Just before serving, tear up nearly all the sage leaves and add to the cooled butter. Warm gently for 1–2 minutes and also warm the mushroom mixture and squash. Stack up the pasta separated by a layer of squash and a layer of mushrooms. Spoon over the sage butter and garnish with the remaining sage.

MASTERCHEF **PASTA, NOODLES, AND GNOCCHI** KNOW-HOW: See **Make Pasta Dough** 469
MASTERCHEF **PASTA, NOODLES, AND GNOCCHI** KNOW-HOW: See **Stretch Pasta Dough by Hand** 470

THAI PRAWN SOUP WITH LEMONGRASS

IWAN THOMAS Celebrity finalist 2009

16 large raw TIGER PRAWNS, shells on

1 litre (1¾ pints) CHICKEN STOCK

2 stalks fresh LEMONGRASS, lightly pounded, cut into
2.5cm (1in) lengths

50g (1¾oz) fresh GALANGAL, sliced

10 KAFFIR LIME LEAVES, shredded

500g (1lb 2oz) ENOKI MUSHROOMS

4 tbsp NAM PLA (Thai fish sauce)

3 tbsp NAM PRIK PAO (chilli paste in oil)

4 tbsp LIME JUICE

5 fresh THAI (BIRD'S EYE) CHILLIES, crushed

TO GARNISH

10g (¼oz) CORIANDER, torn

1 small RED PEPPER, deseeded and
cut into fine ribbons

PREPARATION TIME
10 minutes

COOKING TIME
15 minutes

SERVES 4

1 Wash the prawns and shell them without removing the tails.

2 Bring the chicken stock to the boil in a large saucepan. Add the lemongrass, galangal, and lime leaves.

3 Bring back to the boil, then add the enoki mushrooms, nam pla, nam prik pao, and lime juice. Add the prawns and fresh chillies.

4 As soon as the prawns turn pink (about 2 minutes), serve the soup garnished with the coriander and strips of red pepper.

CRISPY SQUID WITH GREEN PEPPERCORN AND CHILLI DRESSING

SUSIE CARTER Quarter-finalist 2006

4 medium SQUID, cleaned

juice of 1 LIME

SALT and freshly ground BLACK PEPPER

GROUNDNUT OIL for deep-frying

3 tbsp CORNFLOUR

FOR THE DRESSING

2 tbsp fresh GREEN PEPPERCORNS

1 RED CHILLI, deseeded and finely chopped

3cm (1¼in) piece fresh ROOT GINGER, finely grated

2 GARLIC CLOVES, crushed

3 tbsp NAM PLA (Thai fish sauce)

3 tbsp RICE VINEGAR

75g (2½oz) CASTER SUGAR

2 tsp SOY SAUCE

juice of 1 LIME

TO SERVE

4 slices of LIME

CORIANDER LEAVES

PREPARATION TIME
15 minutes

COOKING TIME
5 minutes

SERVES 4

1 To make the dressing, put all the ingredients in a small pan and simmer, stirring, until the sugar has dissolved and the mixture has thickened. Leave to cool.

2 Open out the body sac of the squid and cut each one into about 8 rectangles. With the inside facing up, score a diamond pattern with a sharp knife, taking care not to cut all the way through. Douse with lime juice, season well with salt and pepper, and leave to cure for 2 minutes.

3 Heat plenty of groundnut oil in a large saucepan or deep fat fryer to 180°C (350°F).

4 Dry the squid thoroughly on kitchen paper then toss with the cornflour. Shake off the excess and deep fry in batches for 2 minutes until golden and crisp. Drain on kitchen paper then quickly toss with a few spoonfuls of the dressing and serve immediately with a slice of lime on the side and coriander to garnish.

SMOKED MACKEREL PÂTÉ

Inspired by **STEVEN WALLIS** Champion 2007

250g (9oz) COLD-SMOKED MACKEREL FILLETS

50g (1¾oz) CRÈME FRAÎCHE

25g (scant 1oz) MASCARPONE CHEESE

3 stems of FENNEL FRONDS, plus extra to garnish

grated zest and juice of 1 LIME

grated zest of ½ ORANGE

FLEUR DE SEL

½ tsp CORIANDER SEEDS, toasted

3 tbsp HAZELNUT OIL

SALT and freshly ground BLACK PEPPER

½ tsp SUGAR

4 tsp MUSCAT VINEGAR

3 CHICORY HEADS

25g (scant 1oz) HAZELNUTS, toasted and finely chopped

BABY CHERVIL, to garnish

PEA SHOOT TENDRILS, to garnish

PREPARATION TIME

20 minutes, plus chilling

SERVES 4

1 Finely pick through the smoked mackerel to remove any bones, remove the skin, and break the flesh into pieces in a food processor. Add the crème fraîche, mascarpone cheese, fennel fronds, lime and orange zest, and the lime juice. Season with the fleur de sel and blend to a smooth pâté consistency. Chill for 30 minutes.

2 To prepare the vinaigrette, mix together the coriander seeds and hazelnut oil, season with salt and pepper, and add the sugar. Then add the Muscat vinegar, whisk well, and set aside.

3 To serve, trim the chicory leaves by cutting a good third of the leaves from the end. Allow 3 leaves per person. Spoon in a neat quenelle of pâté onto the cut end of each leaf. Drizzle over the vinaigrette, and scatter over the chopped hazelnuts. Finish with a pinch of fleur de sel and baby chervil leaves, fennel fronds, and pea shoot tendrils.

SMOKED HADDOCK TIMBALE
WITH POACHED QUAIL'S EGG

CHRISTINE HAMILTON Celebrity finalist 2010

4 BABY BEETROOTS (or 1 mature
   beetroot, peeled and quartered)
SALT and freshly ground BLACK
   PEPPER
splash of OLIVE OIL
2–3 sprigs of THYME (optional)
BUTTER for greasing
150g (5½oz) SMOKED HADDOCK
   FILLET, skin removed
400ml (14fl oz) DOUBLE CREAM
4 EGG YOLKS
2 tbsp CHOPPED DILL
2 tbsp CHOPPED CHIVES
4 QUAIL'S EGGS

FOR THE SALAD DRESSING
1 tbsp LEMON JUICE
½ tbsp OLIVE OIL
½ tbsp WALNUT OIL
½ tbsp WHOLEGRAIN MUSTARD
1 tbsp CASTER SUGAR
ground BLACK PEPPER

TO SERVE
small bag of ROCKET and
   WATERCRESS
50g (1¾oz) WALNUT PIECES

PREPARATION TIME
15 minutes

COOKING TIME
30 minutes

SERVES 4

1 Preheat the oven to 170°C (340°F/Gas 3–4). Season the beetroots with salt and pepper and wrap tightly in kitchen foil with olive oil and thyme (if using). Roast in a corner of the oven for 30 minutes.

2 Butter 4 timbale moulds. Poach the haddock lightly for 2–3 minutes in 200ml (7fl oz) of cream. Drain and reserve the cream.

3 In a bowl, whisk together the reserved and remaining cream, egg yolks, dill, chives, and a good pinch of black pepper.

4 Break the haddock into pieces with a fork and divide between the timbale moulds. Pour the cream mixture into each mould.

5 Place the moulds in a deep roasting tray or oven dish. Add 3–4cm (1¼–1½in) of water to the tray or dish before placing it in the preheated oven on a high shelf. Bake for 20 minutes, or until the timbales are set and do not wobble when moved.

6 Meanwhile, poach the quail's eggs by breaking each gently into a pan of just-simmering water and poaching for 30 seconds. When cooked, plunge into iced water.

7 In a small bowl, whisk together all the ingredients for the lemon and walnut dressing.

8 Remove the timbales from the oven and allow to cool before unmoulding. Arrange the dressed salad leaves on each plate, with the diced beetroot, and sprinkle over the finely chopped walnut. Position a timbale in the centre and place a poached quail's egg on top.

SPINACH AND RICOTTA RAVIOLI WITH WALNUT PESTO AND A CREAM AND BASIL SAUCE

CHRIS GATES Finalist 2009

FOR THE PASTA
150g (5½oz) TIPO "00" FLOUR,
   plus extra to dust
350g (12oz) SEMOLINA FLOUR
2 large EGGS
10 EGG YOLKS

FOR THE FILLING
20g (¾oz) BUTTER
200g (7oz) SPINACH
SALT and freshly ground
   BLACK PEPPER
350g (12oz) RICOTTA or soft
   GOAT'S CHEESE
grated zest of 1 LEMON

FOR THE PESTO
30g (1oz) WALNUTS
1 bunch of BASIL
1 GARLIC CLOVE, chopped
25g (scant 1oz) PARMESAN CHEESE,
   freshly grated
OLIVE OIL

FOR THE SAUCE
1 SHALLOT, finely chopped
1 tbsp OLIVE OIL
500ml (16fl oz) DOUBLE CREAM
juice of 1 LEMON

PREPARATION TIME
1 hour 15 minutes

COOKING TIME
1 hour

SERVES 4

1 To make the pasta, blitz all of the ingredients in a food processor until you have a mixture the consistency of breadcrumbs. Empty onto a floured surface and knead into a silky dough. Wrap in cling film and leave to rest in the refrigerator for about 1 hour.

2 Meanwhile, make the filling. Melt the butter in a large pan and wilt the spinach. Season with salt and pepper. Squeeze out any water and place in a bowl. Add the ricotta and lemon zest and season to taste.

3 For the pesto, toast the walnuts in a dry pan until golden. Using a pestle and mortar, break them up with the garlic and basil leaves, reserving the stalks. Add the Parmesan, loosen with oil, and season.

4 For the cream sauce, sauté the chopped shallot in a pan with the oil until softened. Add the reserved basil stalks and soften for 3–4 minutes. Add the cream and allow to reduce slightly. Season with salt and pepper and add the lemon juice.

5 Using a pasta machine, roll out the pasta to the thinnest setting. Make 2 rectangular dough sheets. Place scoops of the filling on top of the first dough sheet at intervals about 5cm (2in) apart. Brush round the filling with a little water and top with the second sheet of dough. Using your fingers, press round the filling to remove any air. Cut out the ravioli, using a fluted pastry cutter about 5cm (2in) in diameter.

6 Cook the ravioli in boiling salted water for about 5 minutes. Drain and serve on warm plates with the cream sauce and pesto spooned over and a scattering of basil leaves as a garnish.

MASTERCHEF **PASTA, NOODLES, AND GNOCCHI** KNOW-HOW: See **Use a Pasta Machine** 472

MASTERCHEF **PASTA, NOODLES, AND GNOCCHI** KNOW-HOW: See **Assemble Ravioli** 474

SEARED TUNA WITH AN ASIAN GLAZE

ANGELA KENNY Semi-finalist 2009

4 CARROTS

4 COURGETTES

8 tbsp DARK SOY SAUCE

4 LIMES

6 tbsp DEMERARA SUGAR

12–16 CHARLOTTE POTATOES,
   peeled and sliced into discs

60ml (2fl oz) WHITE MISO PASTE

60ml (2fl oz) MIRIN

90ml (3½fl oz) DRY SAKE

2 tbsp RICE WINE VINEGAR

1 tbsp OIL

4 TUNA STEAKS, 175–200g (6–7oz) each

SALT and freshly ground BLACK PEPPER

PREPARATION TIME
20 minutes

COOKING TIME
8 minutes

SERVES 4

1 With a potato peeler, shave the carrots and courgettes into long strips. Place in a mixing bowl with 3 tbsp soy sauce, the juice and zest of 1½ limes, and 4 tbsp sugar.

2 Put the potatoes in a large pan with boiling water to cover and the white miso paste. Cook for about 10 minutes until the potatoes are tender and then drain.

3 Place the mirin, sake, remaining sugar and soy sauce, rice wine vinegar, and the juice and zest of the remaining limes in a frying pan over a medium heat and reduce to a syrup consistency – about 10 minutes.

4 Season the tuna with salt and pepper. Heat another frying pan until hot, add the tuna, and sear on both sides for about 3 minutes.

5 Once the tuna is cooked, transfer it to the frying pan containing the glaze and turn to coat it. Heat the ribbon vegetables in the glaze for 2 minutes, then serve with the tuna and potatoes.

SPICED BATTERED FISH AND CHIPS

DHRUV BAKER Champion 2010

4 JOHN DORY FILLETS,
   or other WHITE FISH,
   approx. 150g (5½oz) each
handful of CORIANDER,
   roughly chopped, to garnish

FOR THE MUSHY PEAS

250g (9oz) DRIED SPLIT GREEN
   or YELLOW PEAS
2 ONIONS, chopped
2 BAY LEAVES
SALT and freshly ground
   BLACK PEPPER
handful of CORIANDER, chopped
1–2 RED CHILLIES,
   deseeded and chopped
1–2 GREEN CHILLIES,
   deseeded and chopped
juice of 2–3 LIMES
300g (10oz) frozen or fresh PEAS

FOR THE BROWN SAUCE

2 tbsp TAMARIND PASTE

4 tsp CASTER SUGAR
juice of 2 LIMES
pinch of CHILLI POWDER

FOR THE BATTER

150g (5½oz) PLAIN FLOUR
2 tsp BAKING POWDER
½ tsp FENNEL SEEDS
¼ tsp TURMERIC
¼ tsp CHILLI POWDER
¼ tsp ground CORIANDER
¼ tsp ground CUMIN
¼ tsp BROWN MUSTARD SEEDS
½ tsp GINGER PASTE,
   or freshly grated ROOT GINGER
½ tsp GARLIC PASTE,
   or 1 GARLIC CLOVE, finely crushed

FOR THE CHIPS

4–6 large MARIS PIPER POTATOES,
   peeled and cut into chips
GROUNDNUT OIL for deep frying

PREPARATION TIME
40 minutes

COOKING TIME
50 minutes

SERVES 4

1 Put the dried peas in a saucepan with 1 litre (1¾ pints) of water, the onions, bay leaves, and some black pepper. Boil for 1¼ hours or until the peas are tender and mushy, adding more water if necessary. Add the coriander, chillies, and lime juice. In another pan, boil the frozen or fresh peas for 4–5 minutes or until just tender, then drain and crush, using a fork. Stir into the split peas and season with salt.

2 For the sauce, put the tamarind paste in a small pan with the sugar, lime juice, and 4 tbsp of water. Add the chilli powder. Boil over medium-high heat for 5 minutes or until reduced to a sticky sauce.

3 Parboil the chips in a pan of boiling water for 5 minutes, then drain. Preheat a deep-fat fryer or deep saucepan two-thirds filled with oil to 160°C (325°F). Cook the chips in batches for 5–6 minutes, then drain on kitchen paper. Increase the temperature of the oil to 180°C (350°F) and return the chips to the pan to crisp and turn golden. Toss in salt.

4 For the batter, mix the flour, baking powder, spices, ginger, and garlic with 150–170ml (5–6fl oz) iced water until smooth. Dip 2 pieces of fish in batter and deep fry for 7–8 minutes, turning once or twice. Drain and set aside to keep warm, then repeat with the remaining fish.

5 Serve the battered fish with the chips and mushy peas alongside. Drizzle a little brown sauce over and garnish the plates with coriander.

MASTERCHEF **VEGETABLES** KNOW-HOW: See **Deseed and Cut Chillies** 371
MASTERCHEF **VEGETABLES** KNOW-HOW: See **Make Chips** 373

BEEF WELLINGTON WITH MASH, CREAMED SAVOY CABBAGE, AND AN OXTAIL JUS

LIZ McCLARNON Celebrity champion 2008

4 fillets of BEEF, about
   175g (6oz) each

3 MARIS PIPER POTATOES,
   peeled and chopped

4 large stoneless PRUNES

4 tsp MANGO CHUTNEY

2 STREAKY BACON RASHERS,
   cut in half

250g (9oz) ready-made PUFF PASTRY

200g (7oz) CHESTNUT MUSHROOMS,
   chopped

75g (2½oz) SALTED BUTTER

SALT and freshly ground
   BLACK PEPPER

2 tsp TRUFFLE OIL

½ SAVOY CABBAGE, shredded

400ml (14fl oz) DOUBLE CREAM

1 tbsp OLIVE OIL

3 sprigs of THYME

2 sprigs of ROSEMARY

FOR THE OXTAIL JUS

2 GARLIC CLOVES, chopped

1 SHALLOT, chopped

1 tbsp OLIVE OIL

3 sprigs of FLAT-LEAF PARSLEY,
   chopped

300ml (10fl oz) PORT

200ml (7fl oz) OXTAIL STOCK,
   plus 4 tbsp

PREPARATION TIME
40 minutes

COOKING TIME
1 hour

SERVES 4

1 Preheat the oven to 200°C (400°F/Gas 6). Bring a large saucepan of salted water to the boil, add the potatoes and simmer for 20 minutes, or until cooked. Drain and keep warm.

2 For the oxtail jus, put the garlic cloves and shallot in a frying pan with the oil and parsley. Add the port, bring to the boil, and reduce by three-quarters. Then add the stock and reduce by half. Keep warm.

3 Fill the hole in each prune with the chutney and roll in a piece of streaky bacon. Pierce with a cocktail stick and cook on a baking tray in the oven for 7 minutes. Remove from the oven and keep warm.

4 Roll out the pastry and cut out four 8cm (3¼in) diameter circles. Put them on a floured baking sheet, glaze with a little milk, then cook in the oven for 12 minutes, until golden. Remove and keep warm.

5 Meanwhile, cook the mushrooms in 25g (scant 1oz) of the butter in a saucepan, add seasoning and the truffle oil. Keep warm.

6 Put the cabbage in 300ml (10fl oz) of the double cream in a saucepan, and add seasoning. Cook for 10–12 minutes until tender.

7 Mash the potatoes with the rest of the double cream and butter.

8 Cover the beef in the olive oil and salt and pepper. Heat a frying pan and when hot, seal the beef for a few seconds on each side. Transfer to a roasting tin, add the thyme and rosemary, and spoon the extra stock over the top. Put in the oven for 6 minutes.

9 To assemble, place a puff pastry circle on each plate. Score a circle in the top, push it down, and fill with mushrooms. Add some creamed cabbage, a prune in bacon, and quenelles of mash. Place a fillet of beef on top, add the jus, and serve.

THAI BEEF MASSAMAN CURRY
WITH JASMINE RICE

ALIX CARWOOD Quarter-finalist 2008

500g (1lb 2oz) LEAN RUMP STEAK,
   cut into bite-sized chunks
5 CLOVES
10 CARDAMOM PODS
3 tbsp VEGETABLE OIL
400ml can COCONUT MILK
2 tbsp NAM PLA (Thai fish sauce)
175ml (6fl oz) BEEF STOCK
60g (2oz) unsalted PEANUTS, skinned
1 large MARIS PIPER POTATO, peeled
   and cut into chunks
1.5cm (½in) piece fresh
   ROOT GINGER
1–2 tbsp PALM SUGAR
1–2 tbsp TAMARIND PASTE

FOR THE CURRY PASTE
1 RED CHILLI
1 stalk of LEMONGRASS

1cm (½in) GALANGAL or 1 tsp
   GALANGAL IN SUNFLOWER OIL
5 CLOVES
1 CINNAMON STICK
10 CARDAMOM PODS
3 GARLIC CLOVES
3 SHALLOTS
large handful of CORIANDER
3 tbsp OLIVE OIL

TO SERVE
300g (10oz) JASMINE RICE
unsalted PEANUTS, skinned
CORIANDER LEAVES, to garnish

PREPARATION TIME
25 minutes

COOKING TIME
55 minutes

SERVES 4

1 To make the curry paste, put all the ingredients in a food processor with a little olive oil and blend until they form a paste.

2 For the beef curry, put the cloves and cardamom in a frying pan and dry fry to release the fragrance. Remove and set aside.

3 Put a little of the vegetable oil in the pan and fry 5 tbsp of the curry paste over a medium heat for 5 minutes until the fragrance is released. Add the beef and fry until browned. Then add the remaining ingredients to the pan and bring to the boil. Reduce to a simmer and cook for about 45 minutes until the beef is tender and the sauce is reduced.

4 Bring a pan of water to the boil. Add a pinch of salt and then the jasmine rice. Reduce the heat and leave to simmer for about 10 minutes until the rice is cooked through.

5 Serve the curry in a bowl, sprinkled with peanuts, with the jasmine rice to one side, garnished with coriander.

LAMB SAMOSAS

DAKSHA MISTRY Finalist 2006

250g (9oz) MINCED LAMB

½ ONION, finely chopped

1 GARLIC CLOVE, finely chopped

½ tsp CURRY POWDER

¼ tsp CHILLI POWDER

½ tsp GROUND TURMERIC

¼ tsp ground roasted CUMIN SEEDS

½ GREEN CHILLI, deseeded and finely chopped

1 tbsp chopped CORIANDER

¼ tsp grated fresh ROOT GINGER

½ tsp SALT

freshly ground BLACK PEPPER

squeeze of LEMON JUICE

1 litre (1¾ pints) SUNFLOWER OIL,
    for deep-frying

4 sprigs of CORIANDER, to garnish

FOR THE PASTRY

115g (4oz) PLAIN FLOUR

1 tsp SALT

1 tbsp SUNFLOWER OIL

about 3 tbsp warm WATER

PREPARATION TIME
50 minutes

COOKING TIME
15 minutes

SERVES 4

1 To make the pastry, mix the flour and salt in a bowl. Make a well in the centre and add the oil and enough water to make a firm dough. Knead the dough on a floured surface until smooth and roll into a ball. Cover in cling film and set aside at room temperature for 30 minutes.

2 For the filling, put all the ingredients except the oil and coriander sprigs into a bowl and mix thoroughly with your hands.

3 Divide the pastry into 6 equal pieces. Roll each piece into a ball and cover with cling film to stop them from drying out. Roll each ball of pastry into a 12.5cm (5in) circle and then divide into 2 equal semicircles with a knife.

4 Place a level tbsp of the mixture on one half circle of the semicircle of pastry. Then fold the other half circle across the filling to form a triangle. Dampen the edges with water and gently seal the open edges. Repeat for the other samosas.

5 Heat the oil in a large saucepan. To test when the oil is hot enough, drop a small piece of bread into it and as soon as it starts to sizzle, remove it and start frying the samosas, 4 at a time. Cook each batch for about 5 minutes, turning occasionally, or until the samosas are crisp and brown. Remove them from the pan, drain on kitchen paper, and serve 2 or 3 samosas per person while still warm, garnished with the coriander.

ROAST MOROCCAN LAMB WITH COUSCOUS AND HARISSA SAUCE

HELEN GILMOUR Quarter-finalist 2007

2 cannons of LAMB, about 350g (12oz) each

FOR THE MARINADE

200ml (7fl oz) OLIVE OIL

juice of ½ LEMON

1 ONION, finely chopped

3 tbsp chopped FLAT-LEAF PARSLEY

3 tbsp chopped MINT

5 tbsp chopped CORIANDER

1½ tsp ground CUMIN

1 tsp PAPRIKA

1 tsp SEA SALT and freshly ground BLACK PEPPER

FOR THE COUSCOUS

100g (3½oz) MEDIUM GRAIN COUSCOUS

6 DRIED APRICOTS, chopped

50g (1¾oz) GOLDEN SULTANAS

25g (scant 1oz) SALTED BUTTER

200ml (7fl oz) CHICKEN STOCK

25g (scant 1oz) flaked ALMONDS

20g (¾oz) MINT, finely chopped

20g (¾oz) CORIANDER, finely chopped

200g (7oz) can CHICKPEAS

25g (scant 1oz) nibbed PISTACHIOS

½ tsp ground CINNAMON

3 tbsp OLIVE OIL (optional)

FOR THE HARISSA SAUCE

3 tbsp ROSE HARISSA PASTE

2 tbsp PLAIN YOGURT

PREPARATION TIME
1 hour, plus marinating

COOKING TIME
30 minutes

SERVES 4

1 Combine all the marinade ingredients, pour over the lamb, and set aside to marinate for a minimum of 2 hours, or overnight if you can.

2 Prepare the couscous. Place the couscous, apricots, and sultanas in a bowl. Add the butter, and pour over the chicken stock so there is just enough to cover the grains. Cover with cling film and set aside for 10 minutes to allow the stock to be absorbed.

3 Toast the almonds in a dry pan until golden and set aside in a bowl. Add the mint and coriander.

4 Fluff the couscous with a fork and add half the chickpeas and stir through. Add the almonds and herbs, and then the pistachios and mix thoroughly. Finally, add the cinnamon and season with salt and pepper, and add some olive oil, if required.

5 For the harissa sauce, mix the harissa paste with the yogurt and warm it in a small saucepan over a low heat, but do not overheat as it may split.

6 Heat a frying pan until hot and cook the lamb for 8–10 minutes. Remove from the pan, cover with foil, and leave to rest for 5 minutes.

7 To assemble, divide the couscous between 4 plates and place slices of lamb and a spoonful of the harissa sauce alongside. A spoonful of cacik is the perfect accompaniment.

LOIN OF VENISON WITH CELERIAC PURÉE, BRAISED CABBAGE, AND REDCURRANT JUS

ALEX RUSHMER Finalist 2010

700g (1lb 9oz) LOIN OF VENISON

1 tbsp OLIVE OIL

knob of BUTTER

100g (3½oz) PORCINI or WILD
   MUSHROOMS, cut into thick slices

FOR THE CABBAGE

knob of BUTTER

1 small SHALLOT, diced

300g (10oz) RED CABBAGE,
   quartered, cored, and sliced

1 APPLE, cored, peeled, and sliced

1 tbsp CLEAR HONEY

3 tbsp RED WINE VINEGAR

100ml (3½fl oz) RED WINE

200ml (7fl oz) CHICKEN STOCK

SALT and freshly ground
   BLACK PEPPER

FOR THE CELERIAC

1 CELERIAC, approx. 800g (1¾lb)

juice of 1 LEMON

3 tbsp DOUBLE CREAM

25g (scant 1oz) BUTTER

500ml (16fl oz) VEGETABLE OIL

FOR THE JUS

knob of BUTTER

1 SHALLOT, diced

8 JUNIPER BERRIES

50g (1¾oz) REDCURRANTS

150ml (5fl oz) PORT

150ml (5fl oz) VEAL STOCK

2 tsp REDCURRANT JELLY

PREPARATION TIME
20 minutes

COOKING TIME
1 hour 30 minutes

SERVES 4

1 For the cabbage, melt the butter in a large heavy saucepan. Add the shallot and cook for about 5 minutes to soften. Add the remaining ingredients and season. Cover with greaseproof paper and a lid, and braise over a very low heat for 1½ hours, stirring occasionally.

2 Peel the celeriac and shave off 4 strips to make crisps. Put in a bowl of iced lemon water and set aside. Dice the rest. Put in a pan with water to cover, salt, and lemon juice and bring to the boil. Simmer for 15–20 minutes or until soft. Drain and transfer to a blender or food processor. Add the cream, butter, and seasoning and purée. Keep warm.

3 For the jus, melt the butter in a pan. Cook the shallot for 3 minutes to soften. Add the berries and redcurrants and cook for 1 minute, then stir in the port and reduce by half. Pour in the stock and reduce again. Stir in the jelly and pass through a sieve into a pan to keep warm.

4 Season the venison and fry in the oil for 10–15 minutes, turning once. Cook longer if you prefer your meat less pink. Remove the venison from the pan, leave to rest, and then slice. Add the butter and mushrooms to the pan and fry for about 2 minutes to cook through.

5 Just before serving, drain and dry the celeriac shavings. Deep-fry in the vegetable oil for 2–3 minutes until crisp. Drain on kitchen paper. Spoon the purée and cabbage onto 4 plates and top with the venison and mushrooms. Drizzle over the sauce and garnish with the crisps.

PAN-FRIED CHICKEN BREAST
WITH SESAME SEEDS AND A MANGO HOLLANDAISE

JAYE WAKELIN Quarter-finalist 2007

4 CHICKEN BREASTS, skinned

2 large EGG YOLKS

SALT and freshly ground BLACK PEPPER

1 tbsp LEMON JUICE

1 tbsp WHITE WINE VINEGAR

125g (4½oz) SALTED BUTTER

1 ripe MANGO, peeled, stoned, and chopped

2 tbsp SESAME SEEDS

1 tbsp GROUNDNUT OIL

25g (scant 1oz) BUTTER

400g (14oz) PURPLE SPROUTING BROCCOLI

PREPARATION TIME
15 minutes

COOKING TIME
20 minutes

SERVES 4

1 Remove the chicken from the refrigerator at least 30 minutes before preparation.

2 To make the Hollandaise, place the egg yolks in a blender with salt and pepper to taste and blend thoroughly. Heat the lemon juice and vinegar to simmering point in a small saucepan, then remove the pan from the heat. Switch on the blender again and pour the hot lemon liquid through the vent in the top of it in a steady stream. Switch off the blender.

3 In the same saucepan, melt the butter over a low heat. With the blender running as before, add the butter to the egg mixture in a steady stream. The mixture should now look like runny mayonnaise. Pour it out into a clean bowl.

4 Add the chopped mango to the blender and blitz until smooth and puréed. Stir into the Hollandaise, cover with cling film, and set aside.

5 Spread the sesame seeds over a plate and press the chicken breasts onto them, coating each one evenly. Melt the oil and butter in a frying pan over a medium heat, taking care that the butter doesn't brown. Add the chicken breasts and fry gently on both sides until cooked through – about 5–8 minutes on each side. At this point the butter in the pan will look brown but will not have burnt. Meanwhile, steam the broccoli until tender – about 8 minutes.

6 Return the Mango Hollandaise to a clean saucepan and reheat gently, taking care not to let it bubble and separate. Put the sliced chicken breasts on plates and serve with the Hollandaise spooned over. This dish goes well with any stir-fried Chinese greens or purple sprouting broccoli with a little soy sauce.

RHUBARB CRUMBLE TART
WITH SYLLABUB AND RHUBARB SYRUP

DICK STRAWBRIDGE Celebrity finalist 2010

225g (8oz) SUGAR, plus 3 tbsp

450g (1lb) RHUBARB, cut into
1cm (½in) pieces

2 pieces of STEM GINGER, finely diced

FOR THE NUT CRUST

50g (1¾oz) blanched HAZELNUTS,
toasted

25g (scant 1oz) ICING SUGAR

100g (3½oz) PLAIN FLOUR

50g (1¾oz) BUTTER

½ tsp VANILLA EXTRACT

1 small EGG, beaten

FOR THE CRUMBLE TOPPING

100g (3½oz) PLAIN FLOUR

50g (1¾oz) BUTTER

25g (scant 1oz) DEMERARA SUGAR

finely grated zest of 1 LEMON

FOR THE SYLLABUB

300ml (10fl oz) DOUBLE CREAM

1–2 tbsp GINGER WINE or BRANDY

2 tbsp GINGER SYRUP from the stem
ginger jar

1 piece of STEM GINGER, finely sliced

PREPARATION TIME
45 minutes, plus chilling

COOKING TIME
1 hour

SERVES 4

1 First make a syrup by dissolving 225g (8oz) of the sugar in a saucepan with 300ml (10fl oz) of boiling water. Preheat the oven to 180°C (350°F/Gas 4). Add half the rhubarb to the syrup, bring to the boil, then leave until completely cold. Put the remaining rhubarb in an ovenproof dish and sprinkle over 3 tbsp of sugar. Bake in the oven for about 20 minutes or until softened. Allow to cool, then drain and mix with the slices of stem ginger, reserving 8 slices for decoration. Strain the cold rhubarb syrup into a jug and chill.

2 For the nut crust, put the nuts and sugar in a food processor and mix briefly to combine. Add the remaining ingredients except the egg and mix on the pulse setting. With the machine running, gradually pour in the egg and mix to form a ball. Wrap in cling film and chill for 30 minutes. Divide into 4 equal pieces and press into the base of four 10cm (4in) tart tins. Chill for 10 minutes.

3 Increase the oven heat to 190°C (375°G/Gas 5). Cook the tarts for about 8–10 minutes or until pale golden. Meanwhile, make the crumble. Put all the ingredients in a food processor and mix briefly to form crumbs. Spread out on a baking sheet and cook for 8–10 minutes or until pale golden. Give the crumble a stir halfway through cooking.

4 Divide the rhubarb between tart cases and top with the crumble. Bake for 10 minutes or until heated through.

5 For the syllabub, put the cream, wine, and ginger syrup into a bowl and whisk to form soft peaks. Chill for 10 minutes.

6 Serve the tarts warm with the syllabub, decorating the syllabub with slices of stem ginger. Place a cup of pink rhubarb syrup alongside.

RICE CRISPIE CAKE WITH CHOCOLATE MOUSSE, CHERRY SORBET, AND CHERRIES IN KIRSCH

DAVID COULSON Professionals finalist 2010

FOR THE SORBET

100g (3½ oz) CASTER SUGAR

400g (14 oz) jar of GRIOTINES or BLACK CHERRIES IN KIRSCH

FOR THE CAKE

50g (1¾ oz) DARK CHOCOLATE (68% cocoa solids)

30g (1oz) RICE CRISPIES

1 tbsp GOLDEN SYRUP

100g (3½ oz) CONDENSED MILK

1 packet of CRACKLE CRYSTALS

FOR THE MOUSSE

75g (2½ oz) DARK CHOCOLATE (68% cocoa solids)

2 EGGS, separated

100ml (3½ fl oz) DOUBLE CREAM

FOR THE POACHING SYRUP

150ml (5fl oz) reserved KIRSCH SYRUP from the jar of cherries

1 tbsp CASTER SUGAR

1 STAR ANISE

1 CINNAMON STICK

PREPARATION TIME
50 minutes, plus freezing

SERVES 4

1 To make the sorbet, put the sugar in a saucepan with 100ml (3½ fl oz) of water. Gently heat to dissolve the sugar, then boil for 1 minute to make a stock syrup. Drain the jar of cherries. Set aside 4 cherries and reserve the Kirsch syrup for poaching them.

2 Add the remaining cherries to the stock syrup and blend in a liquidizer or food processor until smooth. Pour into an ice-cream maker and churn. Transfer to a suitable container and freeze.

3 To make the cake, melt the chocolate in a glass bowl set over a pan of simmering water. Stir in the rice crispies, syrup, and condensed milk and add the crackle crystals. Divide the crispie cake between 4 glass dessert dishes and set aside, but not in the refrigerator.

4 For the mousse, melt the chocolate and stir in the egg yolks. Softly whip the cream and fold into the chocolate mix. Beat the egg whites until stiff and fold into the mix until well combined. Spoon the mousse into the glasses on top of the crispie mixture.

5 Put the reserved Kirsch in a pan and stir in the sugar. Add the reserved cherries, the star anise, and the cinnamon stick. Simmer for 5 minutes. Remove the cherries and spices with a slotted spoon and reduce the sauce to a syrup. Reserve the cherries and discard the spices.

6 To finish, use a melonball scoop to put a small scoop of the sorbet on top of the mousse and decorate with a poached cherry. Serve immediately with the syrup in a jug alongside.

EXPLODING LEMON MACAROONS

TIM KINNAIRD Finalist 2010

FOR THE MACAROONS

180g (6oz) CASTER SUGAR

3 tbsp WATER

4 EGG WHITES, near their sell-by date

180g (6oz) ground ALMONDS

180g (6oz) ICING SUGAR

1 tsp YELLOW FOOD COLOURING

FOR THE LEMON CURD

4 EGG YOLKS

grated zest and juice of 6 LEMONS

70g (2¼ fl oz) CASTER SUGAR

70g (2¼ fl oz) SALTED BUTTER

TO SERVE

POPPING CANDY (optional)

PREPARATION TIME
55 minutes, plus standing
and chilling

COOKING TIME
25 minutes

SERVES 4

1 Preheat the oven to 150°C (300°F/Gas 2) and line 2–3 baking sheets with baking parchment.

2 To make the macaroons, dissolve the sugar in 3 tbsp of water over low heat for about 8 minutes, stirring occasionally. Increase the heat and allow the sugar to boil for about 10 minutes, without stirring, until it reaches 118°C (244°F) – "soft boil" temperature.

3 Whisk the egg whites in a free-standing mixer until they start to foam. Still mixing, gradually add the sugar syrup in a steady stream until the sugar is incorporated and the egg whites form stiff peaks.

4 In a separate bowl, mix together the ground almonds, icing sugar, 165g (5½oz) of the egg whites, and the food colouring. Mix together until the meringue flows like lava.

5 Pipe 5cm (2in) circles of the meringue mixture onto the baking parchment with at least 2cm (¾in) gaps between each circle. Leave for 45 minutes for the shells to dry a little and a crust to form.

6 Bake in the oven for about 15 minutes. Remove from the oven to cool and then gently remove from the paper.

7 While the biscuits are resting, make the lemon curd. Put the egg yolks, lemon zest and juice, and caster sugar into a saucepan and heat gently with half the butter for about 10 minutes until the curd thickens.

8 Strain the lemon curd into a bowl to remove the zest and whisk in the remaining butter. Chill in the refrigerator until the curd is firm and the biscuits are cool.

9 Sandwich pairs of macaroons with lemon curd and put them back in the refrigerator to chill, preferably overnight.

10 Remove the macaroons from the refrigerator an hour before serving. Slightly moisten them by lightly brushing them with a moistened pastry brush and sprinkle with popping candy (if using).

MASTERCHEF **EGGS AND DAIRY PRODUCTS** KNOW-HOW: See **Separate Yolks and Whites** 428

MASTERCHEF **EGGS AND DAIRY PRODUCTS** KNOW-HOW: See **Whisk Egg Whites** 429

MASTERCHEF **EGGS AND DAIRY PRODUCTS** KNOW-HOW: See **Shape Meringues** 435

ALMOND PANNA COTTA WITH POACHED TAMARILLOS AND BERRIES

LISA FAULKNER Celebrity champion 2010

4 leaves of GELATINE
250ml (8fl oz) WHOLE MILK
250ml (8fl oz) DOUBLE CREAM
1 VANILLA POD
50g (1¾oz) CASTER SUGAR
few drops of ALMOND EXTRACT

FOR THE TAMARILLOS
100g (3½oz) CASTER SUGAR
1 VANILLA POD
1 CINNAMON STICK
1 BAY LEAF
4 TAMARILLOS, halved lengthways

FOR THE BERRIES
50g (1¾oz) CASTER SUGAR
60ml (2fl oz) CASSIS
50g (1¾oz) RASPBERRIES
50g (1¾oz) BLUEBERRIES

PREPARATION TIME
30 minutes, plus chilling

COOKING TIME
40 minutes

SERVES 4

1 To make the panna cotta, first soak the gelatine in cold water for 10 minutes to soften. Pour the milk and cream into a saucepan, split the vanilla pod, and add to the pan. Bring to the boil, remove from the heat, and allow to infuse for few minutes. Shake off excess water from the gelatine and stir into the pan. Add the sugar, then continue to stir over low heat until completely melted. Take out the vanilla pod and stir in the almond extract.

2 Lightly oil 4 individual pudding basins that will hold 135ml (4½fl oz) of panna cotta then set them on a tray. Pour the mixture into each. Chill for at least 2 hours, or until completely set.

3 For the tamarillos, pour 200ml (7fl oz) water into a saucepan and add the sugar, vanilla, cinnamon, and bay leaf. Cook over low heat until the sugar has dissolved. Increase the heat and, when simmering, add the tamarillos and poach for about 5–10 minutes. Remove from the heat and leave to cool in the syrup.

4 For the berries, pour 100ml (3½fl oz) water into a saucepan, add the sugar and cassis, and bring to the boil. Add the berries and cook slowly for about 30 minutes, stirring occasionally. The mixture should appear syrupy.

5 Dip the pudding basins in hot water for a couple of seconds, then turn out onto the centre of each serving plate. Top with a berry and serve alongside 2 halves of a tamarillo and a spoonful of the poached berries.

MASTERCHEF **FLAVOURINGS** KNOW-HOW: See **Use Gelatine** 391
MASTERCHEF **EGGS AND DAIRY PRODUCTS** KNOW-HOW: See **Whip Cream** 436

BANANA SOUFFLÉ
WITH BLUEBERRY COULIS

NATALIE BRENNER Quarter-finalist 2010

FOR THE COULIS

150g (5½oz) BLUEBERRIES

50g (1¾oz) SUGAR

FOR THE SOUFFLÉS

15g (½oz) UNSALTED BUTTER

4 tsp SUGAR

1 large, ripe BANANA, roughly chopped

1 tbsp CLEAR HONEY

2 large EGGS, whites only

1 tbsp CASTER SUGAR

TO SERVE

ICING SUGAR

1 tbsp DOUBLE CREAM

PREPARATION TIME
30 minutes

COOKING TIME
25 minutes

SERVES 4

1 For the coulis, place the blueberries and sugar in a saucepan with 100ml (3½fl oz) water and bring to the boil. Take off the heat and allow to cool, then blend, using a hand-held blender or by transferring to a food processor, and pass through a sieve. Put back on the heat, bring to the boil, and reduce until syrupy. Set aside to cool.

2 Preheat the oven to 200°C (400°F/Gas 6) and place a baking sheet in the oven to heat. Evenly grease 4 ramekins with the butter, then coat the inside with a layer of sugar.

3 Place the banana in a food processor, add the honey, and blend until smooth.

4 Place the egg whites in a clean, dry bowl and whisk until the whites form soft peaks. Gradually add the caster sugar, whisking all the time, until soft peaks are formed.

5 Using a spatula, fold one-third of the egg whites into the banana mixture relatively vigorously, then very gently fold in the remainder. Spoon the soufflé mix into the ramekins, tap on the work surface to expel any air, and run a finger around the rim to create a "top hat" effect.

6 Put the soufflés on the preheated baking sheet and place in the oven and bake them for 10–12 minutes until risen.

7 To serve, put the coulis in a small jug on each plate. Place the soufflés in the ramekins on the plate, and sprinkle icing sugar on them just before serving.

MASTERCHEF **EGGS AND DAIRY PRODUCTS** KNOW-HOW: See **Whisk Egg Whites** 429

MASTERCHEF **EGGS AND DAIRY PRODUCTS** KNOW-HOW: See **Bake a Soufflé** 432

WHITE CHOCOLATE MOUSSE WITH RASPBERRY AND ELDERFLOWER JELLY

CLAIRE LARA Professionals champion 2010

5 leaves of GELATINE

200ml (7fl oz) DOUBLE CREAM

150g (5½oz) VALRHONA WHITE CHOCOLATE

400g (14oz) RASPBERRIES

150g (5½oz) CASTER SUGAR, plus extra for scattering over the filo sheets

3 tbsp ELDERFLOWER CORDIAL

4 sheets of FILO PASTRY

50g (1¾oz) BUTTER, melted

2 tsp chopped freeze-dried RASPBERRIES

PREPARATION TIME
1 hour, plus chilling

COOKING TIME
30 minutes

SERVES 4

1 Soak 2 of the leaves of gelatine in cold water for at least 10 minutes to soften. Whip the cream until soft peaks form.

2 Melt the chocolate in a bowl set over a pan of barely simmering water, making sure the bowl is clear of the water. Remove the bowl from the pan. While the chocolate is still warm (not hot), squeeze the excess water from the gelatine and stir the gelatine into the chocolate. Whisk the chocolate into the whipped cream and transfer to a piping bag with a plain nozzle. Place in the refrigerator for 20 minutes to set.

3 Meanwhile, place the remaining leaves of gelatine in cold water to soften. Reserving 12 raspberries, whizz the rest of the raspberries to a purée with the sugar in food processor, then pass through a sieve.

Place the raspberry purée and elderflower cordial in a pan and heat gently, then stir in the gelatine. Warm over low heat until the gelatine is dissolved. Pour into mini muffin tins, sit a raspberry on top of each, and put in the refrigerator to set.

4 Preheat the oven to 200°C (400°F/Gas 6). Cut each sheet of filo pastry into 4 rectangles. Brush with melted butter and sugar and bake in the oven for 3 minutes until crispy, then remove and cool. Scatter with freeze-dried raspberries.

5 To serve, on each plate pipe 3–4 lines of mousse on top of a filo rectangle and top with another piece of filo. Repeat twice, finishing with a piece of filo pastry. Serve with the jellies alongside.

DARK CHOCOLATE AND ALMOND TORTE
WITH AMARETTO CREAM, RASPBERRIES, AND PASSION FRUIT

DHRUV BAKER Champion 2010

150g (5½oz) DARK CHOCOLATE
  (70% cocoa solids)
125g (4½oz) UNSALTED BUTTER
5 EGGS, separated
175g (6oz) LIGHT SOFT BROWN SUGAR
175g (6oz) ground ALMONDS
100ml (3½fl oz) AMARETTO, plus
  1 tbsp for amaretto cream
100ml (3½fl oz) DOUBLE CREAM
1 punnet RASPBERRIES
2 PASSION FRUIT, peeled, cut in half,
  and seeds scooped out
ICING SUGAR

PREPARATION TIME
30 minutes

COOKING TIME
30 minutes

MAKES 8 SLICES

1 Preheat the oven to 150°C (300°F/Gas 2). Line the base of a 23cm (9in) diameter springform baking tin with baking parchment and butter the sides.

2 Melt the chocolate and butter in a large bowl placed over a saucepan of simmering water. Once melted, remove from heat and leave to cool slightly.

3 In a separate bowl, whisk the egg whites with a whisk until they form peaks.

4 Mix the sugar and almonds in the chocolate mixture, then stir in the egg yolks and the 100ml (3½fl oz) of amaretto.

5 Finally, fold the egg whites into the chocolate mixture using a metal spoon. Pour the mixture into the prepared tin and bake for about 30 minutes or until firm on top and a skewer comes out clean. Remove the torte from the oven and allow to cool for a few minutes.

6 Whip the cream with a whisk and pour in the remaining amaretto.

7 Put the passion fruit flesh into a blender or food processor and blend to a pulp. Push through a sieve and add icing sugar to taste.

8 To serve, place a slice of the torte on each plate. Drizzle over some passion fruit coulis and add a spoonful of the cream and a few raspberries.

MASTERCHEF **EGGS AND DAIRY PRODUCTS** KNOW-HOW: See **Whisk Egg Whites** `429`

MASTERCHEF **EGGS AND DAIRY PRODUCTS** KNOW-HOW: See **Whip Cream** `436`

HAZELNUT AND RASPBERRY MERINGUE

NADIA SAWALHA Celebrity champion 2007

115g (4oz) whole shelled HAZELNUTS
4 large EGG WHITES
250g (9oz) CASTER SUGAR
1 tsp VANILLA EXTRACT
1 tbsp RASPBERRY VINEGAR
300ml (10fl oz) DOUBLE CREAM
200g (7oz) fresh RASPBERRIES
ICING SUGAR, to dust

PREPARATION TIME
20 minutes

COOKING TIME
40 minutes

SERVES 4

1 Preheat the oven to 160°C (325°F/Gas 3). Butter a 20cm (8in) sandwich tin and line with baking parchment.

2 Halve and dry fry the hazelnuts until lightly toasted, reserving a few.

3 Whisk the egg whites until stiff. Add the sugar 1 tbsp at a time and continue beating until the mixture is very stiff and stands in peaks. Whisk in the vanilla extract and vinegar, then fold in the hazelnuts.

4 Transfer to the sandwich tin. Alternatively, make individual portions by placing dollops of the meringue mix straight on to baking parchment, forming a slight hollow for the filling. Bake in the oven for 20–30 minutes, or until lightly browned and holding its shape. Leave to cool in the tin for 10 minutes then transfer to a serving dish.

5 Whip the cream and pile onto the centre of the meringue when it is completely cold. Place the raspberries. Finely chop the reserved hazelnuts and sprinkle over. Dust with icing sugar just before serving.

MASTERCHEF **EGGS AND DAIRY PRODUCTS** KNOW-HOW: See **Whisk Egg Whites** 429
MASTERCHEF **EGGS AND DAIRY PRODUCTS** KNOW-HOW: See **Whip Cream** 436

STRAWBERRIES WITH SABLÉ BISCUITS AND ORANGE AND LEMON SYLLABUB

JAMES NATHAN Champion 2008

FOR THE SABLÉ BISCUITS

100g (3½oz) PLAIN FLOUR

75g (2½oz) UNSALTED BUTTER

100g (3½oz) GOLDEN CASTER SUGAR

grated zest of 1 LEMON

2 EGG YOLKS

FOR THE SYLLABUB

50g (1¾oz) CASTER SUGAR

grated zest and juice of 1 ORANGE

grated zest and juice of 1 LEMON

300ml (10fl oz) DOUBLE CREAM

FOR THE STRAWBERRY COULIS

350g (12oz) STRAWBERRIES
  (English if possible)

50g (1¾oz) ICING SUGAR

3 tbsp GRAND MARNIER

TO DECORATE

ICING SUGAR, for sprinkling

MINT LEAVES

PREPARATION TIME
40 minutes

COOKING TIME
8 minutes

SERVES 4

1 Preheat the oven to 200°C (400°F/Gas 6). To make the biscuits, mix the flour, butter, sugar, lemon zest, and egg yolks together in a food processor until a soft ball of dough is formed. Rest in the refrigerator for about 30 minutes. Roll out thinly. Cut out 8 biscuits with a 7–8cm (2¾–3¼in) biscuit cutter and bake in the oven on a greased baking tray until golden, about 6–8 minutes.

2 To make the coulis, hull 200g (7oz) of the strawberries. Purée with the icing sugar and Grand Marnier in a food processor. Check for sweetness and adjust if necessary. Pass through a fine sieve and chill the mixture until required.

3 For the syllabub, combine the sugar and zest and juice from the orange and lemon. Whisk the cream until it forms soft peaks. Add the citrus mixture and whisk to firm peaks. Chill until required.

4 To serve, put a swirl of the coulis on each plate. Set a biscuit alongside it. Put a few spoonfuls of syllabub in the centre of the biscuit and surround with the remaining strawberries, halved lengthways to make pillars. Top with another biscuit. Sprinkle with icing sugar and add some mint leaves to finish.

PEARS BELLE HÉLÈNE

STEVEN WALLIS Champion 2007

PREPARATION TIME
20 minutes, plus freezing

COOKING TIME
20 minutes

SERVES 4

FOR THE PEARS

1 tbsp CASTER SUGAR

4 BAY LEAVES

3 CARDAMOM PODS

2 VANILLA PODS

2 COMICE PEARS, with stalks

FOR THE ICE CREAM

300ml (10fl oz) DOUBLE CREAM

200ml (7fl oz) WHOLE MILK

2 VANILLA PODS, slit, seeds scraped
 out but reserved

4 EGG YOLKS

85–100g (3–3½oz) CASTER SUGAR

FOR THE CHOCOLATE SAUCE

1 tsp CASTER SUGAR

300ml (10fl oz) DOUBLE CREAM

2 x 100g (3½oz) bars DARK CHOCOLATE
 (70% cocoa solids)

1 First make the ice cream. Pour the cream and milk into a saucepan. Add the vanilla pods and seeds to the pan and heat gently until steaming but not boiling. Leave to infuse for 5 minutes.

2 Whisk the egg yolks and sugar together until pale and foamy. Remove the vanilla pods and gradually whisk the warm cream into the egg yolk mixture. Return to the pan and cook, stirring, over low heat until a custard thick enough to coat the back of a wooden spoon is formed. Transfer to an ice-cream maker and churn.

3 To cook the pears, pour 300ml (10fl oz) boiling water into a saucepan, add the sugar, and stir to dissolve. Add the bay leaves and cardamom and vanilla pods. Heat gently to boiling point. Peel and core the pears, leaving the stalk intact. Add to the syrup, cover with a lid, and poach gently for 20 minutes or until tender.

4 For the chocolate sauce, put the sugar in a pan with 1 tbsp boiling water and stir until the sugar is dissolved. Set aside. Warm the cream in a heavy pan, add the chocolate piece by piece, and stir very briefly to melt. Remove from the heat and stir in the sugar syrup. Keep warm.

5 To serve, slice the pears in half lengthways, then make vertical cuts about 5mm (¼in) apart. For each diner, scoop out a ball of ice cream the size of a small orange and place in a chilled deep dessert bowl. Carefully lift the pear on top and mould it around the ice cream. Set the bowl on a plate and serve the chocolate sauce on the side.

MASTERCHEF **EGG AND DAIRY PRODUCTS** KNOW-HOW: See **Whip Cream** 436

LAVENDER MOUSSE WITH HOKEY POKEY AND A BLACKBERRY SAUCE

MAT FOLLAS Champion 2009

FOR THE BLACKBERRY SAUCE
300g (10oz) BLACKBERRIES
200g (7oz) CASTER SUGAR

FOR THE LAVENDER MOUSSE
13g (½oz) GELATINE LEAVES, cut into pieces
500ml (16fl oz) WHOLE MILK
5 EGG YOLKS
40g (1½oz) CASTER SUGAR
500ml (16fl oz) WHIPPING CREAM
20g (¾oz) LAVENDER FLOWER HEADS
12 drops LAVENDER ESSENCE

FOR THE HOKEY POKEY
75g (2½oz) CASTER SUGAR
2 tbsp GOLDEN SYRUP
1 tsp BICARBONATE OF SODA

PREPARATION TIME
50 minutes

SERVES 4

1 Set aside 12 blackberries of different sizes for decoration. Then put the remaining blackberries in a pan with the sugar and add 100ml (3½ fl oz) cold water, stir and heat gently until the sugar has dissolved. Bring the sauce to the boil, reduce the heat, and simmer for 5 minutes or until the sauce has reduced by half and thickened. Pass through a sieve, discard the blackberry pulp, and leave to cool.

2 Transfer the sauce into a jug and pour a little into 4 freezerproof glasses, which the mousse will be served in. Put the glasses in the freezer and set the rest of the sauce aside in the refrigerator.

3 For the lavender mousse, put the gelatine in iced water for about 10 minutes to soften. Pour the milk into a saucepan and bring it to the boil. Place the egg yolks and sugar into a bowl and mix. Stir in the milk. Return to the pan, stirring and warming gently for 5 minutes or until the sauce coats the back of a spoon. Drain any excess water from the gelatine and add to the pan and stir until dissolved. Set aside to cool.

4 Whip the cream until stiff peaks are formed. Add the lavender heads and combine. Stir in the lavender essence, a drop at a time, until the flavour is to your taste. Gently fold in the cream.

5 Remove the glasses from the freezer and pour the crème anglaise over the frozen berry sauce. Return to the freezer for 20 minutes.

6 To make the hokey pokey, heat the sugar and golden syrup slowly in a saucepan, stirring constantly for 3 minutes or until the sugar is dissolved. Stir in the bicarbonate of soda and then pour onto a silicone sheet and leave to cool. Put into a plastic bag and gently smash it.

7 To serve, make a line of blackberry sauce on each plate and top with the reserved blackberries. Add the frozen mousses and put a piece of broken hokey pokey in the top of each one and add a small pile of hokey pokey crumbs alongside.

MASTERCHEF **FLAVOURINGS** KNOW-HOW: See **Use Gelatine** 391
MASTERCHEF **EGGS AND DAIRY PRODUCTS** KNOW-HOW: See **Whip Cream** 436

STICKY TOFFEE PUDDING

WENDI PETERS Celebrity finalist 2009

85g (3oz) sugared, stoned DATES, chopped

85g (3oz) LIGHT SOFT BROWN SUGAR

45g (1½oz) UNSALTED BUTTER, softened

1 EGG

115g (4oz) PLAIN FLOUR

1 tsp BICARBONATE OF SODA

1 tbsp VANILLA EXTRACT

FOR THE TOFFEE SAUCE

150g (5½oz) DEMERARA SUGAR

85g (3oz) UNSALTED BUTTER, softened

4 tbsp DOUBLE CREAM

PREPARATION TIME
20 minutes

COOKING TIME
35 minutes

SERVES 4

1 Preheat the oven to 180°C (350°F/Gas 4). Butter a 16 x 12cm (6½ x 5in) ovenproof dish.

2 Put the dates into a bowl and pour over just enough boiling water to cover them.

3 In a separate bowl, cream together the soft brown sugar and the butter. Beat the egg into the creamed mixture with some of the flour before adding the rest of the flour.

4 Add the bicarbonate of soda and vanilla extract to the dates and then stir into the creamed mixture until well mixed. Pour into the ovenproof dish and bake in the oven for 30–35 minutes or until well risen and a cake skewer when inserted comes out clean.

5 Just before the pudding is cooked, make the toffee sauce. Preheat the grill to hot. Put the demerara sugar, butter, and cream into a saucepan and heat gently. Let simmer for 3 minutes. Remove the pudding from the oven, pour over half the sauce, and place under the grill until it bubbles.

6 Serve the pudding while hot with the remaining sauce poured over the top or alongside as an accompaniment.

RHUBARB TARTE TATIN SERVED
WITH MASCARPONE

MARIANNE LUMB Professionals finalist 2009

200g (7oz) ready-made PUFF PASTRY

6 sticks RHUBARB

150g (5½oz) UNSALTED BUTTER, softened

125g (4½oz) granulated SUGAR

grated zest of 1 ORANGE

2 VANILLA PODS, each split and cut into 4 pieces

200g (7oz) MASCARPONE CHEESE

PREPARATION TIME
15 minutes

COOKING TIME
30 minutes

SERVES 4

1 Preheat the oven to 190°C (375°F/Gas 5) and get out 4 heatproof blini pans. Roll the puff pastry to about 3mm (⅛in) thick and cut into 4 discs with a diameter slightly larger than the pans. Prick each disc and leave to chill in the refrigerator.

2 Choose the thicker pieces of rhubarb and cut to fit the 4 pans perfectly in 2 layers. Cover the base of each pan with the butter and then sprinkle over the sugar, orange zest, and a piece of vanilla pod, and then add the rhubarb pieces.

3 Cook the rhubarb on a very high heat on the hob for about 10 minutes to reach a good, bitter caramelization. Check by carefully lifting up the rhubarb with a palette knife, but do not be tempted to stir the rhubarb.

4 Cover each pan carefully with a disc of puff pastry, allowing the pastry to tuck just inside the pans. Place the pans on a baking sheet and cook for 20–30 minutes, or until the puff pastry is perfectly cooked and the tartes have a good caramelization. Remove from the oven and allow to rest for a few minutes.

5 Carefully invert each pan onto a plate, letting the tarte drop gently down. Serve immediately, each topped with a scoop of mascarpone cheese and a remaining piece of vanilla pod, to decorate.

PEAR AND BUTTERSCOTCH
FRANGIPANE TART

SUSIE CARTER Quarter-finalist 2006

50g (1¾oz) CASTER SUGAR

CLOTTED CREAM, to serve

FOR THE BUTTERSCOTCH SAUCE

50g (1¾oz) UNSALTED BUTTER

50g (1¾oz) LIGHT MUSCOVADO SUGAR

2 tbsp GOLDEN SYRUP

2 tbsp DOUBLE CREAM

FOR THE PASTRY

200g (7oz) PLAIN FLOUR

100g (3½oz) BUTTER

1 EGG, beaten

FOR THE TART FILLING

50g (1¾oz) GROUND ALMONDS

50g (1¾oz) CASTER SUGAR

50g (1¾oz) BUTTER

1 EGG

few drops of ALMOND EXTRACT

2 PEARS, with stalks, to serve

PREPARATION TIME
45 minutes

COOKING TIME
40 minutes

SERVES 4

1 To make the butterscotch sauce, put the butter, sugar, and golden syrup into a small saucepan and bring slowly to the boil, stirring. Reduce the heat and simmer for 3 minutes or until thick. Stir in the cream, then remove from the heat and set aside to cool.

2 Make the pastry by rubbing the butter into the flour, then adding enough cold water to bind into a pliable dough. Rest in the refrigerator for 30 minutes, then roll out on a floured surface and use to line 4 tartlet cases about 10cm (4in) in diameter. Trim the excess with scissors, allowing a little to overhang, and prick all over the base with a fork.

3 Preheat the oven to 180°C (350°F/Gas 4). Line each pastry case with baking parchment and bake blind for 10 minutes. Remove the baking parchment and beans, brush the pastry with beaten egg, and return to the oven for 5–10 minutes or until crisp.

4 Spoon 2 tbsp butterscotch sauce into each pastry case and reserve the rest to serve with the finished tarts. To make the frangipane, whisk together all the tart filling ingredients except the pears until light and spoon into the pastry cases to come halfway up the sides.

5 Peel the pears and cut in half through the stalk. Carefully remove the core, then slice along the length like a fan, without cutting all the way through at the stalk end. Use half a pear to top each tartlet, snuggling it down. Bake for 20 minutes or until the pear and frangipane are both cooked. Leave to cool a little.

6 Heat the caster sugar in a small pan, shaking occasionally until it has liquefied and turned light brown. Pour onto a non-stick baking mat in a thin layer and leave to cool for a few minutes. When set, break into shards. Serve the tartlets with a pool of butterscotch sauce, a quenelle of clotted cream, and a caramel shard.

BAKED LIME CHEESECAKE
WITH RUM CREAM

DENNICE RUSSELL Semi-finalist 2009

8 DIGESTIVE BISCUITS, crushed

50g (1¾oz) UNSALTED BUTTER, melted

300g (10oz) MASCARPONE CHEESE

100g (3½oz) RICOTTA CHEESE

1 tbsp PLAIN FLOUR

100g (3½oz) CASTER SUGAR

40g (1½oz) DESICCATED COCONUT

grated zest and juice of 3 LIMES, plus strands of lime
  zest, to decorate

2 EGGS

1 VANILLA POD, scraped

FOR THE RUM CREAM

200ml (7fl oz) DOUBLE CREAM

1 tbsp ICING SUGAR

4 tbsp DARK RUM

PREPARATION TIME
25 minutes

COOKING TIME
25 minutes

SERVES 4

1 Preheat the oven to 180°C (350°F/Gas 4). Mix the biscuits into the melted butter. Place four 10cm (4in) chef's rings on a baking sheet and press in the biscuit mix.

2 Put the cheeses, flour, sugar, coconut, lime juice and zest, eggs, and the seeds of the vanilla pod into a bowl and whisk until blended.

3 Pour onto the biscuit base and bake for 20 minutes, until golden. It should be slightly wobbly in the centre when ready. Leave to cool in the oven.

4 To make the rum cream, put the cream, icing sugar, and rum into a bowl and whisk to form soft peaks.

5 Put the cooled cheesecakes onto serving plates and top with quenelles of rum cream and strands of lime.

MASTERCHEF **FLAVOURINGS** KNOW-HOW: See **Extract Vanilla Seeds** 390

MASTERCHEF **FLAVOURINGS** KNOW-HOW: See **Make Lemon-zest Julienne** 390

MASTERCHEF
KNOW-HOW

ESSENTIAL TOOLS, SKILLS AND INGREDIENTS FOR THE HOME COOK.

KITCHEN KNIVES

QUALITY KNIVES ARE A MUST for every cook. Choose the best you can afford that feel right for you. They should be well-balanced, made of high carbon stainless steel (inferior metal will not give a true, sharp edge), with solid handles that feel comfortable in your hand. Buy from a shop where you can touch and feel them, preferably with an expert on hand to advise you. Here is a selection of the most important ones you will need. Well-chosen knives make food preparation a pleasure.

FILLETING KNIFE

USE FOR FILLETING AND BONING. A slightly flexible knife with a narrow blade for sliding under and round bones, and skin of meat, poultry, and fish.

PARING KNIFE

USE FOR PEELING AND SMALL CUTTING TASKS. It has a short blade for easy manoeuvrability, and a sharp point for removing blemishes.

CARVING KNIFE

USE FOR CARVING SLICES OF MEAT AND POULTRY. It is thinner and longer than a chef's knife for precision cutting of thin slices.

SERRATED UTILITY KNIFE

USE FOR PREPARING TENDER FRUIT AND VEGETABLES. The sharp, serrated edge cuts through soft skin and flesh without damaging it.

CHEF'S KNIFE

SMALL CHEF'S KNIFE

USE FOR CHOPPING AND SLICING. Particularly useful for preparing small amounts of meat, vegetables, or fruit.

ALL-PURPOSE KNIFE

USE FOR GENERAL LIGHT CUTTING. Also known as a utility knife. If not buying a whole range, this is a must-have, multi-purpose utensil.

BREAD KNIFE

USE FOR CUTTING BREAD AND SIMILAR FOODS. The long blade and widely serrated edge make it easy to cut thick or thin, even slices.

SANTOKU KNIFE

USE FOR PRECISION SLICING. The Asian chef's knife is cleverly constructed to slice delicate meats, fish, and vegetables very thinly.

USE FOR A WHOLE RANGE OF TASKS. The tip is for fine chopping or mincing, the middle for general knife jobs, the heel for heavy-duty work.

POTS AND PANS

ESSENTIAL KIT FOR EVERY COOK. Choose pans that are right for you and for your cooker. The look and feel of them are matters of personal preference, but each pan needs particular qualities. Here is some general advice on what to look for.

CHOOSE A SKILLET with flared, not straight, sides. The frying pan should have a handle that is comfortable to hold. It needs a thick base, for even distribution of heat, so meat and poultry brown quickly and efficiently, but not too heavy so you can shake and toss food in the pan easily. Choose one with a lid for covering food when you want to finish dishes in the oven, or stew them in their own juices on the hob.

SKILLET

YOUR STEAMER INSET should be made of stainless steel, with a wide area of tiny holes in the base to allow maximum steam to surround the food. It should be large enough to fit your biggest pan but with graduated sides so it also fits a smaller one. You can buy one as part of a pan set so the lid of the large saucepan also fits the steamer. If not, choose one with a tight-fitting lid to prevent steam escaping, and make sure it will fit snugly over your own pots.

USE YOUR SAUTÉ PAN for frying tender meat, poultry, game, fish, seafood, vegetables, or fruit quickly in just enough oil or butter (or a mixture of both) to coat the base of the pan. Choose a pan with straight sides and a solid base so it conducts and retains the heat well to maintain a high temperature. Move the food by either jerking the pan itself or turning the food with a spatula. Don't toss as often as for stir-frying, though, or the temperature will reduce too much. If you put a lid on the pan you can also use it for braising food.

A DEEP CASSEROLE is an important piece of equipment for serious cooks. Use for soups, stews, braises, and boiling joints or puddings. It should be flameproof and ovenproof so foods can be browned in it on the hob, the liquid added, brought to the boil, then the whole thing put in the oven (or finished on the hob) according to the recipe. Choose the correct sized pot for the amount of food you are cooking. It is no good putting ingredients for 1 or 2 people in a huge, family-sized one. They will dry out as there won't be sufficient liquid to cover them, and there will be much wasted heat in the empty pot.

USE YOUR BAIN MARIE FOR cooking dishes that require gradual and gentle heating not in direct contact with the heat source, such as egg-based sauces (like Hollandaise and beurre blanc), custards, chocolate, and some pâtés and terrines. You can improvise with a bowl or dish that fits snugly over a pan of gently simmering water. A roasting tin half-filled with hot water also works well in the oven.

YOUR SAUCEPANS ARE YOUR trusty friends for all-purpose cooking. You need, at least, a small, medium, and large one for general cooking. A small, non-stick one is also good for boiling milk and making sauces. Choose ones with heavy bases to conduct the heat well and with close-fitting lids. A useful tip if you are throwing out old pans is to keep the small one just for boiling eggs – the calcium deposits do spoil the appearance of the pan in time, even with regular cleaning with vinegar.

WHAT, NO WOK? You are missing out on a simple, healthy, and pleasurable way of cooking. The deep, sloping sides allow the food to be tossed quickly and easily in very little oil. It can also be used for braising, steaming, deep-frying, and tea-smoking.

ADDITIONAL EQUIPMENT

Choose best-quality equipment to hold you in good stead for years. Some items are considered essential – others useful to have if you enjoy particular types of cooking – and have lots of storage space!

THE MUST HAVES

apple corer Choose one with a sharp bottom edge to cut easily into the fruit flesh.

baking tins Buy as you need them. Shallow rectangular and deep square for different tray bakes, and a loaf tin are useful to start.

blender Your food processor or mixer may have one as an attachment, alternatively buy a hand blender.

bun tin A 12-section one is a must for individual cakes, pies, muffins, and Yorkshire puddings.

cake tins A range of sizes are useful: deep round, and/or square, with loose bottoms. You need 2 sandwich tins, too.

carving fork It should have 2 long tines to steady the meat whilst carving, and a protective guard.

grater Choose a multi-sided one with different sized grating slots, and a comfortable handle. A Parmesan grater is also worth having.

electric hand whisk For whisking cream, and egg whites, or instead of a balloon whisk when whisking egg mixtures over a bain marie.

fish slice It should be flexible enough to slide under foods without causing damage, and have a heat-proof handle.

food processor or electric mixer Useful attachments include a whisk, chopper, shredder, and blender.

griddle pan A cast iron, ridged one for char-grilling. You can buy a flat one for making scotch pancakes, griddle, and oat cakes but a heavy skillet will do instead.

mixing bowls Have several of different sizes. A copper one is best for whisking egg whites.

omelette pan Choose a heavy-based, non-stick one. A skillet can be used instead. Use for crêpes too.

pastry brush Bristle ones are traditional, silicone is more practical for all-purpose brushing.

pastry cutters Both fluted and plain ones in graduated sizes are useful.

pestle and mortar White porcelain ones are good all-rounders for looks and efficiency.

pie dish Choose a fairly deep one for top crust pies. It should have a lip all around for the pastry to adhere to.

pie plate For making double-crust pies.

piping (pastry) bag with nozzles For piping and/or filling, choux buns, meringues, and other mixtures.

potato peeler For preparing vegetables, and shaving cheese and chocolate.

pudding basins Choose varying sizes to suit your needs.

ramekins Plain white are the most practical for oven-to-table ware. Buy at least 6.

roasting tin Have at least 2, one for roasting vegetables, one for meat. They should be heavy-duty so can be heated on the hob when necessary.

slotted spoon For removing foods from oil or other liquid.

spatula Rubber or plastic for scraping out; wooden for stirring and turning food.

springform cake tin Good for more delicate cakes that need careful handling.

strainer/strainer insert Use with a stockpot or casserole for making chicken stock or cooking pasta.

Swiss roll tin Use for Swiss rolls and roulades. Also useful as a shallow baking tin.

tart/flan tin Good to have one loose-bottomed one for easy removal, and one deep ceramic one for oven-to-table.

wire rack A large rectangular one is the most practical.

THE MIGHT NEEDS

bamboo steamer Use to steam vegetables, meat, and fish.

cheesecloth (muslin) A new disposable dish cloth will work.

Kugelhopf mould Use any similar sized receptacle.

lobster cracker/small hammer Nut crackers will do.

Madeleine tin Use an ordinary bun tin.

mandolin The best way to slice vegetables thinly, but a sharp knife will do instead.

mezzaluna Really useful for chopping herbs.

oyster knife Any small, sharp-pointed knife will do.

poultry shears The best way to joint poultry or feathered game, but a sharp cook's knife will do.

seafood fork/lobster pick A small cocktail fork or fine skewer will do.

sugar thermometer The best way to test sugar stages.

tweezers Useful for pulling out bones when filleting fish, or for placing intricate garnishes or decorations in place.

ROUND WHITE SEA FISH

BUY Some species are dwindling so only buy those that are sustainably fished. Choose the freshest, best-looking specimens. Look for bright eyes and smooth, glistening skin. If fresh, fish should either have no smell at all, or should smell pleasantly of the sea, with no underlying offensive odour. **STORE** Ideally, fish should be eaten on the day it's bought, but it can be stored for up to 24 hours well-wrapped in the coldest part of the refrigerator. Freeze fish in double-layered freezer bags, with as much air extracted as possible, for up to 3 months.

▲ COLEY

EAT Cuts: Fillets. Good, cheap alternative to cod. Deep-fry, pan-fry in batter or breadcrumbs, bake, steam, poach, in fish pie, fish cakes, and soup. Also available hot smoked (undyed and dyed), dried, or salted. **FLAVOUR PAIRINGS** Butter, milk, beer batter, parsley, chives, bacon, Cheddar cheese. **IN SEASON** April–December

▲ HAKE

EAT Cuts: Fillets, steaks. Some stocks very depleted. Coley or Pollock can be used instead. Pan-fry, roast, poach, sauté, grill. Also available salted or smoked. **FLAVOUR PAIRINGS** Olive oil, smoked paprika, butter, lemon, onions, garlic, tomatoes. **IN SEASON** August–January

LING ▶

EAT Cuts: Whole, fillets, steaks. Buy line-caught from inshore. Steam, pan-fry, grill, or bake. Also available salted or dried. **FLAVOUR PAIRINGS** Onions, garlic, potatoes, leeks, bacon, coriander leaf, parsley, sage, Cheddar cheese. **IN SEASON** August–February

▲ COD

EAT Cuts: Fillets, steaks, loins, fresh and pressed roe. Some successfully farmed. Deep-fry or pan-fry in batter or breadcrumbs, bake, poach, cook in soup or chowder, grill. Also available cold smoked (undyed and dyed), salted, or dried. **FLAVOUR PAIRINGS** Dill, parsley, bay leaf, lemon, olive oil, tomatoes, olives, capers, garlic, breadcrumbs, butter, cheese sauce, cider, white wine. **IN SEASON** May–January

▲ POLLOCK

EAT Cuts: Fillets. Excellent inexpensive alternative to cod and haddock. Roast, deep-fry, bake, poach, steam. Also available salted or smoked. **FLAVOUR PAIRINGS** Tomatoes, chillies, pancetta, basil. **IN SEASON** May–December

▼ HADDOCK

EAT Cuts: Fillets, loin. Pollock or coley are good alternatives. Deep-fry or pan-fry in batter or breadcrumbs (considered sweeter than cod), grill, bake, poach, steam, use in fish pie and for soup. Also available hot smoked (Arbroath smokies), cold smoked (undyed and dyed), or as traditional Finnan haddock. **FLAVOUR PAIRINGS** Parsley, milk, bay leaf, Cheddar cheese, tomatoes, pea purée, garlic, onions. **IN SEASON** May–February

▲ WHITING

EAT Cuts: Whole, fillets (single and butterflied). Steam, pan-fry, grill, bake. Also available salted or smoked. **FLAVOUR PAIRINGS** Tomatoes, chillies, basil, mushrooms, citrus, tartare sauce. **IN SEASON** May–February

◄ SEA BREAM

EAT Cuts: Whole, fillets, thick steaks (larger species). Pan-fry, grill, bake, stuff. **FLAVOUR PAIRINGS** Fennel, Pernod, coriander leaf, lemon, saffron, parsley, garlic. **IN SEASON** June–March, available farmed all year

▲ GREY MULLET

EAT Cuts: Whole, fillets. Pan-fry, roast, bake. Also available dried or salted. The smoked roe is the classic one for taramasalata but it is also available fresh. **FLAVOUR PAIRINGS** Ginger, nutmeg, allspice, chillies, thyme, lemon, lime, anchovies, tomatoes, onions. **IN SEASON** September–May

▲ RED MULLET

EAT Cuts: Whole, fillets. Pan-fry, grill, bake en-papillote. **FLAVOUR PAIRINGS** Citrus, chervil, tarragon, parsley, carrots, celery, courgettes. **IN SEASON** August–April

▲ SEA BASS

EAT Cuts: Whole, fillets. Grill, bake (in a salt crust or en-papillote), pan-fry. **FLAVOUR PAIRINGS** Black bean sauce, soy sauce, ginger, tomatoes, garlic, olive oil, red peppers, olives, aniseed flavours like fennel, caraway, and Pernod. **IN SEASON** July–February, available farmed all year

▼ RED GURNARD

EAT Cuts: Whole, fillets. Grey gurnard also available. Roast, pan-fry, grill. Use cut in pieces in mixed-fish soups and stews. **FLAVOUR PAIRINGS** Olive oil, chorizo, pancetta, garlic, leeks, onions, white wine. **IN SEASON** October–May

▲ JOHN DORY

EAT Cuts: Whole, fillets. Pan-fry, grill, steam, bake, stew. **FLAVOUR PAIRINGS** Garlic, white wine, cream sauces, mushrooms, sage, capers, lemon, crème fraîche. **IN SEASON** September–May

◄ MONKFISH

EAT Cuts: Tail, fillets, steaks, cheeks, shoulder flaps. The liver is considered a delicacy. Pan-fry, roast, grill (fillets or kebabs), stir-fry. **FLAVOUR PAIRINGS** Chorizo, prosciutto crudo, bacon, sage, rosemary, butter, olive oil, lemon, lime, chillies, capers, mushrooms. **IN SEASON** August–January

OILY SEA FISH

BUY Choose line- or net-caught fish from sustainable sources. They should have slippery, shiny, bright-coloured skin and firm flesh. For whole fish the eyes should be bright and the gills prominent, red, and clean. They should have a mild, pleasantly fishy smell. **STORE** Best eaten fresh. Store, well-wrapped, in the coldest part of the refrigerator for up to 24 hours. If not previously frozen, they can be frozen like round white fish for up to 3 months.

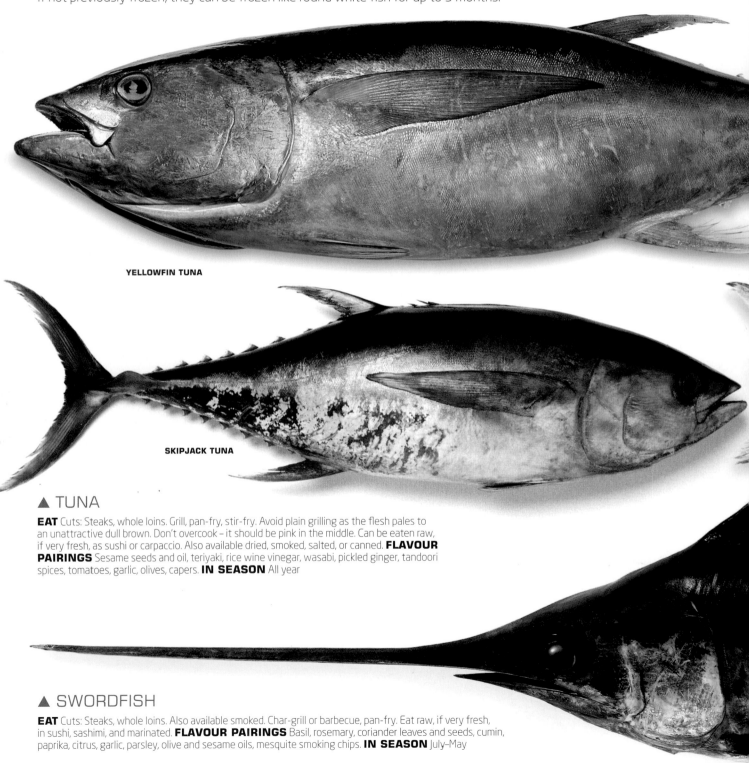

YELLOWFIN TUNA

SKIPJACK TUNA

▲ TUNA

EAT Cuts: Steaks, whole loins. Grill, pan-fry, stir-fry. Avoid plain grilling as the flesh pales to an unattractive dull brown. Don't overcook – it should be pink in the middle. Can be eaten raw, if very fresh, as sushi or carpaccio. Also available dried, smoked, salted, or canned. **FLAVOUR PAIRINGS** Sesame seeds and oil, teriyaki, rice wine vinegar, wasabi, pickled ginger, tandoori spices, tomatoes, garlic, olives, capers. **IN SEASON** All year

▲ SWORDFISH

EAT Cuts: Steaks, whole loins. Also available smoked. Char-grill or barbecue, pan-fry. Eat raw, if very fresh, in sushi, sashimi, and marinated. **FLAVOUR PAIRINGS** Basil, rosemary, coriander leaves and seeds, cumin, paprika, citrus, garlic, parsley, olive and sesame oils, mesquite smoking chips. **IN SEASON** July–May

▲ MACKEREL

EAT Cuts: Whole, fillets. Grill, barbecue, roast, pan-fry. Also available smoked, salted or canned. **FLAVOUR PAIRINGS** Basil, olive oil, garlic, onions, horseradish, mustard, dill, rhubarb, gooseberries. **IN SEASON** August–February.

▼ BONITO

EAT Cuts: Whole, fillets. Grill or barbecue, pan-fry. Dried flakes are used in Japanese soup stock. Also available canned. **FLAVOUR PAIRINGS** Sesame seeds, rice vinegar, mirin, cucumber, daikon, chillies, coriander leaves and seeds, potatoes, onions, green peppers. **IN SEASON** July–April.

◀ ANCHOVY

EAT Cuts: Whole fresh, or preserved marinated, or in salt, brine or oil, in jars or cans, also as paste or essence. Buy sustainably sourced. Pan-fry whole fresh fish. Add preserved to everything from Niçoise salad to pizzas, pasta sauces and bagna cauda dip, where they are 'melted' in olive oil with spices and butter.
FLAVOUR PAIRINGS Sherry vinegar, white wine vinegar, shallots, tomatoes, marjoram, oregano, sage, thyme, parsley, olive oil.
IN SEASON All year

▲ SCAD (HORSE MACKEREL)

EAT Cuts: Whole, fillets. Grill or barbecue, pan-fry.
FLAVOUR PAIRINGS Chilli, ginger, soy sauce, Chinese five-spice powder, coconut milk, tomatoes, peppers.
IN SEASON September–May

SALMON ▶

EAT Cuts: Whole, fillets, steaks. It is recommended not to buy wild salmon as it is becoming rare. Choose good quality farmed salmon from an MSC-rated source instead. Pan-fry, poach, grill, bake. Also available smoked, and the salted roe as red Keta, a caviar substitute.
FLAVOUR PAIRINGS Lemon, butter, Hollandaise sauce, dill, samphire, tarragon, ginger, harissa paste, soy, sesame, chillies, coriander leaves. **IN SEASON** Farmed all year

▲ SPRAT

EAT Cuts: Whole. Either gut it yourself or cook ungutted and hold in your fingers to eat off the bone. Pan-fry, grill, or barbecue. Also available smoked, canned, or salted. **FLAVOUR PAIRINGS** Beetroot, red and white wine vinegar, flat-leaf parsley, coriander leaf and seeds, lemon. **IN SEASON** September–February

◀ SARDINE OR PILCHARD

EAT Cuts: Whole. Pilchards (Cornish sardines) are just large sardines. Pan-fry, grill, barbecue, or bake. Also available smoked, marinated, cured, or canned in olive oil or tomato-based sauce.
FLAVOUR PAIRINGS Olive oil, garlic, lemon, sultanas, pine nuts, parsley, organo, thyme, tomatoes, peppers, chilli, lime, lemon. **IN SEASON** September–February

▲ HERRING

EAT Cuts: Whole, fillets, soft and hard roes. Pan-fry, grill or barbecue, bake, souse or pickle. Tiny immature herrings (and often other fish) are sold as whitebait but are overexploited so best avoided. Also available smoked (kippers, bloaters, buckling), marinated, or canned. **FLAVOUR PAIRINGS** Soured cream, dill, onions, oatmeal, bacon, horseradish, mustard, lemon, capers, parsley. **IN SEASON** All year

▼ SEA TROUT

EAT Cuts: Whole, fillets, steaks. Also known as salmon trout. It is the migratory form of the brown river trout. Poach, steam, grill, pan-fry, bake.
FLAVOUR PAIRINGS Mayonnaise, watercress, Hollandaise sauce, lemon, dill, parsley. **IN SEASON** Wild April–October, available farmed all year

FLAT FISH

BUY Like other fish, they are not all sustainable. Real skate, sadly, is very rare, and wild Atlantic halibut is endangered, so it is now farmed. Many flat fish, however, are thriving but may have minimum size fishing requirements so avoid if small. Choose fish with firm flesh, moist, not slimy skin, and a fresh smell. **STORE** Eat fresh or store, well-wrapped, for up to 24 hours in the coldest part of the refrigerator. Freeze whole or fillets (unless previously frozen) for up to 3 months.

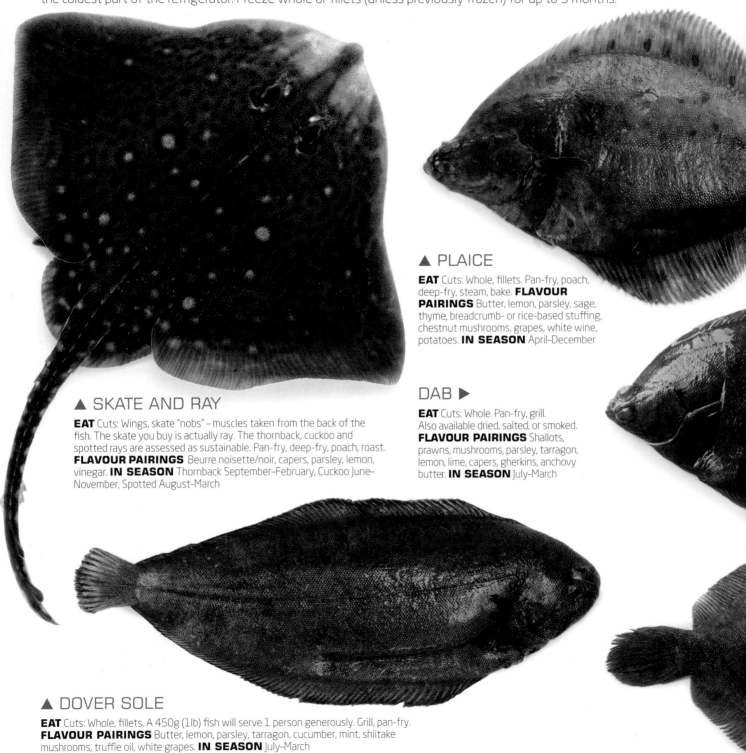

▲ PLAICE

EAT Cuts: Whole, fillets. Pan-fry, poach, deep-fry, steam, bake. **FLAVOUR PAIRINGS** Butter, lemon, parsley, sage, thyme, breadcrumb- or rice-based stuffing, chestnut mushrooms, grapes, white wine, potatoes. **IN SEASON** April–December

▲ SKATE AND RAY

EAT Cuts: Wings, skate "nobs" – muscles taken from the back of the fish. The skate you buy is actually ray. The thornback, cuckoo and spotted rays are assessed as sustainable. Pan-fry, deep-fry, poach, roast. **FLAVOUR PAIRINGS** Beurre noisette/noir, capers, parsley, lemon, vinegar. **IN SEASON** Thornback September–February, Cuckoo June–November, Spotted August–March

DAB ▶

EAT Cuts: Whole. Pan-fry, grill. Also available dried, salted, or smoked. **FLAVOUR PAIRINGS** Shallots, prawns, mushrooms, parsley, tarragon, lemon, lime, capers, gherkins, anchovy butter. **IN SEASON** July–March

▲ DOVER SOLE

EAT Cuts: Whole, fillets. A 450g (1lb) fish will serve 1 person generously. Grill, pan-fry. **FLAVOUR PAIRINGS** Butter, lemon, parsley, tarragon, cucumber, mint, shiitake mushrooms, truffle oil, white grapes. **IN SEASON** July–March

◀ HALIBUT

EAT Cuts: Fillets, steaks. Steam, pan-fry, grill, poach, bake. Also available dried, salted, or cold-smoked. **FLAVOUR PAIRINGS** Butter, beurre blanc, nutmeg, gherkins, capers, lemon, bacon, spicy sausages, charcuterie. **IN SEASON** Farmed all year

TURBOT ▶

EAT Cuts: Fillets, steaks. Steam, pan-fry, bake with a crust, roast, grill. **FLAVOUR PAIRINGS** Wild mushrooms, Champagne, cream, butter, shellfish stock, lemon, prawns, Gruyère cheese, Parmesan. **IN SEASON** Wild September–March, available farmed all year

▲ BRILL

EAT Cuts: Fillets, steaks. Excellent and underrated. Pan-fry, poach, steam, bake with a crust, roast, grill. **FLAVOUR PAIRINGS** Bacon, shallots, wild mushrooms, white wine, garlic, tomatoes, lemon, crab or prawn sauce. **IN SEASON** October–February

◀ LEMON SOLE

EAT Cuts: Whole, fillets. Pan-fry, grill, poach. **FLAVOUR PAIRINGS** Béchamel sauce, parsley, chives, lemon, butter, cider. **IN SEASON** September–March

FRESHWATER FISH

BUY One tends to think of fish being from the sea but, of course, there are many delicious species that grace British and foreign rivers and lakes. Several are now farmed, increasing their sustainability. The skin should be shiny and slippery or even slimy, the flesh firm and moist, not wet. On whole fish, the eyes should be prominent and bright. **STORE** Unless frozen, eat on day or purchase, or store well-wrapped in the bottom of the refrigerator for up to 24 hours. Fresh caught fish can be frozen, gutted, whole or in fillets, for up to 2 months.

◀ TILAPIA

EAT Cuts: Whole, fillets. Also available salted or dried. Pan-fry, deep-fry, steam, bake, barbecue, or grill.
FLAVOUR PAIRINGS Chilli, palm sugar, nam pla (Thai fish sauce), shrimp paste, coriander leaves, coconut, galangal.
IN SEASON Farmed all year

BARRAMUNDI ▶

EAT Cuts: Whole, fillets, steaks, the pearl (cheek) is a speciality. Pan-fry, grill, barbecue, poach, steam. **FLAVOUR PAIRINGS** Pak choi, lime, chilli, fresh herbs, white wine. **IN SEASON** Wild April–August, available farmed all year

▲ CATFISH

EAT Cuts: Whole, fillets. Also available smoked, dried, or salted. Pan-fry, deep-fry, grill, bake, poach. **FLAVOUR PAIRINGS** Cornmeal, sesame seeds, soured cream, mushrooms, spring onions, parsley, bay leaf, thyme. **IN SEASON** Farmed all year

▲ PIKE

EAT Cuts: Whole, fillets. Also available smoked, salted, dried, and the cured roe. Pan-fry, grill, steam, poach, roast. **FLAVOUR PAIRINGS** Unsalted butter, sage, lemon, cream, bay leaf, white wine. **IN SEASON** Closed 15th March–15th June

◄ FRESHWATER BREAM

EAT Cuts: Whole, fillets. Grill, bake. **FLAVOUR PAIRINGS** Thyme, rosemary, fennel, celery, nut oils. **IN SEASON** Wild July–March, available farmed all year

CARP ▶

EAT Cuts: Whole. Smoked, salted and cured roe are also available. Soak in acidulated water to remove slime. Steam, roast, pan-fry, pane (cook in breadcrumbs), bake. **FLAVOUR PAIRINGS** Paprika, butter, capers, dill, garlic, parsley, cornmeal, ginger, rice wine, sesame oil and seeds, fennel. **IN SEASON** Closed 15th March–15th June

◄ RAINBOW TROUT

EAT Cuts: Whole, fillets. Also available hot or cold smoked. Pan-fry, bake, grill, roast. **FLAVOUR PAIRINGS** White wine vinegar, butter, lemon chives, almonds, hazelnuts; Serrano ham, breadcrumbs. **IN SEASON** Wild January–September, available farmed all year

BROWN TROUT ▶

EAT Cuts: Whole, fillets. Pan-fry, bake, grill, roast, barbecue, blue poach in acidulated water (if just caught). **FLAVOUR PAIRINGS** Bouquet garni (parsley, thyme, and bay leaf tied together), watercress-flavoured hollandaise sauce, prawns. **IN SEASON** Wild April–September, available farmed all year

◄ STURGEON

EAT Cuts: Whole, steaks, fillets, female roe highly prized, salted as beluga, osetra, and sevruga caviar. Also available smoked. Some species endangered. Pan-fry, bake, steam and eat raw. **FLAVOUR PAIRINGS** Horseradish, soured cream, beetroot, vinegar, butter, citrus. **IN SEASON** Siberian sturgeon farmed all year

SMOKED, SALTED, AND DRIED FISH

BUY Choose hot-smoked fish that is moist but not slimy and has a strong, pleasant aroma. Pick cold-smoked fish that is dry, glossy, and smells smoked but not too strong. Some salted and dried fish has a pungent smell that is not an indication of poor quality. **STORE** Keep smoked fish well-wrapped in the fridge. Best eaten within 24 hours; vacuum-packed hot-smoked will keep longer. Freeze for up to 2 months. Salted and dried fish can be kept for many months, well wrapped, in a cool, dark place. **IN SEASON** Available all year.

HOT-SMOKED the fish is cooked during smoking in a kiln, after brining or salting

MACKEREL
FILLETS

▲ KILN-SMOKED SALMON

EAT Cuts: Sides, fillets, ready-flaked. Serve cold or add to quiches, pasta, or with scrambled eggs. Make sure it is piping hot before serving, but do not overheat or it will toughen and change in texture. **FLAVOUR PAIRINGS** Eggs, rocket, beetroot, soured cream, horseradish, cream, olive oil, lemon, dill.

▲ MACKEREL

EAT Cuts: Whole, fillets (plain or encrusted with pepper and other toppings). Serve cold or as pâté. Can be flaked and added to other dishes (see kiln-smoked salmon). **FLAVOUR PAIRINGS** Horseradish, mustard, cream and crème fraîche, cream cheese, honey, sesame oil, dill, coriander leaves, beetroot, celeriac, waxy potatoes.

WHOLE
MACKEREL

TROUT
FILLET

WHOLE
TROUT

▲ TROUT

EAT Cuts: Whole, fillets. Best eaten cold or as pâté, but can be flaked and used like kiln-smoked salmon. **FLAVOUR PAIRINGS** Lemon, horseradish, waxy potatoes, rocket, watercress, dill, chives, cream cheese, crème fraîche.

<u>COLD-SMOKED</u> the fish remains raw after being heavily brined and slow-smoked at a low temperature

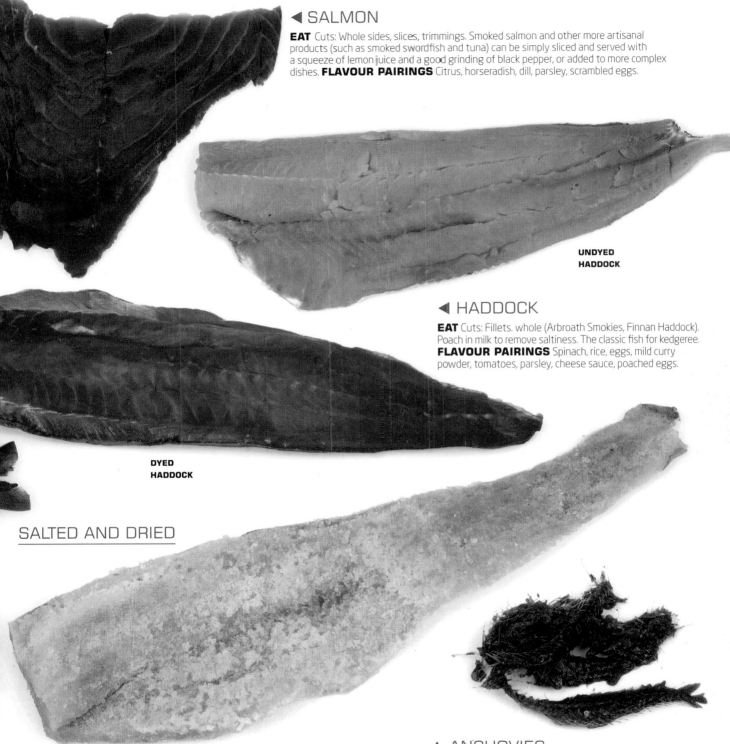

◀ SALMON

EAT Cuts: Whole sides, slices, trimmings. Smoked salmon and other more artisanal products (such as smoked swordfish and tuna) can be simply sliced and served with a squeeze of lemon juice and a good grinding of black pepper, or added to more complex dishes. **FLAVOUR PAIRINGS** Citrus, horseradish, dill, parsley, scrambled eggs.

UNDYED HADDOCK

◀ HADDOCK

EAT Cuts: Fillets. whole (Arbroath Smokies, Finnan Haddock). Poach in milk to remove saltiness. The classic fish for kedgeree. **FLAVOUR PAIRINGS** Spinach, rice, eggs, mild curry powder, tomatoes, parsley, cheese sauce, poached eggs.

DYED HADDOCK

<u>SALTED AND DRIED</u>

▲ ANCHOVIES

EAT Cuts: Fillets. Soak in milk briefly to remove some of the saltiness, soften, and round the flavour. Use on pizzas or to garnish Mediterranean dishes like Salad Niçoise or Pissaladière. **FLAVOUR PAIRINGS** Garlic, onions, tomatoes, chillies, olives, cheese, spinach, pine nuts, butter, olive oil.

▲ SALT COD

EAT Cuts: Fillets, steaks. Soak 36–48 hours in several changes of cold water before use. Poach, bake, casserole, stew. **FLAVOUR PAIRINGS** Olive oil, garlic, parsley, basil, olives, tomatoes, potatoes, citrus, capers, red peppers, chorizo.

GUT A FISH THROUGH THE STOMACH

1 Place the fish on its side. Holding it firmly, make a shallow incision in the underside from just before the fin to the head.

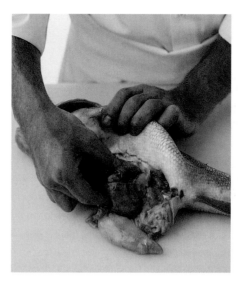

2 Remove the guts using your hands, and cut off the gills, taking care not to cut yourself on them, as they can be very sharp.

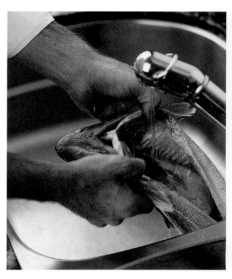

3 Rinse the cavity with cold running water to remove any remaining blood or guts. Pat dry with kitchen paper. The fish can now be scaled.

GUT A FISH THROUGH THE GILLS

1 Hook a finger under the gills to lift them from the base of the head. Using sharp kitchen scissors or a knife, cut off the gills and discard.

2 Hold the fish steady with one hand while you put your fingers through the hole formed by the removed gills and pull out the guts.

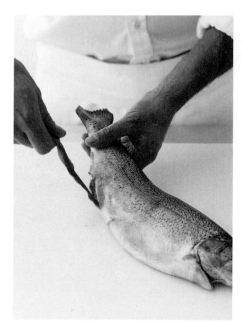

3 Make a small slit in the stomach at the ventral (anal) opening and use your fingers to pull out any remaining guts. Rinse under cold water.

SCALE AND TRIM FISH

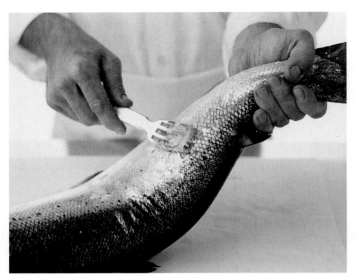

1 Lay the fish on paper on a work surface. Holding the fish by the tail, use a fish scaler or the blunt side of a chef's knife to scrape the scales off, using strokes towards the head. Turn the fish over and repeat.

2 Using a pair of kitchen scissors, and taking care with any sharp spines, remove the dorsal (back) fin. Then cut off the belly fins, and the two on either side of the head.

SKIN A DOVER SOLE

1 Lay the fish dark-side up on a board. Hold the end of the tail, and with a sharp knife, make a small incision through the dark skin at the tail end, cutting at an angle but not all the way through.

2 Using a clean tea towel to give you some grip on the slimy skin, take hold of the flap of skin where you made your incision, and slowly pull the skin away, while holding the tail down with the other hand.

BONE A FLAT FISH

 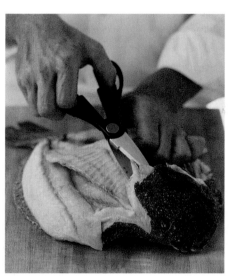 

1 With the fish dark-side up, cut to (not through) the backbone from head to tail. Cut away the flesh one half at a time, to expose the backbone.

2 Slide the knife under the backbone to cut away the flesh. Use scissors to snip each end of the backbone, then cut it through the middle.

3 Lift the backbone pieces from the flesh and discard. Before stuffing, be sure to check for, and remove, any remaining bones.

BONE A ROUND FISH THROUGH THE STOMACH

1 Open the fish by making an incision from the tail to the head. Using the blade of your knife, loosen the backbone (transverse bones) on the top side, then turn the fish over to loosen the other side.

2 Using kitchen scissors, snip the backbone from the head and tail ends. Starting at the tail, peel the bones away from the flesh and discard. Check for, and remove, any remaining bones left in the flesh.

BONE A ROUND FISH FROM THE BACK

1 Cut down the back of the fish, cutting along one side of the backbone from head to tail. Continue cutting into the fish, keeping the knife close on top of the bones. When you reach the belly, don't cut through the skin.

2 Turn the fish over and cut down the back from tail to head, along the other side of the backbone. Continue cutting as before, to cut away the flesh from that side of the backbone too.

3 Using kitchen scissors, snip the backbone at the head and tail ends, then remove it. Pull out the guts (known as the viscera) and discard. Rinse the cavity under cold running water and pat dry.

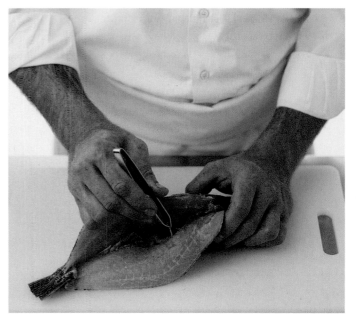

4 Gently open out the stomach cavity and remove any pin bones (the line of tiny bones down each side of the fish) using large tweezers or small needle-nose pliers.

FILLET A FLAT FISH

"Always keep your trim and bones from the flat fish – they make the best fish stock."

JAMES NATHAN

1 Start with a whole fish, skinned, trimmed, and gutted; a Dover sole is shown here. Slice all the way across the base of the head, down to the backbone, to separate the fillet from the head.

2 Starting at the head end, cut along one side of the fish, a short distance from the edge, slicing just above the bone and keeping the knife almost flat. Make the same cut along the outer edge of the other side.

3 Returning to the first side, insert the knife and cut all the way across the fish, with a long stroking action. Release the fillet at the backbone and continue cutting to the other side, until the whole fillet is released.

4 Lift off the fillet in a single piece and then turn the fish over to repeat the process. Smaller types of flat fish, such as Dover sole, are commonly cut into whole fillets and a single fish will be enough for two people.

FILLET A SMALL ROUND FISH

"The most important thing for filleting is a good, sharp, flexible knife."
JAMES NATHAN

1 If you are leaving the skin on the fillets, first scale the fish. Then, with a long, sharp filleting knife, cut into the fish at the head end, behind the gills, cutting at an angle until the blade reaches the backbone.

2 Beginning just behind the head, and near the gills, insert the knife, and keeping it flat, cut the fish along the length of the back, cutting along the top side of the backbone.

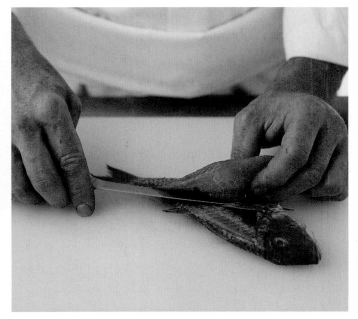

3 Then starting again just behind the head, continue cutting over the bone, keeping the blade as flat as possible, and folding the fillet back as you go. Once you have reached the tail end, remove the fillet.

4 Set the first fillet aside and turn the fish over. Repeat the process to remove the second fillet, but this time make an incision just before the tail and cut towards the head.

PREPARE FLAT FISH

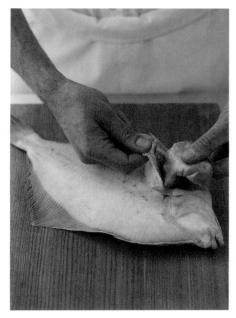

1 Place the fish on a board, dark-side down. Cut along the stomach with a sharp knife and pull out the guts and any roe.

2 Cut off the fins on both sides of the fish with sharp kitchen scissors, taking care not to cut into the body.

3 Put some greaseproof paper underneath the fish and scrape off the scales with a fish scaler or the back of a chef's knife.

4 Use your finger to hook the gills away from the body, and then cut them off with scissors. Rinse the fish under cold running water.

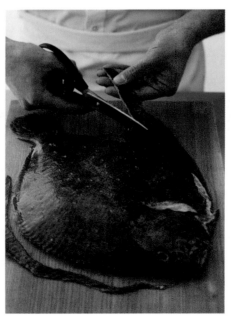

5 To skin the flat fish, place it dark-side up on a board, then using scissors, cut off the fins about 5mm (¼ in) from the body.

6 Turn the fish over and slide a sharp knife just under the skin at the tail end, while you pull the dark skin away with your other hand.

CUT FISH STEAKS

1 Gut the fish through the stomach, then scale it and trim off the fins. Rinse the fish inside and out under cold running water and pat dry with kitchen paper. Cut off the head at a point just behind the gills.

2 Holding the cleaned, dried fish firmly on its side with one hand, use a sharp chef's knife to cut across the body to slice away steaks of the required thickness.

SKIN A FILLET

1 Place the fillet skin-side down. Using a long, sharp knife, make an incision near the tail end, tilting the blade at a slight angle. Carefully cut through the flesh just to, but not through, the skin.

2 Angle the blade of the knife until it is almost flat, and with your other hand, firmly grasp the end of the skin. Keep the knife as close to the skin as possible as you cut, and slowly pull the skin away from the fillet.

SERVE WHOLE COOKED FISH

1 Carefully cut along the top of the fish from head to tail, then starting from the top, gently pull away the skin, working towards the stomach. Remove any dark flesh and scrape away the tiny bones along the back.

2 Using the edge of a spoon, cut down the centre of the fish and carefully lift away the top 2 fillets, one at a time. Break the backbone at the head and tail ends and remove. Replace the top fillets on the fish.

SERVE WHOLE FLAT FISH

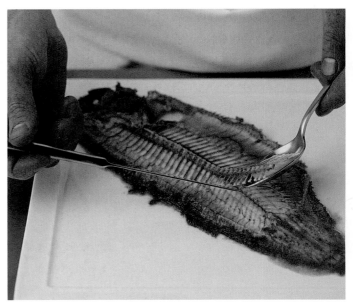

1 Place the fish on a warmed plate. Using a knife and spoon, push away the tiny fin bones from both sides of the fish. Cut along both sides of the backbone with the spoon, just through the flesh as far as the bone.

2 Lift off the top 2 fillets, one at a time and set aside. Lift out the backbone and discard. Check for any stray bones and remove them, then replace the top fillets on the fish.

BAKE FISH IN FOIL

1 Use this technique for baking a whole fish. If your chosen recipe includes a stuffing, spoon it into the cavity, then secure in place with 1 or 2 wooden cocktail sticks.

2 Wrap the fish in lightly oiled or buttered foil to make a well-sealed parcel. Bake in a preheated oven at 180°C (350°F/Gas 4) for 25 minutes for small fish, or 35–40 mins for large fish, or until the flesh along the back is opaque.

STEAM FISH

1 To use a bamboo steamer, pour water into a wok to just below where the steamer fits (make sure it doesn't touch the water). Add any flavourings, then bring the water to a simmer. Put the basket in the wok.

2 Put the fish in the steamer and sprinkle over any extra flavourings. Cover tightly, and steam fillets for approximately 3–4 minutes, whole fish up to 350g (12oz) for 6–8 mins, and up to 900g (2lb) for 12–15 mins.

GRILL FISH

1 Brush a grill rack with oil. Add the fish, brush the surface with oil, and season to taste with salt and pepper. Position the grill rack 10cm (4in) from the heat and grill for half the time specified in the recipe.

2 Using a pair of tongs, carefully lift the fish from the rack and turn over. Continue grilling for the remaining time specified, or until the flesh flakes easily when tested with a fork.

PAN-FRY FISH

1 Heat equal amounts of oil and butter in a heavy frying pan over a medium-high heat until foaming. Season the fish, then add it to the pan, skin-side down, and fry for half the time specified in the recipe.

2 Use a spatula or fish slice to turn the pieces over, then continue frying the fish for the remaining cooking time, or until it is light golden brown and the flesh flakes easily when tested with a fork.

BATTER AND FRY FISH

"The batter should have the consistency of very thick double cream. If it's too runny it won't hold to the fish, and if it's too thick you'll get big lumps." **DHRUV BAKER**

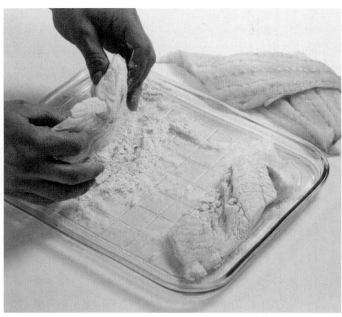

1 Mix the batter by combining 150g (5½oz) plain flour, 2 tsp dried yeast, 1 tbsp sunflower oil, and 180ml (6fl oz) beer, and leave to stand for 30 minutes. Put 2 tbsp seasoned flour in a dish and coat the pieces of fish.

2 Beat the egg white in a medium metal bowl until stiff peaks form when the whisk is lifted. Gently fold the whisked egg white into the batter, using a wooden spoon, until combined.

3 Using a 2-pronged fork, dip a piece of fish in the batter, turning to coat thoroughly. Lift out the fish and hold it over the bowl for 5 seconds so excess batter can drip off.

4 Heat enough groundnut or other oil for deep frying to 190°C (375°F). Carefully lower the fish, 1 or pieces at a time into the oil and deep-fry, turning once, for 6–8 minutes, or until golden brown and crisp.

SHELLFISH, OTHER SEAFOOD, AND SPECIALITIES

BUY Shellfish, seafood, and other creatures should look fresh, shells should be unbroken, and bivalves shut (or will close when tapped sharply). There should be signs of life in all live creatures. Crabs and lobsters should feel heavy for their size. All seafood should smell pleasantly of the sea. **STORE** Unless frozen, eat on day of purchase. Live crustaceans and molluscs can be stored briefly below 3°C in a lightly covered bowl towards the bottom of the refrigerator. Cover live lobsters or crabs with a damp tea towel or seaweed to prevent dehydration.

▼ LOBSTER

EAT Available live whole, or cooked, whole and tail meat, fresh or frozen. For live, freeze for 2 hours to stun, then boil 10 minutes per 450g (1lb), split and grill, bake or eat cold. **FLAVOUR PAIRINGS** Mayonnaise, brandy, white wine, sherry, citrus, Parmesan, cream, chilli, tarragon, parsley, chives, salad leaves, shallots. **IN SEASON** October–June

▲ BROWN CRAB

EAT Available occasionally live, mostly cooked whole and claws, ready dressed in shell, white crabmeat, frozen and canned. Toss into salads, réchauffé in pasta and rice dishes, sauté, in soups and sandwiches. **FLAVOUR PAIRINGS** Mayonnaise, chilli, lemon, parsley, dill, potatoes, butter, Worcestershire sauce, anchovies. **IN SEASON** July–March

▲ FRESH WATER CRAYFISH

EAT Available whole, live or cooked, or frozen cooked, and tails. Native white ones (pictured) are endangered. Buy farmed signal crayfish. For live, freeze for 45 minutes to stun, then boil for 5 minutes, or sauté. **FLAVOUR PAIRINGS** Melted butter, salad leaves, mayonnaise, citrus. **IN SEASON** Farmed all year

▲ LANGOUSTINE (DUBLIN BAY PRAWN)

EAT Available whole, live, or cooked, shelled tails, breaded scampi, fresh or frozen. Boil, pan-fry, poach, deep-fry (breaded scampi). **FLAVOUR PAIRINGS** Mayonnaise, citrus, tomatoes, garlic, butter, tarragon, lovage, parsley, chives, tartare sauce. **IN SEASON** December–August

▲ BROWN SHRIMP

EAT Available whole, raw, or cooked. Plunge raw in boiling, salted water briefly until they turn brown. Fiddly to peel but delicious. Traditionally potted.
FLAVOUR PAIRINGS Butter, lemon, nutmeg, mace, cayenne, Tabasco. **IN SEASON** All year

▲ NORTH ATLANTIC PRAWN

EAT Usually available cooked, whole or shelled, fresh, frozen, or canned. Eat cold in salads or sandwiches, or sauté very briefly. **FLAVOUR PAIRINGS** Mayonnaise, Marie Rose sauce, garlic, butter, citrus, chilli, avocado, melon, cucumber. **IN SEASON** November–May

▲ TIGER PRAWN

EAT Available raw and cooked, peeled and unpeeled, fresh or frozen. Sauté, steam, grill or barbecue, bake, stir-fry, deep-fry battered as tempura. **FLAVOUR PAIRINGS** Mayonnaise, garlic, chilli, curry spices, capers, paprika, citrus, butter, tamari, soy sauce, coconut, sesame seeds.
IN SEASON Farmed all year

◄ OCTOPUS

EAT Available fresh or frozen, whole, or prepared (may be tumbled – ready tenderised – if not, beat with a meat mallet before cooking). Also available canned, marinated, smoked or dried. Braise or stew. Blanch baby octopus briefly, then marinate to serve. **FLAVOUR PAIRINGS** Red wine, onions, balsamic vinegar, parsley, sage, rosemary, paprika, chilli, olive oil, soy sauce, sesame oil, rice vinegar.
IN SEASON August–November

▲ SQUID

EAT Available baby or large, fresh whole, frozen tubes and rings, battered or crumbed rings. Also smoked or canned. Pan-fry, stir-fry, deep-fry, griddle, barbecue, braise, casserole, stew, stuff, also raw in sushi. **FLAVOUR PAIRINGS** Garlic, turmeric, black pepper, spring onions, chillies, other seafood, olive oil, citrus, tomatoes, mayonnaise.
IN SEASON June–November

▲ PERIWINKLE

EAT Available live or cooked in the shell, shucked fresh, and pickled in vinegar. Rinse live ones in salt water before boiling for 3–5 minutes. Pick off the sucker, then extract the meat with a winkle picker or pin. **FLAVOUR PAIRINGS** Chilli vinegar, malt vinegar, lemon juice, garlic butter, watercress. **IN SEASON** July–January

▲ WHELK

EAT Available live and cooked in the shell. Rinse live ones in salted water before boiling for 10–12 minutes. Pick off sucker and extract the meat with a pin or small fork. Eat, or crumb-coat and fry first. **FLAVOUR PAIRINGS** Malt vinegar, garlic butter, parsley, tarragon, chives. **IN SEASON** January–September

▲ COCKLE

EAT Available live in the shell, or cooked and shucked, frozen, in jars in brine or vinegar. **FLAVOUR PAIRINGS** Malt vinegar, parsley, capers, gherkins, cucumber. **IN SEASON** September–February

▲ RAZOR CLAM

EAT Available live in the shell. Best lightly steamed or grilled (the flesh toughens if overcooked). Good served in their shells with flavoured butter or a sauce. **FLAVOUR PAIRINGS** Garlic, butter, parsley, coriander leaves, white wine, shallots, cream, chilli. **IN SEASON** October–April

▲ CLAM

EAT Available live in the shell, or shucked frozen, canned, or as clam juice. There are several species (surf clams pictured). Chop large clams or mince in chowder, shuck smaller specimens and enjoy them raw, or steam open to add to soups, pasta, or rice. **FLAVOUR PAIRINGS** Cream, onions, garlic, white wine, chives, parsley, oregano, thyme, bay leaf, tomatoes. **IN SEASON** October–April

COMMON MUSSELS

GREEN-LIPPED MUSSELS

◄ MUSSELS

EAT Available live in the shell, cooked fresh, frozen, canned, in vinegar, or smoked. Green-lipped usually sold cooked on half shell, or frozen. Steam, bake, grill, stuff. Remove the shell if adding to soups or stews. **FLAVOUR PAIRINGS** White wine, cider, Pernod, butter, garlic, cream, shallots, chillies, fennel, ginger, lemon grass, parsley, coriander leaves, dill, rosemary. **IN SEASON** Wild October–March, available farmed all year

KING SCALLOP

QUEEN SCALLOP

▲ SEA URCHIN

EAT Available whole, live. Also fermented to make sea urchin paste. Eat raw, bake with eggs, or add to creamy fish sauces. **FLAVOUR PAIRINGS** Lemon, black pepper, eggs, cream. **IN SEASON** Available all year (best September–April)

◀ SCALLOPS

EAT Available in the shell, prepared on half shell, prepared and trimmed (processed). Also frozen (with or without coral), canned, smoked, or dried. Pan-fry (fresh and smoked), steam, poach, grill, or barbecue. **FLAVOUR PAIRINGS** Bacon, chorizo, black pudding, red peppers, red onion, olive oil, sesame oil, black beans, spring onions, chillies, ginger, cream, bay leaf, parsley. **IN SEASON** King October–March; Queen June–September

PACIFIC OYSTERS

◀ OYSTERS

EAT Available live in the shell, smoked, and canned. Shuck and serve raw with their juice in the half shell, deep-fry, pan-fry, poach, grill, bake. **FLAVOUR PAIRINGS** (Raw) red wine vinegar, shallots, Tabasco, lemon juice; (cooked) anchovy essence, butter, spinach, cream, Parmesan cheese. **IN SEASON** Native September–April, Pacific farmed all year

NATIVE OYSTERS

SNAILS ▲

EAT Available live in the shell but often bought ready-cooked vacuum-packed with their shells, or canned with shells separately. If live, they need purging for several days before boiling. Once cooked, bake in garlic butter, or add shucked ones to tarts or terrines. **FLAVOUR PAIRINGS** Garlic butter with lemon or rosemary, olive oil with red wine vinegar and black pepper. **IN SEASON** Available farmed all year

▲ ABALONE

EAT Available fresh in the shell, frozen meat/steaks ready tenderized, canned, dried, salted. Tenderize fresh by pounding before cooking. Sauté or pan-fry briefly. Add dried to soup and simmer a long time to add flavour. **FLAVOUR PAIRINGS** Shiitake mushrooms, sesame, soy sauce, ginger, garlic, butter, parsley, oyster sauce. **IN SEASON** Restricted wild harvest, available farmed all year

▲ FROGS' LEGS

EAT Available fresh or frozen. Avoid wild, buy farmed. Pan-fry, add to soup. **FLAVOUR PAIRINGS** Butter, lemon, garlic, black pepper, Calvados, cream, apple, mixed herbs. **IN SEASON** Available farmed all year (best April–October)

CLEAN A LIVE LOBSTER

1 Keep the the claws closed with rubber bands. Hold the lobster firmly on a board. Push the tip of a heavy chef's knife into the head and quickly bring the blade down towards the board, splitting the lobster in two.

2 Hold the lobster's body with one hand, while you remove the claws with the other. Do this either by twisting the claws off, or if that is not possible, by cutting them off with the chef's knife.

3 Now separate the main sections of the lobster by firmly holding the body with one hand, and the head the other. Then twist them in opposite directions and pull apart.

4 Using a spoon, remove the tomalley (the green coloured liver) and any coral (the black roe) from the head and tail sections, and set aside to use in a sauce or stuffing. You can now cook the tail section and claws.

CLEAN A LIVE BLUE CRAB

  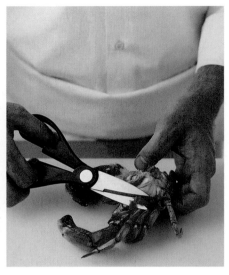

1 Hold the crab on its back, insert the tip of a chef's knife directly behind the eyes, and quickly bring the blade down. Pull and twist off the tail.

2 Holding down the central part of the body and the leg section with one hand, pull off the top shell with the other.

3 Using kitchen scissors, cut off the gills and remove the spongy bag behind the eyes. Cut the crab in half, or into quarters.

CLEAN A LIVE SOFT-SHELL CRAB

 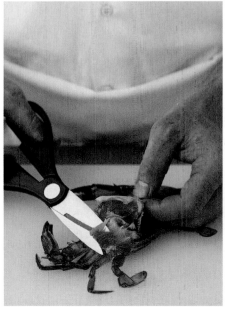 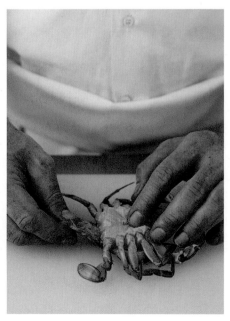

1 Hold the crab firmly, then using sharp kitchen scissors, make a cut across the front of the crab to remove the eyes and mouth.

2 Now pull the top shell away slightly, so that you can cut away and discard the gills from both sides of the body.

3 Turn the crab onto its back. Unfold the tail flap (the apron) and pull it off. This procedure also removes the guts (viscera).

EXTRACT THE MEAT FROM A COOKED LOBSTER

1 Rinse the lobster under cold running water and pat dry with kitchen paper, then place on a cutting board. Take hold of the tail and twist it sharply away from the body to detach it.

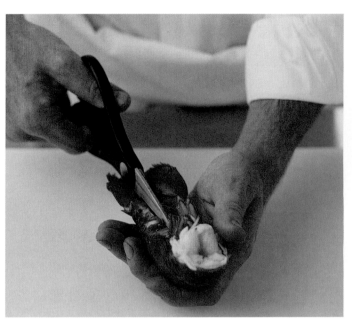

2 Set the lobster's body aside and turn the tail over with the shell-side down. Using a pair of sharp kitchen scissors, and beginning at the far end of the tail, cut down the centre towards the thickest part.

3 Using your thumbs, pull the shell apart along the line where you cut it with scissors, and fold the shell back. You should now be able to extract the meat in one piece.

4 To remove the meat from the claws, crack them open with a lobster cracker or a small hammer. Once the shell has been opened, extract the meat inside carefully, and discard any attached membrane.

DRESS A COOKED CRAB

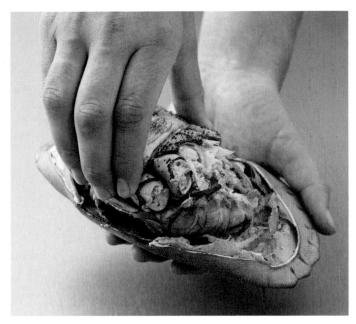

1 Pull away the claws and legs and set aside, then twist off the tail flap and discard. To separate the body from the carapace, crack it under the tail, then prise the two sections apart, pulling the body from the tail end.

2 Remove the gills (dead man's fingers) attached to the main body, and check for stray gills left in the carapace. Remove the stomach sac as well, which will either be attached to the body or in the carapace.

3 Cut the body of the crab into quarters and pick out the white meat, using a seafood fork or lobster pick. Remove any pieces of shell or membrane. Scoop out the brown meat from the carapace with a spoon.

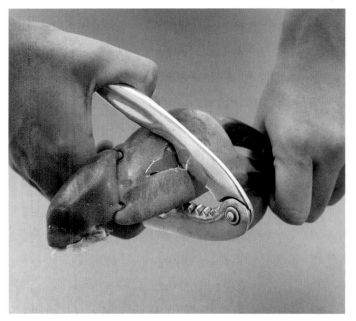

4 Break the shell of the claws with a lobster, or nut cracker. Extract the meat, and remove the cartilage, then check for any shell or membrane. Crack the legs across their narrowest part, then pick the meat with a fork.

CLEAN MUSSELS

"Always check each one before cooking. If you give them a little squeeze, you should see them closing up – if they haven't done that in about 30 seconds, you know to discard them." **JAMES NATHAN**

1 As mussels are cooked, and often served in their shells, they must be thoroughly cleaned. Scrub the mussels under cold running water to brush away any grit, and scrape off barnacles with a small knife.

2 Live mussels usually have a fibrous attachment called a "beard" which needs to be removed. Pinch the stringy thread between your finger and thumb and firmly jerk it away from the mussel shell.

PREPARE PRAWNS

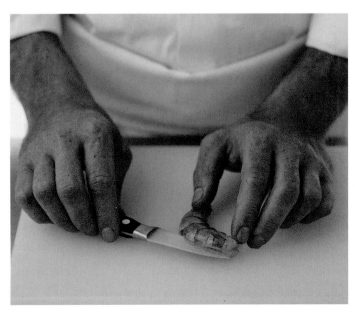

1 To remove the intestinal vein, cut lightly along the back of the prawn with a paring knife. Remove the vein with your fingers or the knife tip, and rinse the prawn under cold running water.

2 To butterfly a prawn, cut along the deveined back and splay it open, but take care not to cut all the way through. Rinse under cold running water and pat dry with kitchen paper.

PREPARE SCALLOPS

"The best tool for this job is just a simple bread and butter knife." **JAMES NATHAN**

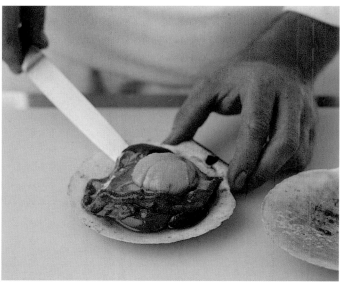

1 Scrub the shell under cold running water before you open the scallop. Slide a knife between the top and bottom shell to open it, then carefully detach the scallop from the bottom shell with the knife.

2 Pull away and discard the viscera and frilled membrane. You can leave the cream and orange coral (roe) attached to the scallop, or remove it too if you wish. Gently rinse the scallop in cold running water.

PICK COOKED CRAYFISH

1 Crayfish should be cooked in a large pan of boiling water or flavoured broth for 5–7 minutes and then removed to cool. When they are cool enough to handle, simply break off the head section.

2 Now hold the tail between your thumb and forefinger, and gently squeeze the tail until you hear the shell crack. Remove the meat in one piece by carefully pulling away the sides of the shell.

OPEN OYSTERS

"To make the oysters easier for your guests to eat, just snip under where the inductor muscle was, loosen up the oyster, and turn it over." **JAMES NATHAN**

1 Hold the oyster flat in a towel, and insert the tip of an oyster knife into the hinge to open the shell. Keep the blade close to the top of the shell so the oyster is not damaged. Cut the muscle, and lift off the top shell.

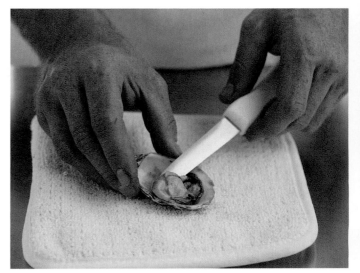

2 Detach the oyster from the bottom shell by carefully sliding the blade of your knife beneath the oyster. Oysters can be served raw on the half shell (scrub the shells thoroughly before opening), or removed and cooked.

OPEN CLAMS

1 Clean the clams under cold running water and discard any open ones. Place the clam in a towel to protect your fingers, then insert the tip of a long sharp knife and twist to force the shells apart.

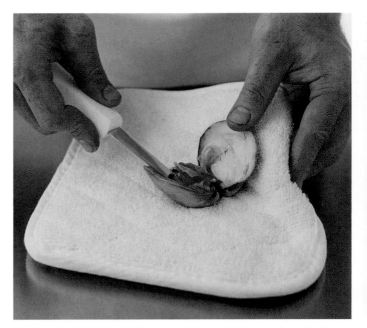

2 Using the tip of your knife, sever the muscle that attaches the clam to the shell, and release the clam. If using soft-shell clams, remove and discard the dark membrane before serving.

CLEAN SQUID

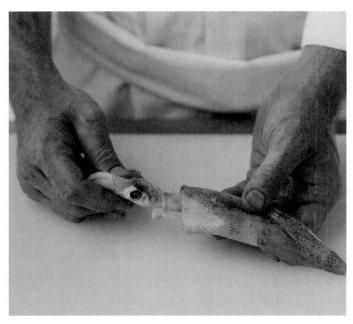

1 First pull the mantle (the body) and tentacles apart. The head, viscera, and ink sac will come away with the tentacles. The black "ink" can be used to flavour and colour sauces, pasta, and rice.

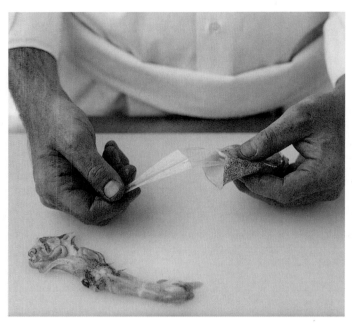

2 Next, push a forefinger into the body cavity, to extract the transparent, plastic-like quill (the inner lining). Hook your finger around it. pull it out and discard.

3 Separate the tentacles from the head, cutting above the eye. Discard the head and viscera, but retain the ink sac if required by your chosen recipe. (Be sure to use it immediately though, or discard.)

4 Open the tentacles to pull out the ball-shaped beak and discard it. Rinse the tentacles and mantle under cold running water, then pat dry with kitchen paper. The squid is ready to be cooked.

POULTRY

BUY Intensively farmed poultry is cheaper than organic or free-range birds but doesn't have the same flavour or texture. Buy poultry from a quality source, and check that the meat is plump and not dry. The bird should have a clean fresh smell, and the skin should have no tears or bruising. If corn-fed it will be yellow, if not the flesh should be pale pink with whitish skin. Also available frozen and smoked. **STORE** Put in a sealed container in the bottom of the fridge, so that it can't touch or drip on other foods. If the bird has giblets, remove and store separately. Cook within 2 days. Freeze fresh poultry for up to 12 months (3 months for giblets). Thaw completely before cooking.

WHOLE CHICKEN ▶

EAT Roast, pot-roast, poach. Stuff the neck end, if liked or, when roasting, put a whole onion and/or fresh herbs/lemon in the body cavity for added flavour.
FLAVOUR PAIRINGS Sage and onion or parsley and thyme stuffing, lemon, honey, barbecue sauce, Cajun spices, Tandoori spices, paprika, bread sauce, redcurrant jelly, cider, white wine.

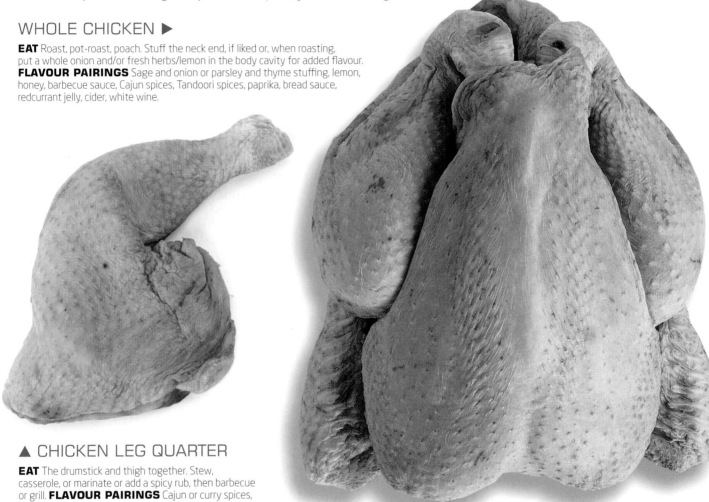

▲ CHICKEN LEG QUARTER

EAT The drumstick and thigh together. Stew, casserole, or marinate or add a spicy rub, then barbecue or grill. **FLAVOUR PAIRINGS** Cajun or curry spices, thyme, tarragon, chives, garlic, lardons, red or white wine, cider, mushrooms, tomatoes.

◀ CHICKEN BREAST QUARTER

EAT The whole breast with the wing and part of the rib cage and backbone attached. Use in the same way as the leg quarter; particularly good stewed with cider, or dipped in milk then flavoured breadcrumbs and oven-fried in sizzling oil. **FLAVOUR PAIRINGS** As for leg quarter, but also bananas, bacon, sweetcorn, soured cream, chives.

▲ CHICKEN DRUMSTICK

EAT The end of the leg, excellent finger food. Roast, grill, or barbecue plain, marinated, or basted with sauce. **FLAVOUR PAIRINGS** Butter, olive oil, garlic, barbecue sauce, sweet and sour sauce, cumin, garam masala, curry paste, harissa paste, chilli, Worcestershire sauce, honey, lemon.

▲ CHICKEN THIGH

EAT Cheaper than breasts, sold with or without skin, boned or whole. Roast plain (boned can be stuffed first), casserole, curry, braise. **FLAVOUR PAIRINGS** Curry spices, pesto, olive oil, chopped fresh herbs, garlic, mirepoix.

▲ CHICKEN WING

EAT Popular barbecued as buffalo wings and for making stock. **FLAVOUR PAIRINGS** Chinese five-spice powder, soy sauce, barbecue sauce, jerk seasoning, Cajun spices, garam masala.

▲ CHICKEN SUPREME

EAT The breast with part of the wing bone attached. Sold with or without skin. Good for stuffing before cooking (like chicken kiev), then coat in egg and crumbs, pan-fry, bake. **FLAVOUR PAIRINGS** Butter, fresh herbs, garlic, cream, white wine, brandy, white grapes, mushrooms.

▲ CHICKEN BREAST

EAT One of the most popular cuts, being tender and easy to cook. Available with or without skin. Can be cooked whole, cut in strips or cubes, or beaten flat as escalopes. Stir-fry, pan-fry, grill (with skin or wrapped in bacon), stew, or casserole. **FLAVOUR PAIRINGS** Thai green curry paste, coconut, nam pla, ginger, oyster sauce, black bean sauce, bacon/pancetta, chorizo, prawns.

▲ POULTRY LIVER

EAT Fresh or frozen. Trim, chop, and sauté until cooked but soft. Serve on bruschetta or salad leaves, with pasta or rice, or in pâtés and terrines. Slice fresh foie gras and quickly fry, or, if preserved, served chilled. **FLAVOUR PAIRINGS** Butter, garlic, shallots, woody herbs, bacon, eggs, truffles, figs, prunes, Sauternes, sherry.

▲ POUSSIN

EAT The French name for young chicken. Sold 4–6 weeks old. Roast, bake, or simmer whole or stuffed birds; grill, fry, or barbecue spatchcocked ones. **FLAVOUR PAIRINGS** Bacon, garlic, shallots, tomatoes, citrus, mushrooms, saffron, lemon grass, kaffir lime, rosemary, thyme, tarragon, bay leaf, pesto, soy sauce, white wine, barbecue sauce.

◀ WHOLE DUCK

EAT Roast or pot-roast whole, or cut in portions. Prick with a fork and rest on a trivet in a roasting tin to allow fat to drain away. **FLAVOUR PAIRINGS** Sage, onion, garlic, spring onions, apples, oranges, turnips, ginger, cherries, soy sauce, hoisin sauce, honey, vinegar, wine, peas, baby white onions, lettuce. **IN SEASON** All year

▲ DUCK BREAST

EAT Sold with or without skin and in goujons. If cooking with skin, score or prick it, then pan-fry skin-side down or grill skin-side up to melt and release fat. Use a little oil or butter if cooking without skin. Good in warm salads. Stir-fry goujons. **FLAVOUR PAIRINGS** Berries, currants, pomegranate, baby leaves, cherry tomatoes, cucumber, red onion, olives, fruit vinegar, olive oil, pomegranate syrup.

▲ DUCK CROWN

EAT A convenient joint for carving – it is the breast (the choicest part) with wings, no legs. Best roasted but can be braised. **FLAVOUR PAIRINGS** The same as for the whole bird, but try rubbing with smoked sea salt before cooking.

▲ DUCK LEG PORTION

EAT Grill, fry, roast, casserole, or use to make confit. Prick the skin before cooking to release the fat. **FLAVOUR PAIRINGS** All the above plus juniper berries, coriander seeds, thyme for confit.

WHOLE GOOSE ▶

EAT Stuff neck end only. Roast. Goose leg confit is also available. Can be jointed and braised, or casseroled. **FLAVOUR PAIRINGS** Apples, onions, red cabbage, tomatoes, white beans, spicy sausages, ginger, sage oatmeal, almonds, apricots, prunes, soy sauce, red wine. **IN SEASON** September–December (some for Michaelmas in September but most bred for Christmas)

WHOLE TURKEY ▶

EAT Roast (stuff neck end only). Pot-roast or poach smaller birds. **FLAVOUR PAIRINGS** Chestnuts, cranberries, thyme, parsley, sage, tarragon, bacon, sausagemeat, root vegetables, brussels sprouts. **IN SEASON** All year, some speciality birds reared just for Easter and Christmas

◀ TURKEY STEAK

EAT Thick slices cut from the breast or top of the leg. Pan-fry, poach, or cut in strips or dice, then stir-fry or casserole. Good beaten flat for escalopes, coated in egg and breadcrumbs (or stuffing mix), then fried. **FLAVOUR PAIRINGS** Ham, cheese (for topping), peppers, tomatoes, mushrooms, sage, tarragon, thyme, parsley, chives, oregano, redcurrant jelly.

◀ TURKEY CROWN

EAT Also called bone-in saddle, good for those who don't like dark meat, and easier to cook than a whole bird. Best roasted. Try masking in bacon or putting flavoured butter or oily paste under the skin to keep it moist. Turkey breast joint and boned roll also available. The legs and thighs are also sold separately. **FLAVOUR PAIRINGS** As for whole bird, but also pancetta, garlic butter, tarragon butter, pesto, tapenade.

GAME BIRDS

BUY Wild game should only be bought in season. Buy from reliable sources and don't accept any illegally shot birds. Quail are farmed. Game birds may have a strong smell but shouldn't be rancid. The flesh should be firm and the skin taught. Avoid if bruised or those with badly shot breasts. Guinea fowl (not shown as not, technically, game birds) should be cooked like chicken. **STORE** Remove all giblets and store separately. Wrap well and store on a plate at the bottom of the fridge for 2–3 days. Birds can be frozen for 6 months, giblets for 3 months.

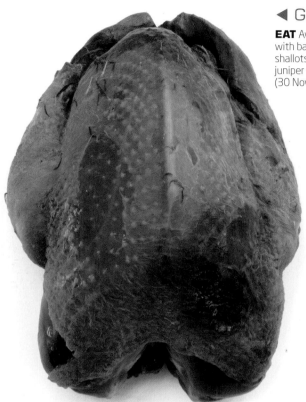

◀ GROUSE

EAT Available whole or as boned breasts. Allow 1 whole bird or 2 breasts per person. Bard (cover) with bacon and roast whole, pan-fry, grill, or braise. **FLAVOUR PAIRINGS** Bacon, ham, celery, shallots, watercress, wild mushrooms, game chips, bread sauce, buttered crumbs, orange, honey, juniper berries, redcurrants, cranberries, whisky, wine. **IN SEASON** 12 August–10 December (30 November in Northern Ireland)

▲ PARTRIDGE

EAT Sold whole. Roast (bard with bacon first), pan-fry, grill, braise. Allow 1 bird per person. **FLAVOUR PAIRINGS** Bacon, cream, cabbage, watercress, lentils, shallots, wild mushrooms, grapes, lemon, pears, quinces, redcurrants, chestnuts, walnuts, turnips, kohl rabi, juniper berries, sage, chocolate, wine. **IN SEASON** 1 September–1 February (31 January in Northern Ireland)

▲ WOODCOCK

EAT Available whole. Roast boned and stuffed, or whole; spatchcock to grill or pan-fry. It is traditionally roasted undrawn, with the beaked head pushed into the body to truss it, usually served on a fried or toasted croûte. Allow 1 bird per person. **FLAVOUR PAIRINGS** Butter, bacon, cream, shallots, garlic, watercress, ginger, bay leaf, parsley, thyme, nutmeg, lemon, apples, grapes, soy sauce, Madeira. **IN SEASON** 1 October– 31 January

▲ QUAIL

EAT Available whole. Bard with bacon and roast, halve or spatchcock to grill, pan-fry, or braise. Allow 1 or 2 birds per person. **FLAVOUR PAIRINGS** Bacon, butter, cream, peppers, mushrooms, truffle, quinces, grapes, cherries, prunes, almonds, honey, cumin, cinnamon, brandy, white and red wine. **IN SEASON** Farmed all year

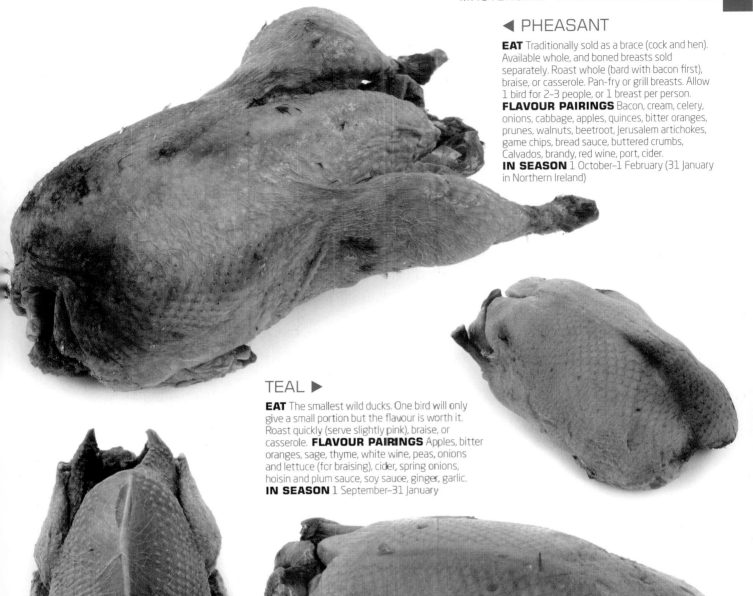

◀ PHEASANT

EAT Traditionally sold as a brace (cock and hen). Available whole, and boned breasts sold separately. Roast whole (bard with bacon first), braise, or casserole. Pan-fry or grill breasts. Allow 1 bird for 2–3 people, or 1 breast per person.
FLAVOUR PAIRINGS Bacon, cream, celery, onions, cabbage, apples, quinces, bitter oranges, prunes, walnuts, beetroot, Jerusalem artichokes, game chips, bread sauce, buttered crumbs, Calvados, brandy, red wine, port, cider.
IN SEASON 1 October–1 February (31 January in Northern Ireland)

TEAL ▶

EAT The smallest wild ducks. One bird will only give a small portion but the flavour is worth it. Roast quickly (serve slightly pink), braise, or casserole. **FLAVOUR PAIRINGS** Apples, bitter oranges, sage, thyme, white wine, peas, onions and lettuce (for braising), cider, spring onions, hoisin and plum sauce, soy sauce, ginger, garlic.
IN SEASON 1 September–31 January

▲ WOOD PIGEON

EAT Pigeons and squabs are sold whole, as crowns, or as boned breasts. Allow 1 bird or 2–3 breasts per person. Stew, casserole, or cook in pies. Quickly roast young birds. Pan-fry or grill breasts (serve pink). **FLAVOUR PAIRINGS** Bacon, cream, red cabbage, mushrooms, spinach, chilli, garlic, orange, redcurrants, blueberries, juniper berries, chocolate, honey, soy sauce, red wine.
IN SEASON All year (best February–May)

▲ MALLARD

EAT Sold whole or as pairs of breasts. Grill or fry breasts (cook rare), and thinly slice to serve. Roast whole young birds. Braise, stew, or casserole older ones. Allow 1 breast or 1 bird between 2–3 people.
FLAVOUR PAIRINGS Ginger, garlic, mushrooms, onions, coriander leaf, parsley, sage, apples, bitter oranges, plums, cherries, redcurrants, cider, red wine, soy sauce. **IN SEASON** 1 September–31 January

JOINT A CHICKEN

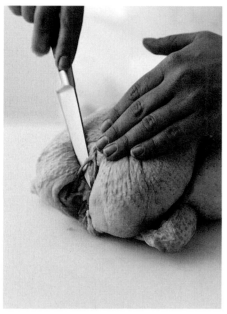

1 To remove the wishbone, scrape the flesh away from it, using a sharp knife, then twist it with your fingers and discard.

2 With the chicken breast-side up on a board, use a sharp knife to cut through the thigh joint and separate the leg from the rest of the bird.

3 Now pull the leg back to dislocate the leg joint. You should hear a distinct popping sound when the ball separates from the socket.

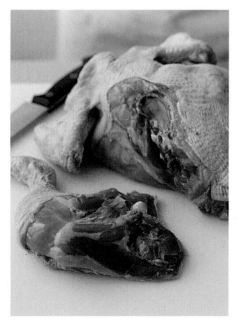

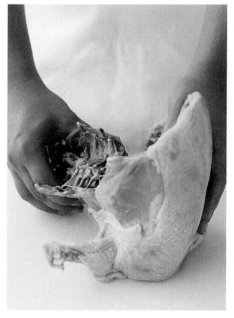

4 If there is any skin or meat still attached to the bird's body, use your knife to free it. Repeat steps 2 and 3 to remove the other leg.

5 Pull the wing straight, then cut through the middle joint with poultry shears to remove the winglet. Repeat for the other winglet.

6 Now grasp the backbone with your hands and firmly pull it away from the upper part of the body (the 2 breasts and wings).

7 To remove the lower end of the backbone, use poultry shears to cut it away from the remaining body.

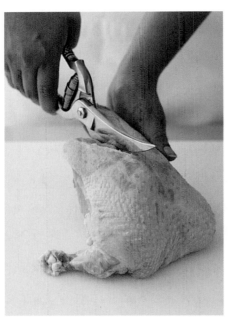

8 Starting at the neck, use poultry shears to cut all the way through the backbone to separate the breasts.

9 The chicken is now cut into 4 pieces. Any leftover bones (such as the backbone) can be used to make chicken stock.

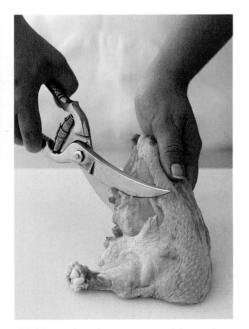

10 Use poultry shears to cut each breast in half diagonally, producing one breast and one wing. Repeat to separate the other breast.

11 Cut each leg through the knee joint (above the drumstick) that connects to the thigh, and cut through to separate.

12 Now, there are two drumsticks, two thighs, two wings, and two breasts. The chicken is divided into 8 pieces.

BONE A CHICKEN BREAST

1 Working from the widest end of the breast, (the wing) use sharp poultry shears to cut away the backbone and ribs.

2 Now use a sharp knife to cut the meat away from the bone. To create a neat fillet, carefully follow the shape of the breastbone.

3 There will be a small inner fillet on the underside of the breast. To remove it, cut away any connecting membrane.

BONE A LEG

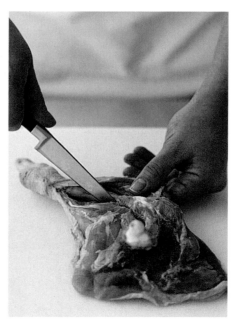

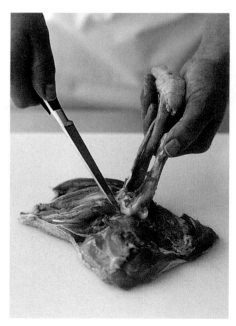

1 Place the leg skin-side down on a board. Using a sharp knife, cut the flesh away from the start of the thigh bone and work down.

2 Using the same technique, start from the knuckle and cut all the way down the length of the drumstick.

3 Lift the bones up from the central knuckle joint. Then using short strokes with the tip of your knife, remove the 2 bones from the flesh.

BONE A THIGH

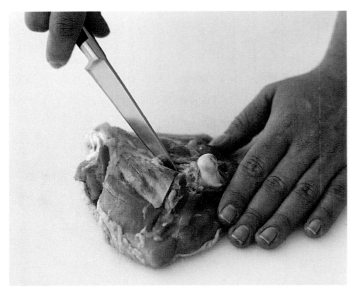

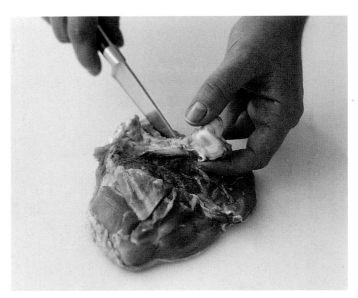

1 Place the thigh skin-side down on a cutting board. Using a small, sharp knife, pierce the flesh at one end of the thigh bone and carefully cut away the flesh to expose it.

2 Make another small incision through the flesh, following the contour of the exposed bone. Cut around the bone to cut it completely free from the flesh and discard, or use for stock.

BONE A DRUMSTICK

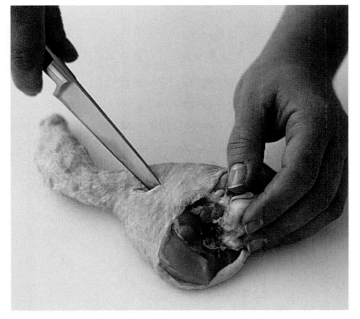

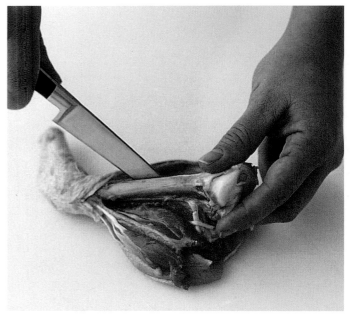

1 Holding the drumstick steady, and starting in the middle of the drumstick, insert the tip of your knife until you locate the bone. Slice along the bone in both directions to expose it fully.

2 Open the flesh out and using short strokes to minimise tearing, neatly cut around the bone to free it completely from the flesh and discard, or use for stock.

SPATCHCOCK A BIRD FOR GRILLING

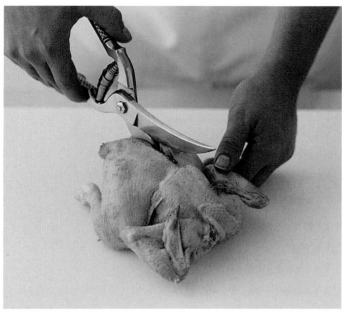

1 Place the bird upside down. Cut along one side of the backbone using sharp poultry shears, then do the same along the other side, and take out the backbone. Open out the two halves and turn the bird over.

2 Press down on the bird with both hands to flatten it out to a more uniform thickness. This will help both to tenderize the meat and make sure that it cooks more evenly.

3 Once flattened out, use a sharp knife to cut a few slashes into the legs and thighs. This will help the heat to penetrate the dense flesh of the thigh and leg meat more thoroughly.

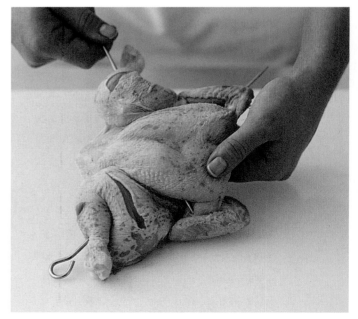

4 Push a metal skewer through the right leg to the left wing, and another one through the left leg to the right wing, to form an "X" shape. The spatchcocked bird can now be marinated before being grilled or roasted.

DEEP-FRY CHICKEN

1 Cream butter and herbs or other flavourings according to your chosen recipe. Shape into a block, wrap in foil and freeze.

2 Flatten the chicken breasts by placing each one between 2 sheets of cling film before flattening out gently with a rolling pin.

3 Divide the butter into 4 pieces and put one in the centre of each flattened chicken breast. Roll the escalope tightly around the butter.

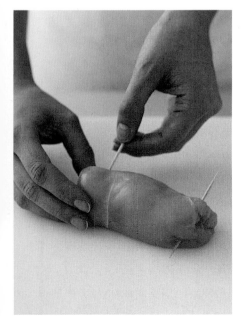

4 Once the escalope is tightly rolled, with no butter mixture showing, secure it at each end with a cocktail stick.

5 Coat the chicken in lightly beaten egg, then roll the meat in breadcrumbs and leave the coated parcels to set in the refrigerator.

6 In a deep-frying pan, heat some sunflower or vegetable oil to 190°C (375°F). Fry the chicken for about 10 minutes, until golden.

STUFF A CHICKEN BREAST

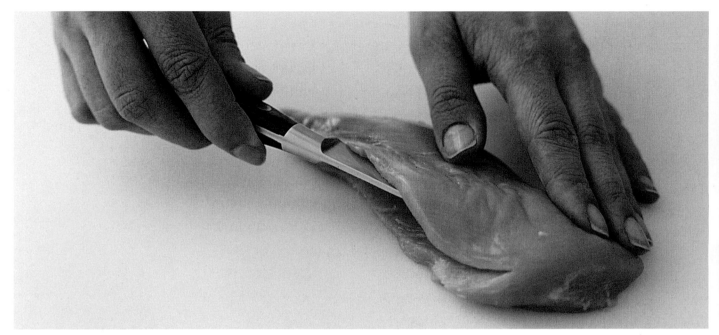

1 With one hand lightly pressing on the chicken breast to keep it in place, use a sharp knife to cut a pocket about 4cm (1½in) deep in the side of the breast fillet. Take care not to pierce the flesh all the way through to the other side.

2 Holding back one side of the chicken breast, press the stuffing from your chosen recipe into the pocket. Do this firmly, but take care not to overfill, then roll the flesh back so that it closes over the stuffing neatly.

BREAD AND FRY POULTRY OR MEAT ESCALOPES

1 Place each fillet between 2 pieces of cling film, then pound them with a rolling pin (without too much pressure on any one point) until the fillets have increased in area and reached an even thickness.

2 Remove the cling film and season the fillets to taste with salt, pepper, and freshly chopped herbs. Dip the seasoned fillets into beaten egg, coating each side evenly.

3 Turn the fillets in breadcrumbs, pressing an even coat to both sides. Repeat the process with the remaining fillets and cook immediately, or cover, and leave to set in the refrigerator for 10–15 minutes.

4 Heat 1cm (½in) of oil in a frying pan until hot and fry the fillets for 4–5 minutes on each side until cooked through (test with a sharp knife to ensure that there are no pink juices). Drain on kitchen paper.

REST, CARVE, AND PORTION

1 Allow the cooked chicken to rest in a warm place for 15 minutes, covered with foil. This allows the juices to flow throughout the bird and helps to keep the meat moist.

2 Transfer the bird to a cutting board, breast-side up. Remove the legs by cutting the skin between the leg and the body and pushing the blade down to where the leg bone joins the body.

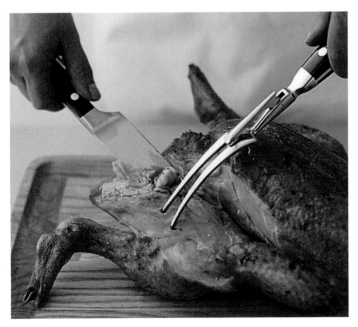

3 Work the blade from side to side a little to loosen the joint, then with a slight sawing motion, push the blade through the joint, cutting the leg free. Transfer the leg to a warmed plate and repeat with the other leg.

4 Remove a breast by cutting as if you are dividing the bird in half, just to one side of the breastbone. As the blade hits the bone, cut along the bone; remove all the meat; repeat on the other side.

5 Place one breast cut-side down on the cutting board. Using horizontal strokes, slice the breast into as many pieces as possible, leaving the wing with a section of breast meat attached.

6 Carve each leg by cutting it in half through the joint at the midway point. You shouldn't need to cut through any bone. As you reach the joint, work the blade into the joint to separate the pieces.

MARINATE CHICKEN

1 Mix the marinade ingredients in a bowl. In another bowl large enough to hold the chicken in a single layer, coat the chicken with the marinade. Cover the bowl and chill in the refrigerator for a minimum of 1 hour.

2 Dry-marinating, which involves no liquid, is an extension of the process of seasoning poultry. The mixture should be left on the bird for at least 1 hour for it to penetrate the meat more than just skin-deep.

BEEF

BUY Best quality beef indicates its origin and breed. Dark red meat will have been matured (3–4 weeks) so should be more tender with good flavour. Muscle meat that is marbled with fat cooks and tastes best, but avoid excessive fat round the edge. **STORE** Keep on the bottom shelf of the refrigerator, well-wrapped on a plate to catch any drips, joints and steaks up to 3 days, and mince and offal for no more than 2 days. Freeze joints and steaks for up to 12 months, stewing or braising meat 8 months, mince 3 months. **IN SEASON** All year.

▶ SIRLOIN JOINT

EAT The finest joint, when sold on the bone, it can include the eye of the fillet the other side of the bone (like T-bone steak). Also sold boned and rolled. Roast. **FLAVOUR PAIRINGS** English mustard, horseradish, Yorkshire puddings, parsnips and other root vegetables.

▲ FILLET STEAK

EAT Very lean and tender, but less flavour than sirloin or rump. Roast whole, wrap in pastry (Beef Wellington), or slice into thick steaks and grill or pan-fry. Serve raw as carpaccio and steak tartare. **FLAVOUR PAIRINGS** Any of the other steak flavourings, liver pâté, port sauce, oysters (stuff with before grilling), soy sauce, oyster sauce, ginger, Cajun spices, garlic.

▲ SIRLOIN STEAK

EAT Tender, well-flavoured, marbled with fat, and best well matured. Grill or pan-fry. **FLAVOUR PAIRINGS** Peppers, onions, olives, savoury butters (see T-bone), green or black peppercorn sauce, Béarnaise sauce.

◀ T-BONE STEAK

EAT Thick slice of sirloin cut down through the bone, hence the 'T' shape, with sirloin one side and fillet the other. Grill or pan-fry. **FLAVOUR PAIRINGS** Savoury butters – anchovy, parsley, mixed herb and garlic, oregano, chilli.

▲ RUMP STEAK

EAT Best well matured to tenderize. Excellent flavour, thick and juicy. Try marinading in red wine and herbs. **FLAVOUR PAIRINGS** Fried onions, potato chips, mushrooms, French mustard, red wine sauce.

▲ CHUCK OR SHOULDER

EAT Can be sold as a joint but usually diced as stewing steak, or minced. Stew, curry, casserole, braise. Cook ox liver or heart in the same way. **FLAVOUR PAIRINGS** Onions, garlic, tomatoes, mushrooms, aubergines, carrots, celery, Indian curry spices, Thai red curry paste, star anise, chilli, cinnamon, ginger.

▲ SILVERSIDE

EAT Less expensive joint. Roast, pot-roast, or stew with carrots (boiled beef and carrots). Also sold salted. **FLAVOUR PAIRINGS** Mustard, carrots, parsnips, onion, red wine, cinnamon, olives, tomatoes.

▲ BRISKET

EAT Inexpensive joint, full of flavour, that needs long slow cooking. Trim excess fat before cooking. Also sold salted. **FLAVOUR PAIRINGS** Mustard, root vegetables, mushrooms, bay leaf, bouquet garni, rosemary, thyme, parsley.

◄ OXTAIL

EAT Cook long and slow until meltingly tender for soups or stews. Best cooled quickly, chilled overnight, then fat removed before re-heating. Look out for other beef offal; ox heart, liver, tripe, tongue, and kidney. **FLAVOUR PAIRINGS** Bacon, celery, parsnip, carrot, swede, onions, nutmeg, cumin, allspice, mustard, red wine, brown beer, soy sauce.

LAMB AND MUTTON

BUY Lambs are animals up to a year old. Hoggets are lambs 1–2 years and then they become mutton. Native lamb increases in size through the year; imported meat, which arrives fresh or frozen, can be any size. Lamb should have just a thin covering of hard white fat. Trim the excess before cooking. Young lamb is the most tender, mutton has the best flavour. **STORE** Keep wrapped, on a plate to catch any drips, in the bottom of the fridge for up to 3 days. Freeze joints and chops up to 12 months, diced meat 8 months, mince 3 months. **IN SEASON** May–September, imported all year.

▲ RACK

EAT Best end of neck. Sold as individual cutlets or as a rack roast. Two tied together are a guard of honour (bones entwined) or crown roast (back to back in a round). It should have the backbone chined (removed) to allow chops to be carved between the ribs. Allow 2–3 chops per person (depending on size). Roast with or without a crust (try breadcrumbs, olives and herbs); serve pink. **FLAVOUR PAIRINGS** Garlic, rosemary, mint, honey, olives, harissa paste, aubergines, yogurt, baby spring vegetables.

▲ NECK

EAT Trim sinews before cooking. Quickly roast whole, or cut in slices and pan-fry very quickly. **FLAVOUR PAIRINGS** Mint, oregano, garlic, cinnamon, star anise, dried fruit, haricot beans, spring onions, dill, lemon.

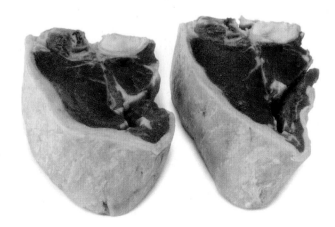

▲ LOIN CHOPS

EAT Double loin chops (pictured) have fillet one side of the bone and loin the other (like T-bone steak). Pan-fry, grill, braise, or roast. **FLAVOUR PAIRINGS** Mint jelly, tomatoes, onions, garlic, oregano.

▲ NOISETTES

EAT Boned and tied loin chops are very tender. Grill, pan-fry, or roast. **FLAVOUR PAIRINGS** Red wine, port, redcurrants, rosemary, lemon, garlic.

▶ LEG

EAT Whole or half. Roast or slow-roast. Try rubbing with paprika, dried oregano, garlic, and seasoning before cooking. Also available as steaks to grill or pan-fry. **FLAVOUR PAIRINGS** Garlic, oregano and potatoes (Greek-style slow-roast), mint sauce/jelly, redcurrant jelly, roast onions or leeks, onion sauce, celery, carrots, paprika, flageolet beans.

▲ KIDNEY

EAT Remove outer membrane, halve, snip out white core with scissors. Sauté or grill and serve in a sauce (don't overcook), braise or add to hotpots. Slice liver and cook the same way. **FLAVOUR PAIRINGS** Cream, shallots, mushrooms, lemon, brandy, sherry, mustard, Worcestershire sauce, tomatoes, sausages, bacon.

▶ SHANK

EAT Shanks need long slow cooking, so braise or casserole. Lamb's hearts can be cooked the same way. **FLAVOUR PAIRINGS** Turnips, carrots, celery, leeks, tomato purée, redcurrant or mint jelly, white, red, or rosé wine.

◀ MUTTON SHOULDER

EAT Mutton shoulder is usually simmered (known as boiled), or diced for curries, stews, and casseroles. Lamb shoulder is roasted, or diced or minced and used the same way. **FLAVOUR PAIRINGS** Caper or onion sauce (boiled mutton), turnips, carrots, leeks, yogurt, aubergines, cinnamon, apricots, prunes, raisins, curry spices, oregano, mint, rosemary, pearl barley.

PORK

BUY Choose outdoor-reared pork for best flavour and on welfare grounds. All pork should be pink (pale or more deeply coloured, depending on the cut), not grey or red. The fat should be soft and white. The whole animal commercially roasted – hog roast – is now popular for parties and festivals. **STORE** Keep wrapped, on a plate to catch any drips, in the bottom of the refrigerator, for up to 3 days. Freeze joints, chops, and steaks up to 9 months, diced meat and belly slices 4 months, mince 3 months.

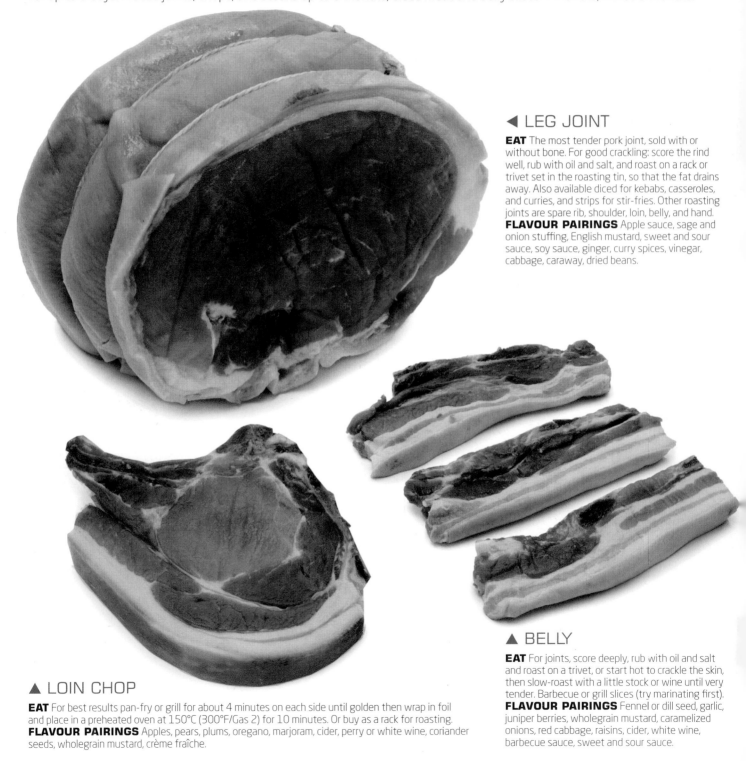

◀ LEG JOINT

EAT The most tender pork joint, sold with or without bone. For good crackling: score the rind well, rub with oil and salt, and roast on a rack or trivet set in the roasting tin, so that the fat drains away. Also available diced for kebabs, casseroles, and curries, and strips for stir-fries. Other roasting joints are spare rib, shoulder, loin, belly, and hand.
FLAVOUR PAIRINGS Apple sauce, sage and onion stuffing, English mustard, sweet and sour sauce, soy sauce, ginger, curry spices, vinegar, cabbage, caraway, dried beans.

▲ BELLY

EAT For joints, score deeply, rub with oil and salt and roast on a trivet, or start hot to crackle the skin, then slow-roast with a little stock or wine until very tender. Barbecue or grill slices (try marinating first).
FLAVOUR PAIRINGS Fennel or dill seed, garlic, juniper berries, wholegrain mustard, caramelized onions, red cabbage, raisins, cider, white wine, barbecue sauce, sweet and sour sauce.

▲ LOIN CHOP

EAT For best results pan-fry or grill for about 4 minutes on each side until golden then wrap in foil and place in a preheated oven at 150°C (300°F/Gas 2) for 10 minutes. Or buy as a rack for roasting.
FLAVOUR PAIRINGS Apples, pears, plums, oregano, marjoram, cider, perry or white wine, coriander seeds, wholegrain mustard, crème fraîche.

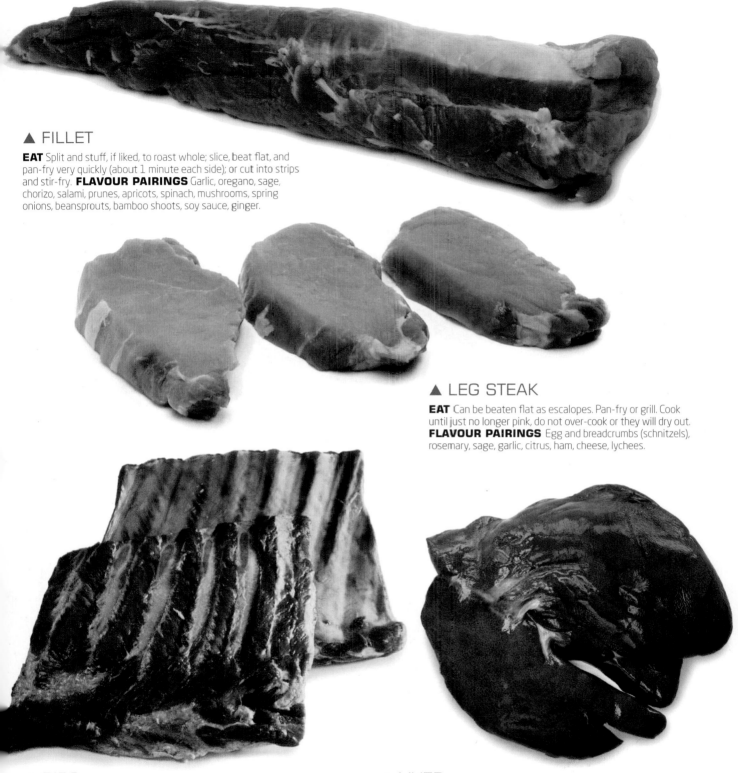

▲ FILLET

EAT Split and stuff, if liked, to roast whole; slice, beat flat, and pan-fry very quickly (about 1 minute each side); or cut into strips and stir-fry. **FLAVOUR PAIRINGS** Garlic, oregano, sage, chorizo, salami, prunes, apricots, spinach, mushrooms, spring onions, beansprouts, bamboo shoots, soy sauce, ginger.

▲ LEG STEAK

EAT Can be beaten flat as escalopes. Pan-fry or grill. Cook until just no longer pink, do not over-cook or they will dry out. **FLAVOUR PAIRINGS** Egg and breadcrumbs (schnitzels), rosemary, sage, garlic, citrus, ham, cheese, lychees.

▲ RIBS

EAT Chinese ribs are the trimmed ribs, sold as a rack or individually cut. Do not confuse with spare rib joints or chops. **FLAVOUR PAIRINGS** Barbecue sauce, chilli, soy sauce, honey, citrus, pineapple, Worcestershire sauce, tomatoes, Chinese five-spice powder.

▲ LIVER

EAT Soak in milk to remove its strong taste before frying. Braise, casserole, use in pâtés and terrines. Look out for kidneys, cheeks, ears, and trotters to braise, too. **FLAVOUR PAIRINGS** Sage, onions, bacon, juniper berries, hazelnuts, watercress, brandy, mushrooms, red wine, cider, root vegetables.

GOAT, RABBIT, VENISON, AND VEAL

BUY All these meats are lower in fat than the others. Rose veal is from calves reared with their mothers, with access to grass and grain. For white veal they are taken away and reared solely on milk. Either should be lean, pale coloured, and firm. Goat is interchangeable with lamb. Young goat is called Chevron. Venison is farmed all year, but several species are shot in the wild during the hunting season (the dates are different in each country of the UK, by species and for bucks or does). Rabbit is also farmed but wild rabbit is becoming widely available too. **STORE** Keep wrapped, on a plate to catch any drips, at the bottom of the refrigerator. Use within 2–3 days. Freeze veal, goat, or venison joints up to 12 months, steaks, chops, or diced meat up to 8 months, rabbit for up to 6 months and mince up to 3 months. **IN SEASON** All year, except wild venison (available July–April) and wild rabbit (July–December).

GOAT

▼ WHOLE KID

EAT Barbecue or slow-roast whole, or bone, stuff, and roll before roasting. Baste well as there is very little fat. **FLAVOUR PAIRINGS** Red wine, olive and nut oils, chilli oil, cumin, cinnamon, garlic, honey, mint, oregano, onions, leeks.

▲ LEG STEAK

EAT Fry or grill. Braise (if older). Leg joints also available, best slow-roasted.
FLAVOUR PAIRINGS Cinnamon, cumin, ginger, allspice, jerk seasoning, onions, oranges, redcurrant jelly.

▲ DICED

EAT Cut from the leg or shoulder. Curry, braise, casserole.
FLAVOUR PAIRINGS Yogurt, curry powder, fenugreek, chilli, vinegar, honey, soy sauce, spring onions, root vegetables.

RABBIT

▶ WHOLE RABBIT

EAT Usually jointed into 5 or 6 pieces before cooking. The saddle and legs are the best parts. Grill, roast, braise, stew, cook in a pie.
FLAVOUR PAIRINGS Bacon, carrots, fennel, celery, sweetcorn, mushrooms, tomatoes, olives, coriander leaf, parsley, rosemary, thyme, lemon, prunes, mustard, soy sauce, cider, white wine.

VENISON

▲ ROLLED HAUNCH

EAT Haunches from smaller deer may be roasted whole, or boned, or sliced into steaks. Large haunches can be left on the bone but are usually parted into individual muscles or paves, rolled, and tied. Roast (cook pink), braise.
FLAVOUR PAIRINGS Guinness, red wine, port, redcurrant jelly, prunes, juniper berries, bay leaf, thyme, cream, chanterelle mushrooms.

▲ FILLET OR TENDERLOIN

EAT The boned out saddle (back) yields the fillet and the loin. They are often confused, but the loin is thicker so takes longer to cook. Roast or braise whole. Pan-fry, grill, or barbecue steaks. **FLAVOUR PAIRINGS** Bacon, pears, cream, fennel, red cabbage, pomegranate, berries, pine nuts, red wine, vermouth.

VEAL

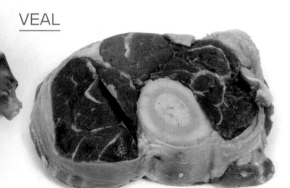

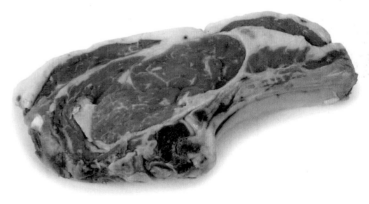

▲ OSSO BUCCO

EAT Thick slices of shin/shank become meltingly tender when slow-cooked. The marrow from the bone enriches the sauce, or is eaten with a teaspoon.
FLAVOUR PAIRINGS Tomatoes, white wine, gremolata (chopped parsley, garlic, anchovy fillets, and lemon zest), Risotto alla Milanese.

▲ LOIN CHOP

EAT Similar to a T-bone steak and still a large chop. Grill or fry. **FLAVOUR PAIRINGS** Tarragon or parsley butter, garlic, rosemary, sage, white wine, cream, brandy, lemon, shallots.

◀ ESCALOPE

EAT This leg cut is beaten flat and either rolled round a filling before frying or braising, or coated in egg and breadcrumbs (Weiner Schnitzel) and pan-fried. The leg (and shoulder) can also be diced. **FLAVOUR PAIRINGS** Egg and breadcrumbs, Parmesan cheese, melting cheeses, ham, cream, mushrooms, sorrel, spinach, gherkins, capers, tomato sauce, potato salad.

MEAT ESSENTIALS

USE THIS CHART TO IDENTIFY THE BEST WAY TO COOK THE MOST POPULAR CUTS OF VEAL, VENISON, AND RABBIT.

MEAT COOKING CHART

VEAL	DESCRIPTION	GRILL/BARBECUE
Sirloin/Loin	Also called fillet or chump end. Prime roasting joint, bone-in, or boneless. Loin chops are a popular veal cut.	Preheat grill or barbecue. Chops: brush with melted butter or oil. Grill or barbecue 2–3 minutes each side for pink, 5–6 minutes for well-done.
Leg	Topside (cushion) is a prime roasting joint. Thick steaks are cut from the topside or rump. Thin slices, beaten flat, are escalopes. Tender, lean, diced leg is good for kebabs or quick casseroles.	Preheat grill or barbecue. Leg steaks: grill or barbecue as loin chops. Escalopes: brush with oil, season, grill or barbecue 2 minutes each side. Diced leg: marinate first, if liked. Thread on kebab skewers, grill, or barbecue 6–8 minutes, turning frequently.
Fillet	Lean and very tender cooked whole or in steaks.	Grill or barbecue fillet steak as loin chop.

VENISON		
Haunch (back leg)	From small deer it may be the whole leg. From larger ones, usually cut in smaller joints and rolled, or cut in pavés or steaks, or diced.	From young deer only. Preheat grill or barbecue. Steaks: brush with oil or melted butter. Brown both sides quickly. Grill 1½ minutes on each side (rare), 2 minutes on each side (medium). Wrap in foil and leave in a warm place to rest for 5 minutes. Do not overcook or will become tough. Diced meat: marinate first. Thread on skewers. Grill 3–4 minutes, turning occasionally.
Fillet or Tenderloin/ Loin	Whole or steaks.	Grill or barbecue loin steaks as for haunch steaks.
Saddle	Highly prized back joint of fillets and loins jointed by backbone.	Not recommended.
Mince	Lean trimmings with fat and sinew removed before mincing.	Preheat grill or barbecue. Press well-seasoned mince on oiled skewers, or form burgers. Brush with oil, grill or barbecue 8–10 minutes, turning once or twice until no longer pink.

RABBIT		
Whole, Jointed	Wild rabbits usually sold whole. Females and small males make best eating. Farmed also sold jointed.	Joints from young wild, or farmed rabbits. Marinate first. Preheat grill or barbecue. Cook for 8–10 minutes, turning occasionally.

FRY	ROAST	BRAISE/STEW/CASSEROLE
Fry in butter (or butter and oil) for 2–3 minutes each side for pink, 5–6 minutes for well-done.	Brush with oil. Season with pepper. Roast at 200°C (400°F/Gas 6) for 20 minutes per 450g (1lb) plus 20 minutes for pink, 30 minutes per lb plus 30 minutes for well done. Rest 10–15 minutes.	Chops: brown on both sides. Add browned vegetables, liquid, and flavourings. Cover and cook at 180°C (350°F/Gas 4) for 1½–2 hours, joints for the same.
Escalopes: egg and crumb, stuff and roll, sandwich in pairs with filling, or coat in batter. Fry in oil (or butter and oil) for 3 minutes each side. If uncoated, fry 2 minutes each side. Diced meat: fry 5 minutes, stirring and turning.	Cook as loin for 20 minutes per 450g (1lb) plus 20 minutes for pink, 30 minutes per lb plus 30 minutes for well done. Rest 10–15 minutes.	Cook thick steaks, cubes, or whole joints as for sirloin/loin. Steaks: cook for 1 hour. Diced leg: cook for 1–1½ hours. Joints: cook for 1½–2 hours.
Fry fillet steak as loin chop.	Roast whole fillet as loin but for 15 minutes per 450g (1lb) plus 15 minutes for pink, 25 minutes per 450g (1lb) plus 25 minutes for well-done.	Braise fillet steaks as leg steaks; whole fillets as diced leg.
From young deer only. Steaks: fry quickly in butter (or butter and oil) 1 minute each side (rare), 2 minutes each side (medium) then wrap in foil and finish in a low oven (150°C/300°F/Gas 2) for 10 minutes. Diced meat: fry quickly in butter (or butter and oil) for 3 minutes, stirring. Remove and make sauce.	From young deer only. For pink meat: measure diameter of rolled haunch. Preheat oven to 230°C (450°F/Gas 8). Brown 2½ minutes per 1cm (½in) then reduce heat to 110°C (225°F/Gas ¼). Roast for 3 minutes per 1cm (½in) then rest for 3 minutes per 1cm (½in).	Bone-in and boneless joints (young deer): brown meat, add vegetables, liquid, and flavourings. Cook at 190°C/375°F/Gas 5 for 1½–2 hours. Steaks: cook as joints for 1½ hours. Diced meat: cook at 160°C (325°F/Gas 3) for 1½ hours. Joints and steaks (older deer): cook at 180°C (350°F/Gas 4) for 2–3 hours.
Fry steaks as for haunch.	Roast loin joint as for haunch joint.	Cook as for haunch joint from young deer.
Not recommended.	Roast as haunch joint.	Cook as haunch from young deer.
Fry meatballs or burgers in hot oil (or butter and oil) for 8–10 minutes, until cooked through, turning once or twice.	Not recommended.	Brown mince and vegetables. Add liquid and flavourings. Cover and cook at 160°C (325°F/Gas 3) for 1½–2 hours.
Not recommended.	Joints from young wild, or farmed rabbits. Marinate first. Roast in a preheated oven at 200°C (400°F/Gas 6) for 25–30 minutes, basting occasionally.	Young wild or farmed rabbits: brown all over in hot oil or butter and oil. Add vegetables, liquid, and flavourings. Cook at 160°C (325°F/Gas 3) for 1–1½ hours. Older wild rabbits: cook at 150°C (300°F/Gas 2) for 2 hours until tender.

CURED AND AIR-DRIED MEATS

BUY There are hundreds of cured and air-dried meats, made using a wide variety of cuts and techniques: these are the most common ones used in cooking. Sold by weight, from delicatessens, butchers, and supermarkets, most are also available pre-packed. **STORE** Unopened packs will keep several weeks (check sell-by date) in the refrigerator; unpackaged or opened packs should be eaten within a week.

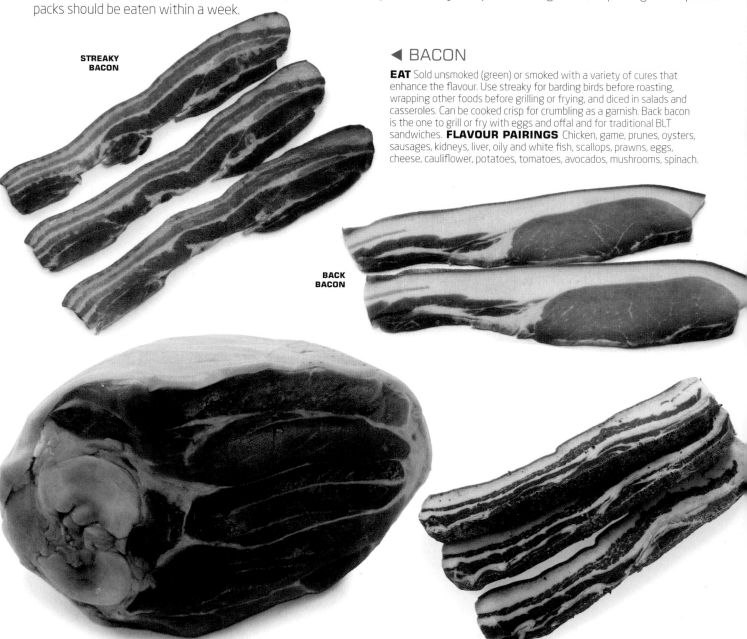

STREAKY BACON

BACK BACON

◄ BACON

EAT Sold unsmoked (green) or smoked with a variety of cures that enhance the flavour. Use streaky for barding birds before roasting, wrapping other foods before grilling or frying, and diced in salads and casseroles. Can be cooked crisp for crumbling as a garnish. Back bacon is the one to grill or fry with eggs and offal and for traditional BLT sandwiches. **FLAVOUR PAIRINGS** Chicken, game, prunes, oysters, sausages, kidneys, liver, oily and white fish, scallops, prawns, eggs, cheese, cauliflower, potatoes, tomatoes, avocados, mushrooms, spinach.

▲ GAMMON/HAM

EAT Available smoked or unsmoked, raw as steaks, or thick rashers to fry or grill, or as joints (with or without the bone) to boil or roast. Heavily salted joints should be soaked in several changes of cold water before cooking. It is also sold cooked ready to eat, hot or cold. **FLAVOUR PAIRINGS** Pineapple, dried fruits, mustard, cloves, honey, onion, bay leaf, parsley sauce, butter beans, carrots, tomatoes, eggs, cheeses.

▲ PANCETTA

EAT Use in pasta sauces, casseroles, risottos, and soups, to top pizzas, and to wrap fish and poultry before grilling or pan-frying. Thinly sliced rolled pancetta can be served as an antipasto. **FLAVOUR PAIRINGS** Cheeses, asparagus, tomatoes, chillies, sweet peppers, bacon, chicken, game birds, meaty white fish, onions, garlic, eggs, cream, white beans.

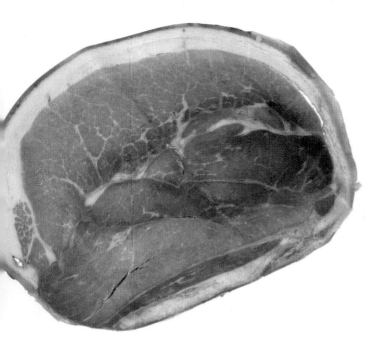

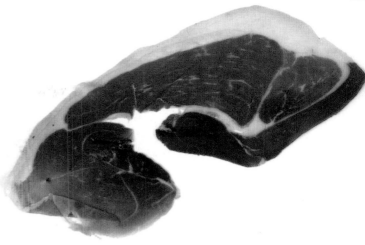

▲ PROSCIUTTO CRUDO

EAT The most widely known of the dry-cured hams. There are many regional cures, including the famous Parma, considered to be the best, and St Daniele from Friuli. Usually sold very thinly sliced. Serve as an antipasto, in sandwiches, salads or added at the last minute to cooked dishes. Use to wrap fish or meat before grilling, pan-frying, or baking. **FLAVOUR PAIRINGS** Parmesan, mozzarella, gherkins, figs, melon, asparagus, tomatoes, olives.

▲ JAMBON DE PARIS

EAT Also known as Jambon blanc, the common French brine-cured boneless ham is usually sold already boiled. It is the favourite cooked ham in France for quick meals and sandwiches. **FLAVOUR PAIRINGS** French and grainy mustards, Gruyère cheese, chips, buckwheat crêpes, eggs, tomatoes.

▲ JAMÓN SERRANO

EAT Meaning "Mountain Ham" in Spanish, these salted and air-cured hams have many regional variations. They have a sweet, rich flavour and chewy texture. Eat in tapas or like prosciutto crudo. **FLAVOUR PAIRINGS** Olives, gherkins, Manchego cheese, figs, rustic bread, nutmeg, eggs, red wine.

▲ BRESAOLA

EAT To make this well-known antipasto, boned beef from the hind leg is salted and flavoured with juniper berries and herbs for a few days, then air-dried. Valtellina in the Italian Alps is the centre of production. **FLAVOUR PAIRINGS** Olive oil, tomatoes, Parmesan, gherkins, olives, celeriac remoulade, rocket, mozzarella, rustic bread.

▲ JAMÓN IBERICO

EAT A highly esteemed Spanish ham from black Iberian pigs, it is salted then air-dried for 1–2 years. The best comes from pigs grazed in the native oak forests, to produce wonderfully flavoured meat. Best enjoyed raw. **FLAVOUR PAIRINGS** Fino sherry (chilled), rustic bread, asparagus, scrambled eggs, baby broad beans, melon, figs, tomato and garlic bread (Pan con Tomate).

SAUSAGES

BUY There are hundreds of sausages made in the world, some fresh, some cooked and some semi-dried. Here is a selection, readily available and popular with chefs. Fresh are usually bought whole. Cooked and dried, or semi-dried are available whole or sliced. Fresh and cooked should be moist and smell pleasant. Dried may have a strong but not unpleasant smell, and the white powder on the exterior improves the flavour. **STORE** Wrap or leave in the packaging in the refrigerator. Use fresh within a few days, and cooked within a week. Dried and semi-dried will keep a long time (whole sausages don't need refrigerating; they can be hung in a cool, dry place). Fresh and cooked sausages can be frozen for up to 2 months.

THICK PORK
SAUSAGES

PORK
CHIPOLATAS

▲ PORK SAUSAGE

EAT The traditional British banger available plain, well-seasoned, with herbs, spices, or other flavourings, as either thick sausages or thinner chipolatas. They must contain at least 42 per cent pork but the higher the meat content, the better quality the sausage. They can be made of other meats, such as lamb or venison. Dry-fry, grill, barbecue, bake, casserole. **FLAVOUR PAIRINGS** Potatoes, white beans, onions, apples, sage, mustard, tomato ketchup, cider, cabbage, tomatoes, mushrooms, Yorkshire pudding.

▲ TOULOUSE SAUSAGE

EAT Made from pork shoulder and belly, this coarse-textured sausage is one of the classic ingredients of cassoulet. Casserole, grill, fry.
FLAVOUR PAIRINGS White beans, belly pork, duck confit, celery, onions, tomatoes, garlic, cloves, bay leaf, flat leaf parsley.

▲ CUMBERLAND SAUSAGE

EAT Sold in a continuous coil, Cumberland sausage has a high chopped pork content, which gives it a firm, dense, meaty texture. Fry, grill, or barbecue.
FLAVOUR PAIRINGS Mustards, tomato sauce, barbecue sauce, chilli sauce, shallots, rosemary, red wine, white beans.

▲ BEEF SAUSAGE

EAT Generally leaner than pork sausages with a drier texture. They may need extra fat when frying, then drain well before serving. They are also popular in casseroles. **FLAVOUR PAIRINGS** Onions, root vegetables, tomatoes, peppers, red beans, oregano, paprika, chilli, cumin, coriander seed and leaf, brown beer, mustard, Worcestershire sauce, barbecue sauce.

▲ SALAME DI GENOA

EAT Made from pork and veal, moistened with red wine, this garlicky, peppery air-dried sausage has a high fat content. The casing is usually pulled off before eating. Slice thinly for appetizers, in salads, scatter over pizzas, use to flavour sauces, rice dishes, stews, and pastries. **FLAVOUR PAIRINGS** Parmesan, mozzarella, rocket, spinach, tomatoes, olives, gherkins, rustic bread.

▲ CHORIZO

EAT Semi-dried and dried Spanish chorizo are generally made from pork and pork fat, spiced with smoked paprika to give either spicy (picante) or mild, sweet (dulce) flavours. The semi-dried are sliced or diced and sautéed, then often added to other dishes; the fatter, dried ones are sliced and eaten cold. **FLAVOUR PAIRINGS** Chicken, seafood, pork, mushrooms, peppers, aubergines, courgettes, pasta, white beans, chickpeas, rice, chimichurri sauce (parsley, sherry vinegar, oregano, chilli , olive oil).

▲ BLACK PUDDING

EAT Made from pig's blood, oatmeal or breadcrumbs, pork fat, onions and other flavourings, black pudding is a favourite with chefs in many dishes It is also fried as part of a British breakfast. **FLAVOUR PAIRINGS** Bacon, eggs, scallops, halibut, turbot, lamb, pork, venison, rabbit, raisins, red wine, chickpeas, white beans, lentils, potatoes.

▲ WHITE PUDDING

EAT Made of highly seasoned pork fat and oatmeal, white pudding usually contains no meat. In Scotland it is called mealie pudding and, when scooped out of the casing, skirlie. Slice or leave whole and pan-fry, or deep-fry in batter. **FLAVOUR PAIRINGS** Black pudding, tomatoes, eggs, bacon, toasted or fried bread, white beans, scallops, halibut, or other meaty fish.

▲ BOUDIN NOIR

EAT The French version of black pudding contains little or no cereal but usually has diced pork fat and sometimes meat as well as apple, onion, chestnut, or other ingredients. Usually served sliced and fried. **FLAVOUR PAIRINGS** Walnuts, pears, apples, oranges, chestnuts, cabbage, white wine, red wine, Dijon and grainy mustards.

▲ BOUDIN BLANC

EAT Made from a mixture of pork, chicken, veal, and rabbit, enriched with cream and eggs, they are sold ready-poached, but are still, usually, fried or grilled. **FLAVOUR PAIRINGS** Caramelized onions, leeks, red wine, brandy, port, tomatoes, wild mushrooms, spinach, black truffles, cream.

BUTTERFLY A LEG OF LAMB

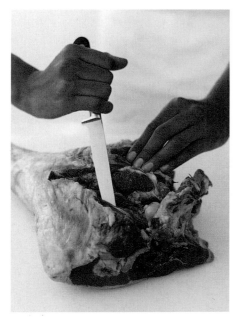

1 Place the lamb fleshiest-side down. Locate the pelvis and hold firmly, while using a sharp, long-bladed knife to cut around the leg bone.

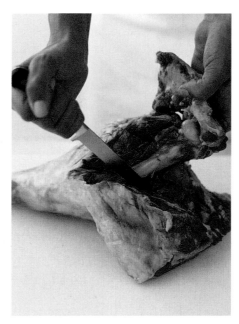

2 Cut from the pelvis to the bottom of the leg. Using short strokes (to prevent tearing), work the knife around the bone to release it.

3 Keeping close to the bone, continue using short strokes, then cut away the flesh from around the ball and socket joint and the shank.

4 Now cut through the sinew and tendons. All 3 bones (the pelvis, thigh, and shank) should come away in one piece.

5 Open out the leg so that the meat lies flat on the board. With short strokes, cut through the thick meaty pieces on either side.

6 Open out the flesh of the butterflied leg. Cut thin fillets from thicker areas and fold them over thinner parts to ensure more even cooking.

BONE A SADDLE OF LAMB

1 Using a sharp knife, cut away the membrane covering the fatty side of the saddle, then turn it over. Working from the centre, cut 2 fillets from either side of the backbone and reserve to cook alongside the saddle.

2 Loosen the outside edge of one side of the backbone using short, slicing strokes. Working from the side edge towards the centre, release the side of the backbone. Repeat with the other side.

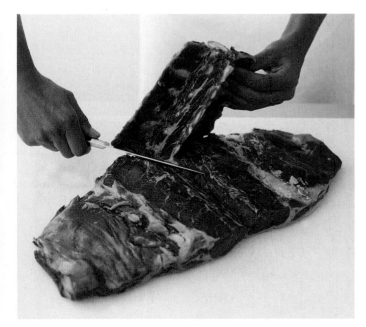

3 Starting at one end, use short, slicing strokes to cut under and around the backbone. As the bone is gradually released from the flesh, lift it away, and cut beneath it.

4 Work from the centre outwards, to cut away the meat and fat from the outer flaps. When the flaps are clean, square off the edges. Turn the saddle over, score through the fat on the other side, and cook as desired.

FRENCH TRIM A RACK OF LAMB

"Keep the bone to make your own stock. Roast it off with shallots and garlic, add some water, and then boil it up for a few hours, and you get yourself a nice little lamb stock."

DANIEL GRAHAM

1 Remove the blade bone by cutting under the skin along the edge of the cut. Then, slice horizontally from the skin, tight against the backbone, down to the ribs. Turn the cut vertically and chop the backbone away.

2 Now trim off the elastin and any flank meat. To form the "rack", expose about 5cm (2in) of the bone at the thin end of the ribs. Make a horizontal cut down to the ribs all the way across, and slice away the meat above.

3 Remove the meat between the ribs by cutting down the length of the exposed portion of rib, getting the knife tight against the bone, then cut across and slice up along the edge of the next rib.

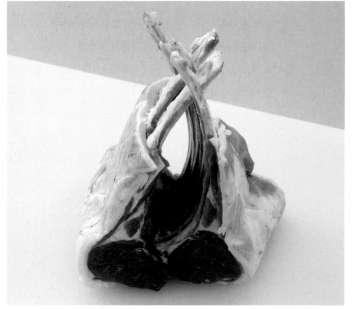

4 If serving two people, a traditional method is to form a "guard of honour" by chopping the rack in two and intersecting the bones. For four people, tie two racks of lamb together, skin-side in, to form a "crown".

TUNNEL BONE A LEG OF LAMB

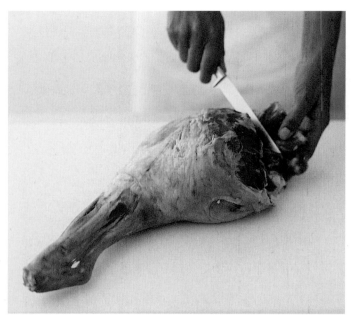

1 With the fleshiest side down, place the lamb on a board. At the top of the leg, find the pelvic bone and hold it firmly while you work around it. Use the tip of your knife close to the bone and expose it with small cuts.

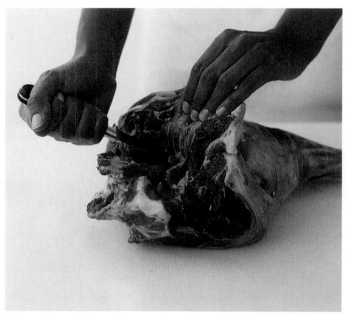

2 Once the pelvic bone is exposed, work your way inside the leg, cutting all the way down the thighbone to the bottom. Keep readjusting your hold, and turning the meat to ensure that your knife stays close to the bone.

3 When you reach the base of the thighbone at the ball and socket joint, firmly grip the thighbone. Cut through the ball and socket joint, and pull the thighbone to work it free. Repeat the process with the shank bone.

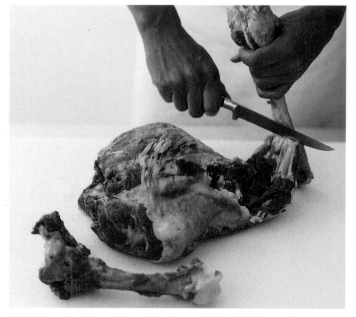

4 Pull the shank bone through to the outside of the leg so that you can access it more easily. Continue working around the bone with your knife until it comes away and the leg is entirely free of bones.

COOK STEAKS TO PERFECTION

"With any steak, you should start cooking it when it's at room temperature so it's not such a shock when it goes into the hot pan." **STEVE GROVES**

1 For a very rare steak, cook the meat for 2–3 minutes, until just seared on both sides. The steak should feel very soft when pressed, and the interior should be reddish purple when the meat is sliced.

2 To cook a rare steak, look for the point where drops of blood come to the surface, then turn the steak over and cook for a total of 6–8 minutes. It should feel soft and spongy, and the interior should be red.

3 For a medium-rare steak, cook for a total of 8–10 minutes, but turn the meat when drops of juice are first visible. The steak should offer resistance when pressed, and be pink in the centre.

4 A well done steak needs to be cooked for 12–14 minutes in total. Turn the meat when drops of juice are clearly visible. The steak should feel firm and be uniformly brown throughout.

5 Heat the grill pan (alternatively a grill or a barbecue) over a high heat. Brush both sides of the steaks with oil, and season with salt and freshly ground black pepper.

6 When the pan is very hot, place the steaks diagonally across the ridges. Cook for half the desired time, (turning 45 degrees to create the diamond pattern) then turn the steaks over. Remove them and allow to rest.

CARVE ROAST BEEF

1 Place the roast on a cutting board with the ends of the ribs facing up. Holding the meat steady with a carving fork, use a sawing action to cut downwards against the sides of the bones.

2 Remove the bones and position the meat fat-side up on the board. With a sawing action, cut downwards, across the grain of the meat, into slices of your desired thickness. Reserve the pan juices to make a gravy.

CABBAGES

BUY There are winter, spring, summer, and autumn varieties. Look for solid heads with a clean, fresh smell, and no yellowing leaves. The cut end should be moist not dry. **STORE** Keep whole heads for several weeks in plastic bags in the vegetable drawer of the refrigerator. Once cut, they deteriorate and lose nutrients. Shred, blanch, and freeze for up to 12 months.

▼ SAVOY CABBAGE

EAT The blanched outer leaves are excellent stuffed and braised. Steam, boil, braise, stir-fry. **FLAVOUR PAIRINGS** Bacon, celery, butter, onions, garlic, tomatoes, walnuts, hazelnuts. **IN SEASON** September–February (best December–February)

▲ ROUND GREEN CABBAGE

EAT Steam or boil, but best braised or finely shredded and stir-fried. **FLAVOUR PAIRINGS** Carrots, onions, celery, soy sauce, ginger, garlic, potatoes. **IN SEASON** August–May (best December–March)

▲ KOHL RABI

EAT Available green (white), or purple. Peel and cook like turnips in soups and stews, steam, or boil. **FLAVOUR PAIRINGS** Parsley sauce, star anise, ginger, garlic, tomatoes, lamb, beef, game birds. **IN SEASON** July–November

▲ WHITE CABBAGE

EAT Stir-fry, sauté, braise, shred raw for salads. Also available as coleslaw and fermented as sauerkraut. **FLAVOUR PAIRINGS** Mayonnaise, wine vinegar, mustard, caraway seeds, smoked sausages, pork, ham, carrots, onions, nuts, apples, celery. **IN SEASON** November–June (best December–February)

▲ RED CABBAGE

EAT Braise with an acid like vinegar, wine, or lemon juice to give a vibrant colour. Pickle and shred raw for winter salads. **FLAVOUR PAIRINGS** Vinegars, red wine, brown sugars, apples, pears, raisins, onions, celery, fennel seeds, bacon, ham, pork, liver. **IN SEASON** November–May (best December–February)

▲ BRUSSELS SPROUTS

EAT Steam or lightly boil whole, shred, and stir-fry, or use in salads. **FLAVOUR PAIRINGS** Melted butter, chestnuts, walnuts, hazelnuts, toasted pine nuts, sausages, crispy bacon. **IN SEASON** November–March

FLOWERING GREENS

BUY Choose tight heads with a uniform colour. Avoid any that are discoloured, damaged, or have yellowing leaves. Avoid purple sprouting broccoli with tiny yellow flowers or woody stems. **STORE** Best eaten fresh, but can be stored loosely wrapped in the vegetable drawer of the fridge for 3–4 days. Blanch and freeze florets or broccoli stems for up to 12 months.

▼ PURPLE CAULIFLOWER

EAT Also look out for orange heads. Cut in florets, best steamed to keep its colour. **FLAVOUR PAIRINGS** Béchamel sauce, tomatoes, Parmesan (or other cheeses), bacon. **IN SEASON** All year (best in Autumn)

▲ COMMON CAULIFLOWER

EAT Separate into tiny florets to eat raw for salads and crudités. Boil or steam whole or in florets, add to soup, cook, then bake in a sauce, or deep-fry in batter. **FLAVOUR PAIRINGS** Brown butter, Gruyère, blue or Cheddar cheese (crumbled or in sauce), garlic, olive oil, parsley, lemon. **IN SEASON** All year (best in Autumn)

▲ CHINESE BROCCOLI

EAT Also called Chinese kale, this sometimes has small white flowers. Stir-fry or braise. **FLAVOUR PAIRINGS** Oyster sauce, soy sauce, ginger, garlic, cashew nuts. **IN SEASON** Autumn and Spring

▲ CALABRESE

EAT Blanch tiny florets, or add raw, to salads. For larger florets, boil, steam, or cook, then bake in a sauce. Pare stalks and cut in batonettes to cook and eat, too. **FLAVOUR PAIRINGS** Bacon, anchovies, pesto, chillies, cheese or Béchamel sauce, lemon, garlic, pine nuts, olive oil. **IN SEASON** July–November, imported all year

▲ ROMANESCO

EAT Tastes like mild cauliflower. Cook in the same way. **FLAVOUR PAIRINGS** Olive oil and toasted flaked almonds (to dress), cherry tomatoes, olives, cream, Italian hard cheeses. **IN SEASON** September–November

▲ PURPLE SPROUTING BROCCOLI

EAT White also available. Steam, lightly boil, stir-fry. **FLAVOUR PAIRINGS** Leeks, tomatoes, chillies, butter, olive oil, garlic, Parmesan cheese, spring onions, citrus, Hollandaise sauce. **IN SEASON** January–April, imported in winter

LEAFY GREENS

BUY All have a sweetish flavour with varying hints of bitterness. Choose firm stalks with fresh green leaves. **STORE** Eat fresh or store, wrapped in moist paper in a plastic bag in the vegetable drawer of the refrigerator, for 2–3 days. Shred large leaves, separate stalks from leaves of chard, blanch, and freeze up to 6 months.

▲ WHITE SWISS CHARD

EAT Add young leaves to salads. Steam, braise or stir-fry larger leaves and stalks separately. The leaves can also be used as wrappers; serve the stalks like asparagus. **FLAVOUR PAIRINGS** Ham, garlic, onion, chillies, olive oil, butter, Hollandaise sauce (stalks). **IN SEASON** July–November

▲ RAINBOW CHARD

EAT Use baby leaves in salads. Stir-fry, steam, or boil larger ones like spinach. **FLAVOUR PAIRINGS** Nutmeg, spring onions, toasted almonds and pine nuts, butter, olive oil. **IN SEASON** July–November

▲ SPINACH

EAT Throw baby leaves in salads or scatter over pizzas. Spinach shrinks a great deal when cooked. Steam or wilt with no extra water, or in hot butter, stir-fry. **FLAVOUR PAIRINGS** Bacon, fish, anchovies, eggs, cheeses, yogurt, cream, butter, olive oil, garlic, onions, avocados, mushrooms, lemon, nutmeg, curry spices. **IN SEASON** All year

▲ CAVOLO NERO

EAT Widely used in Tuscan cooking. Good in braises, soups and casseroles. Lightly steam or sauté. **FLAVOUR PAIRINGS** Garlic, onions, chillies, peppers, white beans, spicy sausages, pancetta, potatoes, tomatoes, olive oil. **IN SEASON** September–March

▲ KALE

EAT Red kale is softer than green, curly kale. Blanch young leaves to add to winter salads. Boil, steam, braise, stir-fry, add to soups and stews. **FLAVOUR PAIRINGS** Bacon, ham, venison, sausages, oily fish, clams, eggs, citrus, tomatoes. **IN SEASON** September–March

▲ SPRING GREENS

EAT Boil, steam, braise, stir-fry, add to soups and stews, finely shred and deep-fry for crispy 'seaweed'. **FLAVOUR PAIRINGS** Bacon, ham, lemon, onions, potatoes, salt pork, garlic, Chinese five-spice powder. **IN SEASON** February–April

◄ MUSTARD GREENS

EAT Baby leaves add a distinctive, peppery taste to salads. Steam, stir-fry, stew, braise. **FLAVOUR PAIRINGS** Fish, seafood, ham, pork, chicken, butter, garlic, soy sauce, rice vinegar, ginger, chillies. **IN SEASON** September–March

▲ PAK CHOI (BOK CHOY)

EAT Steam or braise baby ones whole. Chop larger ones and stir-fry or add to soup. Blanch whole leaves and use as wrappers. **FLAVOUR PAIRINGS** Prawns, pork, chicken, spring onions, water chestnuts, mangetout, cashew nuts, soy sauce, oyster sauce, coriander leaves. **IN SEASON** September–March, imported all year

▲ CHINESE SPINACH

EAT Similar to European spinach, eat raw when young, steam or stir-fry older leaves. **FLAVOUR PAIRINGS** Toasted sesame seeds, star anise, mushrooms, eggs, rice, prawns, coriander leaf, chillies, ginger, garlic. **IN SEASON** June–October

▲ CHINESE LEAVES (NAPA CABBAGE)

EAT Shred raw for salads or cut in larger chunks and stir-fry, braise or ferment as Kimchi, a spicy Korean pickle. **FLAVOUR PAIRINGS** Spring onions, ginger, sambal oelek, garlic, sesame seeds, rice vinegar. **IN SEASON** September–December, imported all year

ROOT VEGETABLES

BUY All roots should be dry and fresh-smelling. Avoid any that are wet (usually over-chilled). If bought with leaves intact, they should be fresh, not wilted or discoloured. Twist them off before storing or the roots go limp. **STORE** If unwashed, no need to refrigerate (except salsify, scorzonera, and water chestnut). Store in a cool, dark place for up to a week if small, 2–3 weeks if large. If washed (and salsify, scorzonera and water chestnut), store in a paper bag in the vegetable drawer in the refrigerator for up to 1 week.

▼ CARROTS

EAT Peel maincrop, but only wash and scrub, or scrape, if necessary, young ones. Cut in batonettes for crudités, grate or shave in ribbons for salads. Steam, boil, roast, braise, sauté or stir-fry, add to soups, stews, and casseroles. Also good for cakes and muffins. **FLAVOUR PAIRINGS** Beef, citrus, ginger, celery, chervil, fennel, thyme, parsley, coriander leaf, watercress, peas, pine nuts, cumin, cinnamon, mixed spice, other roots, particularly beetroot, honey. **IN SEASON** Early young carrots, March–September; maincrop, September–February, imported all year

MAINCROP CARROT

BUNCHED CARROTS

YELLOW CARROT

CHANTENAY

PURPLE CARROT

FINGER CARROT

PURPLE SWEDE

YELLOW SWEDE

▲ SWEDE

EAT Cut in batonettes for crudités or grate in salads. Boil, steam, bake, roast, deep-fry as chips. Add to soups, stews, and casseroles. Good alternative mash (on own or with potato) for topping minced meat and fish pies. **FLAVOUR PAIRINGS** Bacon, liver, onions, carrots, cream, butter, lemon, black pepper, nutmeg, thyme. **IN SEASON** October–March, imported all year

WHITE TURNIP

PURPLE TURNIP

▲ TURNIP

EAT Scrub and cook whole if baby, or peel and cut in pieces if larger. Cut in batonettes for crudités and grate in salads. Boil, steam, roast, sauté, or stir-fry, add to soups, stews and casseroles. Good mashed with potatoes. Leaves can be cooked like other greens. **FLAVOUR PAIRINGS** Lamb, bacon, duck, goose, game, cheeses, apples, mushrooms, potatoes, sherry.
IN SEASON Winter crop, all year; baby turnips, June–July

▲ PARSNIP

EAT Peel thinly, remove any woody core from large ones. Cut in batonettes for crudités, steam, or boil, mash, deep-fry as chips or crisps, griddle slices, roast, bake, braise or sauté. Add to soups, stews, and casseroles. Good in cakes. **FLAVOUR PAIRINGS** Butter, curry powder, nutmeg, garlic, parsley, thyme, tarragon, potatoes, beef, walnuts. **IN SEASON** October–March, imported all year

▲ WATER CHESTNUT

EAT Blanch for 5 minutes then peel and slice raw in savoury and fruit salads and for crudités, stir-fry or steam in oriental dishes and, also, add to beef stews and casseroles for added crunch. Also available canned. **FLAVOUR PAIRINGS** Prawns, beef, chicken, pork, pak choi, oyster sauce, soy sauce, ginger, garlic, sesame oil. **IN SEASON** Imported all year

◄ SALSIFY

EAT Known as oyster plant because of its flavour. Peel and drop in acidulated water to prevent discolouration. Grate and use in salads. Boil (add a tablespoon of flour to the water to retain the white colour), steam, bake, roast, sauté, deep-fry, or add to soups, stews, and casseroles. **FLAVOUR PAIRINGS** Italian hard cheeses, Béchamel sauce, onions, shallots, olive oil, lemon, nutmeg, bacon. **IN SEASON** November–February, also imported

▼ SCORZONERA

EAT Known as black salsify, but is a different species. Softer and more delicate than salsify. It becomes sticky when cut, so either wear gloves or boil whole then strip off the skin (good sautéed in butter) or use as salsify. **FLAVOUR PAIRINGS** White wine, hard cheeses, cream, breadcrumbs, parsley, Parma ham. **IN SEASON** November–March (also imported)

▲ LOTUS ROOT

EAT Peel, remove the fibrous sections between the links then slice or cut in chunks. Blanch, then use in salads, or boil, steam, braise, add to soups, stews, and stir-fries. Blanched slices and seeds are also candied and can be pickled. **FLAVOUR PAIRINGS** Citrus, garlic, onion, coriander leaves, chervil, star anise. **IN SEASON** Imported all year

▲ HAMBURG PARSLEY

EAT Grate in salads, or slice for crudités. Bake, roast, braise, boil, steam, pan-fry or stir-fry, add to soups, stews, and root vegetable mixtures. **FLAVOUR PAIRINGS** Chicken, fish, game, eggs, mushrooms, carrots, potatoes, turnips. **IN SEASON** August–April, some imported

▲ CELERIAC

EAT Cut in batonettes for crudités, or shred for salads and remoulade. Put in acidulated water when preparing, to prevent discolouration. Steam, boil, braise, mash (good with potatoes), roast, deep-fry, or bake. Add to soups, stews, and casseroles. **FLAVOUR PAIRINGS** Bacon, beef, oily fish, cheeses, garlic, potatoes, parsley, dill, olive oil, mustard, tomatoes. **IN SEASON** September–March

▼ BEETROOT

EAT Grate raw for salads (good with grated carrot). Don't peel before cooking: bake, roast, boil, or steam whole, then peel. Also good pickled. Leaves can be cooked separately, like red chard. **FLAVOUR PAIRINGS** Bacon, smoked oily fish, goat's cheese, oranges, watercress, baby red chard, rocket, soured cream, nutmeg, horseradish, dill, caraway. **IN SEASON** June–February, imported all year

RED BEETROOT

YELLOW BEETROOT

STRIPED BEETROOT

▶ RADISH

EAT Add to salads and salsas. Red and white ones are good for crudités. Grate daikon as a garnish for sashimi. All can be added to soups or stews like turnip. Daikon and winter radish (not shown) can be pickled. **FLAVOUR PAIRINGS** Smoked fish, cheeses, potatoes, spring onions, chives, parsley, citrus, vinegar, chilli, star anise (in soup and stews). **IN SEASON** April–December, imported all year

CHERRY RADISH

FRENCH BREAKFAST

DAIKON

TUBERS

BUY All tubers should feel heavy for their size, and be firm with no broken skin or evidence of soft spots. Avoid any potatoes with green patches or signs of sprouting. They should all smell earthy and fresh. Choose Jerusalem artichokes with the fewest little knobs as they are easier to clean (and peel, if required). **STORE** Keep in a paper bag or closed basket in a cool (but not cold) dark place. Best used within a week.

▲ KING EDWARD POTATOES

EAT A famous British floury potato. Mash, bake, use for gnocchi or in soup, roast, purée or chip. **FLAVOUR PAIRINGS** Butter, milk, chives, rosemary, celeriac, leeks, onions, spring onions, garlic, olive oil, lemon, hard cheeses. **IN SEASON** September–October, available stored all year

▲ MARIS PIPER POTATOES

EAT A popular British fairly floury potato. Best for chips but also a good all-rounder. **FLAVOUR PAIRINGS** Butter, chives, parsley, curry spices, mayonnaise, tomato ketchup, malt vinegar, Maldon sea salt. **IN SEASON** September–October, available stored all year

▲ NICOLA POTATOES

EAT A German variety with good, waxy flesh, and a buttery flavour. Good sliced and baked in gratins, and to top meat and fish dishes. Also good for salads. **FLAVOUR PAIRINGS** Cream, crème fraîche, yogurt, garlic, nutmeg, Gruyère, Cheddar and blue cheeses, mayonnaise, French dressing, shallots, ham, bacon, pickled, salted and smoked fish. **IN SEASON** July–October, available stored all year

▲ DESIRÉE POTATOES

EAT A Dutch all-purpose variety. Bake, roast, mash, boil, add to soups and stews, deep-fry, or sauté. **FLAVOUR PAIRINGS** Cumin, Cajun spices, nutmeg, and seeds (to coat wedges), eggs, onions, mushrooms, butter, olive and nut oils. **IN SEASON** September–October, available stored all year

▲ ANYA POTATOES

EAT Long, waxy speciality salad potato, a cross between Pink Fir Apple and Desirée. Best boiled or steamed in the skin, but can be sautéed or roasted whole. **FLAVOUR PAIRINGS** Melted butter, pesto, parsley, thyme, mint, chives, olive oil, mustard, wine vinegar, shallots, grated citrus zest. **IN SEASON** May–October, imported most of the year

▲ CHARLOTTE POTATOES

EAT A high-quality French waxy speciality salad potato. Often available ready-washed. Best boiled or steamed in the skin. Good cold. **FLAVOUR PAIRINGS** Melted butter, mint, chives, parsley, mayonnaise, yogurt, olive oil, anchovies, citrus. **IN SEASON** May–October, imported most of the year

▲ JERSEY ROYAL POTATOES

EAT Famous heritage variety from the Channel Islands, eagerly awaited in the UK every spring for its distinctive rich, earthy flavour. **FLAVOUR PAIRINGS** Melted butter, mint, parsley, chives, thyme, spring onions. **IN SEASON** April–June

▲ SWEET POTATO

EAT Cook in their skins or peel first. Boil, steam, mash, bake, roast, sauté, deep-fry as chips or tempura. Also used in cakes, pastries and candied as sweetmeats. **FLAVOUR PAIRINGS** Apples, brown sugars, molasses, ginger, maple syrup, honey, citrus, chilli, nutmeg, Cajun spices, thyme. **IN SEASON** Imported all year

▲ TARO

EAT Steam, boil, sauté, deep-fry, or cook, then purée as a base for soufflés or croquettes. **FLAVOUR PAIRINGS** Sweet potatoes, chilli, star anise, cinnamon, cardamom, toasted sesame oil. **IN SEASON** Imported all year

▼ YAM

EAT Never eat raw. Peel before use (wear gloves as some types irritate the skin). Boil, steam, bake, roast, sauté or deep-fry as chips, add to meat stews.
FLAVOUR PAIRINGS Eggs, cheese, cream, curry powder, coconut, lime.
IN SEASON Imported all year

▲ CASSAVA

EAT Never eat raw. Peel then bake, boil, roast, use in stews, stir-fries or deep fry as crisps. Cassava flour is a thickening agent and made into tapioca. **FLAVOUR PAIRINGS** Butter, garlic, citrus, coriander seeds and leaves, chilli. **IN SEASON** Imported all year

▲ JICAMA

EAT Can be difficult to digest, so introduce slowly to the diet. Grate, dice, or julienne to add to savoury and fruit salads (try the Mexican way of sprinkling with lime juice and chilli powder), steam, boil, bake, stir-fry, sauté, braise, or pickle. **FLAVOUR PAIRINGS** Chilli, lime, avocado, mango, onions, tomatoes, coriander leaves. **IN SEASON** Imported all year (best autumn to spring)

◀ JERUSALEM ARTICHOKE

EAT Can be difficult for some to digest. Slice raw as crudités, grate or chop in salads (toss in lemon juice to prevent discolouration). Boil, steam, purée, use for gratins, roast, stir-fry, sauté, or deep-fry for crisps or chips. **FLAVOUR PAIRINGS** Béchamel or Hollandaise sauce, butter, cream, ginger, nutmeg, lovage, parsley, lemon, spring onions, crispy bacon, pheasant and other game.
IN SEASON October–March (best November–February)

VEGETABLE ESSENTIALS

CHOOSING VEGETABLES AT THEIR PEAK, STORING THEM WELL, AND COOKING THEM CAREFULLY WILL MAXIMIZE THEIR FLAVOUR AND BRING OUT THE BEST IN THEM.

BUY

Vegetables are the foundation of a healthy diet, and they are at their freshest, tastiest, and most nutritious when they are in season and locally grown by sustainable methods. In season, vegetables reach their flavour peak, and this is also when they are most abundant and most economical. Local farmers are likely to grow the most flavourful varieties, including heritage varieties that have been selected by generations of farmers and gardeners for their superior qualities. Local growers are often organic or sustainable, too, choosing farming methods that protect the environment and preserve the soil's natural fertility without the use of chemicals.

Good colour Buy vegetables that have bright, vibrant colours with no yellowing – especially in cauliflowers and leafy greens. There should be no bruising, discolouration, blemishes, soft spots, cuts, or pits, and no suggestion of mould growth.

Firmness The vegetable should feel firm and heavy in the hand; lighter vegetables may be drying out.

Tight skin Loose skin also indicates that the vegetable is drying out, so look for taut, firm skin.

Fresh ends To ensure freshness and the quality it implies, check the cut ends of vegetables that have been harvested from a root or mother plant. The cut should look fresh and moist, not dried out, and leaves should be glossy and mid-ribs turgid.

Smell The vegetable should have a clean, fresh smell.

STORE

Different vegetables store for varying lengths of time, depending on their type. See individual ingredients for storage times.

Delicate leafy vegetables store best wrapped loosely in a moist paper towel inside a closed plastic bag or refrigerator-storage container.

Root vegetables such as carrots and parsnips keep well in an open, plastic bag in the salad drawer of the fridge.

Vegetables such as bell peppers and cabbage store well in paper bags rolled shut and placed in the salad drawer.

Potatoes store best at room temperature in the dark.

Onions are best stored in a basket at room temperature.

Tomatoes should be kept at room temperature and will continue to ripen when placed on a windowsill.

Hard vegetables such as carrots, beans, broccoli, peas, and sweetcorn, can all be frozen. Freeze cut and prepared vegetables on the day you buy them to retain all their flavours, textures, and nutrients.

VEGETABLE COOKING CHART

| VEGETABLE | BOILING | | | STEAMING |
	TIMES (IN MINUTES)	COLD/BOILING START	COOK COVERED?	TIMES (IN MINUTES)
Artichoke bottoms	20–30	cold start	no	15–20
Artichoke whole	20–40	cold start	no	25–35
Artichoke baby	15–18	cold start	no	15–20
Asparagus	3–4	boiling start	no	4–10
Beans, green	2–8	boiling start	no	5–12
Beetroot, whole	30–60	cold start	yes	30–60
Broccoli florets	2–3	boiling start	no	5–10
Brussels sprouts	5–12	boiling start	no	10–15
Cabbage, quartered	5–15	boiling start	no	6–15
Carrots, baby	3–4	boiling start	yes	10
Carrots, sliced/diced	5–10	boiling start	yes	8–10
Cauliflower florets	2–3	boiling start	no	5–8
Celeriac, cubed/wedges	8–10	cold start	no	8–10
Corn-on-the-cob	3–4	boiling start	no	6–10
Greens, hearty, sliced	5–7	boiling start	no	10–12
Leeks, whole/halved	10–15	boiling start	no	12–15
Mangetout	2–3	boiling start	no	5–10
Peas, fresh	3–5	boiling start	no	5–10
Potatoes, boilling/new	10–25	cold start	no	15–35
Potatoes, floury, cubed	15–20	cold start	no	15–35
Spinach	1–2	boiling start	no	3–4
Squashes, summer, sliced	5–8	boiling start	no	5–10
Squashes, winter, pieces	12–15	boiling start	yes	15–30
Swede, thickly sliced	8–12	cold start	yes	10–15
Sweet potatoes, cubed	15–35	cold start	yes	30–45
Turnip, thickly sliced/cubed	8–12	cold start	yes	10–15

STEMS, SHOOTS, AND FLOWERS

BUY Stems should be firm and plump; buds of asparagus, and artichoke leaves tight shut. Cut ends should look fresh with no dry spots. Avoid any that are wilting, damaged, or discoloured. **STORE** All are best eaten fresh but can be stored in a plastic or paper bag in the vegetable box in the refrigerator; asparagus, artichokes, and cardoons up to 3 days; celery and fennel up to 2 weeks. Blanch and freeze asparagus and artichokes up to 12 months; celery and cardoons 9 months; fennel 6 months.

GREEN ASPARAGUS

◀ GREEN ASPARAGUS

EAT British is considered amongst the finest in the world. Steam, boil, griddle, roast. Eat hot or cold. Also available frozen and canned. Look out for sprue, the thinning of the early crops, which is slim and tender and often cheaper. **FLAVOUR PAIRINGS** Olive oil, butter, coarse sea salt, Parmesan or Grana Padano shavings, balsamic glaze or vinegar, Hollandaise sauce, Mornay sauce, bacon, anchovies, salmon, pesto, vinaigrette, citrus, eggs. **IN SEASON** April–June, imported all year

▲ WHITE ASPARAGUS

EAT Deprived of light as they emerge from the ground, so blanched white. Sweeter and creamier in texture than green. Best steamed or boiled and served cold. Not so popular in the UK. Also available bottled and canned. **FLAVOUR PAIRINGS** Vinaigrette, mayonnaise, garlic, quail's eggs, smoked salmon, Hollandaise sauce. **IN SEASON** May–September

ASPARAGUS SPRUE

GLOBE ARTICHOKE

BABY ARTICHOKE

◀ GLOBE ARTICHOKES

EAT Serve fresh, cooked, or preserved hearts as an antipasto or in salads, pizza toppings, risottos, or pasta dishes. Steam or boil heads and serve hot or cold with melted butter, a sauce, or dressing, or cook, then remove the centres, stuff with a savoury stuffing or salsa, then bake or serve cold. Eat baby artichokes whole, halved, or quartered, raw, grilled, roasted, deep-fried, or steamed. **FLAVOUR PAIRINGS** Vinaigrette, butter, Hollandaise sauce, herbs, cured and dried meats, anchovies, shellfish, tomatoes, chillies, mushrooms, cheeses, cream, garlic, lemon, white truffles. **IN SEASON** June–October

◀ CELERY

EAT Serve batonettes for crudités. Stuff pieces with soft cheese or pastes. Dice in sandwiches, salads, stuffings, soups, stews, and casseroles. Steam, braise, or bake hearts. **FLAVOUR PAIRINGS** Béchamel or Hollandaise sauces, cheeses, onions, cabbage, lemon, walnuts, apples, pears. **IN SEASON** September–February, imported all year

PEAR PALM HEARTS ▶

EAT Available fresh or canned. Cut in thin slices for salads and platters. Steam, stir-fry, grill, sauté, or stew. **FLAVOUR PAIRINGS** Cured and dried meats, shellfish, lime, vinaigrette, tomatoes, baby salad leaves, soy sauce, wasabi, sesame oil, ginger, avocados, tropical fruits. **IN SEASON** Imported all year

▲ FLORENCE FENNEL

EAT Slice or shred for salads. Cut in batonettes for crudités. Boil, steam, roast, braise, or griddle in quarters or thick slices. Cook baby fennel whole. **FLAVOUR PAIRINGS** Cheeses, fish and seafood, veal, chicken, dried and cured meats, citrus, preserved lemon (roasted with), Pernod, Puy lentils, herbs, mayonnaise. **IN SEASON** July–October, imported most of the year

▲ CARDOONS

EAT Use a potato peeler to pare stalks to remove strings (do the same for outer celery stalks). Cut in batonettes for crudités (good with bagna cauda, the Italian anchovy dip). Boil, steam, braise, stew, sauté, or use for soup. **FLAVOUR PAIRINGS** Veal, anchovies, olive oil, hard cheeses, butter, cream, lemon, almonds. **IN SEASON** June–September

PEAS, BEANS, AND OTHER PODS

BUY Those with edible pods should be bright green and snap easily. Those for shelling should be plump but not over-full. Swollen beans and peas will be tough and mealy textured. Choose corn cobs with moist, bright green husks and creamy yellow kernels rather than deep gold, or the sugar will already have turned to starch. **STORE** Best eaten fresh but can be kept for 1–2 days in a plastic bag in the vegetable drawer in the refrigerator. Blanch, then freeze for up to 12 months.

▲ MANGETOUT

EAT Steam or use these sweet, crisp, flat pods as crudités, in salads or stir-fries. **FLAVOUR PAIRINGS** Almonds, chicken, mushrooms, soy sauce, garlic, ginger, sherry, rice wine, Chinese five-spice powder. **IN SEASON** June–October, imported all year

▲ SUGAR SNAP PEAS

EAT Crunchy and sweet, use whole, or thickly slice for crudités and warm salads, or stir-fry or steam. **FLAVOUR PAIRINGS** Toasted sesame seeds, chillies, sesame oil, ginger, soy sauce, soft cheeses, oyster mushrooms, radishes, mint. **IN SEASON** June–October, imported all year

▲ GARDEN PEAS

EAT Raw in salads or cooked as a vegetable. Boil or steam until just tender, purée, or use for soup. Also available frozen (and canned but they lose their colour and texture). Look for pea shoots, the tender tops of the plants, to add to salads, too. **FLAVOUR PAIRINGS** Bacon, ham, fish, duck, baby onions, lettuce, mint, thyme, chervil, mushrooms. **IN SEASON** June–October

▲ BABY CORN

EAT Whole or halve as crudités, stir-fry, boil, steam, braise, slice and add to soups, stews, and casseroles. **FLAVOUR PAIRINGS** Baby vegetables, sesame oil, soy sauce, chicken, fish, duck, gammon, garlic, butter, olive oil. **IN SEASON** August–September, imported all year

▲ SWEETCORN

EAT Roast whole in the husk, or shuck first, then boil, roast, grill or barbecue. Boil, braise, bake, or sauté kernels, or add to soups and stews. Also available frozen and kernels in cans. **FLAVOUR PAIRINGS** Bacon, potatoes, butter, cheese, cream, chillies, citrus. **IN SEASON** August–September, imported all year

▲ RUNNER BEANS

EAT String and thinly slice diagonally. Boil, steam, use for pickles and chutneys. Available frozen. **FLAVOUR PAIRINGS** Bacon, mushrooms, onions, tomatoes, red wine vinegar, honey, olive oil, cashew nuts.
IN SEASON July–October, imported most of the year

▲ HELDA BEANS

EAT No need to string. Top and tail, and cut in chunks or diagonal slices. Boil, steam, stir-fry. **FLAVOUR PAIRINGS** Citrus, melted butter, walnuts, nut oils, toasted sesame seeds, tomatoes. **IN SEASON** June–October, imported all year

▲ BROAD BEANS

EAT Shell, then boil or steam, purée, or make into soup. Pop beans out of their skins before eating, if preferred. Available frozen and canned.
FLAVOUR PAIRINGS Bacon, ham, fish, lamb, chicken, game, spinach, onions, cream, Béchamel sauce. **IN SEASON** May–August

▲ FRENCH BEANS

EAT Top and tail. Cook whole or cut in short lengths. Blanch for salads, steam, or boil. Available frozen and canned. **FLAVOUR PAIRINGS** Eggs, shallots, red wine vinegar, olive oil, tomatoes, garlic, olives, oily fish, new potatoes.
IN SEASON June–October, imported all year

▲ EDAMAME BEANS

EAT Raw (if young), steam or boil. Chew the whole pod or squeeze out the fresh soya beans. Also available frozen, shelled, or whole.
FLAVOUR PAIRINGS Coarse sea salt, harissa paste, lamb, chicken, fish, soy sauce, ginger, garlic, chillies. **IN SEASON** June–September

▲ YELLOW WAX BEANS

EAT Rich buttery flavour. Top and tail, then steam or boil. **FLAVOUR PAIRINGS** Tomatoes, garlic, onions, olive oil, chorizo, mushrooms. **IN SEASON** June–November

▲ OKRA

EAT Can eat raw but usually steam, stew, or bake in a sauce, coat in batter or cornmeal, and deep-fry or stir-fry. They have a mucilaginous quality when cooked. Can be pickled. Available frozen and canned. **FLAVOUR PAIRINGS** Butter, garlic, chillies, curry spices, coconut, green peppers, tomatoes.
IN SEASON December–March, imported all year

SQUASHES, CUCUMBERS, AND CHAYOTE

BUY All these members of the gourd family should be firm, feel heavy for their size, and have unblemished skins. Choose small summer squashes – like courgettes – for best texture and flavour. The skin of winter squashes should be hard (if a thumb nail can pierce it, it won't be sweet and ripe). **STORE** Keep winter squashes in a cool dark place for up to 3 months. Keep the rest in the vegetable drawer of the refrigerator. Remove any plastic film on cucumbers first, store for up to 1 week; summer squashes up to 5 days. Wrap chayote tightly in a paper bag first, to keep for several weeks.

▲ MARROW

EAT An overgrown courgette, stuff and bake whole or in slices, roast in chunks, or steam. **FLAVOUR PAIRINGS** Sausage, mince or rice and herbs for stuffing, tomatoes, melted butter, Cheddar and Parmesan cheeses, Béchamel sauce, thyme, oregano, sage, parsley. **IN SEASON** August–October

◄ SPAGHETTI MARROW

EAT Best pricked, boiled whole then split, the fibres scooped out and dressed like spaghetti. **FLAVOUR PAIRINGS** Fresh tomato sauce, Bolognese sauce, olive oil, melted butter, Parmesan cheese, anchovies, mushrooms. **IN SEASON** August–October

▲ PUMPKIN

EAT Peel large ones before cooking. Steam or boil then purée for soups and pumpkin pie, sauté, roast or bake (small halves seeds removed). Also available canned. **FLAVOUR PAIRINGS** Blue and Cheddar cheeses, toasted pumpkin oil, butter, pumpkin seeds, walnuts, sage, rosemary, thyme, ginger, nutmeg, cinnamon, cumin, tomatoes. **IN SEASON** September–November

▲ RED ONION SQUASH

EAT Flavour reminiscent of chestnuts. Roast, add to soups or sweet dishes. **FLAVOUR PAIRINGS** Red onions, chestnuts, garlic, olive oil, butter, nigella seeds, cinnamon, nutmeg, cloves. **IN SEASON** September–December

▲ BOTTLE GOURD

EAT Peel and slice, or cut in chunks. This winter squash holds its shape well in curries and stir-fries. **FLAVOUR PAIRINGS** Coconut milk, tamarind, mustard seeds, curry leaves, cumin, coriander seed and leaf, ginger, chilli, star anise, tomatoes, onions, garlic, lentils. **IN SEASON** Imported all year

▲ BUTTERNUT

EAT Interchangeable with acorn. Halve and stuff or peel, cut in chunks and roast, steam, boil, or purée. Also good on pizzas, in pasta, risotto, and orzotto. **FLAVOUR PAIRINGS** Goat's cheese, Cheddar, Gruyère, and blue cheeses, garlic, ginger, maple syrup, honey, apples, pears, sage, thyme, rosemary, beetroot. **IN SEASON** September–December, imported all year

▲ ACORN

EAT Alternative to butternut. Halve and stuff, then bake, or peel, cut in chunks and roast, steam, boil, or purée. Try baking, filled with a herby cheese custard. **FLAVOUR PAIRINGS** Soft white cheeses, Parmesan cheese, eggs, garlic, maple syrup, honey, parsley, sage, thyme, apples, pears, quinces. **IN SEASON** September–December

▲ BITTER MELON

EAT Scoop out the seeds, blanch, then salt, and leave 30 minutes before rinsing and cooking to remove bitterness. Braise, steam or stir-fry. Also available canned. **FLAVOUR PAIRINGS** Pork, fish and shellfish, soy sauce, ginger, garlic, spring onions, black bean sauce, oyster sauce. **IN SEASON** Imported all year

▲ TURK'S TURBAN

EAT Large cavity so good eaten whole. Cut slice off top and scoop out seeds. Oil outside, wrap in foil, roast, then scoop out some flesh, mix with stuffing, stuff back in and bake. Also roast in wedges. **FLAVOUR PAIRINGS** Butter, olive oil, Cheddar and goat's cheeses, breadcrumbs, rice, onions, sage, thyme, cream, bacon, ham. **IN SEASON** September–December

◄ CROWN PRINCE

EAT Roast, then purée for soups and cakes, or as a ravioli filling. **FLAVOUR PAIRINGS** Butter, eggs, nutmeg, cinnamon, mixed spice, muscovado sugar, sage, onions, ricotta cheese. **IN SEASON** September–December

◀ COURGETTES

EAT Available as green and yellow. Flowers can be stuffed, or dipped in batter and fried. Grate or shave in ribbons for salads, cook baby ones whole, halve and stuff, then bake, or slice or cut in batonettes and steam, boil, braise, dip in batter and deep-fry, stir-fry, griddle or sauté. **FLAVOUR PAIRINGS** Olive oil, coarse sea salt, sweet peppers, aubergines, onions, garlic, tomatoes, curry spices, basil, parsley. **IN SEASON** May–October (flowers May–September), imported all year

YELLOW COURGETTE

GREEN COURGETTE

▲ PATTY PAN

EAT Bake whole (with or without stuffing), slice and steam, sauté or stir-fry. **FLAVOUR PAIRINGS** Melted butter, olive oil, garlic, cumin, coriander, thyme, basil, parsley, bacon, breadcrumbs, chick peas, hard cheeses. **IN SEASON** July–September

▼ CROOKNECK

EAT Has sweeter flesh than ordinary courgettes. Cook as for courgettes. **FLAVOUR PAIRINGS** Olive oil, butter, cream, Cheddar, Gruyère, and Parmesan cheeses, bacon, white beans, tomatoes. **IN SEASON** July–September

▲ ROUND SQUASH

EAT Steam or stir-fry small ones whole, or halve and stuff larger ones before baking. **FLAVOUR PAIRINGS** As for courgettes, or try prawns or crab and rice stuffing with dill, parsley and lemon zest. **IN SEASON** May–October

▲ RIDGE CUCUMBERS

EAT Peel, cut in batonettes for crudités, or slice or dice for salads. Steam, braise, stir-fry, or halve and stuff then bake.
FLAVOUR PAIRINGS Malt, balsamic or red wine vinegar, black pepper, fish, shellfish, cheese sauce, soy sauce, garlic, ginger, cream cheese, root vegetables, spring onions.
IN SEASON June–October (best August–September)

▲ GHERKINS (CORNICHONS)

EAT From the same species as cucumbers, usually sold ready-pickled, often flavoured with dill. Key ingredient in tartare sauce. Serve with pâtés, terrines and fish; as a nibble with drinks, and as a garnish.
FLAVOUR PAIRINGS Capers and caperberries, mayonnaise, parsley, thyme, tarragon, chervil, chicken, poultry and pig's livers, pork, salt beef, most fish.

▲ COMMON GREENHOUSE CUCUMBER

EAT Pare off evenly spaced strips of skin for an attractive finish when slicing. Best for salads, sandwiches and salsas but good grated for chilled soup.
FLAVOUR PAIRINGS Vinegars, yogurt, dill, purslane, garlic, anchovies, cream cheese, feta cheese, fennel, mint, mayonnaise, tomatoes, chillies, avocados, tropical fruits. **IN SEASON** June–October, imported all year

▲ BURPLESS SLICING CUCUMBER

EAT Reputed not to cause digestive problems, so no need to peel. Good sliced, diced or grated in salads, dips and sandwiches. **FLAVOUR PAIRINGS** Yogurt, mint, coriander leaf and seeds, toasted cumin seeds, garlic, spring onions, watercress, mayonnaise. **IN SEASON** July–October

▲ PICKLING CUCUMBER

EAT Small, solid and crisp to keep their texture when pickled. Also good eaten raw, lightly dressed with French dressing or just balsamic vinegar. **FLAVOUR PAIRINGS** Rock salt, malt, white wine, and cider vinegars, coriander seeds, yellow mustard seeds, dried chillies, allspice, ginger, black peppercorns, bay leaf, dill, white onions. **IN SEASON** July–October

▲ CHAYOTE

EAT The skin is edible on small, tender chayote, peel if larger. Steam, sauté, stir-fry, or bake (with or without stuffing), or grate for salads and salsas.
FLAVOUR PAIRINGS Fish, shellfish, rice, garlic, onion, soft and hard cheeses, chillies. **IN SEASON** Imported all year

ONIONS, SHALLOTS, LEEKS, AND GARLIC

BUY Choose firm onions and shallots with the outer papery skin intact and dry. Avoid if wet, stained, or smelling unpleasant. Leeks and spring onions should be crisp with white bases and bright green tops. Leeks should give a little when squeezed; if fat and hard, they will be tough. **STORE** Onions and shallots keep best in a vegetable rack or string bag in a cool dark place. Keep leeks and spring or salad onions in a sealed plastic bag in the vegetable drawer in the refrigerator for up to 5 days.

BROWN ONIONS ▶

EAT The workhorse of the kitchen. Use raw, fry, braise, stew, boil or roast. **FLAVOUR PAIRINGS** Bacon, liver, sausages, steak, lamb, pork, game, fish, curry spices, fresh herbs, tomatoes, all vegetables, cheeses. **IN SEASON** June–March (best June–September), imported all year

◀ WHITE ONIONS

EAT Sweet mild flavour. Good for dishes where onions not fried first, like white stews, risottos, and sauces. Ideal for batter-dipped fried onion rings, too. **FLAVOUR PAIRINGS** Tempura batter, beer batter, veal, chicken, lamb, sage, parsley, thyme, risotto rice, white beans, white wine, spinach, tomatoes. **IN SEASON** June–March (best June –September), imported all year

RED ONIONS ▶

EAT Sweet mild flavour. Use in salads and salsas, roast, or caramelize for marmalade. **FLAVOUR PAIRINGS** Fresh and sun-dried tomatoes, peppers, aubergines, squashes, avocados, bacon, lentils, chick peas, cheeses, oily fish, basil, thyme, bay leaf. **IN SEASON** June–March (best June–September), imported all year

▲ BANANA SHALLOT

EAT Grate or finely chop to add a sweet, subtle flavour to stews, casseroles, braises and soups, or halve and roast. **FLAVOUR PAIRINGS** Butter, balsamic vinegar, white balsamic condiment, red wine, white wine, cream, wild mushrooms, sorrel, thyme, parsley, mussels and other fish and seafood, chicken. **IN SEASON** September–March

▲ WHITE SALAD ONIONS

EAT Mild and sweet, slice or chop for salads, trim and use whole, cooked, or pickled. Use the green tops for garnish. **FLAVOUR PAIRINGS** Cream cheese, cottage cheese, soured cream, crème fraîche, yogurt, radishes, cherry tomatoes, chicken, fish, shellfish. **IN SEASON** March–September (best April–August)

▲ PICKLING/PEARL ONIONS

EAT Mild sweet flavour best for pickling, but also to cook whole in white sauce, and in classic casseroles and stews. **FLAVOUR PAIRINGS** Malt, white or balsamic vinegars, coriander seeds, yellow mustard seeds, dried chillies, black peppercorns, bay leaf, milk, cream, red and white wine, beef, lardons, chicken, pork, lamb, game, fish, peas, cheese, ham. **IN SEASON** June–March (best June–September)

▲ SPRING ONIONS

EAT Chop or slice in salads, salsas, omelettes, stir-fries, and Thai curries. Finely chop and add to mashed potato. **FLAVOUR PAIRINGS** Thai red and green curry pastes, galangal, lemon grass, nam pla, eggs, potatoes, meat, chicken, fish, most cheese. **IN SEASON** March–September (best April–August), imported all year

ROUND SHALLOT ▶

EAT Use as banana or grey shallots, or can be pickled. Try them finely chopped or sliced with cheese and sage in toasted sandwiches. **FLAVOUR PAIRINGS** Malt or balsamic vinegars, coriander seeds, yellow mustard seeds, black peppercorns, cinnamon sticks, chillies, bay leaf. **IN SEASON** September–March

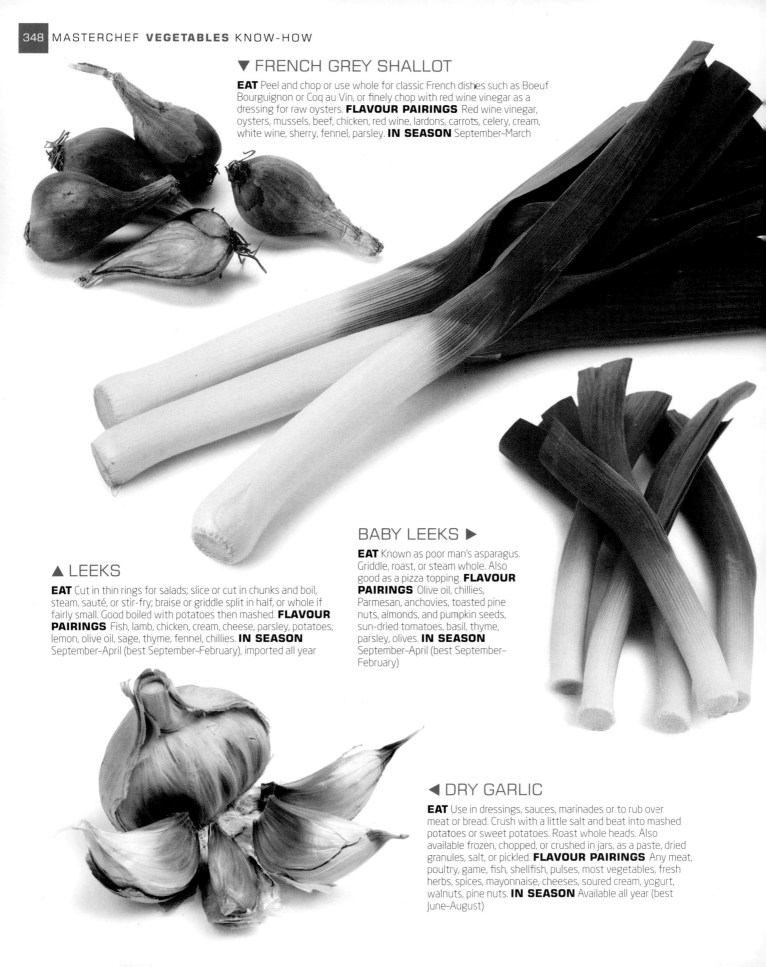

▼ FRENCH GREY SHALLOT

EAT Peel and chop or use whole for classic French dishes such as Boeuf Bourguignon or Coq au Vin, or finely chop with red wine vinegar as a dressing for raw oysters. **FLAVOUR PAIRINGS** Red wine vinegar, oysters, mussels, beef, chicken, red wine, lardons, carrots, celery, cream, white wine, sherry, fennel, parsley. **IN SEASON** September–March

▲ LEEKS

EAT Cut in thin rings for salads; slice or cut in chunks and boil, steam, sauté, or stir-fry; braise or griddle split in half, or whole if fairly small. Good boiled with potatoes then mashed. **FLAVOUR PAIRINGS** Fish, lamb, chicken, cream, cheese, parsley, potatoes, lemon, olive oil, sage, thyme, fennel, chillies. **IN SEASON** September–April (best September–February), imported all year

BABY LEEKS ▶

EAT Known as poor man's asparagus. Griddle, roast, or steam whole. Also good as a pizza topping. **FLAVOUR PAIRINGS** Olive oil, chillies, Parmesan, anchovies, toasted pine nuts, almonds, and pumpkin seeds, sun-dried tomatoes, basil, thyme, parsley, olives. **IN SEASON** September–April (best September–February)

◀ DRY GARLIC

EAT Use in dressings, sauces, marinades or to rub over meat or bread. Crush with a little salt and beat into mashed potatoes or sweet potatoes. Roast whole heads. Also available frozen, chopped, or crushed in jars, as a paste, dried granules, salt, or pickled. **FLAVOUR PAIRINGS** Any meat, poultry, game, fish, shellfish, pulses, most vegetables, fresh herbs, spices, mayonnaise, cheeses, soured cream, yogurt, walnuts, pine nuts. **IN SEASON** Available all year (best June–August)

▼ GREEN GARLIC

EAT Also known as "wet" garlic. Mildly garlicky. Chop or crush and use like spring onions to flavour dips and marinades. Delicious rubbed on rustic bread with beefsteak tomatoes for Pan con Tomate. **FLAVOUR PAIRINGS** tomatoes, soft cheeses, mayonnaise, yogurt, crème fraîche, soured cream, olives, basil, pine nuts, white wine, white balsamic condiment, olive oil, fresh chillies. **IN SEASON** May–September

▲ ELEPHANT GARLIC

EAT Not a true garlic, but related to the leek. It has very large cloves but a surprisingly mild flavour. Use as onions or slice, rub with oil and grill, or roast the cloves whole, pop out of their skins, drizzle with olive oil, sprinkle with coarse sea salt then mash and serve with rustic bread. **FLAVOUR PAIRINGS** Olive oil, coarse sea salt, Butter, wine, cream, mushrooms, thyme, parsley. **IN SEASON** Available all year

▲ RAMSONS (RAMPIONS)

EAT Also called wild garlic and bear's garlic, it gives off a strong garlic smell when crushed. The leaves make a delicious green soup (with potato), an excellent pesto, and are also good in sandwiches, salads, and stir-fries. The flowers can be eaten too. **FLAVOUR PAIRINGS** Olive oil, pine nuts, Parmesan, parsley, thyme, potatoes, onions, sorrel, rocket, tomatoes, water chestnuts, beansprouts, soy sauce, ginger. **IN SEASON** April–June

TREE ONION (EGYPTIAN ONION) ▶

EAT The little bulblets grow at the top of a tall stem, hence their name. They are surprisingly pungent. Good in soups, sautéed, and added to casseroles, used sparingly in salsas and salads, and for pickling. **FLAVOUR PAIRINGS** Beef, chicken, game, cheeses, celery, bay leaf, sage, parsley, pickling spices, malt and red wine vinegar. **IN SEASON** March–October

VEGETABLE FRUITS

BUY Choose unblemished fruits with glossy, firm skin. Avocados should give slightly when gently squeezed in the palm of the hand. **STORE** Aubergines are best eaten fresh but can be stored in a cool dark place for 1–2 days. Ripen green breadfruit in a cool, dark place for 7–10 days. Leave unripe avocados on the windowsill to soften, then store in the fridge for 2–3 days. Tomatoes should be kept in a fruit bowl, not the refrigerator, unless overripe. Peppers and chillies will keep in a paper bag in the refrigerator for up to 2 weeks.

◀ CHERRY TOMATOES

EAT Whole or halved in salads, or as a snack, or lightly crush, stew in olive oil and use as a pizza topping. Also available bottled and semi-dried. **FLAVOUR PAIRINGS** Salad leaves, cucumber, celery, olives, pumpkin and sunflower seeds, red onions, basil, oregano, olive oil, balsamic vinegar, goat's cheese, mozzarella balls, rocket. **IN SEASON** July–October, imported all year

▲ STANDARD GLOBE TOMATOES

EAT Classic fruit that come in green and yellow as well as red varieties. Grill, fry, bake, poach, add to soups, stews and curries, or quarter or slice for salads. Also available dried, as ketchup and sauce. **FLAVOUR PAIRINGS** Bacon, eggs, fish, mushrooms, cheese, parsley, thyme, oregano, sage, cinnamon, garlic, onions, chillies, Thai red curry paste, coconut milk. **IN SEASON** July–October, imported all year

▲ PLUM TOMATOES

EAT Best tomato for sauces and soup, but also keeps its shape well when sliced for grilling or roasting. Use baby ones with pasta. **FLAVOUR PAIRINGS** Basil, oregano, bay, chervil, onions, garlic, bacon, olive oil, orange, celery salt. **IN SEASON** July–October, imported all year

BEEFSTEAK TOMATOES ▶

EAT Slicing tomatoes, but also good to roast, bake (with or without stuffing), sauté, or stew. Also rub on rustic bread with green garlic for the classic Pan con Tomate. **FLAVOUR PAIRINGS** Mozzarella, Parmesan, eggs (bake inside), olives, anchovies, pesto, pine nuts, almonds, rustic bread, green garlic, peppers, courgettes, aubergines, avocados, basil, oregano, marjoram, chervil. **IN SEASON** July–October, imported all year

FUERTE AVOCADO

HASS AVOCADO

▲ AVOCADO

EAT Hass has black skin when ripe and creamy flesh for mashing. Green Fuerte is better for slicing. Best eaten raw but can be made into soup or baked. Slice for sandwiches, mash for guacamole, mix with sugar and cream to make ice cream. Add acid like lemon or lime juice to prevent discolouration.
FLAVOUR PAIRINGS Parma ham, mozzarella, bacon, prawns, tomatoes, spinach, grapefruit, lime, mango, lemon, pineapple, sugar, balsamic vinegar, chillies. **IN SEASON** Imported all year

OVAL DEEP PURPLE AUBERGINE

ITALIAN LONG WHITE AUBERGINE

ITALIAN STRIPED AUBERGINE

ITALIAN ROUND AUBERGINE

▲ AUBERGINE

EAT The most common are large purple ones, but there are also white, stripy and round Italian ones. Slice large ones and griddle, or dip in batter and deep-fry. Dice and pan-fry or stew, or roast whole then purée with spices. Baby purple ones also available to cook whole or split – ideal for curries. **FLAVOUR PAIRINGS** Ham, lamb, beef, mozzarella, feta, hard cheeses, garlic, mushrooms, tomatoes, sweet peppers, lemon, oregano, mint, thyme, chillies, olive oil, cinnamon, curry spices.
IN SEASON June–October, imported all year

YELLOW BELL
PEPPER

RED BELL
PEPPER

GREEN BELL
PEPPER

▲ BELL PEPPERS

EAT Available in varying colours from green through to red. Eat raw, cut into batonettes as crudités, or add to salads. Stuff and bake, roast, griddle, barbecue, stew, sauté, stir-fry, or coat in batter and deep-fry. **FLAVOUR PAIRINGS** Chicken, lamb, beef, pork, anchovies, garlic, onions, sweetcorn, tomatoes, olives, capers, cheese, rosemary, oregano. **IN SEASON** July–October, imported all year

▲ ROMANO PEPPERS

EAT Yellow ones also available. Grill or roast with or without stuffing. **FLAVOUR PAIRINGS** Chorizo and other spicy sausages, soft cheeses, chilli, garlic, basil, parsley, chives, capers. **IN SEASON** July–October, imported all year

◀ PIMENTOS DE PADRÓN

EAT Tiny green peppers from Spain. Most are mild and fruity, one in about 30 is fiery. Sauté in olive oil as a tapas. **FLAVOUR PAIRINGS** Olive oil, sea salt, crusty bread. **IN SEASON** July–November

◀ SCOTCH BONNET CHILLI

EAT Crinkly, rounded chillies in a variety of colours. EXTREMELY HOT. Used in many Caribbean hot sauces and Jerk seasoning. **FLAVOUR PAIRINGS** Chicken, beef, pumpkin and other squashes, potatoes, sweet potatoes, yam, spring onions, garlic, spinach, allspice, bay, coconut milk, lime. **IN SEASON** July–November, imported all year

JALAPEÑO CHILLI ▶

EAT Often sliced and used as a condiment or a pizza topping. Also available pickled. Can be stuffed. MODERATELY HOT. **FLAVOUR PAIRINGS** Beef, spicy sausages, noodles, sweet peppers, courgettes, aubergines, peanuts, cashews, tomatoes, mozzarella, cream cheese, sheep's cheese. **IN SEASON** July–November, imported all year

◀ THAI (BIRDSEYE) CHILLIES

EAT Used fresh and dried, these thin little chillies are red or green. Add to curries and stir-fries or chop for pastes and dips. VERY HOT. **FLAVOUR PAIRINGS** Most spices, coriander leaf, bay leaf, coconut milk, lime, Nam Pla, palm sugar, galangal, spring onions, chicken, beef, pork, lamb, fish. **IN SEASON** July–November, imported all year

▲ HUNGARIAN HOT WAX CHILLI

EAT Fleshy long chilli that can be chopped, sliced or stuffed. Use in salads, stir-fries, braises and pickles. MODERATELY HOT. **FLAVOUR PAIRINGS** Beef, pork, lamb, chicken, seafood, cream cheese, hard cheese, thyme, sage, tomatoes. **IN SEASON** July–November, imported all year

▲ SERRANO CHILLI

EAT Mexican chilli can be stuffed but is often sliced or chopped and used in salsas and soups along with dried chillies. MODERATELY HOT. **FLAVOUR PAIRINGS** Sweet peppers, potatoes, onions, garlic, dried chipotle chillies, avocado, tomatoes, coriander leaf, prawns, steak. **IN SEASON** July–November, imported all year

MUSHROOMS AND TRUFFLES

BUY The mushroom season lasts from late summer to early winter, but some varieties, such as Morel, appear in spring. Many species are now cultivated. If foraging for wild mushrooms, do not eat any unless you are sure they are edible – they can be delicious or deadly! All mushrooms should be fresh and dry, not damaged or slimy. They should smell earthy and sweet.
STORE Keep in the refrigerator in a closed paper bag (never plastic) for up to a week. They dry well and can then be stored for months. Reconstitute by soaking in warm water. Some also available frozen.

▲ CULTIVATED WHITE BUTTON

EAT Buttons become closed cup mushrooms as they grow. Use raw in salads and as crudités. Chop, slice, halve, or quarter to add soups, stews, casseroles, sauces, pasta, and rice dishes. Also available sliced dried and frozen. **FLAVOUR PAIRINGS** Onions, garlic, tomatoes, coriander seeds and leaf, parsley, oregano, lemon, cream, crème fraîche, yogurt, white wine, sherry, steaks, chicken. **IN SEASON** Cultivated all year

▲ BROWN CRIMINI OR CHESTNUT

EAT Young Portabello mushrooms. Meaty, with nutty flavour. Slice raw for salads, sauté, or stir-fry. **FLAVOUR PAIRINGS** Oregano, parsley, marjoram, chives, parsley, coriander leaf and seeds, curry spices, Thai spices, red wine, garlic, bacon, onions. **IN SEASON** Cultivated all year

▲ ENOKI

EAT Cultivated in clumps they have a crisp texture and mild flavour. Good in soups and stir-fries, or raw in salads and sandwiches. **FLAVOUR PAIRINGS** Chicken, prawns, crab, chicken and fish broth, cucumber, celery, carrot, soy sauce, garlic, beansprouts, peppers. **IN SEASON** Cultivated all year

▲ OPEN CUP OR FLAT

EAT Full-grown button mushrooms. They have a firm texture and earthy flavour. Grill, pan-fry, stuff, or bake. **FLAVOUR PAIRINGS** Garlic, cream, white wine, herb stuffings, cheese, pâté, bacon, eggs, parsley. **IN SEASON** Cultivated all year

▲ PORTABELLO

EAT Large, flat, meaty mushrooms. Cook whole, chopped, or sliced. Fry, bake (with or without stuffing), or grill. **FLAVOUR PAIRINGS** Butter, garlic, cream, fresh herbs, white or rosé wine, halloumi and soft cheeses, cider, tomatoes, spring onions. **IN SEASON** Cultivated all year

▲ MOREL

EAT One of the most sought after wild mushrooms. Never eat raw. Often sold dried. Best sautéed. **FLAVOUR PAIRINGS** Butter, olive oil, garlic, asparagus, leeks, cream, white wine, brandy, eggs, chicken, beef, veal, halibut, turbot, monkfish. **IN SEASON** April–May

▲ CHANTERELLE/GIROLLE

EAT Highly acclaimed with a nutty, fruity flavour. Best sautéed. Good in sauces. Also available dried. **FLAVOUR PAIRINGS** Other mushrooms, beef, chicken, fish, seafood, shallots, red wine, sherry, brandy, tomatoes, cheese, ginger, soy sauce, peppers. **IN SEASON** June–January

▲ CEP/PORCINI

EAT Highly revered by chefs. Slice and sauté or add to risottos and pasta dishes. Also available dried. **FLAVOUR PAIRINGS** Risotto rice, pasta, cream, brandy, white wine, leeks, onions, garlic, Parma ham, Parmesan, truffle oil, beef, chicken, game, scallops. **IN SEASON** September–November

▲ OYSTER

EAT Young ones are tender and mild with a slight aniseed flavour. Use in stir-fries and soups. **FLAVOUR PAIRINGS** Eggs, chicken, fish or vegetable broth, noodles, beef, chicken, pork, prawns, crab, spring onions, Chinese five-spice powder, soy sauce, rice wine vinegar. **IN SEASON** Cultivated all year

▲ SHIITAKE

EAT Originally from Japan, with a chewy, meaty texture and good flavour. Stir-fry or add to soups, stews and casseroles. Also available dried. **FLAVOUR PAIRINGS** Pork, chicken, beef, prawns, noodles, rice, soy sauce, ginger, garlic, spring onions, bamboo shoots, water chestnuts, beansprouts, chillies, rice wine, oyster sauce. **IN SEASON** Cultivated all year

▲ WOOD BLEWIT (PIED BLEU)

EAT Faint aniseed smell. Do not eat raw. Good with other mushrooms in soups, stroganoff, risottos, tarts and with pasta. **FLAVOUR PAIRINGS** Cream, crème fraîche, brandy, white wine, rice, pearl barley, lasagne, Italian hard cheeses, thyme, parsley, marjoram. **IN SEASON** September–November, cultivated all year

▲ FIELD

EAT The most common wild mushroom with excellent flavour, especially when mature. Fry or grill. **FLAVOUR PAIRINGS** Bacon, eggs, sausages, steak, venison, risotto rice, cream, crème fraîche. **IN SEASON** September–November

▲ WHITE (ALBA) TRUFFLES

EAT The best are from Piedmont, Italy, with complex earthy aromas and flavours. Grate or shave over hot foods. Also available dried and as flavoured oil. **FLAVOUR PAIRINGS** Eggs, risotto rice, pasta, game birds, scallops, halibut, monkfish, foie gras, potatoes, olive oil, garlic, Parmesan. **IN SEASON** November–February

▲ BLACK (PERIGORD) TRUFFFLES

EAT Delicate fragrance of woodland and chocolate. Shave or grate over hot foods. Also available dried, and as flavoured oil. **FLAVOUR PAIRINGS** Spaghetti, chicken, rabbit, game birds, celeriac, meaty white fish, shellfish, pancetta. **IN SEASON** November–March

SALAD LEAVES

BUY There is an astounding variety of tasty leaves available with overlapping seasons, so there is always a supply of one kind or another to enjoy. Choose fresh-looking leaves with firm hearts, if relevant. Avoid if wilting or bruised. **STORE** Whole heads will keep in the vegetable box in the fridge for a week or more, unwashed leaves will keep in a plastic bag for several days but ready-washed deteriorate more quickly.

WITLOOF CHICORY ▶

EAT Cut a cone shape out of base with a pointed knife to remove bitter core. Add raw to salads or use whole leaves as crudités or vessels for pastes, salsas, nut butters or cream cheese. Stir-fry, grill, braise or bake in gratins. **FLAVOUR PAIRINGS** Bacon, ham, prosciutto crudo, blue, and Cheddar cheeses, nuts, garlic, watercress, olive oil, tomato salsa. **IN SEASON** October–April, imported all year

◀ RADICCHIO

EAT Another variety of chicory. Tear the leaves and add to salads, braise, grill, or add to risottos or pasta dishes. **FLAVOUR PAIRINGS** Pancetta, hazelnuts, walnuts, pine nuts, pumpkin seeds, Italian hard cheeses, ricotta or feta cheese, balsamic vinegar, preserved lemons, anchovies. **IN SEASON** September–March

▲ CURLY ENDIVE (FRISÉE)

EAT The classic for Bistro salad. Tear, rather than cut in pieces. Can be stir-fried too. **FLAVOUR PAIRINGS** Olive oil, croûtons, smoked lardons, red onions, parsley, coriander leaf, chillies, Worcestershire sauce, poached or soft-boiled eggs. **IN SEASON** June–September

▲ ESCAROLE (BATAVIA)

EAT Less bitter than curly endive, usually served in salads. **FLAVOUR PAIRINGS** Balsamic vinegar, fruit vinegars, olive oil, toasted nut and seed oils, mustard, croûtons, eggs, anchovies, avocado, pomegranate, raisins. **IN SEASON** June–September

◀ BUTTERHEAD LETTUCE

EAT Use leaves as soft wrappers for cold mixtures of seafood or avocado. Braise, steam or shred and cook with other vegetables like peas and onions. Tear, don't cut, leaves for salad. **FLAVOUR PAIRINGS** Peas, baby onions, anchovies, cheese, mayonnaise, olive oil, lemon juice, mustard, garlic. **IN SEASON** All year

COS (ROMAINE) ▶

EAT Succulent leaves ideal for burgers, salads, sandwiches and wraps. The classic lettuce for Caesar salad. **FLAVOUR PAIRINGS** Anchovies, eggs, croutons, garlic, Parmesan, chicken, onions, citrus, herbs, honey, mustard. **IN SEASON** June–September, imported all year

◀ RED OAK

EAT Thin soft leaves and crunchy stalks used in typical mesclun mix of leaves and shoots. **FLAVOUR PAIRINGS** Rocket, chicory, chervil, dandelion, purslane, olives, tomatoes, red onions, artichokes, avocado, beetroot, carrots, olive oil, citrus, fruit and wine vinegars. **IN SEASON** April–September

ICEBERG ▶

EAT Crisp but bland. Shred for sandwiches or add to burgers. Braise or blanch, and stuff with meat, fish, chicken or vegetable mixtures, then steam. Use leaves as vessels for mayonnaise-dressed salad mixes. **FLAVOUR PAIRINGS** Seafood, Russian salad, rice or pasta salads, minced chicken, pork, veal or liver, soy sauce, ginger, garlic. **IN SEASON** June–September, imported all year

▲ LITTLE GEM

EAT Sweet baby cos variety, excellent in salads and sandwiches, or halve or quarter, then braise or steam. Use whole leaves as vessels. **FLAVOUR PAIRINGS** Mushrooms, spring onions, garlic, peas, bacon, Italian hard cheeses, tabbouleh, walnuts. **IN SEASON** April–September, imported all year

▲ LOLLO ROSSO

EAT Good for adding contrasting texture and colour to mixed salads. **FLAVOUR PAIRINGS** Pears, apples, pomegranate, blueberries, green salad leaves, cheese, walnuts, toasted pine nuts, pumpkin seeds, olive oil, toasted nut oils, citrus, wine, sherry and cider vinegars, chorizo, salami. **IN SEASON** April–September

▲ ROCKET

EAT Peppery, slightly bitter flavour. Excellent in salads, purée for pesto, add to frittatas, or scatter over pizzas just before serving. **FLAVOUR PAIRINGS** Pine nuts, almonds, olive oil, citrus, garlic, hard and blue cheeses, tomatoes, onions, eggs, potatoes, thyme, basil, rosemary, oregano, lamb's lettuce, watercress. **IN SEASON** All year (best May–October)

◄ DANDELION

EAT Use only young plants. Add leaves to salads or wilt with a hot dressing. Boil, steam, braise, or stir-fry. Roots can be sliced and eaten raw, or baked or roasted whole. Buds that are still inside the crown can be added to pancakes, omelettes, fritters, and frittatas. **FLAVOUR PAIRINGS** Bacon, cheese, garlic, onion, lemon, mustard, olive oil, wine or balsamic vinegar. **IN SEASON** March–May

◄ MIZUNA

EAT Often mixed with other salad leaves, good in sandwiches, as a bed for seafood, with sautéed meats or chicken livers, and as a garnish. Steam or stir-fry briefly, then toss in noodle dishes. **FLAVOUR PAIRINGS** Pork, chicken livers, fish, shellfish, ginger, lemon, sesame oil, olive oil, toasted seeds, tamari. **IN SEASON** All year (best September–May)

LAMB'S LETTUCE (CORN SALAD) ►

EAT . Excellent in warm or cold mixed salads or thrown into sautés at the last minute so it just wilts. **FLAVOUR PAIRINGS** Onions, croûtons, sweetcorn, honey, mustard, cherry tomatoes, toasted seeds, pears, avocados, lardons. **IN SEASON** May–November

▲ WATERCRESS

EAT Use in salads, sandwiches, and as a garnish. Stir-fry or use for soups and sauces. **FLAVOUR PAIRINGS** Cucumber, beetroot, goat's cheese, eggs, salmon, other oily fish, chicken, duck, oranges, potatoes. **IN SEASON** All year

PURSLANE ►

EAT The fleshy leaves are slightly mucilaginous and can be used to thicken soups and stews in the same way as okra. Add leaves to salads, stir-fries, soups, and stews. Pickle in salt and white wine vinegar. The flowers are good in salads and for garnishing. **FLAVOUR PAIRINGS** Beetroot, broad beans, cucumber, spinach, potatoes, tomatoes, eggs, feta cheese, yogurt. **IN SEASON** May–October

◄ SALAD CRESS

EAT The sprouting leaves of cress seeds. Add to salads, sandwiches, and use as a garnish. **FLAVOUR PAIRINGS** Eggs, salmon, sardines, tuna, Cheddar cheese, cream cheese, tomatoes, cucumber. **IN SEASON** All year

PEEL AND DICE AN ONION

1 Using a sharp chef's knife, hold the onion firmly in one hand, then cut the bulb lengthways in half and peel off the skin, leaving the root intact to hold the layers together.

2 Lay one half cut-side down on the board. Hold it in place while you make a few slices into the onion horizontally, making sure that you cut up to, but not through, the root.

3 Hold the horizontally sliced onion firmly, then with the forward tip of your knife, slice down through the layers vertically, cutting as close to the root as possible. Repeat, slicing at regular intervals.

4 Now, cut across the vertical slices that you have just made, to produce an even dice. Use the root to hold the onion steady, then discard this part when the rest of the onion has been diced.

WASH AND CUT LEEKS JULIENNE

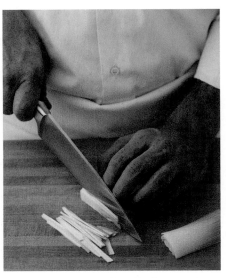

1 With a sharp knife, trim off the root end and some of the dark, green leaf top. Cut the leek in half lengthways and spread the layers apart.

2 Rinse the leek under cold running water to remove the soil that tends to collect between the layers, then pat it dry with kitchen paper.

3 Lay the halved leek flat-side down on the chopping board and slice it into thick or thin strips, according to the recipe.

PEEL AND CHOP GARLIC

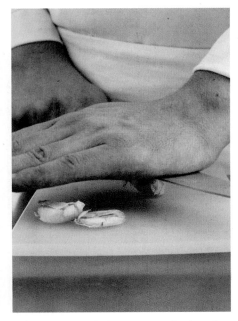

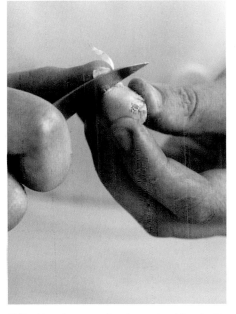

1 Place each garlic clove on a cutting board. Cover with the flat side of a large knife and pound with the palm of your hand.

2 Pushing down on the cloves should make it easier to peel away the papery skin. Discard this, then cut off the ends of each clove.

3 Slice the clove into slivers lengthways, then cut across into tiny chunks. Collect the pieces into a pile and chop again for finer pieces.

SKIN AND DESEED TOMATOES

1 Hold the tomato steady in one hand, while you use a sharp knife to score an "X" through its skin at the base.

2 Completely immerse the tomato in boiling water for around 20 seconds, or until you can see the skin begin to split.

3 Remove the tomato from the boiling water with a slotted spoon and immediately plunge it into iced water to cool it.

4 When the tomato is cool enough to handle, use a paring knife to peel off the skin, starting at the base where you made the "X".

5 Slice the tomato in half, then gently squeeze it in your hand to force the seeds out over a bowl and discard them.

6 Place the now seedless tomato on a board and hold it frmly with one hand while you slice it first into strips and then into dice.

PEEL AND CUT INTO JULIENNE

1 Hold the vegetable firmly in one hand while you peel it thinly using a vegetable peeler or small paring knife. If you are peeling beetroot, you may wish to wear rubber gloves to prevent staining your hands.

2 Place the peeled vegetable on a clean board and hold it steady while you use a chef's knife to trim the sides. Do this as evenly as possible, to form a square shape.

3 Holding the trimmed block gently but firmly, cut it into equal slices of the thickness of 3mm (⅛in) for julienne vegetables, and 5mm (¼in) if you are preparing batonettes.

4 Stack the vegetable slices, just a few at a time to avoid them sliding about, and cut each batch into neat, square-edged batonettes that are the same thickness as the slices.

CUT COURGETTE BATONETTES

1 Place the courgette on a board and cut off both ends. Cut it in half lengthways, then hold the courgette firmly on its side and cut each half again to make slices 5mm (¼in) thick.

2 Now put each slice of courgette flat on the board and cut across it with a sharp chef's knife to make equal-sized batonettes, or sticks with an approximate width of 5mm (¼in).

CUT CARROT BATONETTES

1 Cut each carrot in half crossways. Set a mandolin blade to a 5mm (¼in) thickness and hold it steady. Press the carrot with the other hand (keeping your fingers clear) Slice up and down until the slices are uniform.

2 Stack the carrot slices and neaten them by by cutting the rounded sides away with a sharp knife to achieve a rectangular shape. Then cut the stacked carrot slices lengthways to make strips of equal width.

PREPARE ASPARAGUS

 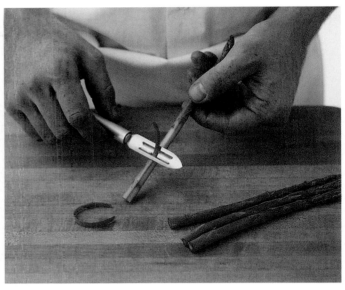

1 With a sharp chef's knife, cut the hard ends from the asparagus spears. If the ends are woody, bend them with your finger until they snap off (they will break at the point where they become more fibrous).

2 To ensure that the asparagus is really tender, hold the tip of the spear very carefully so that you do not bruise it, then use a vegetable peeler to peel off a thin layer of skin from all sides of the stalk.

REMOVE SWEETCORN KERNELS

1 Remove the husks and all the silk thread from the corn-on-the-cob. Rinse the husked corn under cold running water.

2 Place the blunt end on the cutting board. Use a sharp chef's knife and slice straight down the cob. Rotate the cob and repeat.

3 To extract the "milk", hold the cob upright in a bowl and use your knife to scrape down the side. Turn the corn and repeat.

TURN VEGETABLES

1 If necessary, peel the vegetables first, then using a sharp knife, cut them into pieces that are 5cm (2in) long.

2 Now, holding a vegetable piece between your thumb and forefinger, begin slicing off the sides to create a curve.

3 Keep turning the vegetable piece in your hand as you cut. The aim is to create a rugby ball shape with 7 curved sides.

PREPARE A MIREPOIX

1 For stocks and some braised dishes, cut an onion lengthways into quarters, and celery, carrots, and leeks into 5cm (2in) chunks.

2 Braised dishes and stews require smaller chunks, so cut the onion, celery, carrots and leeks into a 2cm (¾in) dice.

3 For dishes with a short cooking time, cut the celery, carrot, and leek into a 5mm (¼in) dice. Dice the onion using the crosshatch method.

CORE AND SHRED CABBAGE

1 Hold the head of the cabbage firmly on the cutting board and use a sharp knife to cut it in half, straight through the stalk end.

2 Cut the halves again through the stalk lengthways, and slice out the core (which will be tough) from each quarter.

3 Working with each quarter at a time, place the wedge cut-side down. Cut across the cabbage, creating broad or fine shreds.

TRIM, WASH, AND DRY SALAD LEAVES

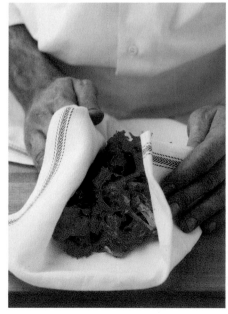

1 Trim the ends of the leaves and discard any discoloured ones. If any of the leaves are tough, cut out the stalk from each one.

2 Place the salad leaves in a colander and rinse under running water or immerse in cool water. Shake them gently to loosen any dirt.

3 Drain the leaves, then gently pat dry with a clean tea towel or kitchen paper. Alternatively, use a salad spinner to remove excess water.

STONE AND REMOVE AVOCADO FLESH

1 Hold the avocado firmly in one hand, then with a chef's knife, slice straight into the avocado, cutting all the way around the stone.

2 Once the avocado has been cut all the way around, gently twist the two halves in opposite directions and separate.

3 Strike the cutting edge of your knife into the stone and lift the knife (wiggling it if necessary) to remove it from the avocado.

1 To release the avocado stone from your knife, use a wooden spoon to carefully prise it away, then discard the stone.

2 Quarter the avocado and hold it very gently to avoid damaging the flesh, then use a paring knife to peel away and discard the skin.

3 To dice an avocado, cut it into neat slices lengthways, then repeat the cuts crossways to the desired size.

PREPARE WHOLE ARTICHOKES

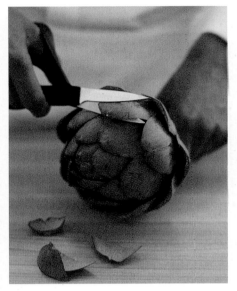

1 Hold the artichoke firmly by the stalk, then with a pair of strong kitchen scissors, snip off the tough tips of the leaves.

2 Now cut through the stalk at the base of the artichoke. Take care to hold the artichoke firmly while you do this.

3 Pull out any tough, darker green leaves and discard. Then cut through the pointed tip. The artichoke is now ready to cook as desired.

PREPARE ARTICHOKE HEARTS

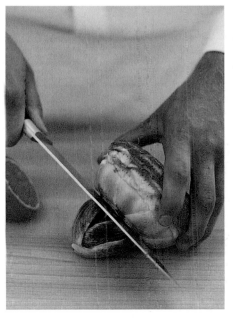

1 Cut or pull away all of the leaves from the whole artichoke first, then cut the stalk from the base and discard.

2 With a sharp knife, cut off the soft middle cone of leaves just above the hairy choke. Rub the flesh with lemon to reduce browning.

3 Trim away the bottom leaves with a paring knife. Scoop out the hairy choke if you plan to cut the heart into pieces for cooking.

PREPARE BELL PEPPERS

1 Place it on its side and cut off the top and bottom. Stand on one of the cut ends and slice in half lengthways. Remove the core and seeds.

2 Open each section and lay them flat on the cutting board. Using a sideways motion, remove the remaining pale, fleshy ribs.

3 Cut the peppers into smaller sections, following the divisions of the pepper. Chop according to the preparation of your dish.

ROAST AND PEEL PEPPERS

1 With a pair of tongs, hold the pepper over an open flame to char the skin. Rotate the pepper and char each side evenly.

2 Put each pepper into a plastic bag, seal, and allow the skins to loosen. When the peppers have cooled, peel away the charred skin.

3 Pull off the stalk, with the core attached, if possible. Discard the pepper seeds and slice the flesh into strips.

DESEED, ROAST, AND GRIND CHILLIES

1 Scraping the seeds out of a chilli will lessen its heat. Cut in half lengthways, then scrape out the seeds with a knife or spoon.

2 To impart a smoky flavour to chillies, dry-roast in a heavy-based frying pan over a high heat. Remove when they begin to darken.

3 Use a mortar and pestle to grind dry-roasted chillies to a powder, or they can be soaked, sieved, and ground to a paste.

DESEED AND CUT CHILLIES

1 Cut the chilli lengthways in half. Using the tip of your knife, scrape out the seeds and remove the membrane and stem.

2 Turn the chilli half flesh-side down and flatten with the palm of your hand. Turn it over again and slice it lengthways into strips.

3 For dice, hold the strips of cut chillies firmly together and carefully slice crossways to make equal-size pieces.

ROAST POTATOES

"Choose the right potato. I always choose King Edwards – they have a really floury texture that's going to make for a perfect roast potato." **STACIE STEWART**

1 Peel and cut the potatoes into equal-sized pieces. Put in a pan with lightly salted cold water to cover, and boil for 10 minutes. Drain and set aside until they are cool enough to handle, then score them with a fork.

2 Heat a roasting pan with a thin layer of sunflower oil, goose, or duck fat in a hot oven at 200°C (400°F/Gas 6). Coat the potatoes in the hot fat and roast for 1 hour, or until crisp. Drain on kitchen paper.

MASH POTATOES

1 Boil the potatoes until they are tender. Drain through a colander, then return them to the pan. Add butter, cream, salt, pepper, and nutmeg to taste. Re-cover the pan and leave for 5 minutes.

2 Using a potato masher, mash the potatoes until they are smooth and fluffy. Adjust the seasoning and add extra butter and cream, if desired. Keep hot until ready to serve.

PAN FRY POTATOES

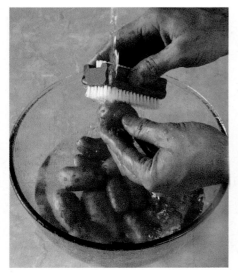

1 If using unpeeled potatoes, scrub them first by washing in water and lightly rubbing with a small vegetable brush to remove any dirt.

2 Heat a thin layer of sunflower or olive oil in a frying pan until hot. On a medium heat, fry a single layer of potato slices for 10 minutes.

3 Using a fish slice or spatula and a knife, turn the slices over and fry until golden and tender. Drain on kitchen paper and season to taste.

MAKE CHIPS

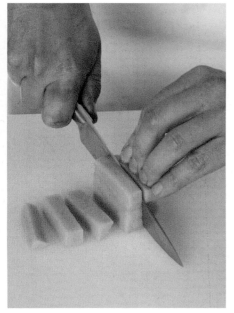

1 The first step to good, chunky chips is cutting large, floury potatoes into slices 1cm (½in) thick and about 7.5cm (3in) long.

2 Heat oil for deep-frying to 160°C (325°F). Add the chips. Fry for 5–6 minutes , until soft, not brown. Remove and drain.

3 Reheat the oil to 180°C (350°F) and fry all the chips again for 2–3 minutes, until crisp and golden. Drain on kitchen paper.

BOIL GREEN VEGETABLES

1 Bring a pan of salted water to the boil. Add the vegetables in small batches to avoid the water temperature being reduced.

2 Return the water to the boil, then reduce the heat and gently simmer the vegetables until they are just tender.

3 Drain through a colander and serve, or to set the green colour and stop the vegetables cooking, rinse under cold running water.

STIR-FRY

1 When the wok (or pan) is hot, add sunflower, rapeseed, or groundnut oil, tilting the pan to spread the oil, then toss in garlic or ginger.

2 Add the desired vegetables and use a spatula to toss continually. Add any meat first, and toss it more slowly to allow it to cook.

3 Some vegetables, such as broccoli, are best steamed for a few minutes. Add a couple of tbsp of water and cover until just tender.

STEAM

1 Bring approximately 2.5 cm (1in) of water to the boil in the bottom pan of a steamer. Place the prepared vegetables in the upper basket and position it above the bottom pan.

2 When the steam rises, cover the pan with a fitted lid and cook until the vegetables are just tender. Test frequently with a knife to ensure that they are tender, but not overcooked.

SAUTÉ FIRM VEGETABLES

1 Set a sauté pan over a high heat. When it is hot, add a thin layer of oil or a small amount of clarified butter. As soon as this has heated, add the vegetables to the pan and keep turning them to cook evenly.

2 Continue turning and tossing the vegetables in the sauté pan. They should gradually take on a light golden brown colour and become tender. Remove from the heat and serve.

HERBS

BUY All herbs should look fresh, whether cut or growing in pots. Avoid any that look wilted or discoloured. Ideally, plant a herb garden or in a window box. Buy dried herbs in small quantities as they lose their fragrance once exposed to the air. Use sparingly as their flavour is concentrated. Also available frozen. **STORE** Best picked and used fresh, but cut can be stored in a plastic bag in the refrigerator for a few days. Freeze sealed bags of cut herbs, whole or chopped, for up to 6 months.

DILL
SEEDS

▲ CHIVES

EAT Always add at the end of cooking. Snip and add to soups, salads (in particular potato), sauces (especially soured cream or yogurt), and use as a garnish. **FLAVOUR PAIRINGS** Avocados, courgettes, potatoes, root vegetables, cream cheese, yogurt, soured cream, eggs, fish, seafood, smoked salmon. **IN SEASON** March–November

▲ DILL

EAT Add at the end of cooking and to salad dressings and creamy sauces for fish and vegetables. Use to flavour pickled fish and cucumber. Add seeds to stuffings, cakes, and breads. **FLAVOUR PAIRINGS** (leaves) Beetroot, broad beans, carrots, celeriac, cucumber, potatoes, spinach, eggs, fish, seafood, (seeds) rice, cabbage, potatoes, pumpkin, vinegars. **IN SEASON** May–September

CELERY
SEEDS

▲ CHERVIL

EAT Scatter over vegetables or add to salads in scrambled eggs or omelettes, in vinaigrette, butter or cream sauces, delicate soups and consommé. **FLAVOUR PAIRINGS** Asparagus, broad beans, green beans, beetroot, carrots, fennel, lettuce peas, potatoes, tomatoes, mushrooms, cream cheese, eggs, fish, seafood, poultry, veal. **IN SEASON** May–October

▲ LEAF CELERY

EAT Excellent way to add the flavour of celery to any dish with just a few leaves or for garnish. Use the seeds sparingly, they are very strong. **FLAVOUR PAIRINGS** Cabbage, potatoes, cucumber, tomatoes, chicken, fish, rice, soy sauce, tofu, soft white cheese. **IN SEASON** May–October

▲ TARRAGON

EAT Use in moderation. Add to green salads or vinaigrette; in marinades; to flavour goat's cheese and feta, in egg dishes, herb butter, and vinegar. **FLAVOUR PAIRINGS** Artichokes, asparagus, courgettes, tomatoes, mushrooms, potatoes, salsify, fish, seafood, poultry, eggs, game, feta, and goat's cheese. **IN SEASON** May–October

▲ CORIANDER

EAT Except when used in curry pastes, best added at end of cooking. Use in curries, stir-fries, soups, pesto, salsas, chutneys, relishes, and as a garnish. **FLAVOUR PAIRINGS** Avocados, sweetcorn, cucumber, root vegetables, onions, chillies, coconut milk, poultry, meat, fish, seafood, citrus, pulses, rice. **IN SEASON** May–October, imported all year

▲ HORSERADISH

EAT Don't cook. As soon as it's grated, mix with lemon juice to preserve colour and pungency. Use in dressings, relishes, sauces, to glaze ham with apricot preserve or honey. Also available grated in jars. **FLAVOUR PAIRINGS** Sausages, beef, gammon, oily and smoked fish, seafood, avocados, beetroot, red cabbage, potatoes, celeriac, apples. **IN SEASON** October–December

FENNEL SEEDS

▲ FENNEL

EAT The leaves, flowers, and pollen give anise fragrance to cold soups, chowders, roast meats and vegetables, and in fish dishes. Add seeds to potatoes, breads, and pickles. **FLAVOUR PAIRINGS** Beetroot, beans, cabbage, leeks, cucumber, tomatoes, potatoes, duck, fish, seafood, pork, lentils, rice. **IN SEASON** May–September

▲ LAVENDER

EAT Infuse flowers in milk, syrup, cream, or wine for baking and desserts and add to jams, jellies, or fruit compôtes. Use chopped flowers and leaves to flavour roast lamb, rabbit, chicken, and pheasant. **FLAVOUR PAIRINGS** Berries, plums, cherries, rhubarb, chicken, lamb, rabbit, pheasant, chocolate. **IN SEASON** March–September

▲ BAY

EAT Add whole to flavour soups, stews, sauces, pickles, milk puddings, and marinades. Thread on kebabs, or use to top terrines or patés before baking. Remove before serving. **FLAVOUR PAIRINGS** Meat, poultry, offal, game, fish, chestnuts, citrus, haricot beans, lentils, rice, tomatoes, mushrooms. **IN SEASON** All year

▲ LOVAGE

EAT Use leaves and stalks instead of celery or parsley in salads, sauces, marinades, soups, stews, casseroles, or with just about any vegetable. **FLAVOUR PAIRINGS** Apples, root vegetables, potatoes, Jerusalem artichokes, courgettes, mushrooms, tomatoes, sweetcorn, Cheddar, Gruyère or cream cheeses, eggs, pulses, fish, meat, poultry, rice. **IN SEASON** May–September

▲ GARDEN MINT

EAT Also called spearmint, the most common mint variety for cooking. Use in sweet and savoury dishes, to flavour and garnish. In some Mediterranean countries, dried is preferred to fresh. **FLAVOUR PAIRINGS** Lamb, duck, potatoes, peas, carrots, tomatoes, cucumber, currants, curries, chocolate, yogurt. **IN SEASON** March–October

▲ SWEET BASIL

EAT It loses flavour quickly, so add at the end of cooking or to cold dishes. It's the classic flavouring for tomato-based dishes, Genoese Pesto, and French Pistou. Best torn or rolled, then chopped. Look out for purple, Thai, and Greek basil too. **FLAVOUR PAIRINGS** Tomatoes, garlic, pine nuts, mozzarella and other cheeses, eggs, aubergines, haricot beans, courgettes, lemon, olives, peas, pizzas, potatoes, rice, raspberries, sweetcorn. **IN SEASON** June–September, imported all year

▲ OREGANO

EAT Popular for flavouring everything from pizzas to baked fish, salads to Mexican bean dishes. **FLAVOUR PAIRINGS** Lamb, beef, chicken, pork, pulses, chilli, cumin, coriander leaf, garlic, tomatoes, aubergines, Cheddar, mozzarella, feta and halloumi cheeses, olives, peppers. **IN SEASON** March–October

▲ SWEET MARJORAM

EAT Similar to oregano but with a more delicate, sweet flavour. Use leaves and flower knots in salads, cream sauces, egg and delicate fish dishes, for marinating fresh cheeses, and as a garnish. **FLAVOUR PAIRINGS** Olive oil, fresh white cheeses, plaice, sole, red mullet, mushrooms, eggs, squashes. **IN SEASON** March–October

▲ SAGE

EAT Use sparingly to flavour rich meats and offal, in toasted sandwiches, stuffings, and polenta. Good as a simple pasta sauce with olive oil, butter, and sea salt. Deep-fry leaves for a few seconds for a garnish. **FLAVOUR PAIRINGS** Pork, duck, goose, veal, chicken, liver, sausages, cheeses, beans, tomatoes, apples, bay leaf, caraway, onions, celery, garlic, lovage, marjoram. **IN SEASON** All year

**CURLY LEAF
PARSLEY**

**FLAT-LEAF
PARSLEY**

▲ PARSLEY

EAT Flat-leaf parsley has a better flavour for adding to dishes, but they are interchangeable. Add chopped at the end of cooking for best flavour. Use stalks for flavouring soups and stews. **FLAVOUR PAIRINGS** Eggs, fish, seafood, chicken, béchamel sauce, lentils, rice, lemon, tomatoes, garlic, onions. **IN SEASON** March–October, imported all year

▲ COMMON SORREL

EAT It has a lemony flavour. Good in salads (add a little honey to the dressing or use balsamic vinegar), shredded in omelettes, baked or scrambled eggs, in cream sauces, and with fish. **FLAVOUR PAIRINGS** Chicken, pork, veal, fish (especially salmon), mussels, eggs, lentils, leeks, lettuce, cucumber, tomatoes, spinach, watercress. **IN SEASON** March–November

▲ THYME

EAT Use in stews, casseroles, stuffings, pies, sauces, pâtés, terrines, and marinades. The flowers make a pretty garnish in sweet and savoury dishes. Lemon thyme can be used in biscuits, breads, and fruit salads. **FLAVOUR PAIRINGS** Lamb, rabbit, chicken, turkey, pulses, aubergines, cabbage, carrots, leeks, wild mushrooms, tomatoes, onions, potatoes, sweetcorn. **IN SEASON** All year

▲ SUMMER SAVORY

EAT Good in salads, soups, stews, casseroles and stuffings. **FLAVOUR PAIRINGS** Rabbit, chicken, oily fish, cheeses, eggs, broad and green beans, pulses, beetroot, cabbage, potatoes. **IN SEASON** May–October

▲ ROSEMARY

EAT Finely chop for soups, stews, casseroles, roast vegetables, meat and fish, in marinades, sautés, and grills. Also good in creams, bakes, and summer drinks. Use whole woody sprigs as skewers for kebabs or as basting brushes. **FLAVOUR PAIRINGS** Poultry, rabbit, pork, lamb, veal, fish, eggs, lentils, squashes, peppers, courgettes, cabbage, potatoes, onions, garlic, citrus, fruit, cream cheese. **IN SEASON** All year

SPICES

BUY Buy spices in small quantities as they lose their fragrance and colour when exposed to the air. Avoid any that look dull or discoloured. Most are available from good supermarkets, but more unusual spices can be found in specialist food shops. For best flavour, grind (or grate as appropriate) whole spices as you need them, rather than using ready-ground.
STORE Keep fresh spices in a sealed container in the refrigerator for up to 2 weeks. Dried, whole, and ground spices should be stored in sealed containers in a cool dark place. Whole dried spices will keep for 1–3 years; ground ones for around 6 months.

CAPERS

CAPERBERRIES

▲ GALANGAL

EAT Similar to ginger, peel and grate, or chop. Soak dried slices then add to soups and stews. Remove before eating. Use in Southeast Asian curries, stews, sambals, satays, soups, and sauces.
FLAVOUR PAIRINGS Chicken, fish, seafood, coconut milk, chillies, fennel, garlic, ginger, lemon grass, lemon, kaffir lime, shallots, tamarind.

▲ CAPERS AND CAPERBERRIES

EAT Both from the caper bush, capers are the pickled or salted buds, and caperberries are the pickled semi-mature fruit. Add towards the end of cooking, or put in cold sauces or dressings. Caperberries can be eaten like olives. **FLAVOUR PAIRINGS** Rich meats, poultry, fish, seafood, globe artichokes, aubergines, green beans, gherkins, olives, potatoes, tomatoes.

BLACK MUSTARD
SEEDS

WHITE (YELLOW)
MUSTARD SEEDS

▲ MUSTARD SEED

EAT Black (and brown) seeds can be dry-roasted or heated in hot oil or ghee to enhance their nutty flavour. Use white (yellow) seeds for pickling and marinades. Powdered yellow mustard is best for rubs, barbecue sauce, and in savoury baking. Prepared mustards are usually served as a condiment, and in sauces, dressings, and glazes. **FLAVOUR PAIRINGS** Beef, rabbit, sausages, chicken, fish, ham, seafood, strong cheeses, cabbage, root vegetables, curries, dals.

▲ PAPRIKA

EAT Available as sweet, hot, or smoked (pimentón). Use sweet or hot in goulash, tagines, soups, and as a garnish; smoked as a rub for grills and roasts, in braises, and pan-fries. **FLAVOUR PAIRINGS** Beef, veal, chicken, duck, vegetables (sweet/hot); sausages, pork, fish, onions, pulses, eggs (smoked).

▲ CHILLI

EAT Use whole dried (there are many varieties, Kashmir shown above), flakes, chilli powder, chilli seasoning, or cayenne (the hottest powder) to add heat and colour (see also fresh chillies p353). **FLAVOUR PAIRINGS** Most spices, bay, coriander leaf, parsley, coconut milk, citrus, meats, poultry, fish, seafood, pulses, tomatoes, avocados, tropical fruits, chocolate.

▲ CINNAMON

EAT Good for flavouring fruity desserts, breads, cakes, and drinks, like coffee, chocolate, tea, mulled wine, and ale. Also good in meat and vegetable tagines and bakes. **FLAVOUR PAIRINGS** Lamb, poultry, aubergines, chocolate, coffee, rice, almonds, apples, apricots, bananas, pears, other sweet spices.

▲ CARAWAY SEED

EAT Use to flavour rye breads, biscuits, cabbage (particularly sauerkraut), seed cakes, sausages, soups, and stews. It is also used in spice blends, such as Harissa paste. **FLAVOUR PAIRINGS** Duck, goose, pork, breads, apples, cabbage, potatoes, root vegetables, tomatoes.

▲ CORIANDER SEED

EAT The basis for many spice blends. Use in vegetable dishes, stews, and French à la grecque dishes, for pickling, marinades, and court-bouillon. **FLAVOUR PAIRINGS** Cumin, chicken, pork, ham, fish, orchard fruits, citrus, mushrooms, onions, potatoes, pulses.

▲ CUMIN

EAT Dry-roast before grinding, or fry in oil to use whole to enhance aroma. Add to soups, curries, and casseroles. Used in numerous spice blends, from Cajun spices to Indian curry powders. **FLAVOUR PAIRINGS** Meats, poultry, cheeses, vegetables, pulses, coriander seed and leaf, chilli, oregano.

◀ PRESERVED LEMONS

EAT Slice and roast with vegetables, meat, chicken, or fish, or chop and add to tagines. Use the salty preserving juice in salad dressings. **FLAVOUR PAIRINGS** Lamb, chicken, fish, rice, cardamom, cloves, allspice, pepper, ginger, cinnamon, coriander leaf, fennel, celery, olives.

▲ KAFFIR LIME LEAVES

EAT If the fresh or dried leaves are to be eaten rather than removed before serving, discard the central rib and shred leaf finely before use. Use in Thai-style salads, curries, fishcakes, soups, and noodle dishes. **FLAVOUR PAIRINGS** Pork, poultry, fish, seafood, mushrooms, noodles, rice, green vegetables, coconut, tropical fruits.

▲ TURMERIC

EAT Use fresh, crushed, or ground turmeric in spice pastes for curries, stews, and vegetable dishes, and to flavour and colour rice and dals.
FLAVOUR PAIRINGS Meat, poultry, fish, eggs, aubergines, beans, lentils, rice, root vegetables, spinach.

▲ CARDAMOM PODS

EAT Lightly bruise and fry, or toast, then grind the seeds before adding to a dish. Split whole pods and add directly to rice. Also used in spice pastes, sweetmeats, pastries, puddings, breads, ice creams, tea, coffee, and chocolate. **FLAVOUR PAIRINGS** Apples, oranges, pears, sweet potatoes, pulses, cinnamon, star anise, cloves.

▲ SAFFRON

EAT Characteristic in Mediterranean fish soups and stews. Also popular in risottos, paellas, biryanis, pilafs, in baking, and to flavour ice cream. Infuse the strands and add early in cooking for a deeper colour; later for stronger fragrance.
FLAVOUR PAIRINGS Chicken, game, fish, seafood, eggs, asparagus, leeks, mushrooms, spinach, squashes, mayonnaise (as rouille).

▲ LEMON GRASS

EAT Finely chop or slice to flavour curries, stews, and stir-fries. Pound with other spices and herbs for curry pastes. **FLAVOUR PAIRINGS** Beef, chicken, pork, fish and seafood, noodles, most vegetables, Thai or European basil, coriander leaf, chilli, galangal, cinnamon, cloves, turmeric, coconut milk.

▲ STAR ANISE

EAT Use in Chinese and Vietnamese soups, stews, broths, and marinades. Also good for fish and seafood dishes, poaching fruit, and to enhance the sweetness of leeks, pumpkin, and root vegetables. **FLAVOUR PAIRINGS** Chicken, beef, oxtail, pork, fish, seafood, tropical fruits, figs, pears, leeks, pumpkin, root vegetables, chilli, cinnamon, coriander seed, fennel seed, garlic, ginger.

▲ CURRY LEAVES

EAT Use in long-simmered South Indian and Sri Lankan curries, then remove or eat with the dish. Use also in a basic tadka to spoon over cooked dal. **FLAVOUR PAIRINGS** Lamb, fish, seafood, lentils, rice, most vegetables, cardamom, chilli, coconut, coriander leaf, cumin, fenugreek seed, garlic.

▲ JUNIPER BERRIES

EAT Crush and add to marinades, stuffings, pâtés, and robust sauces. Also the classic flavouring in gin. **FLAVOUR PAIRINGS** Red meats, game, goose, apples, celery, cabbage, caraway, garlic, marjoram, rosemary, savory, thyme.

▲ SUMAC

EAT It has little taste, but brings out the flavours of foods, much as salt does. Use ground as a condiment. Rub on fish, vegetables, kebabs, and steaks before cooking. Use in chicken and vegetable casseroles, or mix with yogurt and herbs as a dip. **FLAVOUR PAIRINGS** Chicken, lamb, fish, aubergines, chickpeas, lentils, onions, pine nuts, yogurt, coriander leaf, mint, parsley.

▲ POPPY SEED

EAT When baking, sprinkle on or add to breads, bagels, pretzels, and cakes. Use in dressings for noodles or to garnish vegetables. Grind to a paste with honey to fill pastries and sweetmeats. **FLAVOUR PAIRINGS** Aubergines, green beans, cauliflower, courgettes, potatoes, bread, honey.

▲ NIGELLA SEED

EAT Often sold as black onion seed. Add to pilafs, curries, and pickles, or sprinkle alone or with other seeds on breads, savoury pastries, and vegetables before baking. **FLAVOUR PAIRINGS** Allspice, cumin, and sesame seeds, coriander leaf, star anise, pulses, rice, roots, and tubers.

▲ ALLSPICE

EAT Allspice has long been used to preserve meat and fish, and is still used in pickled fish dishes, as well as in other pickles, chutneys, some sausages, and mulled wines and beers. Use in curries and pilafs, too. **FLAVOUR PAIRINGS** Aubergines, onions, squashes, root vegetables, white cabbage, tomatoes, most fruit.

▲ PEPPERCORNS

EAT Use whole black to flavour cooking liquids, stocks, and marinades, and freshly-ground for dressings, sauces, and cooked dishes. Mild pink and green peppercorns, often preserved in brine or vinegar, are good for Steak au Poivre or with chicken and veal (rinse before use). Use sharp white pepper for pale coloured sauces. **FLAVOUR PAIRINGS** Meat, poultry, game, fish and seafood, vegetables, oils, herbs, other spices, salts, some fruits (especially strawberries).

▲ MACE

EAT Similar but lighter than nutmeg. It lifts Béchamel and onion sauces, clear soups, fish stock, potted meat, pâtés, terrrines, cheese soufflés, chocolate drinks, and cream cheese desserts. **FLAVOUR PAIRINGS** Chicken, lamb, veal, milk, eggs, cheeses, carrots, onions, pumpkin, spinach, sweet potato, other sweet spices, bay leaf, thyme.

◀ NUTMEG

EAT Good in many sweet and savoury dishes from vegetable purées, meat stews, and casseroles, to bread sauce, milk puddings, and fruit desserts. Best grated fresh, but can be bought ground. **FLAVOUR PAIRINGS** Chicken, veal, lamb, cabbage, onion, roots and tubers, squashes, spinach, cheese, eggs, milk, rice, couscous, semolina, cardamom, other sweet spices.

▲ GINGER

EAT Add freshly grated to Indian chutneys, relishes, and rice dishes, in stir-fries, soups, sauces, marinades, and tempura dipping sauce. Use pickled ginger with sushi, and fried as a garnish. Use ground ginger in baking for cakes and biscuits, and in desserts. It is also available preserved in syrup or candied. **FLAVOUR PAIRINGS** Fish, seafood, meat, poultry, most vegetables, chilli, coconut, garlic, citrus, soy sauce, orchard fruits, rhubarb.

▲ TAMARIND

EAT Available in block, concentrate, or paste. For block, soak a small piece in hot water for 10 minutes. Stir, strain through a fine sieve, and use the liquid. It adds a sharp tang to curries, sambals, chutneys, marinades and sauces, or mix with salt as a rub for meat. **FLAVOUR PAIRINGS** Chicken, lamb, pork, fish, seafood, lentils, mushrooms, peanuts, most vegetables, chilli, coriander leaf, cumin, galangal, garlic, ginger, turmeric, mustard, soy sauce, palm sugar.

▲ FENUGREEK

EAT A bitter spice, widely used ground in vegetarian Indian cookery, in dals, fish curries, stews, and breads. The seeds are used in pickles, chutneys, and traditional spice blends. **FLAVOUR PAIRINGS** Green and root vegetables, chilli, garlic, fish, chicken, lentils.

▲ SICHUAN PEPPER

EAT Best ground fresh. Remove the seeds from the berries, dry-roast briefly, then grind. Use as a condiment or to flavour meat or poultry for roasting, grilling or frying, and stir-fried vegetables. One of the constituents of Chinese five spice powder. Also available ground. **FLAVOUR PAIRINGS** Black beans, sesame oil and seeds, chilli, star anise, ginger, garlic, citrus, soy sauce.

▲ CLOVES

EAT Use whole or ground with rich meats, in biscuits, pies, cakes, syrups, and preserves, and as a pickling and mulling spice. **FLAVOUR PAIRINGS** Ham, pork, duck, venison, orchard fruits, beetroot, red cabbage, carrots, onions, oranges, squashes, chocolate, cinnamon.

◀ VANILLA PODS

EAT Use whole or split (with or without the seeds scraped into the dish) to flavour sugar, poached fruit, and desserts. Good with chicken and seafood, too. The pods can be rinsed, dried, and reused. Use pure vanilla extract in baking. **FLAVOUR PAIRINGS** Lobster, scallops, mussels, chicken, milk- and cream-based desserts, chocolate, apples, melons, pears, rhubarb, strawberries.

SALTS

BUY Made up of crystals of sodium chloride, these salts can all be used as a condiment or seasoning, but for preserving, choose rock salt or pickling salt. Sea salt is unsuitable for this purpose because of the minerals it contains. It is, however, the one to use for cooking. Fine ground sea salt is labelled simply as cooking salt or *gross sel*. There are also speciality sea salts, see below. Avoid table salt or iodized salt for pickles, as they can cause clouding of the liquid, or darkening of the food.
STORE Salts have an indefinite shelf life, but they should be kept in airtight containers as they will absorb moisture from the atmosphere and become lumpy. If this happens, spread evenly in a baking tray, dry in the oven, and break up the clumps. Iodized salt may turn yellow, but this is harmless.

▲ ROCK SALT CRYSTALS

EAT The commonest form of salt, with a plain, salty taste. It is mined rather than sourced from the sea. The best choice for pickling, and for putting in a salt grinder. **FLAVOUR PAIRINGS** Pickling onions, shallots, green beans, cauliflower, squashes, gherkins, cucumbers, red cabbage, green walnuts.

▲ TABLE SALT

EAT All-purpose refined rock salt, milled to very small grains, with anti-caking agents added to stop it clumping. It has a straightforward salty taste. Use in a salt cellar and for general cooking. Some brands have added iodine. **FLAVOUR PAIRINGS** Meat, fish, vegetables, eggs, pastries, breads, biscuits.

▲ MALDON SEA SALT

EAT Made in Maldon, Essex, for over 200 years. Famous for its lack of bitterness and distinctive, fresh taste of the sea. It is strong, so use sparingly. Scatter over griddled vegetables with a drizzle of olive oil, over chips, or rub on the skins of jacket potatoes before baking. Also available smoked. **FLAVOUR PAIRINGS** All meat, fish, poultry, and vegetables (especially asparagus), aubergines courgettes, peppers, potatoes.

▲ FLEUR DE SEL SEA SALT

EAT The purest form of sea salt derived from the top layer formed in salt pans. The Guérande area of France is famous for it. Use like Maldon sea salt and, again, sparingly, as it has a sharp, pure, salty taste. **FLAVOUR PAIRINGS** All meat, fish, poultry, vegetables, cheeses, grains, pulses, eggs.

▲ CELERY SALT

EAT Ground celery seeds mixed with table salt. It is strong-flavoured so use sparingly to season soups, stews, casseroles, dips, tomato, and cheese dishes. Good rubbed on the skin of chicken or fish before grilling. **FLAVOUR PAIRINGS** Chicken, fish, tomatoes and tomato juice, cheeses, mayonnaise, soured cream, yogurt.

▲ GARLIC SALT

EAT Powdered dried garlic mixed with table salt. Use judiciously to season soups, stews, casseroles, dips, and other dishes when not using fresh garlic. Onion salt can be used in the same way. **FLAVOUR PAIRINGS** Herbs, spices, chicken, meat, fish, cream cheese, yogurt, soured cream, avocados, tomatoes, unsalted butter.

HONEY, SUGARS, AND SYRUPS

BUY The darker the honey, sugar, and syrup, the deeper the flavour. For honey, those high in fructose stay runny, those with more glucose, set. Choose "pure" honey. Multi-floral is cheaper than a mono-floral (a single-blossom one will be identified on the label). When using sugar, select the right one for the job. Brown sugars should be moist and soft.
STORE Keep in a cool dry, dark place. Clear honey and syrups may crystallize during storage; heat gently to dissolve. Sugars, honey, and sugar syrups (except corn) keep indefinitely. Fruit syrups will keep for about a year. Corn syrup is lighter and tends to ferment after around 6 months.

▲ CLEAR HONEY

EAT Use in place of sugar in many recipes, but it's sweeter, so experiment with less. Clear honey mixes easily, so good for drizzling, dressings, glazes, sauces, and syrups. **FLAVOUR PAIRINGS** All meats and poultry, vinegars, oils, tomato purée, garlic, shallots, Worcestershire sauce, soy sauce, mustard, nuts, yogurt, fruits, rosemary, mint. **IN SEASON** June–August (depending on the blossom), imported all year

▲ SET HONEY

EAT Good in biscuits and cakes, to spoon on fruit, or spread on meat or poultry as part of a glaze before baking. **FLAVOUR PAIRINGS** Poultry, game, gammon, bacon, pork, lamb, figs, pineapple, grapefruit, bananas, peanuts, walnuts, almonds. **IN SEASON** June–August (depending on the blossom), imported all year

▲ COMB HONEY

EAT A piece of honey-filled beeswax comb is the most natural way to eat honey. Don't use it for cooking, but it is delicious raw for breakfast or as a tea time treat. **FLAVOUR PAIRINGS** Warm crusty bread, toast, butter. **IN SEASON** June–August (depending on the blossom)

▲ GRANULATED SUGAR

EAT Refined sugar used for sweetening drinks, syrups, preserves, caramel sauce, sweets and confectionery. Preserving sugar has added pectin. **FLAVOUR PAIRINGS** Tea, coffee, chocolate, fruit, creams, nuts.

▲ CASTER SUGAR

EAT A finer version of granulated sugar. White is refined sugar, golden caster is unrefined. Use both for general sweetening, frosting and candying, baking, and desserts. **FLAVOUR PAIRINGS** All fruit, nuts, tomatoes, chocolate, coffee, vanilla, eggs, cream, crème fraîche, yogurt.

▲ ICING SUGAR

EAT Finely ground refined sugar sometimes with anti-caking agent. Use for icings, frostings, sweet butters, delicate sweets, and to dust over cakes and desserts. **FLAVOUR PAIRINGS** Citrus and other fruits, eggs, vanilla, cinnamon, peppermint, almond, chocolate, coffee, cream cheese, caramel, brandy, rum.

▲ DEMERARA SUGAR

EAT Coarse crystal sugar traditionally used to sweeten coffee and for baking rich fruit cakes. Some is coloured refined sugar, look for unrefined. **FLAVOUR PAIRINGS** Coffee, mixed dried fruits, apples, pears, bananas.

▲ MUSCOVADO SUGAR

EAT Dark and light unrefined, moist sugar (dark shown here). Use dark in rich fruit cakes, chutneys, and marinades; light in biscuits and crumbles. Soft brown sugars are refined, with added molasses. **FLAVOUR PAIRINGS** Fruits, vegetables, meats, sweet spices.

▲ JAGGERY AND PALM SUGAR

EAT Jaggery (shown here) is blocks of unrefined palm or cane sugar. Palm sugar comes in blocks, sticky granules, or liquid. **FLAVOUR PAIRINGS** Vegetables, meats, fish, tropical fruits, spices, herbs.

▲ GOLDEN SYRUP

EAT Sticky cane or beet syrup with a distinctive flavour. Classic ingredient of treacle tart and flapjacks. **FLAVOUR PAIRINGS** Ginger, cinnamon, mixed spice, chocolate, butter, oats.

▲ BLACKSTRAP MOLASSES

EAT Unrefined, almost black, thick, slightly bitter syrup for rich cakes and chutneys. **FLAVOUR PAIRINGS** Dried fruits, vegetables, stone and orchard fruits, chillies, spices.

▲ BLACK TREACLE

EAT Runnier than blackstrap molasses and slightly milder. Use in the same way, but also good for treacle toffee, parkin, and gingerbread. **FLAVOUR PAIRINGS** Ginger, cinnamon, cloves, nutmeg, mixed spice, allspice, nuts, oatmeal.

▲ CORN SYRUP

EAT Available as light or dark syrup, similar to golden syrup with a less distinctive taste. Use in the same way. **FLAVOUR PAIRINGS** Ginger, cinnamon, mixed spice, chocolate, butter, oats.

▲ MAPLE SYRUP

EAT Runny syrup from the sap of the maple tree, traditionally served with pancakes and waffles. Maple-flavoured syrup also available. **FLAVOUR PAIRINGS** American-style pancakes, waffles, pineapple, bananas. nuts, chocolate, coffee.

▲ POMEGRANATE SYRUP

EAT Thick, tangy and sweet, also known as pomegranate molasses. Use in sweet and savoury dishes. **FLAVOUR PAIRINGS** Duck, chicken, fish, pork, game, soy sauce, pak choi, courgettes, salad leaves, tropical fruits.

PREPARE SPICES

1 Before use, whole fresh spices such as lemon grass can be bruised with the flat side of a heavy knife and your hand.

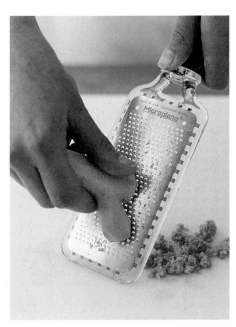

2 Roots like ginger can be finely chopped by hand, but it's often easiest to grate them. Peel off the skin beforehand.

3 Scraping out the seeds from chillies lessens their heat. Wear a pair of rubber or plastic gloves to avoid irritation to your skin.

4 When spices are fried till lightly coloured, their flavour gets trapped in the oil. The oil can then be used along with the spices.

5 To dry-roast spices, place them in an oven preheated to 160°C (325°F/Gas 3), or fry them in a dry pan, till lightly browned.

6 Dried or dry-roasted spices can either be crushed by hand in a pestle and mortar or by machine in a spice mill.

PREPARE HERBS

1 A mezzaluna makes light work of chopping herbs. Rock it from side to side across them until they're chopped to your liking.

2 To strip the leaves of herbs with woody stalks, simply run the thumb and forefinger of one hand along the stalk.

3 For a classic soup flavouring, tie a sprig of thyme and parsley with a bay leaf. You could also include sage or rosemary.

1 To chop the leaves of herbs with tender stalks like basil, and avoid bruising them, roll the leaves together into a tight bunch.

2 Holding the bunch of leaves steady with one hand, slice across them with a sharp chef's knife to create fine shreds.

3 Using the knife in a rocking motion, chop the leaves finely, turning them by 90 degrees halfway through.

EXTRACT VANILLA SEEDS

1 Vanilla pods can be used whole, but the seeds look especially good in creamy desserts. To extract them, put the vanilla pod on a board and using the tip of a sharp knife, cut along the length of the pod.

2 Using the blunt side of a small knife or a teaspoon, scrape along the inside of the pod to collect the sticky seeds. The empty pod can then be used to flavour syrups and sugars.

MAKE LEMON-ZEST JULIENNE

1 Using a peeler, remove strips of the lemon zest, taking off as little of the bitter pith as possible. Try to select unwaxed lemons for this purpose, and always wash and dry the skin before you begin.

2 If any pith remains, use a sharp knife to slice it off by running your knife along the peel away from you. Then, using a rocking motion with your knife, slice the peel into strips.

USE GELATINE

1 Soak the required number of leaves of gelatine in enough cold water, or other liquid, to cover them fully for at least 10 minutes. Squeeze out as much of the water as possible before using.

2 In a saucepan, warm some water or whatever liquid is specified in your chosen recipe. Add the gelatine, and stir to dissolve thoroughly before leaving the solution to cool.

MAKE A SUGAR SYRUP

1 Heat your measured amount of sugar and water over a low heat in a heavy-based pan, without stirring, until dissolved. Use a wet pastry brush to wipe the pan edge to stop grains of sugar sticking.

2 When the sugar has dissolved, bring the syrup slowly to the boil and boil for 2 minutes for basic syrup or to the correct temperature for your recipe, using a sugar thermometer.

MAKE CARAMEL SAUCE

1 Warm 100ml (3½fl oz) liquid glucose in a heavy-based pan over a low heat. Do not boil. Add 125g (4½oz) caster sugar and heat gently until dissolved, then boil until golden. Cool for 1 minute in iced water.

2 While the syrup is still warm, whisk in 25g (scant 1oz) butter and 250ml (8fl oz) softly whipped cream. Return the pan to a low heat and bring gently to the boil until the sauce is smooth, thick, and creamy.

MAKE A GANACHE

1 Chop 100g (3½oz) dark chocolate by placing it on a work surface or chopping board. Select a knife with a serrated edge and use your hand to press down on the blunt side of the blade.

2 Melt the chocolate in a heatproof bowl over a pan of simmering (not boiling) water. Stir with a wooden spoon and add the chocolate to 100ml (3½fl oz) of boiling double cream. Stir again gently from the centre.

PREPARE CHOCOLATE

1 Break the chocolate and chill in the freezer. for a few minutes. Place on a board and using a sharp knife, chop, using a rocking motion.

2 For grating, rub chilled chocolate against the grater, using the widest holes. If it begins to melt, put it back in the freezer and repeat.

3 For curls, spread soft or melted chocolate onto a cool surface. Use the blade of a chef's knife to scrape the chocolate into curls.

MAKE PROFESSIONAL GLOSSY ICING

1 Add 300g (10oz) chopped dark chocolate to a sugar syrup and stir until smooth. Heat to 120°C (225°F) – the mixture should form a "thread" if you dip your fingers in iced water, then the chocolate, and pull apart.

2 Brush the cake with apricot jam melted with a little water. Remove the icing from the heat and tap the pan to remove any air bubbles. Laddle it onto the cake and smooth it out with a warmed metal spatula.

ORCHARD FRUITS

BUY Choose fruit with no bruises. Brown russeting on the skin of some fruit is normal. Apples and Asian pears should smell fragrant. Loquats may have a few brown spots and should feel tender. Pears should give slightly at the stem end. Quinces have a downy skin that becomes smooth as they ripen (any left can be rubbed off). Medlars have a brown, wrinkled skin, and rarely ripen on the tree. Leave to "blet" in a paper bag in a cool, dark place for several weeks until soft. **STORE** Ripe fruit are best refrigerated and put in the fruit bowl as required. Loquats and pears should be eaten as soon as they are ripe. All can be prepared and frozen for up to 12 months.

▲ GRANNY SMITH APPLE

EAT Good all-rounder with green skin and sharp, crunchy flesh. Use in pies, tarts, and cakes, for sauce, in fruit and savoury salads, meat, fish, and cheese dishes. **FLAVOUR PAIRINGS** Cinnamon, mixed spice, cloves, walnuts, almonds, raisins, sultanas, cabbage, cheeses, chicken, pork, duck, game, black pudding, cider, Calvados. **IN SEASON** Imported all year

▲ COX'S ORANGE PIPPIN APPLE

EAT With scented, crisp, sweet flesh and mottled skin, Cox's can be used for cooking as well as eating raw, but are best in salads. Good for juicing and drying. **FLAVOUR PAIRINGS** White or red cabbage, walnuts, almonds, pine nuts, sunflower seeds, fresh and dried fruits, celery, lovage, mayonnaise, vinaigrette, ginger. **IN SEASON** August–February (best August–December)

▲ BRAMLEY APPLE

EAT Large cooking apple that cooks to a fluffy pulp. Best for pies, sauce, baking, fritters, and all types of dessert. Good bottled or in chutneys. **FLAVOUR PAIRINGS** Citrus, almonds, berries, rhubarb, pears, quinces, dried fruit, cinnamon, cloves, mixed spice, nutmeg, vanilla, honey, syrup, demerara sugar, chocolate. **IN SEASON** All year (best October–December)

▲ RED DELICIOUS APPLE

EAT Large fruit with tough, crimson skin and sweet, crumbly flesh. Not good for cooking. **FLAVOUR PAIRINGS** All cheeses, celery, grapes, pork or duck pâté, nuts. **IN SEASON** Imported all year

◀ WILLIAMS' BON CRÉTIEN PEAR

EAT Tender, juicy, and slightly musky, good raw or for preserving. **FLAVOUR PAIRINGS** Red wine, port, brandy, cinnamon, star anise, cloves, ginger, wine vinegar, white and demerara sugar, maple syrup, dried fruits. **IN SEASON** September–February, stored and imported all year

▲ DOYENNE DE COMICE PEAR

EAT Eat raw or cooked in crumbles, pies, and savoury dishes. **FLAVOUR PAIRINGS** Pork, duck, goose, apples, raisins, cinnamon, cloves, ginger, walnuts, goat's and blue cheeses. **IN SEASON** September–March

▲ CONFERENCE PEAR

EAT Good raw or cooked in sweet and savoury dishes. For cooking, choose slightly under-ripe pears. Peel, if liked before use. Use over-ripe fruit in sauces and smoothies. **FLAVOUR PAIRINGS** Game, pork, blue cheese, Parmesan, rocket, watercress, tarragon, celery, walnuts, almonds, cinnamon, ginger, star anise, cardamom, chocolate, vanilla, butterscotch. **IN SEASON** September–February, stored and imported all year

▲ ASIAN PEAR

EAT Peel, if wished, core and slice, or chop. Use in fruit and savoury salads, spicy Asian dishes, or poach in syrup. In Japan they eat them sprinkled with salt. **FLAVOUR PAIRINGS** Beef, papaya, mango, lime, chilli, soy sauce, ginger, cardamom, star anise, rice vinegar, honey. **IN SEASON** July–October, imported most of the year

▲ LOQUAT (NISPEROS)

EAT Halve, remove stone, and scoop out flesh or poach in syrup. Or peel, if liked, and quarter or chop for fruit for savoury salads, sauces, ice cream and cake fillings. **FLAVOUR PAIRINGS** Poultry, prawns, goat's cheese, vanilla ice cream, apples, pears, citrus, ginger, spirits. **IN SEASON** Imported April–June

▲ QUINCE

EAT Peel, core, and chop for sauces and meat dishes, tarts, pies, and crumbles. Purée for mousses and creams. Bottle or make into jams, jellies, or cheese. Use japonica quinces in the same way. **FLAVOUR PAIRINGS** Lamb, pork, chicken, game, hard cheeses (particularly Manchego), apples, pears, ginger, cloves, cinnamon. **IN SEASON** October–November

▲ MEDLAR

EAT When bletted (ripened), peel back the skin and suck or spoon out the flesh. Add pulp to a rich meat sauce or make into jelly, curd, or cheese. **FLAVOUR PAIRINGS** Meat, game, hard cheeses, cinnamon, nutmeg, mixed spice, star anise, red or white wine. **IN SEASON** October–November

STONE FRUITS

BUY Plums, gages, and sloes should have a slight bloom on the skin. They should all feel heavy for their size, and firm, but give slightly when gently pressed. They should never feel squashy. Avoid if rock hard (they may never ripen), if split, wet, with any bruised patches, or with wrinkled skin (except dates, which may be semi-dried). **STORE** If a little firm, keep in a fruit bowl. If ripe, they will keep for a few days in the refigerator in an open paper bag. All except dates can be bottled or frozen in dry sugar or syrup for up to 12 months.

▲ VICTORIA PLUMS

EAT The classic British dessert plum. Delicious raw, or cooked in sauces, soufflés, pies, tarts, cakes, and puddings, or preserved as jam or chutney. **FLAVOUR PAIRINGS** Duck, lamb, pork, gammon, goose, game birds, chilli, Chinese five-spice powder, ginger, soy sauce, garlic, onions, pickling vinegar, almonds, cinnamon, custard, cream, eggs. **IN SEASON** August–October

▲ RED PLUMS

EAT Various large red and purple varieties, mostly imported (Santa Rosa pictured). Red have a better flavour for cooking than purple. Eat fresh, in pies and crumbles, mixed with other fruit, diced in salsas, or as plum sauce. Available canned, and dried as prunes. **FLAVOUR PAIRINGS** Meat, game, avocados, tomatoes, red peppers, cucumber, spring onions, chilli, coriander leaf, lime, garlic, ginger, soy sauce, rice, vinegar, apples, pears, rhubarb, strawberries, custard, clotted cream, ground almonds. **IN SEASON** Imported all year

▲ YELLOW PLUMS

EAT Large imported yellow plums are best raw. Smaller ones, like Coe's Golden Drop (pictured) are good in crumbles, sweet and savoury salads, and salsas. **FLAVOUR PAIRINGS** Sweet peppers, spring onions, cucumber, light muscovado sugar, soft fresh cheeses. **IN SEASON** August, imported all year

▲ OPAL PLUMS

EAT Sweet early-cropper. Good raw but excellent bottled whole in alcohol, and for pies, clafoutis, and desserts. **FLAVOUR PAIRINGS** Brandy, kirsch, red wine, cream, clafoutis batter, light muscovado sugar, butter, almonds. **IN SEASON** August–October

▲ GREENGAGES

EAT Sweet-scented fruit that can be used instead of plums in any dish. **FLAVOUR PAIRINGS** All rich meats and game, ground and flaked almonds, cinnamon, ginger, kirsch, amaretto, brandy, cream, custard. **IN SEASON** August

▲ APRICOTS

EAT Use the natural line on the fruit to cut in half and twist apart. Eat raw as a snack, or in fruit salads or platters. Poach in syrup or wine; purée for fruit sauce; or halve, stuff, and bake. Add to tagines, couscous, roasts, and stuffings. Also available canned, dried, and as jam. **FLAVOUR PAIRINGS** Chicken, lamb, pork, ham, yogurt, cream, custard, oranges, almonds, rice, ginger, vanilla, sweet white wine, amaretto. **IN SEASON** July–August, imported most of the year

▲ DAMSONS

EAT Sharp even when ripe, but excellent in desserts, jams, fruit cheese, soups, wine, and chutney. **FLAVOUR PAIRINGS** Sultanas, apple, garlic, light muscovado sugar, chilli, ginger, cinnamon, pickling vinegar, red wine, ice cream, custard, blackberries. **IN SEASON** August–September

SWEET CHERRIES

SOUR CHERRIES

▲ CHERRIES

EAT Morello are sour cherries with a wonderful flavour for cooking, particularly whenpreserved in alcohol or syrup and in jam. Add sweet cherries whole or stoned to fruit salads, to decorate and fill cakes or in cold and iced desserts. Bake both in pies, tarts, clafoutis, and strudels. Use for soup, or in sweet and savoury sauces. Also sold canned and bottled, in syrup, brandy, or maraschino, and candied (glacé). **FLAVOUR PAIRINGS** Duck, game, almonds, sweet spices, chocolate, citrus, fromage frais, yogurt, brandy, kirsch, grappa. **IN SEASON** June–August, sweet cherries imported most of the year

▲ SLOES

EAT Small back fruit of the Blackthorn. Too sour to eat raw, but good in jam and jelly and to flavour gin or vodka. **FLAVOUR PAIRINGS** Juniper, cinnamon, vanilla, gin, vodka, apples. **IN SEASON** October–November

◀ DATES

EAT Medjool (pictured) is highly-prized. Eat raw, whole or stuffed. Chop and add to rice, couscous, stuffings, stews, and relishes. Also available dried and as syrup. **FLAVOUR PAIRINGS** Poultry, lamb, bacon, cheeses, marzipan, nuts, clotted cream, yogurt, citrus, chocolate. **IN SEASON** Imported most of the year, best November–January

YELLOW-FLESH PEACH

DONUT PEACH

WHITE-FLESH PEACH

▲ PEACHES

EAT Flat donut, yellow- or white-fleshed can all be used in the same way. Best skinned before eating. Halve and grill to garnish savoury dishes; stuff and bake; slice or dice for fruit salads and salsas; purée for ice cream, sorbets and sauces; make into jam or chutney. Also available canned and dried. **FLAVOUR PAIRINGS** Beef, duck, soured cream, yogurt, passion fruit, mangoes, berries, lime, mint, almonds, cinnamon, ginger, nutmeg, chilli, Champagne, sherry, amaretto. **IN SEASON** August–September, imported most of the year

YELLOW-FLESH NECTARINE

WHITE-FLESH NECTARINE

▲ NECTARINES

EAT Similar to peaches (and used the same way) but with smooth skin. Delicious raw with cold meats and in salads and salsas, but also good stuffed and baked. **FLAVOUR PAIRINGS** Chicken, gammon, prosciutto crudo, soft white cheeses like Mascarpone, walnuts, almonds, berries, chilli, cinnamon, vanilla, star anise. **IN SEASON** August–September, imported most of the year

OLIVES

BUY For best flavour, buy olives still with their pits – loose or in jars. Pitted ones are useful for some dishes though. In general look for plump, shiny specimens, although dry salt-cured ones are supposed to look shrivelled. **STORE** Always keep in the refrigerator in sealed containers. Loose ones, or those in salt or brine, should be used within a week or so. Those covered in olive oil will keep for months. If mould appears on the surface, rinse, dry, and cover with fresh oil.

▲ MANZANILLA OLIVES

EAT Large green, silky olives from Seville. Sold stuffed with pimento, too. Traditionally served with chilled fino sherry; also the perfect Martini olive. Good sliced in fish, cheese, and pulse salads. **FLAVOUR PAIRINGS** Dry fino sherry, gin, dry Martini, shellfish, chickpeas, white beans, chorizo, Serrano ham, squid, prawns, crab, Manchego cheese. **IN SEASON** Imported all year

▲ KALAMATA OLIVES

EAT From Greece, with a rich fruity flavour. Good with aperitifs, in salads, and also cooked in stews and casseroles. **FLAVOUR PAIRINGS** White cabbage, tomatoes, cucumber, red onions, sweet peppers, aubergines, Feta cheese, Halloumi cheese, red wine vinegar, olive oil, oregano, preserved lemons, pork, chicken, lamb, pasta, rice. **IN SEASON** Imported all year

◀ DRY SALT-CURED OLIVES

EAT Shrivelled and salty with a strong, olive flavour. Stone and chop, then bake in bread, add to tapenade, pasta sauces, and meat dishes (whole or stoned). **FLAVOUR PAIRINGS** Beef, pork, lamb, spicy sausages, pasta, olive oil, cherry and sun-dried tomatoes, sweet peppers, basil, oregano, parsley. **IN SEASON** Imported all year

◀ PICHOLINE OLIVES

EAT Dusky green olives with a surprising amount of crisp, nutty flesh. Delicious served as an aperitif, but also good chopped in chicken, fish, and rabbit stews, and rice dishes. **FLAVOUR PAIRINGS** Chicken, white and oily fish, rabbit, tomatoes, rice, white wine, sherry, dry vermouth, peppers, white beans, oranges. **IN SEASON** Imported all year

▲ STUFFED GREEN OLIVES

EAT Small green olives are sold pitted and stuffed with pimento, anchovy, lemon, garlic, capers, celery, or almonds. Serve as appetizers or slice in salads. **FLAVOUR PAIRINGS** Fish, meat, poultry, cheeses, pasta, rice, peppers, tomatoes, onions, garlic, sweet spices, herbs. **IN SEASON** Imported all year

▲ NIÇOISE-COQUILLOS

EAT Small and nutty from Provence, France but also grown in Spain and Italy. Often preserved with herbs. Use in classics like Pissaladière and Niçoise salad. **FLAVOUR PAIRINGS** Tomatoes, onions, garlic, anchovies, eggs, green beans, new potatoes, courgettes, capers, caperberries, cinnamon, oregano, herbes de Provence. **IN SEASON** Imported all year

TROPICAL FRUITS

BUY Most should give slightly when lightly squeezed and have a fragrant aroma. Choose bananas according to personal preference. Avoid if soft and dark all over. All unripe fruit can be ripened at room temperature. **STORE** Ripe fruit should be eaten as soon as possible after purchase. All except bananas (and pineapples, unless prepared then put in an airtight container) can be stored in a paper bag in the refrigerator for a few days (bananas go black if too cold). All except dragon fruit can be frozen for up to 12 months as purée (bananas discolour, so use for breads and cakes only and use within 6 months), or in syrup. Freeze passion fruit pulp in ice cube trays to add to ice creams and fruit salads.

▲ KIWI

EAT Halve and spoon out for a snack. Peel and slice or dice for fruit salads and salsas, to decorate pavlovas, pastries and cakes, or as a garnish. **FLAVOUR PAIRINGS** Gammon, chicken, guinea fowl, squid, salmon, swordfish, chillies, orange, strawberries, other tropical fruit. **IN SEASON** Imported all year, best January–August

▲ MANGO

EAT Peel and stone, then slice or chop for salads, salsas, or cakes. Purée for juices, smoothies, sorbets, mousses, and cream. Slice and bottle in syrup. Also available canned, dried, and as chutney. **FLAVOUR PAIRINGS** Chicken, smoked meats, fish, shellfish, green salads, avocados, lime, lemon, chillies, curry spices, coriander leaf, vanilla ice cream, sweet sticky rice, rum. **IN SEASON** Imported all year

▲ PASSION FRUIT

EAT Halve and spoon out the pulp to add to fruit salads and desserts. Sieve to yield juice for dressings, ices, mousses, soufflés, sauces, smoothies, and drinks. **FLAVOUR PAIRINGS** Tuna, venison, game birds, cream, yogurt, custard, oranges, kiwi fruit, strawberries, bananas, peaches, light muscovado sugar, rum, white and sparkling wine. **IN SEASON** Imported October–June

▲ PAPAYA

EAT Peel, halve, and scoop out the seeds. Use in sweet and savoury salads, salsas, and desserts. It contains papain which tenderises meat. When unripe, steam as a vegetable. Also available canned and dried. **FLAVOUR PAIRINGS** Meat, smoked meats, avocados, chillies, lime, lemon, coconut, ginger. **IN SEASON** Imported all year

▲ POMEGRANATE

EAT Use the juicy seeds in sweet and savoury salads, salsas, dressings, cold and iced desserts. Add the juice to soups, stews, desserts, and sauces. Also available as syrup (molasses). **FLAVOUR PAIRINGS** Prawns, lamb, chicken, duck, pheasant, aubergines, figs, almonds, pistachios, couscous, rice. **IN SEASON** Imported October–February

◄ GUAVA

EAT Add to sweet and savoury salads, purée for sauces, smoothies, and pancake fillings, sorbets, and ice cream. Poach or bake for compôtes, desserts, and savoury dishes. Also available canned and dried. **FLAVOUR PAIRINGS** Pork, pheasant, duck, seafood, chicken, cream cheese, apples, pears, lime, chillies, lemon, coconut, ginger, honey. **IN SEASON** Imported all year

PERSIMMON (SHARON FRUIT) ►

EAT Eat whole, or cut off the top and scoop out flesh. Blend for smoothies, add to sauces, cold and iced desserts. If unripe, poach or chop and add to cakes, breads, and muffins. **FLAVOUR PAIRINGS** Ham, pork, game, lime, clotted cream, yogurt, fromage frais, walnuts, ginger, cinnamon, allspice, nutmeg, honey. **IN SEASON** Imported October–April

▲ PINEAPPLE

EAT Peel and slice or dice for savoury and sweet salads, salsas, pastries, and desserts. Add pineapple juice to marinades, drinks, and smoothies. Also available canned, candied, and dried. **FLAVOUR PAIRINGS** Pork, ham, chicken, duck, fish, shellfish, cottage cheese, coconut, ginger, allspice, cinnamon, black pepper, Cointreau, rum, Kirsch. **IN SEASON** Imported all year

▲ DRAGON FRUIT

EAT Do not cook. Best eaten chilled. Halve and scoop out the flesh. Add to fruit salads, or press the juice for sorbets, cocktails, and drinks. **FLAVOUR PAIRINGS** Lime, lemon, other tropical fruits, coconut, sugar, ginger. **IN SEASON** Imported all year

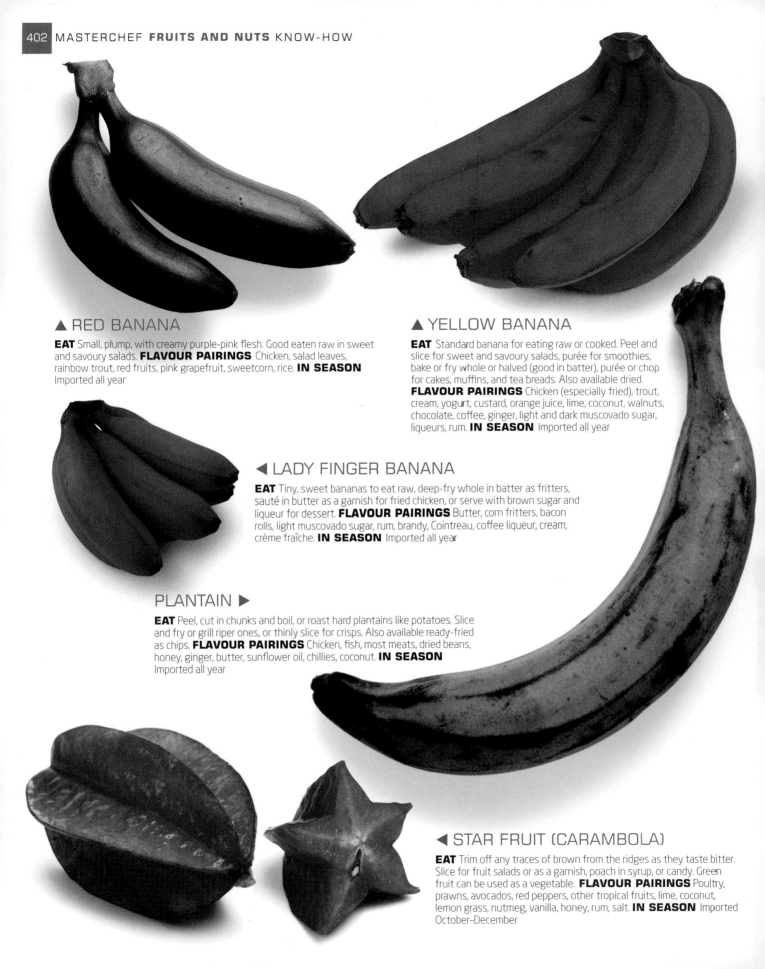

▲ RED BANANA

EAT Small, plump, with creamy purple-pink flesh. Good eaten raw in sweet and savoury salads. **FLAVOUR PAIRINGS** Chicken, salad leaves, rainbow trout, red fruits, pink grapefruit, sweetcorn, rice. **IN SEASON** Imported all year

◄ LADY FINGER BANANA

EAT Tiny, sweet bananas to eat raw, deep-fry whole in batter as fritters, sauté in butter as a garnish for fried chicken, or serve with brown sugar and liqueur for dessert. **FLAVOUR PAIRINGS** Butter, corn fritters, bacon rolls, light muscovado sugar, rum, brandy, Cointreau, coffee liqueur, cream, crème fraîche. **IN SEASON** Imported all year

PLANTAIN ▶

EAT Peel, cut in chunks and boil, or roast hard plantains like potatoes. Slice and fry or grill riper ones, or thinly slice for crisps. Also available ready-fried as chips. **FLAVOUR PAIRINGS** Chicken, fish, most meats, dried beans, honey, ginger, butter, sunflower oil, chillies, coconut. **IN SEASON** Imported all year

▲ YELLOW BANANA

EAT Standard banana for eating raw or cooked. Peel and slice for sweet and savoury salads, purée for smoothies, bake or fry whole or halved (good in batter), purée or chop for cakes, muffins, and tea breads. Also available dried. **FLAVOUR PAIRINGS** Chicken (especially fried), trout, cream, yogurt, custard, orange juice, lime, coconut, walnuts, chocolate, coffee, ginger, light and dark muscovado sugar, liqueurs, rum. **IN SEASON** Imported all year

◄ STAR FRUIT (CARAMBOLA)

EAT Trim off any traces of brown from the ridges as they taste bitter. Slice for fruit salads or as a garnish, poach in syrup, or candy. Green fruit can be used as a vegetable. **FLAVOUR PAIRINGS** Poultry, prawns, avocados, red peppers, other tropical fruits, lime, coconut, lemon grass, nutmeg, vanilla, honey, rum, salt. **IN SEASON** Imported October–December

▲ LYCHEE

EAT Pop out of the shells for a snack. Stone and add to sweet or savoury salads, sweet and sour dishes, and stir-fries. Poach in syrup or purée for ice cream, smoothies, drinks, and dressings. Also available canned. **FLAVOUR PAIRINGS** Pork, duck, chicken, seafood, chillies, avocados, raspberries, coconut, cream, lime, ginger. **IN SEASON** Imported April–June

▲ RAMBUTAN

EAT Peel and eat fresh, use as a garnish, add to savoury or fruit salads, purée for ice cream or sorbet, or poach in syrup. **FLAVOUR PAIRINGS** Pork, duck, avocados, chillies, cream, coconut, vanilla, ginger. **IN SEASON** Imported May–September

▲ TAMARILLO

EAT Also called tree tomato. Cut in half, sprinkle with sugar, chill overnight, then scoop out. Add to ice cream. Peel and stew in savoury dishes and for relishes. Bake or grill for dessert, or add to compôtes. **FLAVOUR PAIRINGS** Roast meats, chicken, fish, curry spices, cream, kiwi fruit, oranges, light muscovado sugar. **IN SEASON** Imported May–October

▲ MANGOSTEEN

EAT Cut off the top and scoop out the flesh, don't eat the pith. Use juice for drinks and sorbets. **FLAVOUR PAIRINGS** Other tropical fruits, strawberries, lemon grass, lemon. **IN SEASON** Imported May–September

▲ CUSTARD APPLE

EAT Remove the seeds and eat fresh, or use in pies, pancakes, stir-fries, and savoury sauces. **FLAVOUR PAIRINGS** Pork, chicken, citrus, yogurt, cinnamon, ginger. **IN SEASON** Imported June–September

▲ DURIAN

EAT Famous for tasting delicious, but smelling awful! Split open and scoop out the pulp round the seeds. Eat with sugar and salt, or purée for shakes and smoothies, or add to cakes. Cook unripe fruit as a vegetable. Roast the seeds. **FLAVOUR PAIRINGS** Milk, cream, coconut, other tropical fruits, curry spices, chillies, sticky rice. **IN SEASON** Imported May–August

◀ PHYSALIS

EAT Peel back the papery casing and eat raw, or dip in chocolate or fondant for petit fours. Poach in syrup, add to cakes and tarts, sauté briefly for savoury dishes, use as a garnish or make into jam. **FLAVOUR PAIRINGS** White fish, scallops, yogurt, other tropical fruits, nuts, lemon, tarragon, chocolate, Cointreau. **IN SEASON** Imported August–October

GRAPES, RHUBARB, AND FIGS

BUY All should be unblemished. Grapes should have a slight bloom. Rhubarb stalks should be firm. The leaves of forced rhubarb should be pale yellow and fresh. Avoid if browning around the stalk end or wrinkling. Figs should feel heavy for their size and just yield without pressing; sugar beads around the stem indicate ripeness. **STORE** Keep in the refrigerator: rhubarb for a week or more, wrapped in moist kitchen paper in a plastic bag; grapes for up to 5 days in an open paper bag; ripe figs for a day or two, but best eaten quickly. If unripe, soften at room temperature. All can be frozen in syrup for up to 12 months.

▲ RED GRAPES

EAT A gourmet, seeded red variety is Muscat Rosada (pictured here). They have a rich, musky flavour. All red grapes (some are seedless) are best eaten fresh to round off a meal, or in fruit salads. **FLAVOUR PAIRINGS** Goat's cheese, Cheddar, Manchego, Port, unblanched almonds, most fruits. **IN SEASON** Imported in spring

▲ GREEN GRAPES

EAT With or without seeds, eat whole or peel, if liked, halve and add to cream and white wine sauces, or to fruit salads. **FLAVOUR PAIRINGS** Chicken, poultry livers, rabbit, flat fish, melon, strawberries, cheeses, walnuts. **IN SEASON** September–October, imported all year

▲ BLACK GRAPES

EAT Good colour and flavour. Halve, de-seed, if necessary, and add to sauces and salads, or serve with cheeses, liver pâtés, and terrines. **FLAVOUR PAIRINGS** Beef, venison, game birds, cheeses, fruits, red wine, port. **IN SEASON** September–October, imported all year.

▼ RHUBARB

EAT Forced rhubarb is tender and pink. Outdoor is coarser and may have tough skin. If so, pull off before cutting into short lengths. Also sold frozen and canned. Use in pies, crumbles, mousses, fools, ice cream, and sauces (particularly for oily fish). **FLAVOUR PAIRINGS** Ginger, cinnamon, vanilla, lavender, strawberries, oranges, plums, brown sugar, custard, mackerel, herring. **IN SEASON** Forced: February–April. Outdoor: April–July

FORCED RHUBARB

OUTDOOR RHUBARB

▲ BROWN TURKEY FIG

EAT Eat whole, including the skin if soft. Add to sweet and savoury salads, stuff for sweetmeats, poach in syrup, bottle, or make into jam. Also sold dried. **FLAVOUR PAIRINGS** Cured meats, yogurt, cream, cheeses, nuts, star anise, marzipan, fortified wine. **IN SEASON** August–September, imported May–December

MELONS

BUY Winter and summer sweet melons and watermelons should all feel heavy for their size. Winter melons have smooth or finely ribbed yellow rind and pale flesh. Summer ones include those with a raised cross-hatch pattern or netting on the rind and have green through to orange flesh. They should yield to gentle pressure round the base and smell fragrant. Watermelons should give a ringing sound when tapped. **STORE** Whole ones will keep in a cool dark place for up to 2 weeks. Keep cut ones in a sealed plastic bag in the refrigerator for up to a week. Freeze balls or cubes in sugar or syrup for up to 6 months.

▲ OGEN

EAT Small summer melon with greenish-yellow skin and green flesh. Good halved and the seeds scooped out, then filled for starter or dessert. **FLAVOUR PAIRINGS** Prawns, crab, lobster, ginger wine, raspberries, framboise liqueur, sorbets, ice cream. **IN SEASON** Imported all year

▲ HONEYDEW

EAT The best known winter variety and the classic choice for melon-boat starters. Good in salads, soups, and jam. **FLAVOUR PAIRINGS** Parma ham, other cured and smoked meats, ground ginger, orange, mint, rosemary, cucumber, herb bread. **IN SEASON** Imported all year

▲ CANTALOUPE (MUSKMELON)

EAT Summer melon with pale orange, very sweet flesh. Good for breakfast or in salads. Note Galia (not pictured) looks similar, but is oval and has light green flesh. **FLAVOUR PAIRINGS** Coconut (fruit and milk), lime, cucumber, mint, fresh cheeses like mozzarella. **IN SEASON** Imported all year

▲ CHARENTAIS

EAT The green ribs on the rind make it look like it comes ready-sectioned. Apricot-orange flesh and delicious fragrance. Excellent dessert summer melon, and good for sorbets and soup. **FLAVOUR PAIRINGS** Tropical fruit, raspberries, strawberries, mint. **IN SEASON** Imported all year

▲ WATERMELON

EAT Serve chilled in wedges, add to a fruit platter or cube for salads and pickle, or make into jam. Roast and salt the seeds. **FLAVOUR PAIRINGS** Chicken, prawns, crab, feta cheese, beetroot, sweet melon, apple, berries, lime, chillies, ginger, mint. **IN SEASON** Imported all year

CITRUS FRUITS

BUY Look for skins that are bright, taut, and glossy. Fruit should feel heavy for its size, and should smell aromatic. Avoid any fruits that look dry or mouldy, or have brown marks. Unwaxed fruit are best if you want to use the peel or zest. **STORE** Keep in a cool place, or uncovered in the refrigerator, for up to 2 weeks; use before the skins shrivel. Smaller fruits will not keep as long as large ones. Freeze peeled segments and slices, or whole small fruits, dry or in syrup for up to 12 months.

PINK
GRAPEFRUIT

▲ POMELO

EAT Delicious in salads and salsas, but make sure you remove all the pith and membrane. Candy the goose-pimpled skin, or add it to marmalade. **FLAVOUR PAIRINGS** Shellfish, smoked fish, poultry, ham, pork, chicory, frisée, celery, spinach, chocolate, cloves, cardamom. **IN SEASON** Imported January–February

RED
GRAPEFRUIT

WHITE
GRAPEFRUIT

▲ GRAPEFRUIT

EAT Halve or segment white, pink, or red grapefruit to eat alone or in salads. Squeeze the juice for drinks, sorbets, and sauces. Grill halves. Use in marmalade or candy the peel. **FLAVOUR PAIRINGS** Chicken, gammon, smoked meats, prawns, avocados, spinach, lemon, mint, ginger, nutmeg, coconut, honey. **IN SEASON** Imported all year

▲ LIME

EAT Squeeze the juice for dressings, salsas, marinades, and drinks. Use the juice and zest in desserts, pies, and baked goods. Also, make into pickles, chutneys, jams, jellies, and marmalade. Also available dried. **FLAVOUR PAIRINGS** Poultry, fish, shellfish, chillies, Tabasco, tomatoes, avocados, lemons, mango, melon, papaya, chocolate, rum, tequila, mint, coriander leaf. **IN SEASON** Imported all year

▲ LEMON

EAT Squeeze the juice for dressings, marinades, drinks, tarts, pies, soups, salsas, fish, curries, and emulsion sauces. Grate the zest for baking and desserts. Add pared zest to casseroles. Chop for marmalade and chutney. **FLAVOUR PAIRINGS** Chicken, veal, fish, shellfish, eggs, artichokes, garlic, olives, cream, sage, tarragon, coriander leaf and seeds, capers, olive oil, gin. **IN SEASON** Imported all year

▲ KUMQUAT

EAT Not a true citrus, but used in similar ways in the kitchen. Eat whole (including the soft skin) or cook with sugar, spices, or spirits to make compôtes and chutneys, or bottle in alcohol. **FLAVOUR PAIRINGS** Shellfish, smoked fish, poultry, ham, pork, duck, chicory, frisée, celery, spinach, chocolate, cloves, cardamom, vodka. **IN SEASON** Imported November–February

▲ MINNEOLA

EAT A mandarin–grapefruit hybrid with sharp, juicy, seedless flesh. Eat as a refreshing snack or use in salads and desserts. **FLAVOUR PAIRINGS** Shellfish, pork, duck, chicory, watercress, celery, rocket, chocolate, cloves, star anise, Cointreau. **IN SEASON** Imported December–February

▲ UGLI

EAT A Jamaican cross between a tangerine, Seville orange, and grapefruit. Halve and eat fresh, or segment and chop and add to rich meats, oily fish, salads, ice creams, and soufflés. Candy the peel. **FLAVOUR PAIRINGS** Oily fish, pork, duck, goose, chicory, frisée, rocket, cream, honey, Kirsch or sherry (over halves). **IN SEASON** Imported November–April

◀ SEVILLE (BITTER) ORANGES

EAT Used mostly for marmalade but also good with rich meats, in spicy fish dishes, desserts, and to flavour white spirits. **FLAVOUR PAIRINGS** Duck, pigeon, pheasant, pork, salmon, tuna, meaty white fish, pancakes, rhubarb, meringue, lemon, grapefruit, gin, vodka, white rum. **IN SEASON** Imported January–March

VALENCIA ORANGES

NAVEL ORANGES

▲ SWEET ORANGES

EAT Valencia, then Navel are the two leading commercial varieties. Grate zest and segment fruit, or squeeze juice, for sauces, soups, with other fruits and vegetables, in casseroles, salads, and sorbets. Use the zest in cakes and biscuits. Also peel and eat raw, or poach in caramelized syrup. Candy the peel and dip in chocolate. **FLAVOUR PAIRINGS** Beef, duck, gammon, liver, scallops, tomatoes, beetroot, black olives, nuts, soy sauce, cloves, cinnamon, fennel, carrots, chicory, frisée, button mushrooms, chocolate, strawberries, brandy. **IN SEASON** Valencias: Imported February–October. Navels: Imported November–May

▲ BLOOD ORANGES

EAT Small oranges with red-flecked flesh that yield a dazzling ruby juice, essential for Sauce Maltaise – with egg yolks and melted butter (or cheat and use red grapefruit) – and sorbets. Use the segmented flesh in sweet and savoury salads. **FLAVOUR PAIRINGS** Egg yolks, butter, baby red chard, beetroot, spring onions, strawberries, raspberries, pineapple, bananas, lemon, lime, walnuts. **IN SEASON** Imported December–May

▲ CLEMENTINE

EAT Peel for a snack or add to salads. Squeeze the juice for smoothies and sorbets. Lightly sauté or grill segments as a side dish. **FLAVOUR PAIRINGS** Shellfish, pork, chicken, duck, spinach, carrots, sweet peppers, salad leaves, almonds, coriander leaf, chocolate, meringues, Grand Marnier. **IN SEASON** Imported all year

▲ SATSUMA

EAT Slightly less sweet than clementines, satsumas can be used the same way but are also good preserved whole in syrup and caramel, with or without alcohol. **FLAVOUR PAIRINGS** Caramel, soft brown sugar, vanilla sugar, brandy, Grand Marnier, vodka, whisky. **IN SEASON** Imported most of the year, best November–January

▲ TANGERINE

EAT Tangerines are varieties of mandarin and have distinctively fragrant, sweet, juicy flesh (Murcott, or honey tangerine, pictured here). Use the zest and juice in desserts, sauces, and for sautéed poultry, pork and fish, and the segments in fruit salads and coleslaw. **FLAVOUR PAIRINGS** Chicken breasts, pork fillet and chops, tuna, salmon, scallops, cabbage, carrots, shallots, cream, honey. **IN SEASON** October–April

CURRANTS AND BERRIES

BUY Choose fruit that are uniformly ripe and unblemished. Avoid red or black fruits that are still green in patches, or bright orange cloudberries (they go yellow as they ripen). Currants and berries do not ripen further after picking. If buying in punnets, avoid any that are stained with juice as this is a sign that the fruit is past its best. **STORE** Better eaten the day of picking or purchase but can be stored in the refrigerator, preferably in a single layer, for a couple of days. Green gooseberries will keep for up to a week. All can be bottled or frozen in dry sugar or syrup for up to 12 months. They soften when thawed so then only use for cooked dishes and purées.

◀ REDCURRANTS

EAT Small fragile berries with a tangy kick. Use for jelly, syrup, in sprigs as a garnish to meat and game, and frosted with egg white and caster sugar to decorate cakes and desserts.
FLAVOUR PAIRINGS Lamb, goat, venison, turkey, goose, duck, game birds, berries, mint, cinnamon, red wine, port, brandy. **IN SEASON** July–August, imported in summer

WHITECURRANTS ▶

EAT Rarer than redcurrants, delicious for dessert on their own or with berries, in jelly, and frosted with egg white and sugar to decorate cakes and desserts. **FLAVOUR PAIRINGS** Raspberries, blueberries, white chocolate, rosemary (in jelly), lemon zest (with sugar to eat raw). **IN SEASON** July–August

▲ BLACKCURRANTS

EAT Excellent for mousses, creams, pies, crumbles, cheesecake toppings, fools, soups, jams, jellies, and cordial. They are very sharp so need cooking and sweetening with sugar, honey, fruit juice, or liqueur before eating. Available bottled, frozen, and canned. **FLAVOUR PAIRINGS** Mint, rosemary, orange, apples, pears, honey, vodka, Cassis, white wine, Champagne. **IN SEASON** July–August, imported in summer

COOKING GOOSEBERRIES

DESSERT GOOSEBERRIES

GOOSEBERRIES ▶

EAT Green ones are sour. Cook with sugar or another sweetener for pies, crumbles, fools, mousses, in jam, and as sauce (particularly good with oily fish). The purple dessert variety is softer and sweeter. Eat raw or cook as above. **FLAVOUR PAIRINGS** Goose, pork, mackerel, herrings, Camembert, cream, lemon, cinnamon, cloves, dill, fennel, elderflowers, honey. **IN SEASON** June–August

◄ RASPBERRIES

EAT Many varieties. Eat raw for dessert, or purée for sauces, cold and iced desserts, soup, and smoothies. Add to savoury and sweet salads, tarts, pies, crumbles, summer pudding, and gâteaux. Use for jam, jelly, and to flavour vinegar and sweetened alcohol. **FLAVOUR PAIRINGS** Duck, goose, venison, game birds, chicken or duck livers, cream, crème fraîche, peaches, other berries, hazelnuts, meringue, almonds, oats, honey, vanilla, cinnamon, red wine, vodka, raspberry vinegar. **IN SEASON** July–November, imported all year

▲ WILD STRAWBERRIES

EAT Also known as fraises des bois, they are found wild and cultivated (then called Alpine strawberries). Exquisite raw or as part of a special dessert, for wonderful flavoured vinegar or liqueur, or added to chilled still or sparkling wine. **FLAVOUR PAIRINGS** Champagne, white or rosé wine, vodka, Cointreau, cream, crème fraîche, eggs, custard, bitter chocolate, red wine or strawberry vinegar. **IN SEASON** June–August

▲ STRAWBERRIES

EAT Many varieties. Dip in melted chocolate, macerate in orange juice or liqueur, top cheesecakes, add to tarts, pies, summer pudding, gâteaux, and shortbread. Purée for coulis, cold and iced desserts, shakes, and smoothies. **FLAVOUR PAIRINGS** Cream, ice cream, curd and other soft white cheeses, cucumber, oranges, melon, rhubarb, other berries, almonds, vanilla, chocolate, black pepper. **IN SEASON** May–September, imported all year

▲ BLACKBERRIES

EAT Wild and cultivated. Add to salads, compôtes, pies, and crumbles. Use for jelly and flavoured vinegar. Purée for mousses, soups, and sauces. Bottle in syrup. **FLAVOUR PAIRINGS** Poultry, game, cream, yogurt, cream cheese, apples, pears, raspberries, almonds, oats, honey, vanilla, cinnamon. **IN SEASON** July–October, imported all year

▲ ROWANBERRIES

EAT Gather after the first frosts, or pick when ripe and freeze for a couple of weeks to remove the bitterness. Must be cooked before eating. Use in sauces, pies, and crumbles, for jelly, wine, and liqueur. **FLAVOUR PAIRINGS** Lamb, mutton, goat, venison, poultry, apples, pears. red wine. **IN SEASON** August–October

▲ LOGANBERRIES

EAT Blackberry-raspberry hybrid with an intense flavour. Use in pies, tarts, summer pudding, and for jam. Purée for ice cream, sorbets, and smoothies. **FLAVOUR PAIRINGS** Apples, pears, bananas, rhubarb, cream, crème fraîche, soft white cheeses, yogurt, almonds. **IN SEASON** July–September

▲ BLUEBERRIES

EAT Serve as a snack or dessert alone, or with cereal for breakfast or in fruit salad. Purée for soups and smoothies. Bake in pies, tarts, crumbles, cobblers, cakes, and muffins. Stew for sweet and savoury sauces, in compôtes, or cheesecake toppings. **FLAVOUR PAIRINGS** Game, cream, crème fraîche, yogurt, citrus, almonds, pistachios, mint, cinnamon, allspice, plain and white chocolate. **IN SEASON** July–August, imported all year

▲ CRANBERRIES

EAT Stew with sugar or honey for sauces and desserts. Add to pies, tarts, muffins, cakes, and parfaits as well as to pâtés, terrines, and stuffings for poultry and meat. Bottle alone or with apples or other berries. Make into jelly and jam. Also available frozen. **FLAVOUR PAIRINGS** Turkey, goose, pork, gammon, oily fish, apples, raspberries, blueberries, oranges, nuts, red wine, brandy, port. **IN SEASON** Imported November–March

▲ MULBERRIES

EAT Gather from the ground when they've dropped when completely ripe. Eat whole, or purée for drinks, cocktails, ice cream, and sorbet. Make into jam or jelly, use to flavour vinegar, gin, white rum, or vodka **FLAVOUR PAIRINGS** Poultry, lamb, game, cream, pears, citrus. **IN SEASON** August–September

▶ ELDERBERRIES

EAT The fruit must be cooked. Add to pies, crumbles, or compôtes with other fruits, or purée for sauces and soups. Use to make cordial, wine, jam, or jelly. Use elderflowers to flavour gooseberries, dip in batter as fritters, or to make cordial or Champagne. **FLAVOUR PAIRINGS** Game, pork, apples, crab apples, strawberries, blackberries, lemon, walnuts, cinnamon, allspice, nutmeg, cloves. **IN SEASON** August–October

DRIED AND CANDIED FRUITS

BUY Look for plump, unblemished, supple dried fruit (except banana chips, which are hard). Avoid if they appear leathery. Most are now sold ready-to-eat but check if they need soaking before use. They are sometimes treated with sulphur dioxide to preserve them further, or may contain added sugar, oil, flavourings, or additives. Check the labels. Candied fruit should be soft and moist. Available all year. **STORE** Once a packet or pot is opened, place in an airtight container and store in a cool, dark, dry place. Dried fruits will keep for 6 months, candied fruit for a year.

▲ RAISINS AND SULTANAS

EAT Raisins are dried black grapes (pictured). Black manukka and muscatels have the best flavour. Sultanas are dried white grapes. Eat as a snack, add to breakfast cereals, in rice and couscous dishes, salads, tagines, curries, cakes, biscuits, muffins, puddings, and chutneys. **FLAVOUR PAIRINGS** Cinnamon, mixed spice, curry spices, coriander leaf, parsley, mint, oats and other grains, cabbage, honey, rum, cream, most fruits, chocolate, nuts.

▲ DRIED CRANBERRY

EAT Often sweetened when dried. Add to breakfast cereals, cakes, biscuits, muffins, sweet or savoury stuffings. **FLAVOUR PAIRINGS** Oats, wheat, barley, millet, rice, breadcrumbs, turkey, duck, goose, pork, chicken, pine nuts, rosemary, thyme, parsley, onions, honey, maple syrup.

▲ DRIED BLUEBERRY

EAT Add to breakfast cereals, cakes, biscuits, muffins, trail mix, sweet and savoury salads. **FLAVOUR PAIRINGS** White and plain chocolate, vanilla, cinnamon, oats, rice, couscous, pistachios, almonds, walnuts, honey.

▲ DRIED CHERRY

EAT Sour cherries are delicious as a snack, or add to breakfast cereals, puddings, pies, muffins, and ice cream. **FLAVOUR PAIRINGS** Almonds, oats and other grains, white soft cheeses, cream, kirsch, amaretto, plain chocolate.

▲ CURRANTS

EAT Dried small black grapes with an intense, slightly bitter flavour. Use alone or with other dried fruits for cakes, puddings, biscuits, and pastries. Also good in hot and cold rice and couscous dishes. **FLAVOUR PAIRINGS** Brown and white sugars, honey, soft white cheeses, other dried fruits, ginger, cinnamon, mixed spice, cardamom, cumin, turmeric, peas, apples, pears, citrus, mint, parsley, rosemary, coriander seed and leaf, basil.

▲ DRIED MANGO

EAT They have a vibrant colour and chewy texture. Delicious as a snack. Chop and add to cakes, biscuits, tea breads, chutney, and jam.
FLAVOUR PAIRINGS Coconut, lime, lemon, apples, pears, peaches, nectarines, strawberries, raspberries, blueberries, vanilla, ginger.

▲ DRIED PEACH

EAT Eat for a snack, soak or poach in wine, fruit juice, or syrup, or chop and add to cakes, biscuits, desserts, savoury and fruit salads, and casseroles.
FLAVOUR PAIRINGS Other dried fruits, hard cheeses, soft blues like Gorgonzola, mozzarella, feta, halloumi, ham, duck, game birds, rice.

▲ DRIED DATES

EAT Available whole or ready-chopped for baking. Stone whole ones and stuff with marzipan or walnuts and honey for a sweetmeat, chop and add to stuffings, cakes, tea breads, biscuits, breakfast cereals, puddings, relishes, and sauces. **FLAVOUR PAIRINGS** Marzipan, walnuts, honey, fruit syrup, golden syrup, molasses, ginger, sweet spices, cooking apples, pears, chocolate.

▲ DRIED APRICOT

EAT Some need soaking before use. Eat as a snack, or add whole, halved, or chopped to casseroles and tagines, stuffings, couscous and rice dishes, sweet and savoury salads; desserts, cakes, biscuits, muffins, pies, and tarts. Unsulphured apricots have a brown colour and more intense flavour.
FLAVOUR PAIRINGS Cinnamon, star anise, nutmeg, curry spices, almonds, brazil nuts, pistachios, walnuts, lamb, pork, chicken, turkey, goose, duck, game, soft cheeses, yogurt, cream, citrus.

▲ DRIED PEAR

EAT Eat as a snack, or poach in wine, cider, fruit juice, or syrup. Chop and add to sweet and savoury salads, to fish stews, and serve with cheeses.
FLAVOUR PAIRINGS Blue and sage-flavoured cheeses, Cheddar, walnuts, bananas, rice, pasta, peas, mushrooms, meaty white fish, ice cream, custard.

◄ PRUNES

EAT Dried plums, with or without stones. Some need soaking before use (cold tea is good). Eat as a snack, or grill with bacon or pancetta wrapped round. Add whole, chopped, or puréed to soups, sauces, stews and casseroles, in stuffings, sweet and savoury pies, hot and cold desserts. Also available canned.
FLAVOUR PAIRINGS Chicken, rabbit, pork, beef, venison, game birds, bacon, cheeses, spinach, other dried fruit, pears, apples, yogurt, cream, custard.

▲ DRIED APPLE

EAT Nibble raw, add to casseroles and compôtes, soak and bake as a garnish with rich meats. Apple chips are excellent added to breakfast cereals.
FLAVOUR PAIRINGS Pork, duck, goose, pheasant, honey, maple syrup, redcurrant jelly, cider, apple juice, dried pears, hard cheeses.

▲ DRIED BANANA

EAT Slices are often coated with sugar or honey. Eat as a snack alone or with nuts, scatter on breakfast cereals, crush and add to biscuits. Small, whole, dried, brown, chewy bananas also available. Eat these as a snack, or chop and add to cakes, muffins, tea breads, stews, soufflés, and dried fruit salads.
FLAVOUR PAIRINGS Yogurt, soft white cheeses, oats and other grains, walnuts, coconut, hazelnuts, other dried fruits, ginger, cinnamon, brandy.

CHOPPED MIXED PEEL

◄ DRIED FIG

EAT Intense flavour. Eat as a snack or stuff for sweetmeats. Chop and add to hot and cold desserts, cakes, biscuits, teabreads, and shortbreads. Use in stuffings or casseroles with poultry and game birds. Soak and stew whole in syrup with or without alcohol and sweet spices.
FLAVOUR PAIRINGS Pork, chicken, duck, goose, game birds, sausages, cheeses, fennel, rum, cider, Pernod, marzipan, star anise.

FLAKED COCONUT

CITRON PEEL

DESICCATED COCONUT

▲ CANDIED PEEL

EAT Chopped, mixed, diced, or sliced candied peel is used in rich fruit and plainer cakes, biscuits, florentines, teabreads, and steamed puddings, particularly Christmas pudding. Candied citron peel is moist and sticky. Chop and use in cakes, marmalades, fruit relishes, jam, and as a sweetmeat.
FLAVOUR PAIRINGS Angelica, glacé cherries, other dried fruits, chocolate, cinnamon, mixed spice, ginger, nutmeg, mace.

▲ DRIED COCONUT

EAT Available sweetened and unsweetened, as shavings (chips), flakes, and shredded (desiccated). Use in baking, curries, breakfast cereals, and anything that requires the flavour of coconut. **FLAVOUR PAIRINGS** Curry spices and spice pastes, pulses, all meats, poultry, fish, dried fruits, tropical fruits, cherries, citrus, oats and other grains, rice, noodles, cream.

NUTS AND SEEDS

BUY Nuts are available in shells, or shelled whole, flaked, chopped, or ground, depending on variety. Buy nuts and seeds in smallish quantities as they have a high fat content so can go rancid. When buying in their shells, they should feel heavy. If light they may be rotten. Shake a coconut, you should hear the water inside. Avoid chestnuts and coconuts with any signs of mould or cracks. Seeds generally need no preparation, but both nuts and seeds can be toasted before use to enhance the flavour. Look out for nut butters too. **STORE** Nuts in their shell will keep for several months. Keep ready-shelled nuts and seeds in airtight plastic or glass containers, in a cool, dark place and use within a few weeks.

▲ ALMONDS

EAT Available in shell or shelled, unblanched or blanched (raw, or roasted and salted), slivered or flaked, chopped, and ground. Eat whole as a snack, or in some baked dishes and salads. Use processed ones in cakes, biscuits, petits fours, meringues, pastries, desserts, praline, almond paste (marzipan), stir-fries, sauces, stews, and curries. **FLAVOUR PAIRINGS** Lamb, chicken, trout, honey, chocolate, apricots, cherries, plums, peaches, nectarines, dried fruits.
IN SEASON October–January, imported shelled all year

▲ BRAZILS

EAT Excellent for snacks. Good chopped or ground in stuffings, biscuits, cakes, and confectionery. **FLAVOUR PAIRINGS** Bananas, dried fruits, chocolate, toffee, maple syrup, molasses. **IN SEASON** Imported in shell October–January, shelled all year

▲ MACADAMIAS

EAT Highly prized roasted and salted as a snack with drinks, or add chopped to biscuits, cakes, pastries, confectionery, ice cream, sweet and savoury salads, and stuffings. **FLAVOUR PAIRINGS** Chicken, white fish, bananas, toffee, coconut, chocolate, maple syrup. **IN SEASON** Imported shelled all year

▲ CASHEWS

EAT A popular nibble, roasted, with or without salt, with drinks. Add raw whole or chopped in stir-fries, curries, stews, casseroles, sweet and savoury salads, biscuits, and confectionery. Grind for nut butter. Also available ready-prepared. **FLAVOUR PAIRINGS** Chicken, beef, white fish, sweetcorn, chilli, smoked paprika, star anise, Thai curry pastes, lemon grass, galangal, ginger, orange, lime. **IN SEASON** Imported shelled all year

▲ PISTACHIOS

EAT Roasted and salted in their shell, they are a popular nibble with drinks. Use blanched unsalted in desserts, cakes, biscuits, sweet pastries, ice cream, sweet sauces, in rice and couscous dishes, pâtés and terrines, sausages, and as a pretty garnish. **FLAVOUR PAIRINGS** Chicken, fish, pork, veal, chocolate, vanilla, raspberries, blueberries, meringues, rice. **IN SEASON** Imported, with and without shells, all year

COBNUTS

HAZELNUTS

▲ HAZELNUTS AND COBNUTS

EAT Hazelnuts are the original wild variety, cobnuts are cultivated. Eat as a snack, or blanch and add whole, chopped, or ground to cakes, biscuits, meringues, sweet and savoury stuffings, pâtés, terrines, and salads. **FLAVOUR PAIRINGS** Game birds, fish, pork, liver, apples, plums, raspberries, cinnamon, coffee, chocolate, cream cheese. **IN SEASON** Green: August. Brown: September–October, imported shelled all year

▲ PINE NUTS

EAT Use extensively in sauces, sweet and savoury salads, roasts, bakes, soups, stews, stuffings, biscuits, cakes, pastries, and desserts. **FLAVOUR PAIRINGS** Chicken, fish, spinach, aubergines, basil, mint, coriander leaf, cinnamon, vanilla, rice, couscous, bulgur, chocolate, honey. **IN SEASON** Imported shelled all year

▲ COCONUT

EAT Coconuts are not, technically, nuts but fruit. Snack on fresh chunks, drink the water. Grate fresh to add to cereals, salads, desserts, ice cream, sweetmeats, curries, biscuits, and cakes. Infuse the flesh to make coconut milk and cream, which is also available canned and powdered. The flesh is also available dried. **FLAVOUR PAIRINGS** Chicken, shellfish, yogurt, chilli, curry spices, Thai curry pastes, rice, citrus, tropical fruits, cherries, vanilla, jaggery. **IN SEASON** Imported all year

▲ CHESTNUTS

EAT They have a high tannin content so should not be eaten raw. Roast in their shells, add whole or chopped in stuffings, casseroles, and braises, or with vegetables, or purée for soups, pastries, and desserts. Also available shelled and vacuum-packed, frozen and canned whole, puréed (sweetened and unsweetened), and candied. **FLAVOUR PAIRINGS** Chicken, turkey, game birds, venison, sausagemeat, Brussels sprouts, onions, nutmeg, vanilla, cinnamon, chocolate. **IN SEASON** September–December

▲ PECAN NUTS

EAT Good raw, halved or chopped, in breads, biscuits, muffins, cakes, pies, pastries, confectionery, ice cream, and in savoury dishes. Serve salted or spiced with drinks. **FLAVOUR PAIRINGS** Chicken, turkey, game birds, eggs, sweet potato, bananas, pears, cinnamon, maple syrup, chocolate, coffee. **IN SEASON** Imported in shell October–March, shelled all year

GREEN WALNUT

ENGLISH WALNUT

▲ PEANUTS

EAT Seeds of a legume, not nuts but used in the same way, raw or roasted and, sometimes, salted as a snack, ground to a paste for peanut butter, or in sauces, soups, stews, curries, stir-fries, noodle dishes, and for biscuits, cakes, trail mix, and confectionery. **FLAVOUR PAIRINGS** Spring onions, wasabi, chilli, peppers, egg and rice noodles, sesame seeds, chocolate, caramel, light muscovado sugar, hard and soft cheeses. **IN SEASON** Imported all year

▲ WALNUTS

EAT Sold in their shells and shelled halves and broken pieces. Add halves or chopped to breakfast cereals, salads, snack mixes, stuffings, breads, cakes, pastries, and to decorate sweetmeats. Grind for soups and sauces. Pickle green ones. **FLAVOUR PAIRINGS** Coffee, chocolate, bananas, pears, dried fruits, cream, blue cheeses, celery, apples, cabbage. **IN SEASON** Green June–July, brown September–January, imported shelled all year

▲ SUNFLOWER SEEDS

EAT Enjoy raw, or toasted and salted, as a snack, on their own, or as part of a trail mix. Use raw or toasted to add flavour and texture to breakfast cereals, porridge, salads, sandwiches, bread, cakes, biscuits, pasta, and rice dishes.
FLAVOUR PAIRINGS Oats, barley, rye, millet, rice, couscous, grated root vegetables, dried fruits, tropical fruits, honey, maple syrup, pomegranate syrup.
IN SEASON Imported all year

▲ LINSEED

EAT Available as dark brown, reddish brown, or golden seeds. Use whole or cracked to add texture and colour. Grind or use the oil for maximum nutritional benefits. Add to porridge, breakfast cereals, flapjacks, biscuits, and bread. Use ground in smoothies. **FLAVOUR PAIRINGS** Oats, rye, rice, couscous, potatoes, almonds, dried fruits, honey, golden or corn syrup, mixed spice.
IN SEASON UK and imported all year

▲ SESAME SEED

EAT Used all over the world in sweet and savoury dishes. Add to rice and noodles, to coat foods before frying, sprinkle over salads and vegetables, add to salads, vegetables, breads, biscuits, pastries, and sweetmeats. Sesame seed paste (tahini) is used in dips, sauces, and dressings, in baking and sweetmeats.
FLAVOUR PAIRINGS Chicken, fish, peanuts, chick peas, spinach, carrots and other root vegetables, noodles, rice, parsley, mint, coriander leaf, chilli, honey, lemon, lime. **IN SEASON** Imported all year

▲ PUMPKIN SEED

EAT Enjoy as a snack, toasted and salted, or spiced. Add raw or toasted to breakfast cereals, salads, stir-fries, pasta and rice dishes, cakes, biscuits, and breads. You can use seeds straight from the squash, fresh or dry-roasted first.
FLAVOUR PAIRINGS Oats, barley, wheat, apricots, pumpkin, chilli, cinnamon, ginger, maple syrup. **IN SEASON** Imported all year

PEEL AND PREPARE APPLES

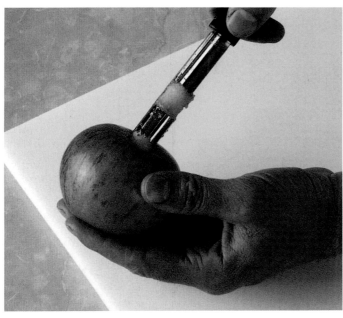

1 Remove the core of an apple by pushing a corer straight into the stalk of the apple and through to the bottom. Twist gently and loosen the core, then pull it out with the corer.

2 Using a peeler or small paring knife, gently remove the skin of the apple (and as little of the flesh as possible) by making a circular path around the fruit from top to bottom.

3 Place the cored apple on its side and hold it steady against a clean cutting board. Using a sharp knife, slice down through the apple. Repeat, making slices of an even thickness.

4 To chop: after slicing, stack the rings, a few at a time. Slice down through the pile, then repeat crossways in the opposite direction, making pieces of about the same size.

CUT A PINEAPPLE

1 With a sharp knife, cut the top and the base from the pineapple. Stand the pineapple upright and cut along the contour of the flesh, removing the skin in long strips from top to bottom.

2 To make the rings, turn the pineapple sideways and cut it into slices of an even thickness. Then use a round metal cutter to remove the hard, fibrous centre of each ring.

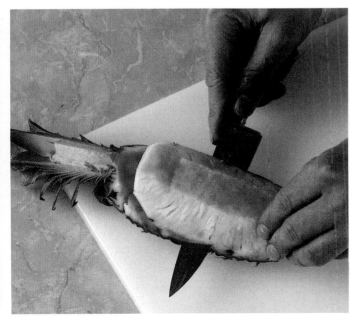

3 Quarter the fruit by cutting from plume end to base, then cut lengthways to remove the core at the centre of each piece. Beginning at the plume end, cut along between the flesh and the skin.

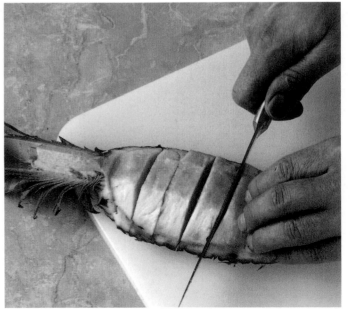

4 Hold the pineapple steady and cut the flesh crossways against the skin, making slices of an even width. Repeat the process, cutting the other quarters into slices.

SEGMENT CITRUS FRUIT

1 With a sharp knife, cut off the top and bottom of the fruit so it can stand upright. Holding it firmly with a fork, slice down and around the flesh, following the contour of the skin. Try to remove as much of the bitter white pith as possible.

2 With one hand, hold the peeled fruit steady on the board, while you use a sharp knife to slice along the lines of the membrane which separates each slice. Repeat slicing between each membrane to remove the segments.

PREPARE A MANGO

"When choosing your mango, just give it a feel to see if there's a little bit of give – if it's rock hard you know it's completely unripe. Again, if it's very soft it's likely to be overripe – you want just a small amount of give when you give it a little press." **DHRUV BAKER**

1 Standing the mango on its side, cut it by running your knife just to one side of the stone; repeat the cut on the other side, so that a single slice remains with the stone encased.

2 With the halves flesh-side up, cut the flesh into strips lengthways, then crossways, cutting to, but not through, the skin. Invert the skin to expose the flesh. Run your knife along the skin to remove the segments.

PEEL SOFT FRUIT

1 Starting at the base, make a cut crossways around the middle of the fruit, just through the skin. Then repeat the cut in the other direction so that the skin is quartered in wedges.

2 Place the fruit in a heatproof bowl and pour over boiling water, then using a slotted spoon, transfer the fruit to a bowl of cold water. When cool, remove the fruit from the water and pull the skin from the flesh.

CHEESES

BUY There are, of course, hundreds of cheeses available, many that are delicious cooked, but we have only selected some of the most popular used for culinary purposes here. All cheese should look and smell fresh. Best to buy pieces freshly cut, when possible. Buy in quantities you can use quickly, but hard cheeses will keep much longer than fresh. **STORE** Keep each cheese separately, well-wrapped, in a sealed container with room to "breathe", in the refrigerator. Freeze full-fat fresh soft cheeses for up to 3 months (don't freeze low-fat varieties); hard, blue, and other soft cheese for 6 months.

▲ CHEDDAR

EAT Choose a well-flavoured farmhouse one for cooking. Use in sandwiches, sauces, soufflés, salads, quiches, melted over potatoes, grated over vegetable dishes, and grilled. **FLAVOUR PAIRINGS** Crusty bread, pickles, chutneys, tomatoes, celery, beetroot, onions, apples, chillies, nuts, sage.

▲ GRANA PADANO AND PARMESAN

EAT Grana Padano (pictured) and Parmiggiano Reggiano (Parmesan) are both hard and grainy with complex, salty flavours. Parmesan is considered superior. Freshly grate or shave over pasta, griddled vegetables, and salads, stir into risottos and soups, use to flavour pesto, or nibble to round off a meal. **FLAVOUR PAIRINGS** Pasta, ravioli, risotto rice, olive oil, butter, sage, basil, parsley, rosemary, garlic, pine nuts, balsamic vinegar, walnuts, pears.

▲ PECORINO

EAT A grainy, salty sheep's milk cheese. Use instead of Parmesan or Grana Padano. Particularly good with tomato-based sauces for pasta. **FLAVOUR PAIRINGS** Tomatoes, sun-dried tomatoes, onions, garlic, prosciutto, oregano, basil, white beans, pasta, olive oil.

▲ GRUYÈRE

EAT One of many sweet, nutty, smooth-textured melting cheeses. Use for fondues, with pasta, gratins, salads, and sauces. Good mixed with other melting cheeses too. **FLAVOUR PAIRINGS** Crudités, kirsch, white wine, potatoes, cauliflower, spinach, onions, garlic, tomatoes, leeks, crusty bread.

▲ GORGONZOLA

EAT Smooth with a sweet, spicy tang. Use in salads, sauces, dips, mousses, soufflés, tarts, risottos, and on pizzas. **FLAVOUR PAIRINGS** Watercress, squashes, leeks, tomatoes, spinach, nuts, fruits, prosciutto, steaks, chicken.

▲ STILTON

EAT It mellows with age. Enjoy to round off a meal, or in soups, dressings, sauces, or potted. **FLAVOUR PAIRINGS** Red wine, port, walnuts, celery, fennel, leeks, potatoes, beetroot, squashes, cream, crème fraîche, unsalted butter, honey, sunflower oil, steaks, chicken, grapes, figs, orchard fruits.

▲ MOZZARELLA

EAT Buffalo mozzarella is the best but also made from cow's milk. Use for salads, to top pizzas, and with pasta. **FLAVOUR PAIRINGS** Tomatoes, avocados, artichokes, olives, Parmesan, basil, oregano, sage, rosemary, mushrooms, prosciutto, spicy sausages, bacon, olive oil, balsamic vinegar.

FETA ▲

EAT Made with goat's or sheep's milk, crumbly, salty, and fresh. It does not melt completely when heated. Crumble or dice for salads, in stuffings, on vegetables, with olives as an appetizer. **FLAVOUR PAIRINGS** Lamb, chicken, tomatoes, onions, cucumber, cabbage, lettuce, aubergines, courgettes, broad beans, olives, olive oil, oregano, mint, thyme, watermelon.

▲ MASCARPONE

EAT Smooth, rich, and creamy – the classic cheese for tiramisu. Also use for cheesecakes, with cream to fill gâteaux or accompany fruit, in pâtés, sweet and savoury stuffings, and pasta sauces. **FLAVOUR PAIRINGS** Tomatoes, artichokes, wild mushrooms, beetroot, stone fruits, berries, citrus, ginger, coffee, chocolate, coffee liqueur, brandy, amaretto.

▲ RICOTTA

EAT Soft whey cheese with a touch of acidity and a delicate lemony aroma. Use in baked pasta dishes, sweet and savoury stuffings, and creamy desserts. **FLAVOUR PAIRINGS** Spinach, peppers, mushrooms, tomatoes, red onions, basil, sage, chilli, berries, stone fruits, figs, fresh dates, bananas, citrus, chocolate, coffee, honey, nutmeg, cinnamon.

TEST AN EGG FOR FRESHNESS

FRESH To test if an egg is fresh, gently drop it into a glass of cold water. A really fresh egg will lie in a horizontal position at the bottom.

BORDERLINE If, after settling, the egg begins to rise in the water at one end, it is not completely fresh, but can still be used.

STALE If the egg bobs up towards the surface of the water in a vertical position, it is stale and should be discarded.

SEPARATE YOLKS AND WHITES

1 Break the eggshell by tapping it against the rim of the bowl. Insert your fingers into the break, and gently pry the two halves apart. Some of the white will escape into the bowl. Remove any shell that falls in too.

2 Gently shift the yolk back and forth between the shell halves, allowing the white to fall into the bowl. Take care to keep the yolk intact. Place the yolk in another bowl and set aside.

WHISK EGG WHITES

1 Place the egg whites in a metal or ceramic bowl that is clean, free of any traces of grease, and completely dry. Begin whisking them slowly, using a small range of motion.

2 Continue whisking steadily, using larger strokes, until the whites have lost their translucency and start to foam. The aim is to incorporate as much air as possible to make the whites expand and increase in volume.

3 Continue incorporating as much air as possible, increasing your speed and range of motion until the whites have mounted to the desired degree and are stiff, but not dry.

4 Test by lifting the whisk away; the peaks should be firm but glossy, and the tips should hang. Take care not to overwhisk the egg whites, or the air bubbles that have formed will collapse.

SOFT- AND HARD-BOIL EGGS

"A good tip is to peel the egg under running water." **STACIE STEWART**

SOFT-BOIL EGGS The whites should be set and the yolks runny. Use a pan large enough to hold the eggs in a single layer. Cover them with at least 5cm (2in) of cold water and set over a high heat. Bring the water to the boil, then lower to a simmer for 2–3 minutes. Remove the eggs.

HARD-BOIL EGGS Both the whites and the yolks should be set. Use the method for soft-boiled eggs, but once the water has boiled, simmer them for 10 minutes. Then run cold water into the pan to stop the cooking process. Peel away and discard the shells when cool enough to handle.

SCRAMBLE EGGS

1 Crack the eggs into a bowl, and remove any fallen shell. Beat the eggs with a fork and season with salt and black pepper.

2 Heat a non-stick pan over medium heat, and add a knob of butter. When the butter has melted, pour in the beaten eggs.

3 Using a wooden spoon, pull the setting egg from the edges into the centre. Continue doing so until it is set to your liking.

POACH EGGS

1 Carefully crack an egg onto a small plate, then slide it into a pan of gently boiling water mixed with a drop of vinegar.

2 Using a slotted spoon, gently lift the white over the yolk until set. Adjust the heat to a gentle boil and poach for 3–5 minutes.

3 Before serving, place the eggs in another pan of gently simmering salted water for 30 seconds to remove the taste of the vinegar.

BAKE A SOUFFLÉ

1 Grease the inside of each soufflé dish and then coat with sugar, biscuit crumbs, or grated cheese. Use sugar or biscuit crumbs for a sweet soufflé, and grated cheese for a savoury soufflé.

2 Whisk the egg whites until holding stiff peaks: if under-whisked the soufflés will not rise. Fold into the base gently, to retain as much air as possible. Add a pinch of salt before mixing for savoury soufflés.

3 Run a finger around the soufflé mix, along the top edge of each ramekin just inside the rim, to give a professional "top hat" effect and help the soufflés rise up straight.

4 Cook the soufflés straight away, placing them on a thoroughly preheated baking tray. Doing this will heat the base of the ramekins so that the soufflés begin to rise as soon as you put them in the oven.

MAKE A CLASSIC OMELETTE

1 Beat and season the eggs. Heat a nonstick frying pan over a moderate heat and melt a knob of butter. As soon as it begins to froth, add the eggs, tilting the pan so that the eggs can spread evenly.

2 Stir the eggs with a fork to distribute them evenly. Stop stirring the eggs just as soon as they are set. Fold the side of the omelette nearest to you halfway over itself.

3 To form a neatly rolled omelette, sharply tap the handle of the pan to encourage the other side of the omelette to curl over and slide to the edge of the pan.

4 When the omelette is cooked to your taste, tilt the pan over a serving plate until the omelette slides out of it onto the plate seam-side down. Serve immediately.

MAKE ITALIAN MERINGUE

"A tip when you're making meringue is to break and separate the eggs the day before, so the egg whites have time to age in the fridge." **TIM KINNAIRD**

1 Dissolve 250g (9oz) caster sugar in 75ml (2½fl oz) water over a low heat to 121°C (248°F). Whisk 4 egg whites until they form soft peaks. Pour the hot sugar syrup into the egg whites whisking continuously.

2 Continue to whisk until the meringue is cold, with a very stiff, smooth, and satiny consistency. Transfer the meringue mixture into a piping or pastry bag fitted with a metal tip.

3 Twist off the loose end of the bag, then squeezing with one hand, pipe the meringue over the surface of the tart. You may find it easier to hold the tip end with your other hand to keep it steady.

4 Italian meringue is far easier and quicker to cook than traditional meringue. Simply place under a preheated grill for a few minutes to lightly brown the top.

MAKE FRENCH MERINGUE

"When making meringue, always make sure that the bowl you are using for the egg whites is spotlessly clean." **TIM KINNAIRD**

1 In a large mixing bowl, whisk 4 egg whites, half of 200g (7oz) caster sugar, and the seeds of 1 vanilla pod at moderate speed.

2 Continue whisking until the mixture becomes smooth, shiny, and firm. Draw the whisk away to check that there are soft peaks.

3 Using a rubber spatula, gently fold in the rest of the sugar. Bake until just golden, then leave to dry in the oven for at least 8 hours.

SHAPE MERINGUE

1 For discs, use a star tip to pipe the meringue in a spiral onto a parchment-covered baking tray. Bake for 1 hour 20 minutes, then let dry.

2 For shells, use a pastry bag with a round tip to pipe the meringue in equal-sized globes. Bake for 1 hour 10 minutes, then let dry.

3 For fingers, use a round tip to pipe the meringue into thin sticks and dust with icing sugar. Bake for 30–35 minutes, then let dry.

WHIP CREAM

1 Remove the cream from the refrigerator and wait for it to reach 5°C (40°F). Set it over ice. Begin whipping slowly, at about 2 strokes per second (or the lowest speed on an electric mixer) until it starts to thicken.

2 To create soft peaks, increase the whipping to a moderate speed and for stiff peaks, continue beating the cream. Test by lifting the beaters or whisk to see if the cream retains its shape.

FILL A PIPING BAG

1 Place your chosen piping nozzle in the bag and pull it through the opening until the bag is tightly surrounding the wider end of the nozzle. Then give the bag a twist to seal and prevent leakage.

2 Holding the bag just above the nozzle with one hand, fold the top of the bag over with your other hand, creating a "collar", and begin spooning in the cream.

MAKE CRÈME PÂTISSIÈRE

1 Over a low heat, bring 250ml (8fl oz) full-fat milk, 25g (scant 1oz) cornflour, 2 split vanilla pods, and 30g (1oz) sugar to the boil, whisking.

2 Whisk 3 egg yolks with 30g (1oz) of sugar in a bowl. Keep whisking, add the hot milk, transfer to the pan and just before boiling, remove to cool.

3 While the pan cools, remove the vanilla pods. Then add 25g (scant 1oz) of butter pieces and whisk into the sauce until smooth and glossy.

MAKE CUSTARD

1 Bring 150ml (5fl oz) full-fat milk, 150ml (5fl oz) double cream, and ½ a vanilla pod (and seeds) to the boil, remove, and chill overnight.

2 Discard the vanilla pod and bring the milk to the boil. Whisk 3 egg yolks and 25g (scant 1oz) sugar together. Pour in the milk, whisking.

3 Pour back into the pan and whisk over a medium heat until thick and smooth. Do not boil.

RICE

BUY Choose clear packets of unbroken grains. In ready-prepared mixes containing wild rice, the grains may be broken or pierced so they cook in a similar time to the other rice in the pack. **STORE** Wholegrain and polished rices will keep in a cool, dry cupboard for over two years. Fragrant varieties become less aromatic, though. Flaked and ground rice and rice flour can be stored for over a year in an airtight container. **IN SEASON** Available all year.

▲ WHITE LONG GRAIN

EAT Basic rice for side dishes, salads, and stuffings. **FLAVOUR PAIRINGS** Any meat, poultry, game, or fish, pulses, root vegetables, sweetcorn, cabbage leaves (for stuffing), peppers, aubergines, squashes, beans, peas, cheeses, salad vegetables, dried fruits, herbs, spices, soy sauce.

▲ SHORT GRAIN RICE

EAT There are superior risotto ones like Italian Arborio and Carnaroli, and basic short, round grain pudding rices. Use for risottos and rice desserts. **FLAVOUR PAIRINGS** Wild and cultivated mushrooms, truffles, peppers, aubergines, tomatoes, peas, squashes, saffron, herbs, onions, garlic, chicken, seafood, cheeses, citrus, white wine, caster sugar, milk, cream, unsalted butter, vanilla, nutmeg, dried fruits.

▲ BASMATI RICE

EAT Fragrant, long-grain variety. Use in biryanis, pilafs, stuffings, salads, and to accompany curries, casseroles, tagines, roast, and baked dishes. **FLAVOUR PAIRINGS** Curry spices, curry leaves, ginger, cinnamon, garlic, coriander leaf, parsley, mint, chives, all meats, poultry, seafood, vegetables, dried fruits, coconut milk, yogurt.

▲ THAI JASMINE RICE

EAT Slightly sticky and fragrant. Use to accompany Thai and Chinese savoury dishes. **FLAVOUR PAIRINGS** Thai curry pastes, lemon grass, galangal, ginger, nam pla, soy sauce, all meat, fish, shellfish, and poultry, all vegetables, coconut milk, tropical fruits, green tea.

▲ RED RICE

EAT Speciality crops, one of the most famous being from Camargue, in Provence, France. Excellent for salads, stuffings and side dishes. **FLAVOUR PAIRINGS** Spring onions, garlic, leeks, puy lentils, fish, shellfish, chicken, courgettes, aubergines, feta cheese, olives, cherry and sun-dried tomatoes, cucumber, sweet peppers, mushrooms, peas, green beans, pine nuts.

▲ BLACK STICKY RICE

EAT Deep purple grains, with a fruity, grassy aroma. Used mostly boiled as a sweet breakfast cereal, in dumplings, stuffings, and for puddings. **FLAVOUR PAIRINGS** Coconut milk, palm sugar, peanuts, red onions, garlic, minced meat, dried prawns, oyster sauce, soy sauce, dried shiitake mushrooms, bananas.

▲ WHITE STICKY RICE

EAT Also known as glutinous or sweet rice. Best steamed or it becomes mushy. Use for sushi.
FLAVOUR PAIRINGS Rice vinegar, wasabi, pickled ginger, nori wraps (seaweed), fresh tuna or salmon, keta (salted salmon roe), prawns, avocados, beansprouts, cucumber, carrot, chicken.

▲ PAELLA RICE

EAT Spanish rices (Bomba, the main variety, Calasparra, and Valencia, the best). Use for Paella.
FLAVOUR PAIRINGS Chicken, shellfish, chorizo, pancetta, white wine, saffron, paprika, chilli, olive oil, onions, garlic, mushrooms, peppers, tomatoes, peas, green beans, parsley, thyme.

▲ FLAKED RICE

EAT Part-cooked before rolling into flakes. Good for milk puddings, or soaked, then fried in sunflower oil either with mirepoix, fresh chillies and spices, or seasoned and mixed with peanuts as a snack.
FLAVOUR PAIRINGS Milk, cream, honey, citrus, vanilla, curry leaves, chillies, mirepoix, peanuts.

▲ GROUND RICE

EAT Slightly grittier than rice flour, use in puddings and mixed with wheat flour in baking to give a crisp texture to shortbread, pastry, and biscuits.
FLAVOUR PAIRINGS Butter, milk, cream, vanilla, almond, lavender, chocolate, dried fruit, cinnamon, nutmeg, mixed spice.

▲ WILD RICE

EAT The seeds of an aquatic grass. Can be eaten alone but often added to basmati, red, or long-grain rice. Also available ready-mixed with them.
FLAVOUR PAIRINGS Game, poultry, salmon, shellfish, eggs, bacon, asparagus, celery, mushrooms, potatoes, squashes, mangoes, nuts.

▲ BROWN RICE

EAT Wholegrain unrefined rice with a chewy texture and nutty flavour. Available in many varieties from basic short-grain and long-grain to speciality rices like Basmati. Use instead of white rices but it takes longer to cook.
FLAVOUR PAIRINGS Chicken, pulses, meat, fish, most vegetables and salad stuffs, dried fruit, curry spices, herbs, milk, cream, honey, vanilla, nutmeg.

▲ RICE FLOUR

EAT White or brown, gluten-free with a slightly gritty texture. Good for coating before frying, and dusting work surfaces for rolling bread or pastry dough. Use, too, for gluten-free breads, cakes, and biscuits, on its own or with other gluten-free flours. **FLAVOUR PAIRINGS** Paprika, chilli, herbs, eggs, butter, honey, vanilla, mixed spice, cocoa, almonds, dried fruit.

OTHER GRAINS

BUY Choose the right grain with the right amount of processing for the job in hand. For instance, you might want toasted buckwheat grains for adding to breakfast cereals or for cooking in a pilaf, you would want buckwheat flour to add flavour to your crêpes or pasta dough. **STORE** Most grains will keep in sealed containers in a cool, dark place for a year or more. Amaranth, millet, and buckwheat flour tend to go bitter after a few months, so buy in small quantities.

▲ BARLEY

EAT Use pearl barley in soups, stews, and orzotto (barley risotto). Boil for pilafs and salads. Cook in milk like porridge and sweeten for breakfast or pudding. Pot barley is the whole grain variety. Barley flour and beremeal (a speciality Scottish flour) are best mixed with wheat flour for baking.
FLAVOUR PAIRINGS Chicken, duck, prawns, beef, lamb, beer, mushrooms, most vegetables, coconut, herbs, spices, apples, blackberries, citrus.

▲ AMARANTH

EAT Highly nutritious, best toasted briefly before use. Boil, then use for pilafs, add to stews, or to rice puddings about 15 minutes before the end of cooking. Simmer in milk like porridge and add chopped fresh or dried fruit. Use the flour with wheat or rye flour for pastry, flat breads, and batters. **FLAVOUR PAIRINGS** Dried beans, cheeses, chicken, chillies, squashes, peas, mushrooms, coconut, corn, honey, chocolate.

▲ QUINOA

EAT High in protein and fat. An excellent alternative to rice, and quicker to cook.
FLAVOUR PAIRINGS Beef, chicken, pulses, cheeses, prawns, chickpeas, chillies, coriander leaf and seed, sweetcorn, nuts, squashes, sweet potatoes, citrus, grapes.

POLENTA

POPCORN

▲ BUCKWHEAT

EAT Strong-flavoured gluten-free grain. Use toasted and boiled for pilafs or salads, or add to rice for added texture and flavour. The flour is used in Japanese soba noodles, and for crêpes, blinis, and pasta doughs (sometimes with wheat flour). **FLAVOUR PAIRINGS** Bacon, eggs, chicken, smoked salmon, caviar, ham, melting cheeses, peanuts, cashew nuts, cucumber, mushrooms, onions, ginger, parsley, rice, soy sauce.

▲ CORN

EAT There are many different varieties for different uses. Cornflour is a fine white powder. Use for thickening and dusting to prevent sticking. Cornmeal is coarser ground; use in baked goods, for crumb coatings, and tortillas. Polenta is very coarse yellow or white cornmeal. Boil to a thick paste as a side dish, or cool and set, then cut into pieces and fry or grill. Also use for cornbread. Popcorn is a special hard variety that explodes and puffs up when heated. **FLAVOUR PAIRINGS** Pulses, beef, bacon, chicken, pork, rabbit, cheeses, peppers, coriander leaf, parsley, citrus, mushrooms, pumpkin, tomatoes, butter, syrups.

▲ MILLET

EAT Whole grains are an excellent alternative to rice. Best toasted before boiling. Flakes make good porridge, or add to muesli or other breakfast cereals, flapjacks, and multigrain doughs. Use millet flour for gluten-free biscuits and crackers.
FLAVOUR PAIRINGS Chicken, salmon, dried beans, eggs, spinach, mushrooms, soy sauce, dried fruit, nuts, oats, other grains, muscovado sugar.

▲ OATS

EAT Use rolled oats for porridge, muesli, flapjacks, biscuits, crumbles, and in bread dough. Use pinhead, coarse, and medium oatmeal for oatcakes, in soups and stews, haggis, porridge, toasted to add to cream crowdie and other desserts, or as a coating for fried fish. Fine oatmeal is good for quick porridge, pancakes, pastry, and puddings.
FLAVOUR PAIRINGS Ham, lamb, sausages, herrings or mackerel, onions, cabbage, stone fruits, berries, dried fruits, cream, syrups, honey.

▲ WHEAT FLOURS

EAT Use strong white or wholemeal flour, high in gluten, for yeast cookery. Plain flour is for general baking and thickening. Choose pastry flour for puff and choux, and self-raising flour for quick cakes, scones, and teabreads. Farina or Tipo "00" is for pasta, gnocchi, and fine cakes. Wheatgerm and bran are also available to add extra goodness to dishes.
FLAVOUR PAIRINGS Nuts, seeds, dried fruits, other grains, vanilla, chocolate, coffee, syrups, honey, jams, butter, oils, herbs, spices.

▲ BULGUR

EAT Whole wheat grains steamed, hulled, dried, and crushed. Traditional for tabbouleh, but good as a base for salads, pilafs, stuffings, soups, and as a side dish. Cracked wheat is similar, but not pre-cooked. Use it in multigrain breads, too.
FLAVOUR PAIRINGS Tomatoes, cucumber, herbs, spring onions, garlic, cumin, cinnamon, lemon, olive oil, feta cheese, olives, dried fruit.

▲ COUSCOUS

EAT Not technically a grain, as it's processed from wheat. Giant couscous and fregola have larger granules, roasted during manufacture, so are less sticky and chewier. Serve as a side dish, plain or with added flavourings, as a base for spicy main courses like Couscous Royale, in salads, stuffings, and cakes. **FLAVOUR PAIRINGS** Olive oil, lamb, chicken, chorizo, fish, chickpeas, coriander leaf, mint, thyme, bay leaf, oregano, garlic, onions, peppers, courgettes, aubergines, tomatoes, chilli, paprika, harissa paste, cumin, cinnamon, dried fruit.

▲ RYE

EAT Cook the grains for nutty pilafs, salads, in stuffings, soups, and bread doughs. Dark and light rye flour is good for baking, particularly bread, with or without wheat flour, and makes delicious Scotch pancakes. Rye flakes are also available for porridge, or adding to muesli, cracker, and bread doughs.
FLAVOUR PAIRINGS Cheeses, ham, crab, smoked salmon, fennel, sauerkraut, honey, maple syrup, oats, oranges, raisins.

◀ SPELT

EAT Use wholegrains for soups, pilafs, salads, and risotto-type dishes. Farro is an Italian variety, often confused with spelt grain and can be used in the same way. Spelt flour is available as white and wholemeal, and is used as an alternative to common wheat. Often tolerated by people with wheat allergies.
FLAVOUR PAIRINGS Lamb, chicken, game, rabbit, fish, wild and cultivated mushrooms, most vegetables and salad stuffs, herbs, cinnamon, nutmeg, mace, caraway, poppy and nigella seeds.

PULSES (DRIED PEAS, BEANS, AND LENTILS)

BUY If buying packets of pulses, inspect for signs of tearing where animals might have been at work. If buying in bulk, pulses should be clean and unbroken and free from dust, grit, or signs of spoilage. Sprouted beans should look crisp and fresh. Avoid if browning. Most kinds of pulses are sold ready-cooked in cans too. Some are sold frozen. **STORE** Keep indefinitely in sealed containers in a cool, dark place. The longer you keep them, the longer they'll need soaking before cooking. All except mung beans, lentils, and split peas should be boiled rapidly for 10 minutes to remove toxins before simmering until tender. Can be frozen, cooked, for up to 6 months.

▲ FLAGEOLET BEANS

EAT Integral to French cuisine, with a creamy texture and delicate flavour. Traditionally served with roast or braised lamb. Good in soups, stews, casseroles, and salads, or serve as a side dish. **FLAVOUR PAIRINGS** Lamb, delicate fish, veal, garlic, shallots, red onions, tomatoes, celery, carrots, fennel, paprika, parsley, sage, thyme.

▲ CANNELLINI BEANS

EAT Italian long white haricot bean, with nutty flavour and smooth texture. Good in salads, soups, and stews. Smaller round haricots are used for baked beans. **FLAVOUR PAIRINGS** Tomatoes, garlic, onions, fennel, cavolo nero, white wine, sage, thyme, eggs, bacon, pork, black pudding.

▲ PINTO BEANS

EAT Earthy flavour and floury texture, used for Mexican re-fried beans and in most chilli dishes. **FLAVOUR PAIRINGS** Eggs, beef, fresh, dried and pickled chillies, onions, garlic, coriander leaf, parsley, oregano, tomatoes, peppers, rice.

▲ BUTTER BEANS

EAT Large and floury, good for soaking up flavours in soups, stews, and braises, and for mashing. **FLAVOUR PAIRINGS** Gammon, pork, chicken, pheasant, chorizo and other sausages, garlic, onions, turmeric, cumin, cloves, turnips, carrots, kale, crème fraîche, tahini, parsley, coriander leaf.

▲ CHICKPEAS

EAT Smooth and buttery when puréed, ideal for dips and sauces, good in patties too. They also keep their shape, so good for long-cooked stews and casseroles. **FLAVOUR PAIRINGS** Garlic, cumin, turmeric, coriander seed and leaf, parsley, mint, chilli, sweet and smoked paprika, cinnamon, cloves, chorizo, tahini, tomatoes, onions, aubergines, peppers, squashes, mushrooms.

MUNG BEANS

MUNG BEAN SPROUTS

▲ MUNG BEANS

EAT Robust yet creamy, good in soups, stews, or casseroles. Most popular sprouted for stir-fries, salads, and sandwiches. **FLAVOUR PAIRINGS** Most vegetables, seafood, chicken, Sichuan pepper, garlic, ginger, soy sauce, rice wine.

SOYA BEAN SPROUTS

SOYA BEANS

▲ SOYA BEANS

EAT Highly nutritious but lack flavour, so good used in spicy stews, terrines, and patties. Also used for making soya products like milk, tofu, miso, and soy sauce. Use the sprouts in stir-fries and salads. **FLAVOUR PAIRINGS** Beans: curry spices, herbs, mango chutney, chillies, mushrooms, root vegetables, kale, cavolo nero. Sprouts: oyster sauce, black bean sauce, hoisin, vinegar, honey, pineapple, peppers, spring onions, garlic, Chinese five-spice powder.

ADZUKI BEANS

ADZUKI BEAN SPROUTS

◄ ADZUKI BEANS

EAT Nutty, slightly sweet and keep their shape when cooked. Good in pilafs, salads, stews, and patties. Use the sprouts in the same way. **FLAVOUR PAIRINGS** Sweet peppers, squashes, sweet potatoes, rice, orzo, chilli, bay, basil, apples, pears, soy sauce.

COOK RICE BY ABSORPTION

1 Put the rice and 1½ times its quantity of water into a saucepan. Bring to the boil, stir once, then simmer uncovered until the water is absorbed. Remove from the heat and cover with a clean tea towel and a lid on top.

2 Leave the rice to steam under the tea towel and saucepan lid for 20 minutes. Remove the tea towel and replace the lid. Leave to stand for 5 minutes, then fluff the rice with a fork and serve.

REHYDRATE INSTANT COUSCOUS

1 Place the couscous in a bowl and pour over twice as much boiling water. Cover with cling film and leave to stand for 5 minutes. Uncover the bowl and fluff up the grains with a fork, then cover again for 5 minutes.

2 Now remove the cling film. Enrich the couscous by adding 1 tbsp of olive oil or a knob of butter, and season to taste. Fluff up the grains again with a fork until they are light and separate. It is ready to serve.

MAKE RISOTTO

"One crucial thing when you're making risotto is to keep your stock just under a boil right next to your rice. If you add cold stock to your rice, you end up cooling the whole thing down and slowing down the cooking process." **ALEX RUSHMER**

1 Heat 900ml (1½ pts) stock in a saucepan to a simmer. In another, wide-bottomed pan, heat 1 tbsp olive oil and 75g (2½oz) butter. Stir in 280g (10oz) risotto rice, coating the grains in the butter and oil.

2 Add one 75ml (2½fl oz) glass of white wine and boil, stirring until absorbed. Then add a ladle of simmering stock and stir until absorbed. Continue adding the hot stock, one ladle at at time, and stirring constantly.

3 Continue adding the stock and stirring with a wooden spoon until the rice is tender, but retains a slight bite. Add a knob of butter, season with salt and pepper to taste, and remove from the heat.

4 The constant stirring releases the starch in the rice, so the risotto should now have a creamy texture. Cover the pan and leave the risotto to rest for about 2 minutes before serving.

MAKE SOFT AND GRILLED POLENTA

1 Bring a large pan of salted water to the boil. Gradually pour in the polenta, whisking quickly and continuously to ensure there are no lumps and the mixture is smooth.

2 Reduce the heat to low and continue cooking for 40–45 minutes, or until the polenta is coming away from the edge of the pan, whisking occasionally. Stir in butter, Parmesan cheese, and season to taste.

3 For grilled polenta, first make soft polenta, but without the butter and cheese. Once thickened, pour it onto a greased baking tray, spread with a spatula, then leave it to set. (Keep up to 4 days, chilled and covered.)

4 When ready to use, turn the tray out onto a board. Cut the polenta into the desired shapes and sizes. Brush the pieces with olive oil, then grill on a hot, ridged grill pan for about 3–5 minutes on each side.

MAKE BLINIS

1 Sift 100g (3½oz) buckwheat flour, ¼ tsp baking powder, and ¼ tsp salt into bowl, add 1 egg yolk, half of 100ml (3½fl oz) milk, and beat together. Add the remaining milk and when smooth, fold in 1 whisked egg white.

2 Heat a flat griddle pan and add a thin layer of vegetable or sesame oil. Cook the blinis in batches, turning them over when bubbles appear on the surface and the edges are firm.

MAKE PANCAKES

1 Make a batter by whisking 200g (7oz) plain flour, 1 tbsp caster sugar, 2 large eggs, and 450ml (15fl oz) whole milk together. Melt a knob of butter in a frying pan, add a ladle of batter and tip it to cover the pan.

2 Cook the pancake for 30–45 seconds then use a metal spatula to peel the pancake loose and check it is golden brown. Then either turn it over by flipping in the air, or use the spatula to do the job.

MIX BREAD DOUGH

1 In a bowl, whisk together 1½ tsp fresh yeast and 350g (12oz) tepid water, (weigh both dry and liquid ingredients in a jug to keep the correct ratio of flour to water) until the yeast has completely dissolved.

2 In a separate bowl, combine 500g (1lb 2oz) strong white flour and 1 tsp salt. Then, using only your hand to stir, mix the yeast liquid together with the dry ingredients.

3 As quickly as possible, mix together to make a soft, sticky dough. Make sure that all the flour is thoroughly combined with the liquid by scraping your hand all around the bowl.

4 Cover the dough with a clean tea towel to keep it moist. Leave to stand for 10 minutes before beginning to knead it, as this should produce a more elastic dough that is easier to work.

KNEAD BREAD DOUGH

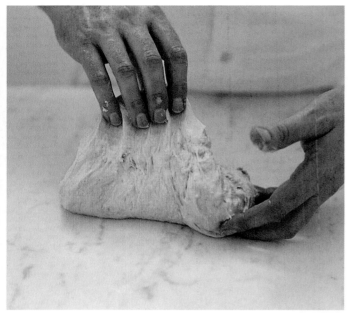

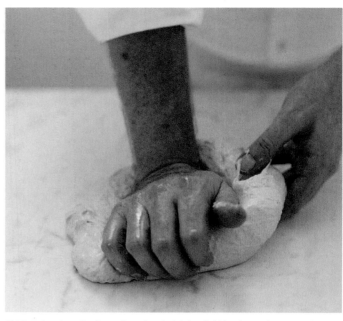

1 Try using a lightly oiled, rather than floured surface for kneading. Rub another 2 tbsp of oil over the dough ball, then fold it in half, bringing the top edge towards you. It will be very sticky and quite soft at this stage.

2 Use the thumb of one hand to hold the fold in place, then use the heel of your stronger hand to gently but firmly push down and away through the centre of the dough to seal the fold and stretch it.

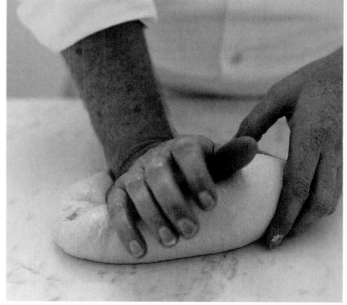

3 Lift the dough and rotate it a quarter turn. Repeat the folding, pushing, and rotating process 10–12 times. Then place the dough in an oiled bowl seam-side down, cover with a cloth, and leave to prove for 10 minutes.

4 Knead the dough in this way again twice, with 10 minutes between each knead. Each time you do this it will require less oil. By the end, the dough will become noticably more elastic and even silken.

MAKE A PIZZA BASE

1 In a bowl, dissolve 14g (½oz) fast-action dried yeast in 360ml (12fl oz) water and 2 tbsp olive oil. On a work surface, make a well in 500g (1lb 2oz) strong plain flour, add the liquid, and bring the flour into the centre.

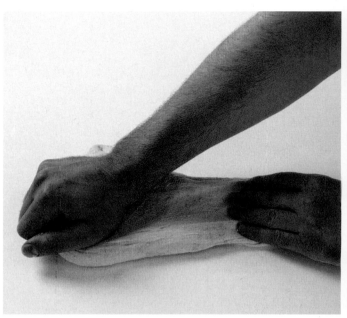

2 Using your hands, combine the flour and liquid and form it into a ball of dough. Knead the dough for 10 minutes, or until smooth. Set the dough aside in a bowl, cover with cling film, and allow to rise.

3 When the dough has doubled in size, turn it out onto a floured surface. Working from the centre outward, roll the dough into a circle. Flip the dough and repeat.

4 Roll the dough circle over the rolling pin and carefully transfer it to a lightly oiled and floured baking tray. Pinch the edges with your thumb and index finger to make a small rim around the edge.

MAKE BRIOCHE DOUGH

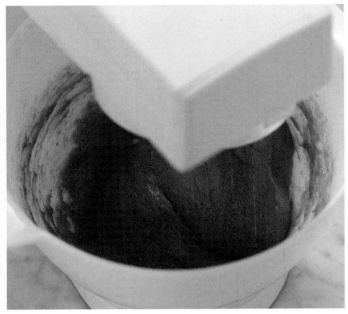

1 In a bowl, mix 375g (13oz) strong white flour, 7g (¼oz) instant dried yeast, and 50g (1¾oz) caster sugar. Using a dough hook, mix on medium speed and gradually add 100ml (3½fl oz) warm milk and 3 eggs.

2 Mix until smooth, then add 1 more egg. Once the dough is mixed and begins to come away from the edges of the bowl, add salt and 175g (6oz) softened unsalted butter (cut into pieces). Mix again.

3 When the dough is smooth, transfer it to another large bowl. Cover with cling film and leave it to sit at room temperature for 2–3 hours, or until it doubles in size. The risen dough will be very sticky.

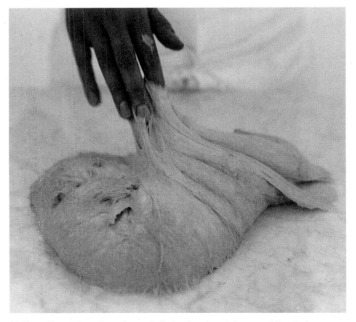

4 On a floured work surface, deflate the dough by punching it down. Return the dough to the bowl, cover with cling film and place in a refrigerator for 1¼ hours. Deflate once more, then shape and bake.

SHORTCRUST PASTRY

"The art of making good shortcrust pastry is to keep everything as cold as possible – ice cold water and cold hands – then your pastry will roll out perfectly." **HANNAH MILES**

1 Sift 175g (6oz) plain white flour and a pinch of salt in a bowl. Add 85g (3oz) cold diced butter, margarine, or other fat. Lightly stir.

2 Using your fingertips, rub together the flour and butter until it forms coarse crumbs. Sprinkle over 2 tbsp iced water.

3 Use your fingers to gather the dough together and roll around to form a ball. Wrap in cling film and chill for 30 minutes before using.

ROUGH PUFF PASTRY

1 In a bowl, combine 250g (9oz) plain flour, 85g (3oz) cold butter, and 85g (3oz) vegetable fat with a knife. Add 150ml (5fl oz) iced water.

2 Add a squeeze of lemon juice, and stir with a knife to bind. Place the dough on a floured board and gently roll out.

3 Fold the top third of the pastry down, the bottom third up, and roll. Turn 90° and repeat the process. Chill for 30 minutes before using.

CHOUX PASTRY

"When you're dealing with pastry, you must always be completely exact in your measurements."

CHRIS GATES

1 Bring 240ml (8fl oz) water and 115g (4oz) diced butter to the boil. Remove from the heat and add 140g (5oz) plain flour and 1 tsp sugar.

2 Beat until smooth, then return the pan to the heat and stir until the dough forms a ball and comes away from the sides of the pan.

3 Remove the pan from the heat. Add 4 eggs, one at a time, beating well. When the mixture easily drops off the spoon it is ready to use.

SWEET SHORTCRUST PASTRY

1 Sift 200g (7oz) plain flour onto a work surface. Make a well in the centre and add 85g (3oz) butter, 4 tbsp sugar, and 3 egg yolks.

2 Using your fingertips, gradually work the flour into the butter and egg mixture to form very rough crumbs.

3 Gather the dough into a ball and knead it lightly until it is pliable, then wrap in cling film and chill for 30 minutes before using.

SHAPE CHOUX PASTE

1 Pipe neat and uniform globes onto a baking sheet, pressing the nozzle gently into the paste at the end to avoid forming a peak.

2 If peaks should form, dip a fork in a little beaten egg to gently flatten them. Lightly brush with beaten egg, then bake.

3 When cooked, the buns should be puffed and golden. Make a small slit in each of the buns to allow the steam to escape, then cool.

4 When cool, cut a small split in the base of each bun. Fill by piping cream or chocolate through the split using a large, plain nozzle.

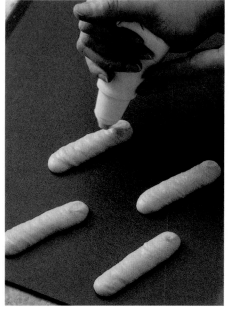

5 To make eclairs, use a plain nozzle to pipe the choux paste in strips, making each "finger" identical in length. Bake, pierce, and cool.

6 To create rings, mark out circles of your chosen size on a baking sheet. Following the circles, pipe choux rings, bake, pierce, and cool.

ROLL OUT PUFF PASTRY

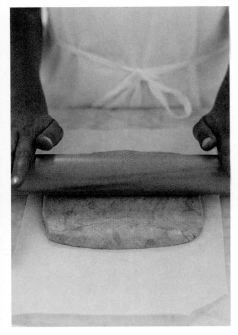

1 On a piece of baking parchment, on a cool, floured, work surface, roll out your ready-made puff pastry dough to a long rectangle.

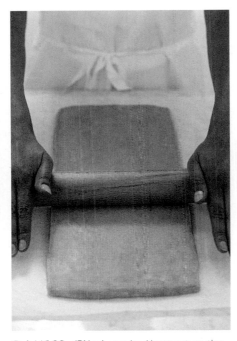

2 Add 100g (3½oz) unsalted butter, turn the parcel over, and slowly but firmly, roll out from the centre again.

3 Using the edge of the baking parchment, fold both the top and the bottom ends of the dough inwards to meet in the centre.

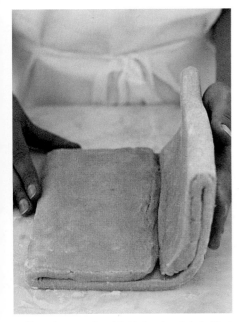

4 Turn the parcel and fold the dough in half at the centre. Using your hands, flatten the parcel slightly, and chill for 30 minutes.

5 Roll the pastry parcel out to a rectangle again, then fold and chill as before. Repeat the process once more.

6 Roll into a rectangle then fold one end to the middle and the other over it. Cover with cling film and chill for 30 minutes before using.

LINE A TART TIN

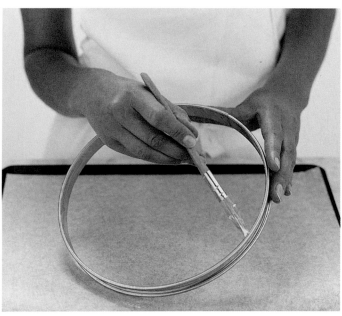

1 Using a pastry brush dipped in a little melted butter, grease the inside of a tart ring or a loose-bottomed tart tin. Place the ring on a large flat baking sheet covered with baking parchment.

2 Sprinkle a little flour on a cool work surface, then lightly dust the pastry ball with flour, and roll out the pastry into a circle larger than your tart ring. Keep rolling out until it is 3–5mm (⅛–¼ in) thick.

3 Ensure that the pastry does not stick to the surface by sliding a flexible spatula underneath it after every few strokes with the rolling pin. Carefully brush away any surplus flour with a dry pastry brush.

4 Use the rolling pin to gather up the pastry by rolling the pastry halfway over it. Then carefully lift the rest of the pastry circle away from the surface to transfer it to the tart ring.

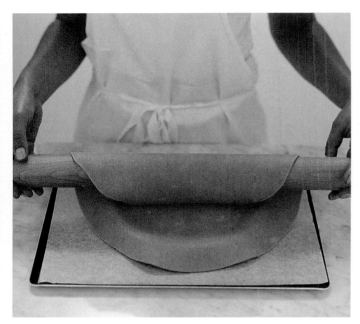

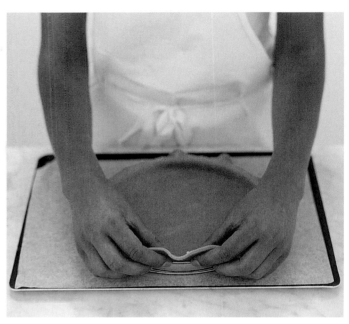

5 Dust off any surplus flour again, and gently unroll the pastry circle across the tart ring, making sure that there is plenty of excess pastry to cover the sides of the ring.

6 Carefully smooth the pastry from the centre of the circle then, using your thumbs and forefingers, gently press the pastry into the inside edge of the ring and and up the sides.

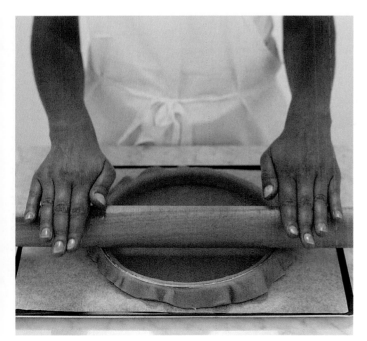

7 Now use your rolling pin to trim away the excess pastry and give a clean edge, by pressing the rolling pin over the top of the tart ring to cut away the pastry hanging over the top.

8 Using your thumbs, carefully press the pastry into and up the sides of the ring again to achieve a smooth fit. Prick the base all over with a fork to allow air to escape. Chill in the refrigerator for 30 minutes before using.

BLIND BAKE

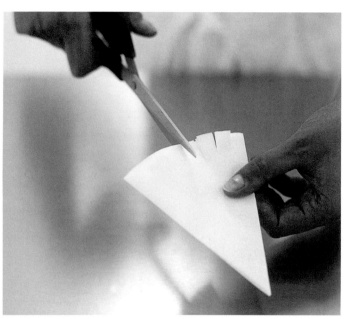

1 Cut a circle of baking parchment slightly larger than the flan ring or tart tin that you are using. Fold the disc in half several times, then clip the outer edge with scissors.

2 Place the pastry in the flan ring and and prick it with a fork, then cover the base and sides of the pastry with the parchment, taking the paper above the sides of the ring. Fill with dried beans or baking beans.

3 Place the shell in the oven and bake according to your recipe's instructions. For a fully baked case, remove the beans and paper, then return the shell to the oven for the required time.

4 Cool the pastry case on a wire rack. Lift off the flan ring (or remove from the tart tin) before, or after filling, according to the recipe directions.

TRIM AND DECORATE PASTRY

 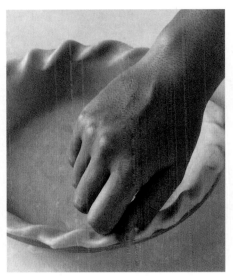 

1 For a forked edge, press the dough to the rim of the dish using the prongs of a fork. Repeat around the edge in even intervals.

2 For a rope edge, pinch the dough between your thumb and the knuckle of your index finger. Place your thumb in the groove and repeat.

3 For a fluted edge, push a finger against the outside edge and pinch the pastry with the other finger and thumb to form a ruffle.

SEAL AND GLAZE PASTRY

1 Apply a melted jelly, jam, or light caramel over the fruit when you remove the tart from the oven to give it a lustrous appearance.

2 For turnovers, brush with an egg wash (1 egg yolk, 1 tbsp water and a pinch of salt) before baking to give a rich, glossy glaze.

3 For a cooked tart, thinly glaze the base of a cooled tart shell with melted plain or white chocolate and allow to set.

MAKE A GENOESE SPONGE

1 Preheat the oven to 190°C (375°F/Gas 5). Sift 200g (8oz) plain flour and set aside. In a heatproof bowl over boiling water, place 6 eggs and 20g (¾oz) honey, and whisk until the mixture is a creamy, pale yellow.

2 Remove from the heat and whisk at a high speed until thick. Add grated zest of ½ lemon, and whisk slowly for 15 minutes. Fold in the flour. Stir 2 tbsp of the mixture into 60g (2¼oz) melted butter, then quickly combine.

3 Pour the mixture into a springform cake tin lined with greaseproof paper. Smooth the top and place it in the oven. Reduce the heat to 175°C (350°F/Gas 4) and bake for 30–40 minutes, or until golden brown.

4 Remove from the oven and leave to cool for 10 minutes. Set on a wire rack and release the springform. To cut layers, place one hand on top of the cake and use a long-bladed, serrated knife to cut through.

ROLL A SPONGE ROULADE

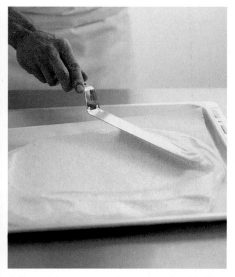  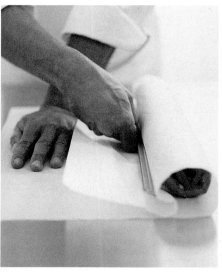

1 Spread the sponge mixture on a lined baking tray. Bake until golden, then put a piece of baking parchment on top and turn out the cake.

2 Slowly peel away the bottom layer of parchment. Fill, and roll, using the second piece of parchment to support the roulade.

3 Fold one half of the paper over the roulade, then push a ruler against the roll to shape it. Remove the paper, and trim the ends to serve.

PREPARE AND LINE A CAKE TIN

1 Melt unsalted butter and use a pastry brush to apply a thin, even layer all over the bottom and sides of the tin, including any corners.

2 Sprinkle a little flour into the tin, then shake and rotate the pan so the flour coats the bottom and sides. Tip away any excess flour.

3 If using a paper liner, instead of flouring, place a fitted piece of baking parchment directly onto the greased bottom.

PASTA

BUY Available fresh or dried, plain white, with egg, wholemeal, or coloured and flavoured with spinach, with olives, with black squid ink, and with tomato. Fresh is not always best; some sauces are better suited to dried pasta and a quality brand will be superior to that of a cheap fresh pasta. A rough texture is a positive attribute indicating that the pasta was made in small batches and that sauces will cling well to it. **STORE** Keep dried pasta in a sealed container in a cool dry place for up to a year. Freshly made pasta keeps for up to 3 days in the fridge, 3 months in the freezer. Bought fresh pasta keeps about a week in the refrigerator – check use-by date. Cooked pasta can be frozen for up to 2 months, it will be slightly softer on thawing.

▲ SPAGHETTI

EAT Long, thin, and round. Use with everything from a simple garlic, chilli, and olive oil dressing to cream or meat sauces. Made from durum wheat and also from alternative flours. Spaghettini is thin spaghetti; use in the same way. **FLAVOUR PAIRINGS** Meat ragùs, meatballs, pesto, olive oil, butter, cream, ham, pancetta, onions, garlic, tomatoes, chillies, shellfish, Parmesan.

◀ VERMICELLI

EAT Very fine durum wheat pasta, like very thin spaghetti. Used in many cuisines outside Italy. Often cooked and layered with fish or vegetable mixtures and baked with a breadcrumb topping or broken into pieces to add to broth (available ready cut too). **FLAVOUR PAIRINGS** Shellfish, sweet peppers, tomatoes, onions, aubergines, courgettes, olives, garlic, basil, oregano, thyme, breadcrumbs, olive oil, chicken, beef and vegetable broths.

◀ TAGLIATELLE

EAT Fresh tagliatelle is sold in strips; dried in nests. Good with rich meat and cream sauces. Dried nests are available in different colours and flavours. Best to choose complementary sauces e.g. black pasta is flavoured with squid or cuttlefish ink so best matched with seafood or vegetables. Fettuccine is a narrower version, sold in lengths. **FLAVOUR PAIRINGS** Cream, crème fraîche, eggs, ham, pancetta, mushrooms, peas, broad beans, fresh and smoked salmon, shellfish, broccoli, classic Bolognese sauce, Parmesan.

▲ PAPPARDELLE

EAT Thick ribbons with wavy or straight edges. Good with chunky meat or fish sauces. **FLAVOUR PAIRINGS** Olive oil, cream, veal, beef, chicken, chicken livers, monkfish, halibut, tuna, fresh and smoked salmon, sage, oregano, basil, parsley, olives, garlic, onions, tomatoes.

▲ ORZO

EAT Italian for barley, beads of pasta used in place of rice in soups, bakes or side dishes. **FLAVOUR PAIRINGS** Chicken, beef and vegetable broths, olive oil, tomatoes, onions, garlic, sweet peppers, olives, cavolo nero, carrots, turnips, mushrooms.

▲ MACARONI

EAT Smooth or ribbed, short or long pasta tubes. Use for macaroni cheese and other baked pasta dishes, such as timbales. **FLAVOUR PAIRINGS** Cheddar, blue cheese, Italian hard cheeses, broccoli, tomatoes, mushrooms, spinach, sweetcorn, tuna, bacon, prosciutto crudo, breadcrumbs, butter.

▲ LASAGNE

EAT Fresh or dried, usually layered with a chunky sauce and topped with Béchamel sauce, then baked. Fresh lasagne can be cooked and folded on plates over a filling and served as open lasagne or open ravioli. **FLAVOUR PAIRINGS** Bolognese sauce, tomato sauce, fish and shellfish, mixed pulses, mushrooms, Mediterranean vegetables, broccoli, Italian hard cheeses, mascarpone.

▲ FARFALLE

EAT Likened to bow ties or butterflies, they're good with simple tomato, or cheese and ham sauces, or in salads and oven-bakes. **FLAVOUR PAIRINGS** Tomatoes, onions, garlic, olive oil, basil, Gorgonzola, cream, Italian hard cheeses, cherry tomatoes, black olives, pesto (as salad dressing), salmon, tuna, pine nuts, spinach.

▲ FUSILLI

EAT Favourite spiral shape for coloured pasta and multigrain combinations (as well as plain). Good in salads and bakes and with chunky vegetable and creamy sauces. **FLAVOUR PAIRINGS** Olive oil, black olives, tomatoes, aubergines, red peppers, onions, garlic, capers, pine nuts, basil, cream, Gorgonzola, mozzarella, Parmesan.

▲ RIGATONE

EAT Large and satisfying, good with meat ragùs and chunky vegetables but also with smooth cream and cheese sauces. **FLAVOUR PAIRINGS** Beef, veal, chicken, ham, pig's liver, olive oil, butter, sage, basil, parsley, onions, tomatoes, sweetcorn, broccoli, beans, spinach, mozzarella, Italian hard cheeses, Gorgonzola.

▲ PENNE

EAT Pasta quills with smooth sides (lisce) or ribbed (regate). Classically paired with tomato and chilli sauces, and also good in salads and pasta bakes. **FLAVOUR PAIRINGS** Olive oil, butter, cream, onions, garlic, sweet peppers, mushrooms, shellfish, chicken, chorizo, beef, veal, tomatoes, fennel, sun-dried tomatoes, basil, parsley, thyme, chillies, Parmesan, mascarpone.

▲ CONCHIGLIE

EAT Shells available in small (add to soups), medium (serve with sauces or in salads), and large (stuff). **FLAVOUR PAIRINGS** Chicken and vegetable broths, tomatoes, onions, garlic, anchovies, prawns and other shellfish, bacon, ham, chicken, sweetcorn, peas, spinach, squashes, rocket, olives, Parmesan, basil, sage.

▲ TROFIE

EAT Speciality of Liguria, handmade with just Tipo "00" flour and water, traditionally served with pesto from the same region. **FLAVOUR PAIRINGS** Basil pesto, olive oil, butter, prawns, goat's cheese, lemon, artichoke hearts, wild mushrooms, courgettes, Parmesan.

▲ RAVIOLI

EAT Stuffed square or round (girasole) pasta cushions, filled with meat, chicken, vegetables, mushrooms, fish, or spinach and ricotta cheese. Serve simply dressed, or with a sauce. **FLAVOUR PAIRINGS** Fresh tomato sauce, butter, olive oil, sage, thyme, parsley, Parmesan, mascarpone.

▲ CAPPELLETTI

EAT Modelled on little hats worn in the middle ages, usually stuffed with meat or cheese. **FLAVOUR PAIRINGS** Butter, olive oil, sage, parsley, garlic, Italian hard cheeses.

▲ LUNETTE

EAT "Little moons", sometimes flavoured with truffles, often stuffed with cheese, or mixtures like broccoli and almonds. **FLAVOUR PAIRINGS** Olive oil, butter, fresh herbs, truffles or truffle oil.

NOODLES

BUY All these noodles cook quickly, so take care to follow packet directions or they will become very soft. All are available dried. If you find a supplier of fresh ones, make sure the shop has a high turnover of trade as they deteriorate quickly.
STORE Fresh ones should be eaten on day of purchase but can be stored in the refrigerator in a plastic bag for a few days if necessary. Dried noodles will keep wrapped, in a cool, dry cupboard for several years.

▲ FLAT RICE NOODLES

EAT Also called rice sticks, they vary in width from a couple of millimetres to about 1 centimetre. Use in Pad Thai, add to stir-fries, or use with steamed dishes. **FLAVOUR PAIRINGS** Shallots, beansprouts, spring onions, chilli, coriander leaf, oyster sauce, nam pla, lime, peanuts, eggs, prawns.

▲ RICE VERMICELLI

EAT Very thin skeins of dried noodles. Use to add soft bulk and texture in many dishes including spring rolls and salads. Try deep-frying dried noodles to puff up and crisp as a garnish for salads, or soak, dry, then deep-fry for crunchy noodles to serve with stir-fries. **FLAVOUR PAIRINGS** Sesame oil and seeds, ginger, chilli, garlic, shiitake mushrooms, spring onions, cabbage, carrots, shellfish, chicken, beef, soy sauce, oyster sauce, beansprouts.

◄ BROWN RICE UDON NOODLES

EAT Often made with wheat flour too, these give a more distinctive flavour and firmer texture to serve in soups, and with salads, stir-fries, steamed, or stewed dishes. **FLAVOUR PAIRINGS** Chilli, ginger, peanut butter, peanut oil, sesame oil, soy sauce, garlic, miso, coconut milk, spring onions, broccoli, carrots, daikon, pak choi and other leafy greens, baby corn, mangetout, green beans.

▲ FINE RICE NOODLES

EAT Thin, straight version of flat rice noodles, suitable for adding to soups and stir-fries.
FLAVOUR PAIRINGS Chicken or beef broth, chicken, beef, prawns, crab, lobster, shiitake mushrooms, sweetcorn, spring onions, soy sauce, ginger, garlic.

▲ WHEAT UDON NOODLES

EAT Plump white noodles with rounded or square-cut edges. Serve in broths and thick curry (katsu) sauces. **FLAVOUR PAIRINGS** Chicken, pork, prawns, garlic, onions, peppers, root and green vegetables, apples, bananas, curry spices, turmeric, honey, tomato ketchup, chicken broth, miso, nam pla, chilli, star anise.

▲ CHINESE WHEAT NOODLES

EAT Round or flat, they are robust and versatile. Ideal for soups and stir-fries. **FLAVOUR PAIRINGS** Beef, poultry, pork, cashew nuts, peanuts, chilli, green peppers, miso, onion, oyster sauce, spinach, Chinese five-spice powder.

▲ BUCKWHEAT (SOBA) NOODLES

EAT Japanese noodles, either exclusively buckwheat, or mixed with wheat flour (milder). Good hot or cold. **FLAVOUR PAIRINGS** Spring onions, shiitake mushrooms, asparagus, mangetout, carrots, celery, peppers, bean sprouts, garlic, lime, soy sauce, peanuts, tahini, chilli, ginger, rice wine, rice vinegar, honey, chicken, prawns.

▲ BEAN THREAD (CELLOPHANE) NOODLES

EAT Made from mung beans and tapioca, particularly good in salads. **FLAVOUR PAIRINGS** Peanut or sunflower oil, sesame oil, rice wine vinegar, soy sauce, chilli, ginger, garlic, cucumber, carrots, radishes, chicken, duck, prawns, lychees, mango, beansprouts.

▲ CHINESE EGG NOODLES

EAT Available in a variety of thicknesses. Famous in Chow Mein, but good in all stir-fries and steamed dishes. **FLAVOUR PAIRINGS** Beef, poultry, pork, prawns, sesame oil, soy sauce, dry sherry, rice wine, spring onions, peppers, Chinese five-spice powder, chilli sauce.

▲ SOMEN NOODLES

EAT Associated with Japanese summer time, they are often eaten cold with a dipping sauce. **FLAVOUR PAIRINGS** Tamari soy sauce, ginger, garlic, rice wine, chilli, spring onions, sesame oil, most vegetables, beef, chicken, pork, fish and shellfish.

▲ INDIAN VERMICELLI

EAT Fine wheat noodles, sold plain or pre-toasted (as most recipes call for them to be browned in ghee before use). Used in some savoury dishes but mostly for milk puddings. **FLAVOUR PAIRINGS** Milk, sugars, honey, cardamom seeds, cumin seeds, saffron, raisins, cashew nuts, pistachios, butter or ghee.

▲ RAMEN NOODLES

EAT Japanese wheat noodles, similar to Chinese ones, served in soups and as an accompaniment. **FLAVOUR PAIRINGS** Chicken or beef broth, chicken, beef, shellfish, shiitake mushrooms, bamboo shoots, daikon, carrots, spring onions, miso, mustard greens, ginger, garlic, tamari soy sauce.

COOK DRIED PASTA

1 Bring a large pan of salted water to the boil and pour in the pasta. Stir once to prevent the pasta sticking to the bottom of the pan.

2 Boil with the pan uncovered, following the recommended cooking time on the pack, or until al dente (remove a spoonful to test).

3 Drain the pasta through a colander, shaking it gently to remove any excess water, and toss with a little oil to prevent it sticking together.

BOIL NOODLES

1 To boil egg, wheat, or buckwheat noodles, bring a large saucepan of water to the boil. Add the noodles, allow the water to return to the boil, then cook until the noodles are softened (about 2 minutes).

2 Drain the noodles in a colander and place them under cold running water. Toss the noodles with a little oil to prevent them from sticking, then proceed with the desired recipe.

MAKE PASTA DOUGH

"The general rule is: for every 100 grams of flour, use 1 egg or 1 egg-worth of liquid."

ANDY OLIVER

1 Pour the pasta flour onto a surface, form a well in the centre, and add the eggs then gently break the yolks with a fork.

2 Beat the eggs lightly with the fork, then slowly begin to draw the flour into the centre to mix with the eggs a little at a time.

3 Once the eggs and the flour have been combined, push any remaining flour into the centre and use your hands to form the dough.

4 Now place the dough on a clean surface and knead it firmly with both hands until it feels semi-soft and holds together.

5 Continue to knead the dough, turning it as you go, for at least 4–5 minutes, or until it feels silky, smooth, and elastic.

6 Wrap the kneaded dough in cling film and place it in the refrigerator (but not the coldest part) to rest for up to an hour.

STRETCH PASTA DOUGH BY HAND

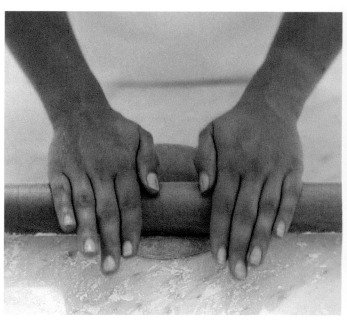

1 Unwrap the dough and cut it in halves, thirds, or quarters. Re-wrap what you are not yet using. Form the dough into a ball, then use your hands to flatten it slightly. Sprinkle the work surface lightly with flour.

2 Place the rolling pin about a third of the way into the circle of dough and gently roll outwards. Continue doing this, and each time you roll outwards, give the dough a quarter turn until it is about 3mm (⅛in) thick.

3 Curl the dough over the rolling pin and roll up about a quarter of it. Hold the dough on the table with your other hand and rolling the pin with a quick forwards-and-backwards motion, unfurl the dough.

4 Repeat the process of curling of the dough over the rolling pin, but take up a bit more dough this time. Hold the other end of the dough with your other hand and use the same unfurling motion at the top.

5 Continue, rolling up a little more of the dough each time, until you have rolled up and unfurled all of it. Roll all the dough up and turn the rolling pin around (left to right, not over) then unroll the dough again.

6 Start the process again, beginning at the opposite end to where you previously began. Repeat this curling, stretching, and unrolling process until the dough is the right thickness for your recipe.

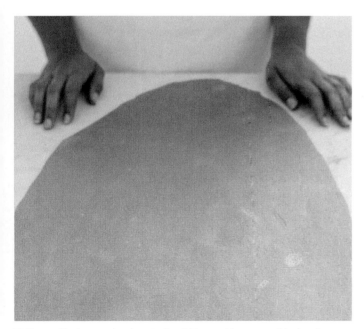

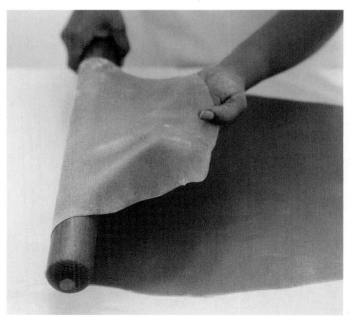

7 For stuffed pasta the dough should be as thin as possible, but it needs to be about 1mm thick for cut pasta. By the end of all this rolling and unrolling, you will have an elongated oval shape called the "sfoglia".

8 If you are making the pasta for stuffed forms, you should use it immediately. If it is to be cut into shapes, let it dry on top of a clean, dry tea towel for about 15–25 minutes.

USE A PASTA MACHINE

1 Flatten the pasta dough into a circle and pass through the pasta machine on the thickest setting 3 times. This will make the dough spread out to fill the full width of the machine.

2 Fold the pasta dough into thirds, then flatten it , and pass through the machine again. Repeat this process 6 times (lightly dusting the dough with flour once or twice to prevent it sticking).

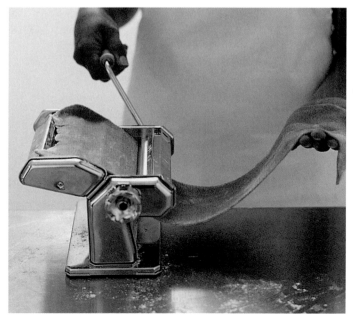

3 Continue to roll the pasta through the machine, decreasing the thickness setting each time. As you turn the handle with one hand, support the dough with the other, as it gradually becomes thinner.

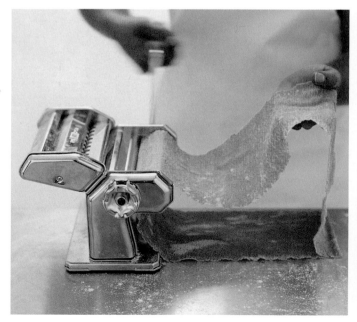

4 To save time, press the edges of the pasta sheet together to create a loop. This will avoid the need to keep removing the dough from the machine and feeding it back in.

MAKE GNOCCHI

"Gnocchi goes well with a hundred different things – punchy sauces, meat sauces, vegetables, ragùs – and is dead easy to make." **TIM KINNAIRD**

1 Gnocchi is made by forming a rough dough out of cooked potato, eggs, and flour. Take each piece of dough and roll it back and forth on a floured work surface to form a cylinder. Ensure you handle it lightly.

2 When the cylinders are evenly formed (they should be about as thick as your forefinger), cut the dough into 3cm (1¼in) pieces, shape into crescents, and press onto the back of a fork to form the indentations.

CUT PASTA DOUGH BY HAND

1 To make rectangular or square shaped pasta, cut the dough to the required size for your recipe. 12x15cm (5x6in) rectangles are the usual size for lasagne or cannelloni.

2 To make pasta noodles, fold the dough into thirds with the folds at the top and bottom, then cut it into strips. 1cm (½in) wide would be the usual size for pappardelle and 5mm (¼in) wide for fettuccine.

ASSEMBLE RAVIOLI

"You want to knock all the air out and make sure it's nice and sealed at the same time. If it isn't sealed or there's a lot of air, then when you come to boil it, it will explode. All your filling will come out, and you'll just be left with a soggy bit of pasta." **CHRIS GATES**

1 Using a pasta machine, roll out a thin sheet of pasta and divide it into two equal lengths. Take one sheet and mark out the number and shape of ravioli, as specified by the recipe, by scoring the pasta with a cutter.

2 Take teaspoonfuls of the filling mixture and carefully place them in the centre of each scored raviolo half. Brush on beaten egg or a little water, to help bind the edges of the ravioli.

3 Now take the second length of rolled-out pasta and carefully lift it over the first sheet, check for alignment, and then place on top. Gently shape round each dollop of filling, getting rid of any air bubbles.

4 Take the pastry cutter and run it around the outside edges of the ravioli sheet to form a neat edge, then cut out each individual raviolo. Lightly press around the edges with your fingertips to seal.

SHAPE TORTELLONI

1 Roll the the pasta dough until it is extremely thin and lay out a sheet 12cm (5in) wide, then trim the edges. Cut the sheet into two equal lengths. Put one half aside and cover with a clean, damp tea towel.

2 Spread another damp tea towel on your work surface and lay the other dough sheet on top. Cut the pasta sheet in half lengthways, then cut across it at equal intervals to create 6cm (2½in) squares.

3 Take one square and turn it over onto the work surface, so that its damp side now faces upwards. Position it like a diamond, rather than a square. Place a teaspoon of filling into the middle of the diamond.

4 Now take the the bottom corner up over the filling to the top corner, so that it forms a triangular shape. Press the edges together and then lift the left and right corners and pinch them together to seal.

OILS

BUY There are hundreds of oils on the market. It is important to use the right one for the job. Here's a selection of favourites used in cookery. Choose cold-pressed oils for flavour and nutritional value. Not all oils are suitable for frying. Those high in polyunsaturated fats have too low a smoking point. **STORE** Olive and seed oils will keep unopened in a cool, dark place for a year or more. However, nut oils should be used within 6 months. All open bottles should be used within 3 months.

▲ EXTRA VIRGIN OLIVE OIL

EAT Highest quality olive oil, the best is cold-pressed. Made from a single olive variety or a blend, filtered or unfiltered, producing a wide difference in flavour and variance in colour from olive green to greenish gold. Choose according to preference. Use when flavour is all-important – as a condiment or drizzle, in dressings, dips, and marinades. Don't waste an expensive oil for frying. **FLAVOUR PAIRINGS** Asparagus, artichokes, aubergines, peppers, tomatoes, baby leeks, onions, shallots, garlic, fresh herbs, olives, capers, fresh cheeses, cured meats, fish and seafood, wines, vinegars, mustards, honey.

▲ VIRGIN OLIVE OIL

EAT Lower quality than extra virgin oil. Use for everyday cooking, when you want a milder-flavoured dressing, or for grilling and sautéing. **FLAVOUR PAIRINGS** Wine, balsamic, and fruit vinegars, Dijon and grainy mustard, white and red wine, citrus, all meats, fish and seafood, poultry, game, vegetables, most dried and fresh fruits, herbs, chilli.

▲ OLIVE/LIGHT OLIVE OIL

EAT A blend of virgin olive oil and a cheaper refined oil to give a "lighter" flavour. Popular with those who aren't so keen on the pronounced flavour of extra virgin oil. Some like it for making mayonnaise. Light does not mean lower in calories. Use for general cooking or mix with a little nut or seed oil (like walnut or toasted pumpkin) in dressings. **FLAVOUR PAIRINGS** All meats, fish, poultry and game, egg yolks, mustard, vegetables, salad stuffs, wine, balsamic or fruit vinegars, lemon juice, honey, nuts, seeds.

▲ GROUNDNUT OIL

EAT The refined oil is almost tasteless and ideal when you don't want added flavour – for frying everything from chips to fritters, and general cooking. **FLAVOUR PAIRINGS** Roots and tubers, leafy greens, onions, meat, fish, poultry, robust herbs like parsley or sage (fried for garnish).

▲ GRAPESEED OIL

EAT Widely used in French cookery and in salad dressings, it has a delicate flavour. Can also be used for frying. **FLAVOUR PAIRINGS** Nuts, seeds, tomatoes, onions, root vegetables, garlic, balsamic, fruit, and herb vinegars, herbs.

▲ RAPESEED OIL

EAT Also known as Canola oil. Good for frying and baking. **FLAVOUR PAIRINGS** Meatballs, patties, burgers, fritters, fish and shellfish, choux pastry (for beignets), onions, potatoes, root vegetables, apples, pears, bananas, pineapple.

▲ SUNFLOWER OIL

EAT Suitable for all cooking and dressings. Cold-pressed is much earthier. Safflower is from the same family of seeds. Use in the same way. **FLAVOUR PAIRINGS** Meats, poultry, game, fish, vegetables, eggs, cream, vinegars, citrus.

▲ PUMPKIN SEED OIL

EAT Toasted has best flavour. Good to finish soups, brush on roast meats, and in salad dressings. **FLAVOUR PAIRINGS** Pork, oily fish, squashes, balsamic, fruit, and wine vinegars, cherry tomatoes, cucumber, spinach, apples, berries.

▲ SESAME OIL

EAT Nutty taste. Use for Chinese cookery and salad dressings. **FLAVOUR PAIRINGS** Sesame seeds, spring onions, garlic, soy sauce, honey, Sichuan pepper, beansprouts, peppers, cucumber, water chestnuts, chicken, fish, shellfish, beef, pork.

▲ WALNUT OIL

EAT Rich, nut flavour and aroma. Use in dressings, drizzled over cooked vegetables, and for stir-fries. **FLAVOUR PAIRINGS** Nuts and seeds, pears, apples, cabbage, celery, root vegetables, spinach, blue and cream cheeses.

▲ HAZELNUT OIL

EAT Subtle flavour of hazelnuts. Delicious in dressings and desserts. Don't use for cooking as it goes bitter. **FLAVOUR PAIRINGS** Beetroot, cherry tomatoes, shallots, baby leaves, fresh soft cheeses, raspberries, oats, rice, vanilla.

▲ TRUFFLE OIL

EAT White truffle oil is stronger. Drizzle over pasta, risotto, grills, and omelettes. Gently fry eggs in black truffle oil, then serve on bruschetta with the oil drizzled over. **FLAVOUR PAIRINGS** Eggs, pasta, risotto rice, fish and shellfish, game birds, fois gras.

▲ CHILLI OIL

EAT All chilli oils are pungent. Use whenever you want their spicy flavour in cooking and dressings. **FLAVOUR PAIRINGS** Tomatoes, mushrooms, onions, garlic, basil, oregano, cheeses, pasta, beef, pork, veal, chicken, seafood, citrus, tropical fruits.

▲ GARLIC OIL

EAT Use for an earthy, garlic flavour. Good in dressings, marinades, and potato dishes. Don't use for frying. **FLAVOUR PAIRINGS** Potatoes, onions, mushrooms, rice, courgettes, pasta, couscous, fish, seafood, chicken.

▲ HERB OILS

EAT Useful if a particular fresh herb is not available. Don't use for cooking at high temperatures. **FLAVOUR PAIRINGS** Most vegetables, pasta, rice, couscous, polenta, fish and seafood, meat, poultry, game, cheeses, tropical fruits.

VINEGARS

BUY Each vinegar has its own particular flavour and is not usually interchangeable, so buy a selection from which to choose. Start with the ones you will use frequently, like, perhaps, basic wine vinegars and a good brown and white balsamic, and then add to the list as recipes call for them. **STORE** Most will keep almost indefinitely in a cool, dark cupboard (but fruit or herb vinegars usually only 2–3 years). Naturally produced wine vinegars that have not been pasteurized may grow a "vinegar mother" – a cluster of vinegar-producing bacteria. Just remove it and or use it to make your own vinegar at home.

▲ WHITE WINE VINEGAR

EAT Delicately sour with fruity undertones. Use in dressings for delicate salads, to make mayonnaise, and to deglaze the pan before making cream sauces for steaks, chops, and cutlets. **FLAVOUR PAIRINGS** Shallots, baby salad leaves, artichoke hearts, avocado, cucumber, mushrooms, fennel, beef, lamb, pork, chicken, white fish, shellfish, white beans, cream, eggs, parsley, sage, lovage, chervil, olive oil, sunflower oil.

▲ RED WINE VINEGAR

EAT Robust and fruity with a good depth of acidity. Use in most culinary applications, particularly stronger-flavoured salads, meat, game, and poultry stews and casseroles. It is also the French choice for making vinaigrette. **FLAVOUR PAIRINGS** Beetroot, carrots, red onions, green beans, mushrooms, beef, venison, pork, lamb, game birds, oily fish, pulses, tarragon, parsley, oregano, rosemary, bay, olive oil, herb oils, toasted seed oils.

▲ SHERRY VINEGAR

EAT Matured for a number of years in wooden barrels. It is full of dried fruit flavours that are good for robust salads, and to marinate pork or veal loin before roasting. **FLAVOUR PAIRINGS** Pork, veal, chicken, duck, salmon, mackerel, sardines, root vegetables, spinach, sorrel, rocket, watercress, radishes, olive oil, nut oils.

▲ MUSCAT VINEGAR

EAT Strong aroma and taste of sweet muscat grapes, from which it is made. Particularly good in fish and seafood dressings, desserts, and fruit sauces. **FLAVOUR PAIRINGS** Smoked mackerel, smoked salmon, lobster, prawns, olive oil, hazelnut oil, chicory, tropical fruits, apples, pears, strawberries, raspberries, nuts.

▲ CIDER VINEGAR

EAT A strong aroma and flavour of apples. Use instead of red or white wine vinegar but particularly good with richer meats and fish. **FLAVOUR PAIRINGS** Duck, chicken, game birds, salmon, trout, mackerel, herring, sea bass and bream, orchard fruits, cabbage, shallots, olive, walnut, toasted sesame and pumpkin oil.

▲ PICKLING VINEGAR

EAT Usually malt vinegar-based, special blends of pickling spices are infused in it ready for making pickles. **FLAVOUR PAIRINGS** Onions, shallots, cucumbers, beetroot, plums, red and white cabbage, cauliflower, carrots, tomatoes, peppers, courgettes, beans, turmeric, mustard powder, garlic, cinnamon, bay leaf, muscovado and other brown sugars, granulated sugar, honey.

▲ HERB VINEGAR

EAT Made by infusing the chosen herb in wine vinegar (tarragon here). Use in dressings and marinades. **FLAVOUR PAIRINGS** Salad stuffs, avocados, peppers, mushrooms, fish, shellfish, carpaccios, fresh cheeses, chicken, olive oil.

▲ FRUIT VINEGAR

EAT Strong flavour of featured fruit (raspberry here). Use for dressings, drizzles, and marinades. **FLAVOUR PAIRINGS** Duck, game, avocados, salad stuffs, beetroot, shallots, basil, rosemary, lavender, parsley, olive, hazelnut, and walnut oils.

▲ BALSAMIC VINEGAR

EAT Good balsamic from Modena contains no caramel or preservatives. Use for drizzles, dressings, savoury sauces, and with fresh and dried fruits **FLAVOUR PAIRINGS** Cheeses, pulses, fruits, vegetables, duck, game birds, rich meats, fish, honey, olive oil.

▲ WHITE BALSAMIC CONDIMENT

EAT It's not a vinegar as it does not have a high enough acidity. It has a sweet, mildly acidic taste. **FLAVOUR PAIRINGS** Fish, shellfish, chicken, artichokes, white asparagus, chicory, celeriac, button mushrooms, olive, sunflower and nut oils.

▲ CHINESE WHITE RICE VINEGAR

EAT Tastes similar to white wine or malt vinegar. Use in sweet and sour dishes, pickles, and as a condiment. **FLAVOUR PAIRINGS** Pork, fish, prawns, chicken, peppers, spring onions, tomatoes, carrots, pineapple, cucumber, ginger, soy sauce.

▲ CHINESE BLACK RICE VINEGAR

EAT Mellow, slightly salty, and smoky. Chinkiang is the best. Use as a dim sum dipping sauce, or as balsamic vinegar. Red rice vinegar is similar but less sweet. **FLAVOUR PAIRINGS** Prawns, chicken, pork, beef, ginger, garlic, chilli, sesame oil, soy sauce.

▲ JAPANESE BROWN RICE VINEGAR

EAT Mellow flavour. Use in dipping sauces and marinades. **FLAVOUR PAIRINGS** Fish, shellfish, chicken, cabbage, daikon, mizuna, lotus root, edamame, cucumber, peppers, corn, okra.

▲ JAPANESE RICE VINEGAR

EAT Mix with salt and sugar for sushi vinegar. Add to tempura batter. **FLAVOUR PAIRINGS** Tofu, seafood, wasabi, ginger, soy sauce, sushi rice, nori, sesame seeds, cucumber, spring onions.

▲ MALT VINEGAR

EAT Strong and sour. Traditional condiment with fish and chips. Use for pickles and chutneys and in some sauces. **FLAVOUR PAIRINGS** Fish, tripe, potatoes, roots, beans, cauliflower, cucumbers, onions, peppers, fruits, bay leaves, pickling spices.

FLAVOURING SAUCES AND PASTES

BUY Check the labels and avoid those containing MSG or that have a long list of additives. For soy sauces, ensure they are authentically fermented from soya beans. For vegetable pastes, choose the longest use by date. **STORE** Keep unopened in a cool, dark cupboard. Once opened, store in the refrigerator. Most will last 3–6 months.

▲ TOMATO PURÉE

EAT Intense tomato flavour. Use generally in soups, stews, casseroles, and sauces. Look for sun-dried tomato paste, passata (sieved tomatoes), and the condiment, tomato ketchup. **FLAVOUR PAIRINGS** All meats, poultry, game, fish, pulses, most vegetables, cheeses, herbs and spices.

▲ WORCESTERSHIRE SAUCE

EAT A smooth sauce with a tangy flavour. Use in traditional British cookery and in a Bloody Mary. **FLAVOUR PAIRINGS** Tomato juice, vodka, celery salt, avocados, minced beef, bacon, mushrooms, mayonnaise, ketchup, Tabasco.

▲ TABASCO

EAT Thin fiery sauce with a salty, sour taste. A green, milder one is also available. Use to spice up soups, stews, casseroles, and dips and add a few drops to a Bloody Mary. Slightly thicker yellow or orange hot chilli sauce can be used the same way. **FLAVOUR PAIRINGS** Most vegetables, poultry, meat, pulses, cheeses, tomato juice, vodka, parsley, coriander leaf, celery salt.

▲ ANCHOVY PASTE

EAT Intense anchovy flavour. Spread on toast or add a dash to enhance meat pâtés, casseroles, and fish dishes. Thinner anchovy essence also available. **FLAVOUR PAIRINGS** Beef, venison, pig's liver, all fish and seafood, tomatoes.

▲ TAHINI PASTE

EAT Thick, smooth sesame seed paste. Essential in chickpea hummus, or use thinned with lemon juice as a dip with falafel. Good in sauces and dressings. **FLAVOUR PAIRINGS** Chickpeas and other pulses, olive oil, citrus, chilli, coriander leaf, mint, oregano, sesame seeds, yogurt.

▲ MISO

EAT Japanese white or red pastes made from fermented soy with wheat, barley, or rice. (White rice miso shown here). Use in soups (with dashi – stock made with dried bonito flakes), dressings, sauces, stir-fries, stews, marinades, and glazes. Miso soup mix, too. **FLAVOUR PAIRINGS** Tuna, salmon, monkfish, veal, ham, poultry, most vegetables, ginger, chilli, garlic.

▲ SOY SAUCE

EAT Use dark soy in general Chinese cooking but particularly "red"-cooked dishes. Also good as gravy browning. Use light soy as a condiment and dipping sauce. **FLAVOUR PAIRINGS** Poultry, all meats, seafood, vegetables, noodles, rice, eggs, Sichuan pepper, ginger, rice vinegar.

▲ TAMARI

EAT Japanese soy sauce. Use as a dipping sauce and in most savoury Japanese dishes. Often served with wasabi (the mustardy paste) as a condiment. **FLAVOUR PAIRINGS** Seafood, chicken, pork, beef, cabbage, daikon, mizuna, lotus root, edamame, cucumber, aubergine, peppers.

▲ OYSTER SAUCE

EAT Only mildly fishy. Use to flavour Chinese meat and vegetable dishes, particularly stir-fries. **FLAVOUR PAIRINGS** Beef, pork, chicken, prawns, aubergines, bean sprouts, pak choi, onions, spring onions, shiitake mushrooms, bamboo shoots, water chestnuts.

▲ BLACK BEAN SAUCE

EAT Mild or fiery. Use in Chinese stir-fries and steamed dishes. Add towards the end of cooking. Use yellow bean sauce in a similar way. **FLAVOUR PAIRINGS** Beef, pork, chicken, most vegetables, garlic, soy sauce.

▲ SWEET CHILLI SAUCE

EAT Sweet and thick, good for dipping or in stir-fries. **FLAVOUR PAIRINGS** Chicken, beef, pork, fish and shellfish, most vegetables, noodles, rice, soy sauce.

▲ HOISIN SAUCE

EAT Thick, sweet yet salty, strong and garlicky. Use as a glaze, a dip, in sauces, or to spread on Chinese pancakes before adding crispy duck. **FLAVOUR PAIRINGS** Duck, chicken, pork, beef, shellfish, noodles, most vegetables, spring rolls.

▲ NAM PLA

EAT Thai fish sauce; smells fishy, tastes salty. Add to dressings, stews, and curries. Asian shrimp paste is stronger, but use the same way. **FLAVOUR PAIRINGS** Curry pastes, galangal, coconut milk, beef, chicken, seafood, vegetables.

▲ SAMBAL OELEK

EAT Strong, salty, and tangy chilli paste. Serve as a relish, in salsas, or to add a kick to many dishes. **FLAVOUR PAIRINGS** Chicken, seafood, pulses, root and green vegetables, bean sprouts, salad vegetables, rice vinegar, white balsamic condiment.

▲ HARISSA PASTE

EAT Fiery chilli paste widely used in North African cookery. Use as a rub, in marinades, and dressings. **FLAVOUR PAIRINGS** Lamb, chicken, tuna, salmon, pulses, rice, edamame beans, broad beans, aubergines, courgettes, peppers, tomato purée.

MAKE FRESH CHICKEN STOCK

1 Roast the chicken bones in the oven for 20 minutes at 200°C (400°F/Gas 6). This will intensify the flavour and colour of the broth.

2 Transfer the bones to a large saucepan. Pour the fat from the roasting pan, add 500ml (16fl oz) water and bring to the boil.

3 Pour the boiling liquid from the roasting pan over the bones and add a further 2 litres (3½ pints) water.

4 Skim off the foam with a ladle or slotted spoon. Add the vegetables and simmer for 3 hours, uncovered.

5 Strain the contents of the saucepan into a bowl; you will find an extra ladleful at the bottom of the pan.

6 Leave the stock uncovered to cool, then use a ladle or spoon to skim off any fat that has settled on the surface.

MAKE CHICKEN CONSOMMÉ

1 To make a clarification mixture, whisk 2 egg whites just enough to loosen them and form a few bubbles. Add 1 tsp tomato purée and mix.

2 Place finely chopped chicken meat, garlic, vegetables, and parsley in a bowl, add the egg white mixture, mix, and refrigerate.

3 Combine the stock with the clarification mixture in a large saucepan. Heat slowly, and stir until the stock comes to the boil.

4 Once the stock reaches boiling point, reduce to a gentle simmer for 1 hour, or until a crust forms. Poke a knife through to check the clarity.

5 When the consommé is clear and the clarification ingredients cooked, strain the soup through a sieve lined with muslin.

6 Season the consommé with salt and white pepper to taste, then garnish with a sprig of fresh chervil and serve.

MAKE FISH STOCK

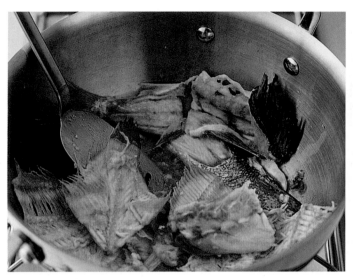

1 On a low heat, melt a knob of butter in a large saucepan or stockpot. Add the fish bones and stir until they smell of cooked fish, taking great care that they do not burn.

2 Add water, vegetables, and seasoning, and bring the liquid to the boil. Skim away any foam on the surface, and simmer for 30–40 minutes before straining through a fine sieve.

MAKE VEGETABLE STOCK

1 Place chopped carrots, celery, onion, and a bouquet garni into a large stockpot. Cover with water and bring to the boil. Reduce the heat and gently simmer the stock for up to 1 hour.

2 Ladle the stock through a fine sieve, pressing the vegetables against the sieve to extract any extra liquid. Season to taste with salt and freshly ground black pepper, let cool, and refrigerate for up to 3 days.

MAKE BEEF STOCK

1 Use either leftover bones from a rib of roast beef, or ask the butcher for a bag of beef bones. Tip the bones into a large roasting tin, add a handful of vegetables, and season. Roast for 30 minutes.

2 Add the roasted bones and vegetables to a large deep pan with some fresh stalks of thyme, rosemary, or a woody herb of your choice, then pour over enough cold water to cover completely.

3 Bring to the liquid to the boil, then reduce to a gentle simmer. Cook with the lid half-on for about 1 hour, skimming any scum that may come to the top of the pan, if necessary.

4 Remove the pan from the heat, then lift the beef bones from the saucepan and discard. Set a sieve over a large heatproof jug and pour the liquid through.

MAKE A VELOUTÉ SAUCE

1 Sweat 4 finely chopped shallots in 15g (½oz) butter over a low heat. Add 300ml (10fl oz) white wine, and 75ml (2½fl oz) vermouth.

2 Bring to the boil, stirring, then reduce the heat and simmer, uncovered, for 25 minutes, or until the liquid has reduced by two-thirds.

3 Now add the stock, stir, and return to the boil. Continue cooking it uncovered, over a high heat for 20 minutes, or until reduced by half.

4 Add 375ml (13fl oz) double cream and stir. Bring to the boil, then reduce the heat and cook until the sauce has reduced by over half.

5 The sauce should now be thick enough to coat the back of a spoon. If it is still too thin to do so, reduce for a further 5 minutes.

6 Strain the sauce through a fine sieve to remove the shallots, then serve, or keep warm in a bain-marie or double boiler.

MAKE A CLASSIC VINAIGRETTE

1 In a clean bowl, combine 2 tsp smooth Dijon mustard, 2 tbsp good-quality vinegar (red or white wine, herb, balsamic, or cider), and freshly ground black pepper.

2 Gradually whisk in 120ml (4fl oz) of extra virgin olive oil, until completely emulsified. Adjust the seasoning if necessary. Serve as a salad dressing, or in place of a heavier sauce for fish, poultry, or pasta.

CLARIFY BUTTER

3 Cut the butter into cubes and place them in a saucepan over a low heat. Keep watch over the butter and take care that it does not burn, as this will destroy the fresh flavour.

4 When the milk solids have completely separated from the fat, skim off any froth and remove from the heat. Carefully pour the clarified butter into a bowl, trying to keep the milk solids in the pan.

MAKE BEURRE BLANC, NOISETTE, OR NOIR

1 Place 2 finely chopped shallots, 3 tbsp white wine vinegar, and 4 tbsp dry white wine in a small pan and bring to the boil.

2 Lower the heat and reduce the liquid until only 1 tbsp of it remains. It should now have a light, syrupy consistency.

3 Over a low heat, add 2 tbsp water, then whisk in 200g (7oz) chilled, cubed butter, a little at a time, until it has emulsified.

4 Season the sauce with salt, white pepper, and lemon juice before serving. For a smoother sauce, strain through a fine sieve.

5 For beurre noisette, heat 50–75g (1¾–2½oz) salted butter for 2 minutes until it turns nutty brown. Add a squeeze of lemon juice.

6 Beurre noir is made in the same way as a beurre noisette, but cook the butter in the pan for 20–30 seconds longer.

MAKE BÉCHAMEL SAUCE

1 Push 4 whole cloves into a halved small onion. Place them in a pan with 600ml (1 pint) of full-fat milk and 1 bay leaf. Bring almost to the boil, then reduce the heat and simmer for 4–5 minutes. Allow to cool.

2 Melt 45g (1½oz) of unsalted butter over a low heat in a separate pan. Add 45g (1½oz) of plain flour, and cook gently for about 30 seconds, using a wooden spoon to stir the mixture into a pale roux.

1 Remove the pan with the roux from the heat. Add the cooled milk mixture through a sieve, and whisk until the sauce is smooth. Return to a medium heat and whisk continuously until the sauce comes to the boil.

2 Reduce the heat, and gently simmer for 20 minutes, or until the sauce is smooth, thickened, and glossy. Season to taste with salt, white pepper, and nutmeg. This recipe will make 600ml (1 pint).

MAKE MAYONNAISE

"Incorporate the oil a tiny bit at a time. If you pour it all in at once, it won't emulsify." **DHRUV BAKER**

1 Whisk 2 egg yolks, 1 tsp Dijon mustard, and 1 tsp vinegar in a bowl. Pour in 250ml (8fl oz) olive oil, drop by drop whisking all the time.

2 Gradually increase the speed of pouring to a steady stream. Once all the oil has been added, stir in 2 tsp freshly squeezed lemon juice.

3 If the mayonnaise "splits", place another egg yolk and 1 tsp mustard in a clean bowl, then trickle in the curdled sauce and whisk together.

SAVE CURDLED MAYONNAISE

1 Curdling may happen because the egg yolks or the oil were too cold when mixed, too much oil was added, or it was done too hastily.

2 To save it, simply place 1 egg yolk into a clean mixing bowl, and very slowly, add in the curdled mayonnaise, whisking continuously.

3 Continue whisking after each ladleful until the curdled mixture is completely smooth and incorporated into the new egg yolk.

MAKE HOLLANDAISE

"It's important to add the butter bit by bit. If you try to tip it all in at once, it won't form that emulsion or lovely smooth finish you are looking for." **DHRUV BAKER**

1 In a small pan, boil 2 tbsp vinegar, 2 tbsp water, and 1 tbsp of white peppercorns. Simmer for 1 minute, or until reduced by one-third.

2 Remove from the heat and leave to chill completely. Strain the liquid into a heatproof bowl, add 4 egg yolks, and whisk.

3 Place the bowl over a pan of simmering water. Whisk the mixture for 5–6 minutes, or until the sauce is thick and creamy.

4 Stand the bowl on a tea towel. Slowly pour in 250g (9oz) of clarified butter and whisk until the sauce is thick, glossy, and smooth.

5 Gently whisk in the juice of half a lemon, and season to taste with freshly ground white pepper, a pinch of cayenne pepper, and salt.

6 The hollandaise is now ready, and should be served immediately. This recipe will make 600ml (1 pint).

FLAVOUR PAIRINGS

In the following section you will find an easy reference guide to some of the ingredients and their flavour pairings featured in this book. It is an ideal at-a-glance guide to how you can combine textures and tastes to create wonderful dishes.

FISH

FISH ALWAYS NEEDS CAREFUL PAIRING BECAUSE SUBTLE FLAVOURS CAN BE OVERPOWERED BY STRONG ACCOMPANIMENTS.

ANCHOVY Sherry vinegar, white wine vinegar, shallots, tomatoes, marjoram, oregano, sage, thyme, parsley, olive oil.

BARRAMUNDI Pak choi, lime, chilli, fresh herbs, white wine.

BONITO Sesame seeds, rice vinegar, mirin, cucumber, daikon, chilli, coriander leaf and seed, potatoes, onions, green peppers.

BRILL Bacon, shallots, wild mushrooms, white wine, garlic, tomatoes, lemon, crab or prawn sauce.

BROWN TROUT Bouquet garni (parsley, thyme and bay leaf tied together), watercress-flavoured Hollandaise sauce, prawns.

CARP Paprika, butter, capers, dill, garlic, parsley, cornmeal, ginger, rice wine, sesame oil and seeds, fennel.

CATFISH Cornmeal, sesame seeds, soured cream, mushrooms, spring onions, parsley, bay leaf, thyme.

COD Dill, parsley, bay leaf, lemon, olive oil, tomatoes, olives, capers, garlic, breadcrumbs, butter, cheese sauce, cider, white wine.

COLEY Butter, milk, beer batter, parsley, chives, bacon, Cheddar cheese.

DAB Shallot, prawns, mushrooms, parsley, tarragon, lemon, lime, capers, gherkins, anchovy butter.

DOVER SOLE Butter, lemon, parsley, tarragon, cucumber, mint, shiitake mushrooms, truffle oil, white grapes.

FRESHWATER BREAM Thyme, rosemary, fennel, celery, nut oils.

GREY MULLET Ginger, nutmeg, allspice, chillies, thyme, lemon, lime, anchovies, tomatoes, onions.

HADDOCK Parsley, milk, bay leaf, Cheddar cheese, tomatoes, pea purée, garlic, onions.

HAKE Olive oil, smoked paprika, butter, lemon, onions, garlic, tomatoes.

HALIBUT Butter, beurre blanc, nutmeg, gherkins, capers, lemon, bacon, spicy sausages, charcuterie.

HERRING Soured cream, dill, onions, oatmeal, bacon, horseradish, mustard, lemon, capers, parsley.

JOHN DORY Garlic, white wine, cream sauces, mushrooms, sage, capers, lemon, crème fraîche.

KILN-SMOKED SALMON Eggs, rocket, beetroot, soured cream, horseradish, cream, chilli, olive oil, lemon, dill.

LEMON SOLE Béchamel sauce, parsley, chives, lemon, butter, white grapes.

LING Onions, garlic, potatoes, leeks, bacon, coriander leaf, parsley, sage, Cheddar cheese.

MACKEREL Basil, olive oil, garlic, onions, horseradish, mustard, dill, rhubarb, gooseberries.

MONKFISH Chorizo, proscuitto crudo, bacon, sage, rosemary, butter, olive oil, lemon, lime, chillies, capers, mushrooms.

PIKE Unsalted butter, sage, lemon, cream, bay leaf, white wine.

PLAICE Butter, lemon, parsley, sage, thyme, breadcrumb- or rice-based stuffing, chestnut mushrooms, grapes, white wine, potatoes.

POLLOCK Tomatoes, chilli, pancetta, basil.

RAINBOW TROUT White wine vinegar, butter, lemon chives, almonds, hazelnuts, Serrano ham, breadcrumbs.

RED GURNARD Olive oil, chorizo, pancetta, garlic, leeks, onions, white wine.

RED MULLET Citrus, chervil, tarragon, parsley, carrots, celery.

SALMON Lemon, butter, Hollandaise sauce, dill, samphire, tarragon, ginger, harissa paste, soy, sesame seeds and oil, chilli, coriander leaves.

SALTED DRIED ANCHOVIES Garlic, onions, tomatoes, olives, cheese, spinach, pine nuts, butter, olive oil, chilli.

SALT COD Olive oil, garlic, parsley, basil, olives, tomatoes, potatoes, citrus, capers, red peppers, chorizo.

SARDINE OR PILCHARD Olive oil, garlic, lemon, sultanas, pine nuts, parsley, oregano, thyme, tomatoes, peppers, chilli, lime, lemon.

SCAD (HORSE MACKEREL) Chilli, ginger, soy sauce, Chinese five-spice powder, coconut milk, tomatoes, peppers.

SEA BASS Black bean sauce, soy sauce, ginger, tomatoes, garlic, olive oil, red peppers, olives, aniseed flavours like fennel, caraway, and Pernod.

SEA BREAM Fennel, Pernod, coriander leaf, lemon, saffron, parsley, garlic.

SEA TROUT Mayonnaise, watercress, Hollandaise sauce, lemon, dill, parsley.

SKATE AND RAY Beurre noisette/noir, capers, parsley, lemon, vinegar.

SMOKED HADDOCK Spinach, rice, eggs, mild curry powder, tomatoes, parsley, cheese sauce, poached eggs.

SMOKED MACKEREL Horseradish, mustard, cream and crème fraîche, cream cheese, honey, sesame oil, dill, coriander leaves, beetroot, celeriac, waxy potatoes.

SMOKED SALMON Citrus, horseradish, dill, parsley, scrambled eggs.

SMOKED TROUT Lemon, horseradish, waxy potatoes, rocket, watercress, dill, chives, cream, crème fraîche.

SPRAT Beetroot, red and white wine vinegar, flat-leaf parsley, coriander leaves and seeds, lemon.

STURGEON Horseradish, soured cream, beetroot, vinegar, butter, citrus.

SWORDFISH Basil, rosemary, coriander leaf and seeds, cumin, paprika, citrus, garlic, parsley, olive and sesame oils, mesquite smoking chips.

TILAPIA Chilli, palm sugar, nam pla (Thai fish sauce), shrimp paste, coriander leaves, coconut, galangal.

TUNA Sesame seeds and oil, teriyaki, rice wine vinegar, wasabi, pickled ginger; tandoori spices, tomatoes, garlic, olives, capers.

TURBOT Wild mushrooms, Champagne, cream, butter, shellfish stock, lemon, prawns, Gruyère and Parmesan cheeses.

WHITING Tomatoes, chillies, basil, mushrooms, citrus, tartare sauce.

SHELLFISH

THE SWEET, INTENSE FLAVOURS OF SOME SHELLFISH CAN TAKE QUITE ROBUST PAIRINGS, OTHERS NEED MORE DELICATE ONES.

ABALONE Shiitake mushrooms, sesame seeds and oil, soy, ginger, garlic, butter, parsley, oyster sauce.

BROWN CRAB Mayonnaise, chilli, lemon, parsley, dill, potatoes, butter, Worcestershire sauce, anchovies.

BROWN SHRIMP Butter, lemon, nutmeg, mace, cayenne, Tabasco.

CLAM Cream, onions, garlic, white wine, chives, parsley, oregano, thyme, bay leaf, tomatoes.

COCKLE Malt vinegar, black pepper, salt, parsley, capers, gherkins, cucumber.

FRESHWATER CRAYFISH Melted butter, salad leaves, mayonnaise, citrus.

FROGS' LEGS Butter, lemon, garlic, black pepper, Calvados, cream, apples, and mixed herbs.

LANGOUSTINE (DUBLIN BAY PRAWN) Mayonnaise, citrus, tomatoes, garlic, butter, tarragon, lovage, parsley, chives, tartare sauce.

LOBSTER Mayonnaise, brandy, white wine, sherry, citrus, Parmesan, cream, chilli, tarragon, parsley, chives, salad leaves, shallots.

MUSSELS White wine, cider, Pernod, butter, garlic, cream, shallots, ginger, fennel, lemon grass, chillies, parsley, coriander leaves, dill, rosemary.

NORTH ATLANTIC PRAWN Mayonnaise, Marie Rose sauce, garlic, butter, citrus, chilli, avocados, melon, tomatoes, cucumber.

OCTOPUS Red wine, onions, balsamic vinegar, parsley, sage, rosemary, paprika, chilli, olive oil, soy sauce, sesame oil, rice vinegar.

OYSTERS (Raw) red wine vinegar, shallots, Tabasco, lemon juice; (Cooked) anchovy essence, butter, spinach, cream, Parmesan cheese.

PERIWINKLE Chilli, vinegar, malt vinegar, salt, black pepper, lemon juice, garlic butter, watercress.

RAZOR CLAM Garlic, butter, parsley, coriander leaves, white wine, shallots, cream, chilli.

SCALLOPS Bacon, chorizo, black pudding, red peppers, red onion, olive oil, sesame oil, black beans, spring onions, ginger, chilli, cream, bay leaf, parsley.

SEA URCHIN Lemon, black pepper, eggs, cream.

SNAILS Garlic butter with lemon or rosemary, olive oil with red wine vinegar and black pepper.

SQUID Garlic, turmeric, black pepper, spring onions, chilies, other seafood, olive oil, breadcrumbs, lemon juice, tomatoes, mayonnaise.

TIGER PRAWN Mayonnaise, garlic, chilli, curry spices, capers, paprika, citrus, butter, tempura dipping sauce, soy sauce, coconut, sesame seeds.

WHELK Malt vinegar, salt, black pepper, garlic butter, parsley, tarragon, chives.

MEAT, POULTRY, AND GAME

FROM HUMBLE SAUSAGES TO SEASONAL GROUSE, THERE ARE MANY EXCITING FLAVOURING POSSIBILITIES.

BEEF AND VEAL

BRISKET Mustard, root vegetables, mushrooms, bay leaf, bouquet garni, rosemary, thyme, parsley.

CHUCK OR SHOULDER Onion, garlic, tomatoes, mushrooms, peppers, aubergines, carrots, celery, Indian curry spices, Thai red curry paste, star anise, chilli, cinnamon, ginger.

FILLET STEAK Any of the other steak flavourings, liver pâté, port sauce, oysters (stuff with, before grilling), soy sauce, oyster sauce, ginger, cajun spices, garlic.

OXTAIL Bacon, celery, parsnips, carrots, swede, onions, peppercorns, nutmeg, cumin, allspice, mustard, red wine, brown beer, soy sauce.

RUMP STEAK Fried onions, Potato chips, mushrooms, French mustard, red wine sauce.

SILVERSIDE Mustard sauce, carrots, parsnips, onions, red wine, cinnamon, olives, tomatoes.

SIRLOIN JOINT English mustard, horseradish sauce or relish, Yorkshire puddings, root vegetables.

SIRLOIN STEAK Peppers, onions, olives, savoury butters (see T-bone), green or black peppercorn sauce, Béarnaise sauce.

T-BONE STEAK Savoury butters – anchovy, parsley, mixed

herb and garlic, oregano, chilli.

VEAL ESCALOPE Egg and breadcrumbs, Parmesan, ham and melting cheeses, cream, mushrooms, sorrel, spinach, gherkins, capers, tomato sauce, potato salad.

VEAL LOIN CHOP Tarragon or parsley butter, garlic and rosemary, white wine, cream, brandy, lemon, shallots.

VEAL OSSO BUCCO Tomatoes, white wine, gremolata (chopped parsley, garlic, anchovy fillets, lemon zest), Risotto alla Milanese.

LAMB AND GOAT

GOAT DICED Yogurt, curry powder, fenugreek, chilli, vinegar, honey, soy sauce, spring onions, root vegetables.

GOAT LEG STEAK Cinnamon, cumin, ginger, allspice, jerk seasoning, onions, oranges, redcurrant jelly.

GOAT WHOLE KID Red wine, olive and nut oils, chilli oil, cumin, cinnamon, garlic, honey, mint, oregano, onions, leeks.

LAMB KIDNEY Cream, shallots, mushrooms, lemon, brandy, sherry, mustard, Worcestershire sauce, tomatoes, sausages, bacon.

LAMB LEG Garlic, oregano and potatoes (Greek-style slow-roast), mint sauce/jelly, redcurrant jelly, roast onions or leeks, onion sauce, celery, carrots, paprika, flageolet beans.

LAMB LOIN CHOPS Mint jelly, tomatoes, onions, garlic, oregano.

LAMB NECK Mint, oregano, garlic, cinnamon, star anise, dried fruit, haricot beans, spring onions, dill, lemon.

LAMB NOISETTES Red wine, port, redcurrants, rosemary, lemon, garlic.

LAMB SHANK Turnips, carrots, celery, leeks, tomato purée, redcurrant or mint jelly, white, red or rosé wine.

LAMB RACK Garlic, rosemary, mint, honey, olives, harissa paste, aubergines, yogurt, baby spring vegetables.

MUTTON SHOULDER Caper sauce (boiled mutton), turnips, carrots, leeks, onions, yogurt, aubergine, cinnamon, apricots, prunes, raisins, curry spices, oregano, mint, rosemary, pearl barley.

PORK

BELLY Fennel or dill seed, garlic, juniper berries, wholegrain mustard, caramelized onions, red cabbage, raisins, cider, white wine, barbecue sauce, sweet and sour sauce.

FILLET Garlic, oregano, sage, chorizo, salami, prunes, apricots, spinach, mushrooms, spring onions, beansprouts, bamboo shoots, soy sauce, ginger.

LEG JOINT Apple sauce, sage and onion stuffing, English mustard, sweet and sour sauce, curry spices, vinegar, cabbage, caraway, dried beans.

LEG STEAK Egg and breadcrumbs (schnitzels), rosemary, sage, garlic, citrus, ham, cheese, lychees.

LIVER Sage, onions, bacon, juniper berries, hazelnuts, watercress, brandy, mushrooms, red wine, cider, root vegetables.

LOIN CHOP Apples, pears, plums, oregano, marjoram, cider, perry or white wine, coriander seeds, wholegrain mustard, crème fraîche.

RIBS Barbecue sauce, chilli, soy sauce, honey, citrus, pineapple, Worcestershire sauce, tomato, Chinese five-spice powder.

POULTRY

CHICKEN BREAST Thai green curry paste, coconut, nam pla, ginger, oyster sauce, black bean sauce, bacon/pancetta, chorizo, prawns.

CHICKEN BREAST QUARTER As for leg quarter, but also fried bananas, bacon rolls, and corn cobs.

CHICKEN DRUMSTICK Butter, olive oil, garlic, barbecue sauce, sweet and sour sauce, cumin, garam masala, curry paste, harissa paste, chilli, Worcestershire sauce, honey, lemon.

CHICKEN LEG QUARTER Cajun or curry spices, thyme, tarragon, chives, garlic, lardons, red or white wine, mushrooms, tomatoes.

CHICKEN SUPREME Butter, herbs, garlic, cream, white wine, brandy, white grapes, mushrooms.

CHICKEN THIGH Curry spices, pesto, olive oil, herbs, garlic, mirepoix.

CHICKEN WING Chinese five-spice powder, soy sauce, barbecue sauce, jerk seasoning, cajun spices, garam masala.

DUCK BREAST Berries, currants, pomegranate, baby leaves, cherry tomatoes, cucumber, red onion, olives, fruit vinegar, olive oil, pomegranate syrup.

DUCK CROWN The same as for the whole bird but try rubbing with smoked sea salt before cooking.

DUCK LEG PORTION As for duck breast, plus juniper berries, coriander seeds, thyme for confit.

POULTRY LIVER Butter, garlic, shallots, woody herbs, bacon, eggs, truffles, figs, prunes, Sauternes, sherry.

POUSSIN Bacon, garlic, shallots, tomatoes, mushrooms, lemon, lime, saffron, lemongrass, kaffir lime leaves, rosemary, thyme, tarragon, bay leaf, soy sauce, white wine, barbecue sauce.

TURKEY CROWN As for whole bird, but also pancetta, garlic butter, tarragon butter, pesto, tapenade.

TURKEY STEAK Ham, cheese (for topping), peppers, tomatoes, mushrooms, sage, tarragon, thyme, parsley, chives, oregano, redcurrant jelly.

WHOLE CHICKEN Sage and onion or parsley and thyme stuffing, lemon, honey, barbecue sauce, cajun spices, Tandoori spices, paprika, bread sauce, redcurrant jelly, cider, white wine.

WHOLE DUCK Sage, onions, garlic, spring onions, apples, oranges, turnips, ginger, cherries, soy sauce, hoisin sauce, honey, vinegar, wine, peas, baby white onions, lettuce.

WHOLE GOOSE Apples, onions, red cabbage, tomatoes, white beans, spicy sausages, ginger, sage, oatmeal, almonds, apricots, prunes, soy sauce, red wine.

WHOLE TURKEY Chestnuts, cranberries, thyme, parsley, sage, tarragon, bacon, sausagemeat, root vegetables.

GAME

GROUSE Bacon, ham, celery, shallots, watercress, wild mushrooms, game chips, bread sauce, buttered crumbs, oranges, honey, juniper berries, redcurrants, cranberries, whisky, wine.

MALLARD Ginger, garlic, mushrooms, onions, swede, coriander leaf, parsley, sage, apples, bitter oranges, plums, cherries, redcurrants, cider, red wine, soy sauce.

PARTRIDGE Bacon, cream, cabbage, watercress, lentils, shallots, wild mushrooms, grapes, citrus, pears, quinces, redcurrants, chestnuts, walnuts, turnips, kohl rabi, juniper berries, sage, chocolate, wine.

PHEASANT Bacon, cream, celery, onions, cabbage, sage, apples, quinces, bitter oranges, prunes, walnuts, beetroot, Jerusalem artichokes, game chips, bread sauce, buttered crumbs, Calvados, brandy, wine.

QUAIL Bacon, butter, cream, sweet peppers, mushrooms, truffles, quinces, grapes, cherries, prunes, almonds, honey, cumin, cinnamon, brandy, white and red wine.

RABBIT, WHOLE Bacon, carrots, fennel, celery, sweetcorn, mushrooms, tomatoes, olives, coriander leaf, parsley, rosemary, thyme, lemon, prunes, mustard, soy sauce, cider, white wine.

TEAL Apples, bitter oranges, sage, thyme, white wine, peas, onions and lettuce (for braising), cider, spring onions, hoisin and plum sauce, soy sauce ginger, garlic.

VENISON FILLET OR TENDERLOIN Bacon, pears, cream, fennel, red cabbage, pomegranate, red berries, pine nuts, red wine, vermouth.

VENISON ROLLED HAUNCH Guinness, red wine, port, redcurrant jelly, prunes, juniper berries, bay leaf, thyme, cream, chanterelle mushrooms.

WOODCOCK Butter, bacon, cream, shallots, garlic, watercress, ginger, bay leaf, parsley, thyme, nutmeg, lemon, apples, grapes, soy sauce, Madeira.

WOODPIGEON Bacon, cream, red cabbage, mushrooms, spinach, chilli, garlic, orange, redcurrants, blueberries, juniper berries, chocolate, honey, soy sauce, red wine.

CURED AND AIR-DRIED MEATS

BACON Chicken, game, prunes, oysters, sausages, kidneys, liver, oily and white fish, scallops, prawns, eggs, cheese, cauliflower, potatoes, tomatoes, avocados, mushrooms, spinach.

BRESAOLA Olive oil, tomatoes, Parmesan, gherkins, olives, celeriac remoulade, rocket, mozzarella, rustic bread.

GAMMON/HAM Eggs, pineapple, dried fruits, mustard, cloves, honey, onion, bay leaf, parsley sauce, butter beans, carrots, tomatoes, eggs, cheeses.

JAMBON DE PARIS French and grainy mustard, Gruyère cheese, chips, buckwheat crêpes, eggs, tomatoes.

JAMÓN IBERICO Fino sherry (chilled), rustic bread, asparagus, scrambled eggs, baby broad beans, tomato and garlic bread (pan con tomate).

JAMÓN SERRANO Olives, gherkins, Manchego cheese, figs, rustic bread, nutmeg, eggs, red wine.

PANCETTA Parmesan, asparagus, tomatoes, chilli, bacon, onions, garlic, eggs, cream, white beans.

PROSCUITTO CRUDO Parmesan, mozzarella, gherkins, figs, melon, asparagus, tomatoes, olives.

SAUSAGES

BEEF SAUSAGE Onions, root vegetables, tomatoes, peppers, red beans, oregano, paprika, chilli, cumin, coriander seed and leaf, brown beer, mustard, Worcestershire sauce, barbecue sauce.

BLACK PUDDING Scallops, halibut, turbot, lamb, pork, venison, rabbit, raisins, red wine, chickpeas, white beans, lentils, bacon, eggs, potatoes.

BOUDIN BLANC Caramelized onions, red wine, brandy, port, tomatoes, wild mushrooms, spinach, black truffles, cream.

BOUDIN NOIR Walnuts, pears, apples, oranges, chestnuts, cabbage, white wine, red wine, Dijon and grainy mustards.

CHORIZO Chicken, seafood, pork, mushrooms, peppers, aubergines, courgettes, pasta, white beans, chickpeas, rice, chimichurri sauce (parsley, sherry vinegar, oregano, chilli, olive oil).

CUMBERLAND SAUSAGE Mustard, tomato sauce, barbecue sauce, chilli sauce, shallots, rosemary, red wine, white beans.

PORK SAUSAGE Potatoes, white beans, onions, apples, sage, mustard, tomato ketchup, cider, cabbage, tomatoes, mushrooms, Yorkshire pudding.

SALAME DI GENOA Parmesan, mozzarella, rocket, spinach, tomatoes, olives, gherkins.

TOULOUSE SAUSAGE White beans, belly pork, duck confit, celery, onions, tomatoes, garlic, cloves, bay leaf, flat leaf parsley.

WHITE PUDDING Batter, black pudding, tomatoes, eggs, bacon, toasted or fried bread, white beans, scallops, halibut or other meaty fish.

VEGETABLES

VEGETABLES ADD TASTE AND TEXTURE THEMSELVES, BUT CAN ALSO BE COMPLEMENTED BY EXCITING FLAVOUR COMBINATIONS.

CABBAGES, FLOWERING, AND LEAFY GREENS

BRUSSELS SPROUTS Melted butter, chestnuts, walnuts, hazelnuts, toasted pine nuts, sausages, crispy bacon.

CALABRESE Bacon, anchovies, pesto, chillies, cheese or Béchamel sauce, lemon, garlic, pine nuts, olive oil.

CAVOLO NERO Garlic, onions, peppers, white beans, spicy sausages, pancetta, potatoes, tomatoes, olive oil, chilli.

CHINESE BROCCOLI Oyster sauce, soy sauce, ginger, garlic, cashew nuts.

CHINESE LEAVES (NAPA CABBAGE) Spring onions, ginger, sambal oelek, garlic, sesame seeds, rice vinegar.

CHINESE SPINACH Toasted sesame seeds, star anise, mushrooms, eggs, rice, prawns, coriander leaf, chillies, ginger, garlic.

COMMON CAULIFLOWER Brown butter, Gruyère, blue or Cheddar cheese (crumbled or in sauce), garlic, olive oil, parsley, lemon.

KALE Bacon, ham, venison, sausages, oily fish, clams, eggs, citrus, tomatoes.

KOHL RABI Parsley sauce, star anise, ginger, garlic, tomatoes, lamb, beef, game birds.

MUSTARD GREENS Fish, seafood, ham, pork, chicken, butter, garlic, soy sauce, rice vinegar, ginger, chillies.

PAK CHOI Prawns, pork, chicken, spring onions, water chestnuts, mangetout, cashew nuts, soy sauce, oyster sauce, coriander leaves.

PURPLE CAULIFLOWER Béchamel sauce, tomatoes, Parmesan (or other cheeses), bacon.

PURPLE SPROUTING BROCCOLI Leeks, tomatoes, chillies, butter, olive oil, garlic, Parmesan, spring onions, citrus, Hollandaise sauce.

RAINBOW CHARD Nutmeg, spring onions, toasted almonds and pine nuts, butter, olive oil.

RED CABBAGE Vinegar, red wine, brown sugar, apples, pears, raisins, onions, fennel seeds, caraway seeds, bacon, ham, pork, liver.

ROMANESCO Olive oil and toasted flaked almonds (to dress), cherry tomatoes, olives, cream, Italian hard cheeses.

ROUND GREEN CABBAGE Carrots, onions, celery, soy sauce, ginger, garlic, potatoes.

SAVOY CABBAGE Bacon, celery, butter, onions, garlic, tomatoes, walnuts, hazelnuts.

SPINACH Bacon, fish, anchovies, eggs, cheeses, yogurt, cream, butter, olive oil, garlic, onions, avocados, mushrooms, lemon, nutmeg, curry spices.

SPRING GREENS Bacon, ham, lemon, onions, potatoes, salt pork, garlic, Chinese five-spice powder.

WHITE CABBAGE Mayonnaise, wine vinegar, mustard, caraway seeds, smoked sausages, pork, ham, carrots, onions, nuts, apples, celery.

SALAD LEAVES

BUTTERHEAD LETTUCE Peas, baby onions, anchovies, cheese, mayonnaise, olive oil, lemon juice, mustard, garlic.

COS (ROMAINE) LETTUCE Anchovies, eggs, croûtons, garlic, Parmesan, chicken, onions, citrus, herbs, honey, mustard.

CURLY ENDIVE (FRISÉE) Olive oil, croûtons, smoked lardons, red onions, parsley, coriander leaf, chillies, Worcestershire sauce, poached or soft-boiled eggs.

DANDELION Bacon, cheese, garlic, onions, lemon, mustard, olive oil, wine or balsamic vinegar.

ESCAROLE (BATAVIA) Balsamic vinegar, fruit vinegars, olive oil, toasted nut and seed oils, mustard, croûtons, eggs, anchovies, avocados, pomegranate, raisins.

ICEBERG LETTUCE Seafood, Russian salad, rice or pasta salads, tabbouleh, minced chicken, pork, veal or liver, soy sauce, ginger, garlic.

LAMB'S LETTUCE (CORN SALAD) Onions, croûtons, sweetcorn, honey, mustard, cherry tomatoes, toasted seeds, pears, avocados, lardons.

LITTLE GEM LETTUCE Mushrooms, spring onions, garlic, peas, bacon, Italian hard cheeses, cottage cheese, walnuts.

LOLLO ROSSO Pears, apples, pomegranate, blueberries, cheeses, walnuts, toasted pine nuts, pumpkin seeds, olive oil, toasted nut oils, citrus, wine, sherry and cider vinegars, chorizo, salami.

MIZUNA Pork, chicken livers, fish, shellfish, ginger, lemon, sesame oil, olive oil, toasted seeds, tamari.

PURSLANE Beetroot, broad beans, cucumber, spinach, potatoes, tomatoes, eggs, feta cheese, yogurt.

RADICCHIO Pancetta, hazelnuts, walnuts, pine nuts, pumpkin seeds, Italian hard cheeses, ricotta or feta cheese, balsamic vinegar, preserved lemons, anchovies.

RED OAK LETTUCE Rocket, chicory, chervil, dandelion, purslane, olives, tomatoes, red onions, artichokes, avocados, beetroot, carrots, olive oil, citrus, fruit and wine vinegars.

ROCKET Pine nuts, almonds, olive oil, citrus, garlic, hard and blue cheeses, tomatoes, onions, eggs, potatoes, thyme, basil, rosemary, oregano, lamb's lettuce, watercress.

SALAD CRESS Eggs, salmon, sardines, tuna, Cheddar cheese, cream cheese, tomatoes, cucumber.

WATERCRESS Cucumber, beetroot, goat's cheese, eggs, salmon, other oily fish, chicken, duck, oranges, potatoes.

WHITE SWISS CHARD Ham, garlic, onions, chillies, olive oil, butter (leaves), Hollandaise sauce (stalks).

WITLOOF CHICORY Bacon, ham, prosciutto crudo, blue and Cheddar cheese, nuts, garlic, watercress, olive oil, tomato salsa.

STEMS, SHOOTS, AND FLOWERS

CARDOONS Veal, anchovies, olive oil, hard cheeses, butter, cream, lemon, almonds.

CELERY Béchamel or Hollandaise sauces, cheeses, onions, cabbage, lemon, walnuts, apples, pears.

FLORENCE FENNEL Cheeses, fish, seafood, veal, chicken, dried and cured meats, citrus, preserved lemon (roasted with), Pernod, Puy lentils, herbs, mayonnaise.

GLOBE ARTICHOKES Vinaigrette, butter, Hollandaise sauce, herbs, cured and dried meats, anchovies, shellfish, tomatoes, chillies, mushrooms, cheeses, cream, garlic, lemon, white truffles.

GREEN ASPARAGUS Olive oil, butter, coarse sea salt, Parmesan or Grana Padano shavings, balsamic glaze or vinegar, Hollandaise sauce, Mornay sauce, bacon, anchovies, salmon, pesto, vinaigrette, citrus, eggs.

PEAR PALM HEARTS Cured and dried meats, shellfish, lime, vinaigrette, tomatoes, baby salad leaves, soy sauce, wasabi, sesame oil, ginger, avocados, tropical fruits.

WHITE ASPARAGUS Vinaigrette, mayonnaise, garlic, quail's eggs, smoked salmon, Hollandaise sauce.

ROOT VEGETABLES AND TUBERS

ANYA POTATOES Melted butter, pesto, parsley, thyme, mint, chives, olive oil, mustard, wine vinegar, shallots, grated citrus zest.

BEETROOT Bacon, smoked oily fish, goat's and other cheeses, oranges, watercress, baby red chard, baby spinach and rocket, soured cream, nutmeg, horseradish, dill, caraway.

CARROTS Beef, citrus, ginger, celery, chervil, fennel, thyme, parsley, coriander leaf, watercress, peas, pine nuts, cumin, cinnamon, mixed spice, other roots, particularly beetroot, honey.

CASSAVA Butter, garlic, citrus, coriander seeds and leaves, chilli.

CELERIAC Bacon, beef, oily fish, cheeses, garlic, potatoes, parsley, dill, olive oil, mustard, tomatoes.

CHARLOTTE POTATOES Melted butter, mint, chives, parsley, mayonnaise, yogurt, olive oil, anchovies, citrus.

DESIRÉE POTATOES Cumin, cajun spices, nutmeg and seeds (to coat wedges), eggs, onions, mushrooms, butter, olive and nut oils.

HAMBURG PARSLEY Chicken, fish, game, eggs, mushrooms, carrots, potatoes, turnips.

JERSEY ROYAL POTATOES Melted butter, mint, parsley, chives, thyme, spring onions.

JERUSALEM ARTICHOKE Béchamel or Hollandaise sauce, butter, cream, ginger, nutmeg, lovage, parsley, lemon juice, spring onions, crispy bacon, pheasant and other game.

JICAMA Chilli, lime, avocados, mangos, onions, tomatoes, coriander leaf.

KING EDWARD POTATOES Butter, milk, chives, rosemary, celeriac, leeks, onions, spring onions, garlic, olive oil, lemon, hard cheeses.

LOTUS ROOT Citrus, garlic, onions, coriander leaves, chervil, star anise.

MARIS PIPER POTATOES Butter, chives, parsley, curry spices, mayonnaise, tomato ketchup, malt vinegar, Maldon sea salt.

NICOLA POTATOES Cream, crème fraîche, yogurt, garlic, nutmeg, Gruyère, Cheddar, blue cheeses, mayonnaise, French dressing, shallots, ham, bacon, pickled, salted and smoked fish.

PARSNIP Butter, curry powder, nutmeg, garlic, parsley, thyme, tarragon, potatoes, beef, walnuts.

RADISH Smoked fish, cheese, potatoes, spring onions, chives, parsley, citrus, vinegar, chilli, star anise.

SALSIFY Italian hard cheeses, Béchamel sauce, onions, shallots, olive oil, lemon, nutmeg, bacon.

SCORZONERA White wine, hard cheeses, cream, breadcrumbs, parsley, Parma ham.

SWEDE Bacon, liver, onions, carrots, cream, butter, lemon, black pepper, nutmeg, thyme.

SWEET POTATO Apples, brown sugar, molasses, ginger, maple syrup, honey, citrus, chilli, nutmeg, cajun spices, thyme.

TARO Sweet potatoes, chilli, star anise, cinnamon, cardamom, toasted sesame oil.

TURNIP Lamb, bacon, duck, goose, game, cheese, apples, mushrooms, potatoes, sherry.

WATER CHESTNUT Prawns, beef, chicken, pork, pak choi, oyster sauce, soy sauce, ginger, garlic, sesame oil.

YAM Eggs, cheese, cream, curry powder, coconut, lime.

SQUASHES, CUCUMBERS, AND CHAYOTE

ACORN SQUASH Cheddar, blue cheeses, Gruyère, eggs, garlic, ginger, maple syrup, honey, sage, thyme, apples, pears, quinces.

BITTER MELON SQUASH Pork, fish, shellfish, soy sauce, ginger, garlic, spring onions, black bean sauce, oyster sauce.

BOTTLE GOURD Coconut milk, tamarind, mustard seeds, curry leaves, cumin, coriander seeds and leaf, ginger, chilli, star anise, tomatoes, onions, garlic, red lentils.

BURPLESS SLICING CUCUMBER Yogurt, mint, coriander leaf and seeds, toasted cumin seeds, garlic, spring onions, watercress, mayonnaise.

BUTTERNUT SQUASH Goat's cheese, Cheddar, blue cheeses, Gruyère, garlic, ginger, maple syrup, honey, apples, pears, sage, thyme, rosemary, beetroot.

CHAYOTE Fish, shellfish, rice, garlic, onions, soft and hard cheeses, chillies.

COMMON GREENHOUSE CUCUMBER Vinegars, yogurt, dill, garlic, milk (for soup), anchovies, cream cheese, feta cheese, fennel, mint, mayonnaise, tomatoes, chillies, avocado, tropical fruits.

COURGETTES Olive oil, coarse sea salt, sweet peppers, aubergines, onions, garlic, tomatoes, curry spices, basil, parsley.

CROOKNECK SQUASH Olive oil, butter, cream, Cheddar, Gruyère, Parmesan, bacon, white beans, tomatoes.

CROWN PRINCE SQUASH Butter, eggs, nutmeg, cinnamon, mixed spice, muscovado sugar, sage, onions, ricotta cheese.

GHERKINS (CORNICHONS) Capers and caperberries, mayonnaise, parsley, thyme, tarragon, chervil, chicken, poultry and pig's livers, pork, salt beef, most fish.

MARROW Sausage, mince or rice and herbs for stuffing, tomatoes, melted butter, hard cheeses, béchamel sauce, thyme, oregano, sage, parsley.

PATTY PAN SQUASH Melted butter, olive oil, garlic, cumin, coriander, thyme, basil, parsley, bacon, breadcrumbs, chickpeas, hard cheeses.

PICKLING CUCUMBER Rock salt, malt or white wine vinegar, coriander seeds, yellow mustard seeds, dried chillies, allspice, ginger, black peppercorns, bay leaf, dill, white onions.

PUMPKIN Blue and Cheddar cheeses, toasted pumpkin oil, butter, pumpkin seeds, walnuts, sage, rosemary, thyme, ginger, nutmeg, cinnamon, cumin, tomatoes.

RED ONION SQUASH Red onions, chestnuts, garlic, olive oil, butter, nigella seeds, cinnamon, nutmeg, cloves.

RIDGE CUCUMBER Malt, balsamic, or red wine vinegar, black pepper, fish, shellfish, cheese sauce, soy sauce, garlic, ginger, cream cheese, root vegetables, spring onions.

ROUND SQUASH As for courgettes, or try prawns or crab and rice stuffing with dill, parsley, and lemon zest.

SPAGHETTI MARROW Fresh tomato sauce, Bolognese sauce, olive oil, melted butter, Parmesan, anchovies, mushrooms.

TURK'S TURBAN SQUASH Butter, olive oil, Cheddar or goat's cheeses, breadcrumbs, rice, onions, sage, thyme, cream, bacon, ham.

ONIONS, SHALLOTS, LEEKS, AND GARLIC

BABY LEEKS Olive oil, chillies, Parmesan, anchovies, toasted pine nuts, almonds and pumpkin seeds, sun-dried tomatoes, basil, thyme, parsley, olives.

BANANA SHALLOT Butter, balsamic vinegar, white balsamic condiment, red wine, white wine, cream, wild mushrooms, sorrel, thyme, parsley, mussels and other fish and seafood, chicken.

BROWN ONIONS Bacon, liver, sausages, steak, lamb, pork, game, fish, curry spices, herbs, tomatoes, all vegetables, cheeses.

DRY GARLIC Any meat, poultry or game, fish, shellfish, pulses, most vegetables, herbs, spices, mayonnaise, cheeses, soured cream, yogurt, walnuts, pine nuts.

ELEPHANT GARLIC Olive oil, coarse sea salt, butter, wine, cream, mushrooms, thyme, parsley.

FRENCH GREY SHALLOT Red wine vinegar, oysters, mussels, beef, chicken, red wine, lardons, carrots, celery, cream, white wine, sherry, fennel, parsley.

GREEN GARLIC Tomatoes, soft cheeses, mayonnaise, yogurt, crème fraîche, soured cream, olives, basil, pine nuts, white wine, white balsamic condiment, olive oil, fresh chillies.

LEEKS Fish, lamb, chicken, cream, cheese, parsley, potatoes, lemon, olive oil, sage, thyme, fennel, chillies.

PICKLING/PEARL ONIONS Malt, white or balsamic vinegar, coriander seeds, yellow mustard seeds, dried chillies, black peppercorns, bay leaf, milk, cream, red and white wine, beef, lardons, chicken, pork, lamb, game, fish, peas, cheese, ham.

RAMSONS (RAMPIONS) Olive oil, pine nuts, Parmesan, parsley, thyme, potatoes, onions, sorrel, rocket, tomatoes, water chestnuts, beansprouts, soy sauce, ginger.

RED ONIONS Fresh and sun-dried tomatoes, peppers, aubergines, squashes, avocados, bacon, lentils, chickpeas, cheeses, oily fish, basil, thyme, bay leaf.

ROUND SHALLOT Malt or balsamic vinegar, coriander seeds, yellow mustard seeds, black peppercorns, cinnamon, chillies, bay leaf.

SPRING ONIONS Thai red and green curry pastes, galangal, lemon grass, nam pla, eggs, potatoes, meat, chicken, fish, most cheese.

TREE ONION (EGYPTIAN ONION) Beef, chicken, game, cheeses, celery, bay leaf, sage, parsley, pickling spices, malt and red wine vinegar.

WHITE ONIONS Tempura batter, beer batter, veal, chicken, lamb, sage, parsley, thyme, risotto rice, white beans, white wine, spinach, tomatoes.

WHITE SALAD ONIONS Cream cheese, cottage cheese, soured cream, crème fraîche, yogurt, radishes, cherry tomatoes, chicken, fish, shellfish.

PEAS, BEANS, AND OTHER PODS

BABY CORN Baby vegetables, sesame oil, soy sauce, chicken, fish, duck, gammon, garlic, butter, olive oil.

BROAD BEANS Bacon, ham, fish, lamb, chicken, game, spinach, onions, cream, béchamel sauce.

EDAMAME BEANS Coarse sea salt, harissa paste, lamb, chicken, fish, soy sauce, ginger, garlic, chillies.

FRENCH BEANS Eggs, shallots, red wine vinegar, olive oil, tomatoes, garlic, olives, oily fish, new potatoes.

GARDEN PEAS Bacon, ham, fish, duck, baby onions, lettuce, mint, thyme, chervil, mushrooms.

HELDA BEANS Citrus, melted butter, walnuts, nut oils, toasted sesame seeds, tomatoes.

MANGETOUT Almonds, chicken, mushrooms, soy sauce, garlic, ginger, sherry, rice wine, Chinese five-spice powder.

OKRA Butter, garlic, chillies, curry spices, coconut, green peppers, tomatoes.

RUNNER BEANS Bacon, mushrooms, onions, tomatoes, red wine vinegar, honey, olive oil, cashew nuts.

SUGAR SNAP PEAS Toasted sesame seeds, chillies, sesame oil, ginger, soy sauce, soft cheeses, oyster mushrooms, radishes, mint.

SWEETCORN Bacon, potatoes, butter, cheese, cream, chillies, citrus.

YELLOW WAX BEANS Tomatoes, garlic, onions, olive oil, chorizo, mushrooms.

VEGETABLE FRUITS

AUBERGINE Ham, lamb, beef, mozzarella, feta, hard cheeses, garlic, mushrooms, tomatoes, sweet peppers, lemon, oregano, mint, thyme, chillies, olive oil, cinnamon, curry spices.

AVOCADO Parma ham, mozzarella, bacon, prawns, tomatoes, spinach, grapefruit, lime, mango, lemon, pineapple, sugar, balsamic vinegar, chillies.

BEEFSTEAK TOMATOES Mozzarella, Parmesan, eggs (bake inside), olives, anchovies, pesto, pine nuts, almonds, rustic bread, green garlic, peppers, courgettes, aubergines, avocados, basil, oregano, marjoram, chervil.

BELL PEPPERS Chicken, lamb, beef, pork, anchovies, garlic, onions, sweetcorn, tomatoes, olives, capers, cheeses, rosemary, oregano.

CHERRY TOMATOES Salad leaves, cucumber, celery, olives, pumpkin and sunflower seeds, red onions, basil, oregano, olive oil, balsamic vinegar, goat's cheese, mozzarella balls, rocket.

HUNGARIAN HOT WAX CHILLI Beef, pork, lamb, chicken, seafood, cream cheese, hard cheeses, thyme, sage, tomatoes.

JALAPEÑO CHILLI Beef, spicy sausages, noodles, sweet peppers, courgettes, aubergines, peanuts, cashews, tomatoes, mozzarella, cream cheese, sheep's cheese.

PIMIENTOS DE PADRÓN Olive oil, sea salt, crusty bread.

PLUM TOMATOES Basil, oregano, bay, chervil, onions, garlic, bacon, olive oil, oranges, celery salt.

ROMANO PEPPERS Chorizo and other spicy sausages, soft cheeses, chilli, garlic, basil, parsley, chives, capers.

SCOTCH BONNET CHILLI Chicken, beef, squashes, potatoes, sweet potatoes, yam, spring onions, garlic, spinach, allspice, bay leaf, coconut milk, lime.

SERRANO CHILLI Sweet peppers, potatoes, onions, garlic, dried chipotle chillies, avocados, tomatoes, coriander leaf, prawns, steak.

STANDARD GLOBE TOMATOES Bacon, eggs, fish, mushrooms, cheese, parsley, thyme, oregano, sage, cinnamon, garlic, onions, chilli, Thai red curry paste, coconut milk.

THAI (BIRDSEYE) CHILLIES Most spices, coriander leaf, bay leaf, coconut milk, lime, nam pla, palm sugar, galangal, spring onions, chicken, beef, pork, lamb, fish.

MUSHROOMS AND TRUFFLES

BLACK (PERIGORD) TRUFFLES Spaghetti, chicken, rabbit, game birds, celeriac, meaty white fish, shellfish, pancetta.

BROWN CRIMINI OR CHESTNUT MUSHROOMS Oregano, parsley, marjoram, chives, parsley, coriander leaf and seeds, curry spices, Thai spices, red wine, garlic, bacon, onions.

CEP/PORCINI MUSHROOMS Risotto rice, pasta, cream, brandy, white wine, leeks, onions, garlic, Parma ham, Parmesan, truffle oil, beef, chicken, game, scallops.

CULTIVATED WHITE BUTTON MUSHROOMS Onions, garlic, tomatoes, coriander seeds and leaf, parsley, oregano, lemon, cream, crème fraîche, yogurt, white wine, sherry,

steaks, chicken.

ENOKI MUSHROOMS Chicken, prawns, crab, chicken and fish broth, cucumber, celery, carrot, soy sauce, garlic, beansprouts, peppers.

FIELD MUSHROOMS Bacon, eggs, sausages, steak, venison, risotto rice, cream, crème fraîche.

MOREL MUSHROOMS Butter, olive oil, garlic, asparagus, leeks, cream, white wine, brandy, eggs, chicken, beef, veal, halibut, turbot, monkfish.

OPEN CUP OR FLAT MUSHROOMS Garlic, cream, white wine, herb stuffings, cheese, pâté, bacon, eggs, parsley.

OYSTER MUSHROOMS Eggs, chicken, fish or vegetable broth, noodles, beef, chicken, pork, prawns, crab, spring onions, Chinese five-spice powder, soy sauce, rice wine vinegar.

PORTABELLO MUSHROOMS Butter, garlic, cream, herbs, white or rosé wine, halloumi and soft cheeses, cider, tomatoes, spring onions.

SHIITAKE MUSHROOMS Pork, chicken, beef, prawns, noodles, rice, soy sauce, ginger, garlic, spring onions, bamboo shoots, water chestnuts, beansprouts, chillies, rice wine, oyster sauce.

WHITE (ALBA) TRUFFLES Eggs, risotto rice, pasta, game birds, scallops, halibut, monkfish, fois gras, potatoes, olive oil, garlic, Parmesan.

WOOD BLEWIT (PIED BLEU) MUSHROOMS Cream, crème fraîche, brandy, white wine, rice, pearl barley, lasagne, Italian hard cheeses, thyme, parsley, marjoram.

HERBS

HERBS ADD FABULOUS FRAGRANCE TO DISHES, BUT IT IS IMPORTANT TO CHOOSE THE RIGHT ONES FOR THE JOB.

BAY Beef, chicken, game, lamb, ham, offal, fish, chestnuts, citrus, haricot beans, lentils, rice, tomatoes, mushrooms.

CHERVIL Asparagus, broad beans, green beans, beetroot, carrots, fennel, lettuce, peas, potatoes, tomatoes, mushrooms, cream cheese, eggs, fish, seafood, poultry, veal.

CHIVES Avocados, courgettes, potatoes, root vegetables, cream cheese, yogurt, soured cream, eggs, fish, seafood, smoked salmon.

COMMON SORREL Chicken, pork, veal, fish (especially salmon), mussels, eggs, lentils, leeks, lettuce, cucumber, tomatoes, spinach, watercress.

CORIANDER LEAF Avocados, cucumber, root vegetables, sweetcorn, coconut milk, fish, seafood, beef, lamb, pork, poultry, citrus, pulses, rice, chillies, onions.

DILL (leaves) Beetroot, broad beans, carrots, celeriac, courgettes, cucumber, potatoes, spinach, eggs, fish, seafood; (seeds) rice, cabbage, onions, potatoes, pumpkin, vinegar.

FENNEL Beetroot, beans, cabbage, leeks, cucumber,

tomatoes, potatoes, duck, fish, seafood, pork, lentils, rice.

GARDEN MINT Lamb, duck, potatoes, peas, carrots, tomatoes, cucumber, currants, curries, chocolate, yogurt.

HORSERADISH Apples, beef, baked gammon or ham, sausages, oily and smoked fish, seafood, avocados, beetroot, red cabbage, potatoes.

LAVENDER Berries, plums, cherries, rhubarb, chicken, lamb, rabbit, pheasant, chocolate.

LEAF CELERY Cabbage, potatoes, cucumber, tomatoes, chicken, fish, rice, soy sauce, tofu, soft white cheeses.

LOVAGE Apples, root vegetables, potatoes, Jerusalem artichokes, courgettes, mushrooms, tomatoes, sweetcorn, Cheddar, Gruyère, cream cheeses, eggs, pulses, fish, meat, poultry, rice.

OREGANO Lamb, beef, chicken, pork, pulses, chilli, cumin, coriander leaf, garlic, tomatoes, aubergines, Cheddar, mozzarella, feta and halloumi cheeses, olives, peppers.

PARSLEY Eggs, fish, seafood, chicken, béchamel sauce, lentils, rice, lemon, tomatoes, garlic, onions.

ROSEMARY Poultry, rabbit, pork, lamb, veal, fish, eggs, lentils, squashes, peppers, courgettes, cabbage, potatoes, onions, garlic, citrus, fruit, cream cheese.

SAGE Pork, duck, goose, veal, chicken, liver, sausages, cheeses, beans, tomatoes, apples, bay leaf, caraway, onions, celery, garlic, lovage, marjoram.

SUMMER SAVORY Rabbit, chicken, oily fish, cheeses, eggs, broad and green beans, pulses, beetroot, cabbage, potatoes.

SWEET BASIL Tomatoes, garlic, pine nuts, mozzarella and other cheeses, eggs, aubergines, haricot beans, courgettes, citrus, olives, peas, pizzas, potatoes, rice, raspberries, sweetcorn.

SWEET MARJORAM Olive oil, feta, mozzarella and halloumi cheeses, plaice, sole, red mullet, mushrooms, eggs, squashes.

TARRAGON Artichokes, asparagus, courgettes, tomatoes, mushrooms, potatoes, salsify, fish, seafood, poultry, eggs, game, feta and goat's cheeses.

THYME Lamb, rabbit, chicken, turkey, pulses, aubergines, cabbage, carrots, leeks, wild mushrooms, tomatoes, onions, potatoes, sweetcorn.

SPICES

FOR SUBTLETY OR A BIG KICK, SPICES USED JUDICIOUSLY ADD AN EXTRA SENSATIONAL DIMENSION TO MANY DISHES.

ALLSPICE Aubergines, onions, squashes, root vegetables, white cabbage, tomatoes, most fruit.

CAPERS AND CAPERBERRIES Rich meats, poultry, fish, seafood, globe artichokes, aubergines, green beans, gherkins, olives, potatoes, tomatoes.

CARAWAY SEEDS Duck, goose, pork, breads and cakes, apples, cabbage, potatoes, root vegetables, tomatoes.

CARDAMOM PODS Apples, oranges, pears, sweet potatoes, pulses, cinnamon, star anise, cloves.

CHILLI Most spices, bay leaf, coriander leaves, parsley, coconut milk, citrus, meat, poultry, fish, seafood, pulses, tomatoes, avocados, mangoes, papayas, chocolate.

CINNAMON Lamb, poultry, aubergines, chocolate, coffee, rice, almonds, apples, apricots, bananas, pears, other sweet spices.

CLOVES Ham, pork, duck, venison, orchard fruits, beetroot, red cabbage, carrots, onions, oranges, squashes, chocolate, cinnamon.

CORIANDER SEEDS Cumin, chicken, pork, ham, fish, orchard fruits, citrus, mushrooms, onions, potatoes, pulses.

CUMIN Coriander seeds and leaves, chilli, oregano, chicken, lamb, hard and soft cheeses, most vegetables, pulses.

CURRY LEAVES Lamb, fish, seafood, lentils, rice, most vegetables, cardamom, chilli, coconut, coriander leaves, cumin, fenugreek seed, garlic.

FENUGREEK Green and root vegetables, chillies, garlic, fish, chicken, lentils.

GALANGAL Chicken, fish, seafood, chilli, coconut milk, fennel, garlic, ginger, lemon grass, lemon, kaffir lime leaves, shallots, tamarind.

GINGER Fish, seafood, meat, poultry, most vegetables, chilli, coconut, garlic, citrus, soy sauce, orchard fruits, rhubarb.

JUNIPER BERRIES Red meats, game, goose, apples, celery, cabbage, caraway, garlic, marjoram, rosemary, savoury, thyme.

KAFFIR LIME LEAVES Pork, poultry, fish, seafood, mushrooms, noodles, rice, green vegetables, coconut, tropical fruits.

LEMON GRASS Beef, chicken, pork, fish, seafood, noodles, most vegetables, Thai or European basil, coriander leaves, chilli, galangal, cinnamon, cloves, turmeric, coconut milk.

MACE Chicken, lamb, veal, milk, eggs, cheeses, carrots, onions, pumpkin, spinach, sweet potatoes, other sweet spices, bay leaf, thyme.

MUSTARD SEEDS Beef, rabbit, sausages, chicken, fish, ham, seafood, strong cheeses, cabbage, root vegetables, curries, dals.

NIGELLA SEED Allspice, cumin and sesame seeds, coriander leaf, star anise, pulses, rice, roots and tubers.

NUTMEG Chicken, veal, lamb, cabbage, onions, roots and tubers, squashes, spinach, cheeses, eggs, milk, rice, couscous, semolina, cardamom, other sweet spices.

PAPRIKA (sweet/hot) Beef, veal, chicken, duck, vegetables; (smoked) sausages, pork, fish, onions, pulses, eggs.

PEPPERCORNS Meat, poultry, game, fish, seafood, vegetables, oils, herbs, spices, salts, some fruits (especially strawberries).

POPPY SEED Aubergines, green beans, cauliflower, courgettes, potatoes, bread, honey.

PRESERVED LEMONS Lamb, chicken, fish, rice,

cardamom, cloves, allspice, pepper, ginger, cinnamon, coriander leaf, fennel, celery, olives.

SAFFRON Chicken, game, fish, seafood, eggs, asparagus, leeks, mushrooms, spinach, squashes, mayonnaise (as rouille).

SICHUAN PEPPER Black beans, chilli, citrus, garlic, ginger, sesame oil and seeds, soy sauce, star anise.

STAR ANISE Chicken, beef, oxtail, pork, fish, seafood, tropical fruits, figs, pears, leeks, pumpkin, root vegetables, chilli, cinnamon, coriander seed, fennel seed, garlic, ginger.

SUMAC Chicken, lamb, fish, seafood, aubergines, chickpeas, lentils, onions, pine nuts, yogurt, coriander, mint, parsley.

TAMARIND Chicken, lamb, pork, fish and shellfish, lentils, mushrooms, peanuts, most vegetables, chilli, coriander leaves, cumin, galangal, garlic, turmeric, mustard, soy sauce, palm sugar.

TURMERIC Meat, poultry, fish, eggs, aubergines, beans, lentils, rice, root vegetables, spinach.

VANILLA PODS Lobster, scallops, mussels, chicken, milk- and cream-based desserts, chocolate, apples, melons, pears, rhubarb, strawberries.

FRUIT

FRUIT COMPLEMENTS SO MANY SWEET AND SAVOURY FOODS, ADDING COLOUR, TEXTURE, AND DEPTH OF FLAVOUR.

ORCHARD FRUITS

ASIAN PEARS Beef, papaya, mango, lime, chilli, soy sauce, ginger, cardamom, star anise, rice vinegar, honey.

BRAMLEY APPLES Citrus, almonds, berries, rhubarb, pears, quinces, dried fruit, cinnamon, cloves, mixed spice, nutmeg, vanilla, honey, syrup, demerara sugar, chocolate.

BROWN TURKEY FIG Cured meats, yogurt, cream, cheeses, nuts, star anise, marzipan, fortified wine.

CONFERENCE PEAR Game, pork, blue cheeses, Parmesan, rocket, watercress, tarragon, celery, walnuts, almonds, cinnamon, ginger, star anise, cardamom, chocolate, vanilla, butterscotch.

COX'S ORANGE PIPPIN APPLES White or red cabbage, walnuts, almonds, pine nuts, sunflower seeds, fresh and dried fruits, celery, lovage, mayonnaise, vinaigrette, ginger.

DOYENNE DE COMICE PEAR Pork, duck, goose, apples, raisins, cinnamon, cloves, ginger, walnuts, goat's and blue cheeses.

GRANNY SMITH APPLES Cinnamon, mixed spice, cloves, walnuts, almonds, raisins, sultanas, cabbage, cheeses, chicken, pork, duck, game, black pudding, cider, Calvados.

LOQUAT (NISPEROS) Poultry, prawns, goat's cheese, vanilla ice cream, apples, pears, citrus, ginger, spirits.

MEDLAR Meat, game, hard cheeses, cinnamon, nutmeg, mixed spice, star anise, red or white wine.

QUINCE Lamb, pork, chicken, game, hard cheeses (particularly Manchego), apples, pears, ginger, cloves, cinnamon.

RED DELICIOUS APPLES All cheeses, celery, grapes, pork or duck pâté, nuts.

WILLIAMS' BON CRETIEN PEAR Red wine, port, brandy, cinnamon, star anise, cloves, ginger, wine vinegar, white and demerara sugar, maple syrup, dried fruits.

STONE FRUITS

APRICOTS Lamb, pork, chicken, ham, yogurt, cream, custard, oranges, almonds, rice, ginger, vanilla, sweet white wine, amaretto.

BLACK GRAPES Beef, venison, game birds, cheeses, fruits, red wine, port.

CHERRIES Duck, game, almonds, sweet spices, chocolate, citrus, fromage frais, yogurt, brandy, Kirsch, grappa.

DAMSONS Sultanas, apples, garlic, light muscovado sugar, chilli, ginger, cinnamon, pickling vinegar, red wine, ice cream, custard, blackberries.

DATES Poultry, lamb, bacon, cheeses, marzipan, nuts, clotted cream, yogurt, citrus, chocolate.

DRY SALT-CURED OLIVES Beef, pork, lamb, spicy sausages, pasta, olive oil, cherry and sun-dried tomatoes, sweet peppers, basil, oregano, parsley.

GREEN GRAPES Chicken, poultry livers, rabbit, flat fish, melon, strawberries, cheeses, walnuts.

GREENGAGES All rich meats and game, ground and flaked almonds, cinnamon, ginger, Kirsch, amaretto, brandy, cream, custard.

KALAMATA OLIVES White cabbage, tomatoes, cucumber, red onions, sweet peppers, aubergines, feta cheese, halloumi cheese, red wine vinegar, olive oil, oregano, preserved lemons, pork, chicken, lamb, pasta, rice.

MANZANILLA OLIVES Dry fino sherry, gin, dry martini, shellfish, chickpeas, white beans, chorizo, Serrano ham, squid, prawns, crab, Manchego cheese.

NECTARINES Chicken, gammon, prosciutto crudo, soft white cheeses like mascarpone, walnuts, almonds, berries, chilli, cinnamon, vanilla, star anise.

NIÇOISE-COQUILLOS OLIVES Tomatoes, onions, garlic, anchovies, eggs, green beans, new potatoes, courgettes, capers, caperberries, cinnamon, oregano, Herbes de Provence.

OPAL PLUMS Brandy, Kirsch, red wine, cream, clafoutis batter, light muscovado sugar, butter, almonds.

PEACHES Beef, duck, soured cream, yogurt, passion fruit, mangoes, berries, lime, mint, almonds, cinnamon, ginger, nutmeg, chilli, Champagne, sherry, amaretto.

PICHOLINE OLIVES Chicken, white and oily fish, rabbit, tomatoes, rice, white wine, sherry, dry vermouth, peppers, white beans, oranges.

RED GRAPES Goat's cheese, Cheddar, Manchego, Port, unblanched almonds, most fruits.

RED PLUMS Meat, game, avocados, tomatoes, red peppers, cucumber, spring onions, chilli, coriander leaf, lime, garlic, ginger, soy sauce, rice, red wine or malt vinegar, apples, pears, rhubarb, strawberries, custard, clotted cream, ground almonds (for crumble topping and in strudels).

SLOES Juniper, cinnamon, vanilla, gin, vodka, apples.

STUFFED GREEN OLIVES Fish, meat, poultry, cheeses, pasta, rice, peppers, tomatoes, onions, garlic, sweet spices, herbs.

VICTORIA PLUMS Duck, lamb, pork, gammon, goose, game birds, chilli, Chinese five-spice powder, ginger, soy sauce, garlic, onions, pickling vinegar, almonds, cinnamon, custard, cream, eggs.

YELLOW PLUMS Sweet peppers, spring onions, white balsamic condiment, cucumber, light muscovado sugar, soft fresh cheeses, fromage frais.

CURRANTS AND BERRIES

BLACKBERRIES Poultry, game, cream, crème fraîche, yogurt, soft white cheeses, apples, pears, hazelnuts, raspberries, almonds, oats, honey, vanilla, cinnamon.

BLACKCURRANTS Mint, rosemary, oranges, apples, pears, honey, vodka, Cassis, white wine, Champagne.

BLUEBERRIES Game, cream, crème fraîche, yogurt, citrus, almonds, pistachios, mint, cinnamon, allspice, plain and white chocolate.

CRANBERRIES Turkey, goose, pork, gammon, oily fish, apples, oranges, raspberries, blueberries, nuts, red wine, brandy, port.

ELDERBERRIES Game, pork, apples, crab apples, strawberries, blackberries, lemon, walnuts, cinnamon, allspice, nutmeg, cloves.

GOOSEBERRIES Goose, pork, mackerel, herrings, Camembert, cream, lemon, cinnamon, cloves, dill, fennel, elderflowers, honey.

LOGANBERRIES Apples, pears, bananas, rhubarb, cream, crème fraîche, fromage frais, soft white cheeses, yogurt, almonds.

MULBERRIES Poultry, lamb, game, cream, pears, citrus.

RASPBERRIES Duck, goose, venison, game birds, chicken or duck livers, cream, crème fraîche, peaches, other berries, hazelnuts, meringue, almonds, oats, honey, vanilla, cinnamon, red wine, vodka, raspberry vinegar.

REDCURRANTS Lamb, goat, venison, turkey, goose, duck, game birds, raspberries, strawberries, loganberries, mint, cinnamon, red wine, port, brandy.

ROWANBERRIES Lamb, mutton, goat, venison, poultry, apples, pears, red wine.

STRAWBERRIES Cream, ice cream, curd and other soft white cheeses, cucumber, oranges, melon, rhubarb, other berries, almonds, vanilla, chocolate, black pepper.

WHITECURRANTS Raspberries, blueberries, white chocolate, rosemary (in jelly), lemon zest (with sugar to eat raw).

WILD STRAWBERRIES Champagne, white or rosé wine, vodka, Cointreau, cream, crème fraîche, eggs, custard, bitter chocolate, red wine or strawberry vinegar.

CITRUS FRUITS

BLOOD ORANGE Egg yolks, butter, baby red chard, beetroot, spring onions, strawberries, raspberries, pineapple, bananas, lemon, lime, walnuts.

CLEMENTINE Shellfish, pork, chicken, duck, spinach, carrots, sweet peppers, salad leaves, almonds, coriander leaf, chocolate, meringue, Grand Marnier.

GRAPEFRUIT Chicken, gammon, smoked meats, prawns, avocados, spinach, lemon, mint, ginger, nutmeg, coconut, honey.

KUMQUAT Shellfish, smoked fish, poultry, ham, pork, duck, chicory, frisée, celery, spinach, chocolate, cloves, cardamom, vodka.

LEMON Chicken, veal, fish, shellfish, eggs, butter, artichokes, garlic, olives, cream, sage, tarragon, coriander leaf and seeds, capers, olive oil, gin.

LIME Poultry, fish, shellfish, chillies, Tabasco, tomatoes, avocados, lemons, mangos, melons, papayas, chocolate, rum, tequila, mint, coriander leaf.

MINNEOLA Shellfish, pork, duck, chicory, watercress, celery, rocket, chocolate, cloves, star anise, Cointreau.

POMELO Shellfish, smoked fish, poultry, ham, pork, chicory, frisée, celery, spinach, chocolate, cloves, cardamom.

SATSUMA Caramel, soft brown sugar, vanilla sugar, brandy, Grand Marnier, vodka, whisky.

SEVILLE (BITTER) ORANGE Duck, pigeon, pheasant, pork, salmon, tuna, meaty white fish, pancakes, rhubarb, meringue, lemon, grapefruit, gin, vodka, white rum.

SWEET ORANGE Beef, duck, gammon, liver, scallops, tomatoes, beetroot, black olives, nuts, soy sauce, cloves, cinnamon, fennel, carrots, chicory, frisée, button mushrooms, chocolate, strawberries, brandy.

TANGERINE Chicken breasts, pork fillet and chops, tuna, salmon, scallops, cabbage, carrots, shallots, cream, honey.

UGLI Oily fish, pork, duck, goose, chicory, frisée, rocket, cream, honey, kirsch, or sherry (over halves).

MELONS

CANTALOUPE (MUSKMELON) Coconut (fruit and milk), lime, cucumber, mint, fresh cheeses like mozzarella.

CHARENTAIS MELON Tropical fruit, raspberries, strawberries, mint.

HONEYDEW MELON Parma ham, other cured and smoked meats, ground ginger, orange, mint, rosemary, cucumber, herb bread.

OGEN MELON Prawns, crab, lobster, ginger wine, raspberries, framboise liqueur, sorbets, ice cream.

WATERMELON Chicken, prawns, crab, feta cheese, beetroot, sweet melons, apple, berries, lime, chillies, ginger, mint.

TROPICAL FRUITS

CUSTARD APPLE Pork, chicken, citrus, yogurt, cinnamon, ginger.

DRAGON FRUIT Lime, lemon, other tropical fruits, coconut, sugar, ginger.

DURIAN Milk, cream, coconut, other tropical fruits, curry spices, chillies, sticky rice.

GUAVA Pork, pheasant, duck, seafood, chicken, cream cheese, apples, pears, lime, chillies, lemon, coconut, ginger, honey.

KIWI Gammon, chicken, guinea fowl, squid, salmon, swordfish, chillies, oranges, strawberries, other tropical fruit.

LADY FINGER BANANA Butter, corn fritters, bacon rolls, light muscovado sugar, rum, brandy, Cointreau, coffee liqueur, cream, crème fraîche.

LYCHEE Pork, duck, chicken, seafood, chillies, avocados, raspberries, coconut, cream, lime, ginger.

MANGO Chicken, smoked meats, fish, shellfish, green salads, avocados, lime, lemon, chillies, curry spices, coriander leaves, vanilla ice cream, sweet sticky rice, rum.

MANGOSTEEN Other tropical fruits, strawberries, lemon grass, lemon.

PAPAYA Meat, smoked meats, avocados, chillies, lime, lemon, coconut, ginger.

PASSION FRUIT Tuna, venison, game birds, cream, yogurt, custard, oranges, kiwi fruit, strawberries, bananas, peaches, light muscovado sugar, rum, white and sparkling wine.

PERSIMMON (SHARON FRUIT) Ham, pork, game, lime, clotted cream, yogurt, fromage frais, walnuts, ginger, cinnamon, allspice, nutmeg, honey.

PHYSALIS White fish, scallops, yogurt, other tropical fruits, nuts, lemon, tarragon, chocolate, Cointreau.

PINEAPPLE Pork, ham, chicken, duck, fish, shellfish, cottage cheese, coconut, ginger, allspice, cinnamon, black pepper, Cointreau, rum, kirsch.

PLANTAIN Chicken, fish, most meats, dried beans, honey, ginger, butter, sunflower oil, chillies, coconut.

POMEGRANATE Prawns, lamb, chicken, duck, pheasant, aubergines, figs, almonds, pistachios, couscous, rice.

RAMBUTAN Pork, duck, avocados, chillies, cream, coconut, vanilla, ginger.

RED BANANA Chicken, salad leaves, rainbow trout, red fruits, pink grapefruit, sweetcorn, rice.

STAR FRUIT (CARAMBOLA) Poultry, prawns, avocados, red peppers, other tropical fruits, lime, coconut, lemon grass, nutmeg, vanilla, honey, rum, salt.

TAMARILLO Roast meats, chicken, fish, curry spices, cream, kiwi fruit, oranges, light muscovado sugar.

YELLOW BANANA Chicken (especially fried), trout, cream, yogurt, custard, orange juice, lime, coconut, walnuts, chocolate, coffee, ginger, light and dark muscovado sugar, liqueurs, rum.

DRIED AND CANDIED FRUITS

CANDIED PEEL Angelica, glacé cherries, other dried fruits, chocolate, cinnamon, mixed spice, ginger, nutmeg, mace, light and dark muscovado sugar.

CURRANTS Dark and light muscovado sugars, honey, soft white cheeses, other dried fruits, ginger, cinnamon, mixed spice, cardamom, cumin, turmeric, peas, apples, pears, mint, rosemary, parsley, coriander seed and leaf, basil, rice, citrus.

DRIED APPLE Pork, duck, goose, pheasant, honey, maple syrup, redcurrant jelly, cider, apple juice, dried pears, hard cheeses.

DRIED APRICOTS Cinnamon, star anise, nutmeg, curry spices, almonds, brazil nuts, pistachios, walnuts, lamb, pork, chicken, turkey, goose, duck, game, soft cheeses, yogurt, cream, citrus.

DRIED BANANA Yogurt, fromage frais, oats, soft white cheeses, wheat, barley, millet, walnuts, coconut, hazelnuts, other dried fruits, ginger, cinnamon, brandy.

DRIED BLUEBERRY White and plain chocolate, vanilla, cinnamon, oats, rice, couscous, pistachios, almonds, walnuts, honey.

DRIED CHERRY Oats and other grains, white soft cheeses, almonds, kirsch, amaretto, cream, plain chocolate.

DRIED COCONUT Curry spices and spice pastes, pulses, all meats, poultry, fish, dried fruits, tropical fruits, cherries, citrus, oats and other cereals, rice, noodles, cream.

DRIED CRANBERRY Oats, wheat, barley, millet, rice, breadcrumbs, turkey, duck, goose, pork, chicken, pine nuts, rosemary, thyme, parsley, onions, honey, maple syrup.

DRIED DATES Marzipan, walnuts, honey, fruit syrup, golden syrup, molasses, ginger, cinnamon, allspice, mixed spice, mace, cooking apples, pears, chocolate.

DRIED FIG Pork, chicken, duck, goose, game birds, sausages, cheeses, rum, cider, Pernod, marzipan, star anise, fennel.

DRIED MANGO Coconut, lime, lemon, apples, pears, peaches, nectarines, strawberries, raspberries, blueberries, vanilla, ginger.

DRIED PEACH Other dried fruits, cheeses, particularly Gorgonzola, mozzarella, feta and halloumi, ham, duck, game birds, rice.

DRIED PEAR Blue cheeses, sage-flavoured cheeses, Cheddar, walnuts, bananas, rice, pasta, peas, mushrooms, meaty white fish, ice cream, custard.

PRUNES Chicken, rabbit, pork, beef, venison, game birds, bacon, cheeses, spinach, other dried fruit, pears, apples, cream, custard.

RAISINS AND SULTANAS Oats, wheat, chilli, cinnamon, star anise, mixed spice, curry spices, coriander leaf, parsley, chives, mint, honey, rum, cream, most fruits, cabbage, nuts.

INDEX

Entries in roman indicate recipes.

A

abalone 279
acorn squash 343
adzuki beans 443
allspice 383
almonds 416
   almond panna cotta 218
   dark chocolate and almond torte 224
   exploding lemon macaroons 216
   pear and butterscotch frangipane
      tart 238
amaranth 440
anchovies 256, 263
   salad Niçoise 32
   spaghetti puttanesca 110
anchovy paste 480
apples 394
   apple pie 130
   apple sauce 67
   crêpes with caramelized apples and
      chocolate 144
   dried apples 415
   preparation 420
   roast quail 90
   tarte Tatin 145
apricots 397
   dried apricots 414
   watercress and apricot stuffing 72
artichoke hearts: preparation 369
   veal Milanese 60
artichokes see globe artichokes; Jerusalem
   artichokes
Asian pears 395
asparagus 338
   chargrilled asparagus with Hollandaise 120
   preparation 365
aubergines 351
   ratatouille 122
avocados 351
   guacamole 128
   preparation 368

B

baby corn 340
bacon 314
   coarse meat terrine 80
   quiche Lorraine 26
bain maries 248
Baker, Dhruv 198, 275, 423, 491
baking blind 460
balsamic vinegar 479
bananas 402
   banana cream pie 153
   banana soufflé with blueberry coulis 220
   dried bananas 415
barbecuing see grilling
barding game birds 92
barley 440
barramundi 260

basil 378
   spinach and ricotta ravioli with a cream and
      basil sauce 194
basmati rice 438
bass see sea bass
basting poultry 72–3
batter, frying fish 275
bay leaves 377
bean sprouts 443
bean thread noodles 467
beans, dried 442–4
beansprouts: pad thai 104
béarnaise, châteaubriand with 45
béchamel sauce 489
beef: beef strogonoff 44
   beef Wellington with mash 200
   boeuf bourguignon 46
   carving 323
   châteaubriand with béarnaise 45
   cooking steaks 322–3
   cuts 40, 304–5
   flavour pairings 493–4
   pappardelle alla Bolognese 109
   roast rib of beef 38
   roasting 38–42
   steak and kidney pie 56
   steak au poivre 57
   stock 485
   Thai beef massaman curry 202
beef sausages 316
beetroot 332
berries 410-11
beurre blanc 488
beurre noir 488
beurre noisette 488
biscuits: sablé biscuits 228
   shortbread 175
   tuile biscuits 176
bisque, lobster 14
bitter melon 343
black bean sauce 481
black beans 444
black-eyed beans 444
Black Forest gâteau 162
black pudding 317
black sticky rice 438
blackberries 411
   lavender mousse with a blackberry
      sauce 232
blackcurrants 410
blackstrap molasses 387
blanquette de veau 62
blinis 449
blueberries 412
   banana soufflé with blueberry coulis 220
   blueberry crumble 150
   dried blueberries 413
boeuf bourguignon 46
boiling: eggs 430
   green vegetables 374
   noodles 468
bok choy see pak choi
Bolognese sauce 109
boning: chicken 296–7
   fish 266–7
   saddle of lamb 319

   tunnel boning leg of lamb 321
bonito 255
borlotti beans 444
bottle gourds 342
boudin blanc 317
boudin noir 317
bouillabaisse 10
braising: rabbit 313
   veal 313
   venison 313
Brazil nuts 416
bread: bread and butter pudding 132
   croque monsieur 23
   kneading dough 451
   mixing dough 450
   summer pudding 154
bream, freshwater 261
   see also sea bream
Brenner, Natalie 220
bresaola 315
brill 259
brioche, making dough 453
broad beans 341
broccoli, Chinese 325
broccoli, purple sprouting 325
   pan-fried chicken breast with sesame
      seeds 210
brown crab 276
brown rice 439
brown shrimp 277
brown trout 261
brownies, chocolate 164
Brussels sprouts 324
buckwheat 440
buckwheat flour: blinis 449
buckwheat noodles 467
bulgur 441
   tabbouleh 118
butter 425
   beurre blanc 488
   beurre noir 488
   beurre noisette 488
   clarifying 487
   Hollandaise 491
   sage butter 184
butter beans 442
butterflying leg of lamb 318
butternut squash 343
butterscotch: pear and butterscotch
   frangipane tart 238

C

cabbage 324
   beef Wellington with mash, creamed
      Savoy cabbage 200
   coleslaw 115
   coring and shredding 367
   see also red cabbage
cakes: Black Forest gâteau 162
   carrot cake 166
   chocolate brownies 164
   Genoese sponge 462
   madeleines 170
   marble cake 165
   preparing and lining tins 463
   red velvet cupcakes 160

Victoria sponge cake 178
    see also gâteau
calabrese 325
candied peel 415
cannellini beans 442
    minestrone 16
caperberries 380
capers 380
cappelletti 465
caramel: caramel sauce 392
    classic crème brûlée 138
    crème caramel 140
    hokey pokey 232
    pear and butterscotch frangipane tart 238
    sticky toffee pudding 234
    sugar syrup 391
caraway seeds 381
cardamom 382
cardoons 339
carp 261
carrots 328
    batonettes 364
    carrot cake 166
    seared tuna with an Asian glaze 196
Carter, Susie 188, 238
carving: beef 323
    chicken 302–3
Carwood, Alix 202
cashew nuts 416
cassava 335
casserole dishes 247
casseroles *see* stews and casseroles
cassoulet 58
caster sugar 386
catfish 260
cauliflower 325
cavolo nero 326
celeriac 331
    loin of venison with celeriac purée 208
celery 339
celery leaf 376
celery salt 385
celery seeds 376
cellophane noodles 467
ceps 355
chanterelles 355
châteaubriand with béarnaise 45
chayote 345
Cheddar cheese 426
cheese 426–7
    cheese soufflé 24
    croque monsieur 23
    goat's cheese and red onion tart 182
    macaroni cheese 101
    pasta alla carbonara 112
    spinach and ricotta ravioli 194
    see also mascarpone cheese
cheesecake, baked lime 240
cherries 397
    Black Forest gâteau 162
    cherry clafoutis 137
    dried cherries 413
    rice crispie cake with chocolate mousse,
        cherry sorbet, and cherries in Kirsch 214
chervil 376
chestnut mushrooms 354

chestnuts 418
chicken 288–9
    boning 296–7
    breading and frying escalopes 301
    carving 302–3
    chicken cacciatore 76
    chicken Kiev 78
    chicken tikka masala 86
    consommé 483
    coq au vin 82
    deep-frying 299
    flavour pairings 494
    jointing 294–5
    marinating 302
    pan-fried chicken breast with sesame
        seeds 210
    roast chicken 70
    roasting times 70
    southern fried chicken 87
    stock 482
    stuffing breasts 300
    tandoori chicken 84
    Thai green chicken curry 88
chicken liver pâté 79
chickpeas 442
    roast Moroccan lamb with couscous 206
chicory 356
chilli oil 477
chilli sauce 481
chillies 353, 381
    crispy squid with green peppercorn and chilli
dressing 188
    preparation 371
    rouille 10
Chinese broccoli 325
Chinese leaves 327
Chinese noodles 466, 467
Chinese rice vinegar 479
Chinese spinach 327
chips 126, 373
    spiced battered fish and chips 198
chives 376
chocolate: Black Forest gâteau 162
    chocolate and walnut roulade 136
    chocolate brownies 164
    chocolate fondants 134
    chocolate mousse 142
    crêpes with caramelized apples and
        chocolate 144
    dark chocolate and almond torte 224
    ganache 392
    glossy icing 393
    marble cake 165
    pears Belle Hélène 230
    preparation 393
    profiteroles 156
    rice crispie cake with chocolate mousse 214
    white chocolate mousse 222
chops 306, 308, 311
chorizo 317
choux pastry 455, 456
    profiteroles 156
    shaping 456
Christmas pudding, traditional 133
cider vinegar 478
cinnamon 381

citrus fruits 406–9
    segmenting 422
    see also oranges, lemon etc
clafoutis, cherry 137
clams 278
    linguine alle vongole 102
    opening 286
clarifying butter 487
clementines 409
clotted cream 425
cloves 384
cobnuts 417
cockles 278
coconut 417
coconut, dried 415
coconut milk: Thai beef massaman curry 202
    Thai green chicken curry 88
cod 250
    salt cod 263
coffee: quick tiramisu 158
cold-smoked fish 263
coleslaw 115
coley 250
conchiglie 465
consommé, chicken 483
coq au vin 82
coriander 377
coriander seeds 381
corn 440
corn syrup 387
cornichons 345
coulis: blueberry 220
    passion fruit 224
    raspberry 136
Coulson, David 214
courgettes 344
    batonettes 364
    ratatouille 122
    seared tuna with an Asian glaze 196
couscous 441
    rehydrating 446
    roast Moroccan lamb with couscous 206
crab 276
    cleaning 281
    dressing 283
crackling 67
cranberries 412
cranberries, dried 413
crayfish 276
    preparing 285
cream 425
    almond panna cotta 218
    banana cream pie 153
    Black Forest gâteau 162
    classic crème brûlée 138
    ganache 392
    hazelnut and raspberry meringue 22
    lavender mousse 232
    quick tiramisu 158
    rum cream 240
    syllabub 212
    whipping 436
    see also ice cream
crème brûlée, classic 138
crème caramel 140
crème fraîche 425

crème pâtissière 437
crêpes with caramelized apples and
    chocolate 144
crimini mushrooms 354
crookneck squashes 344
croque monsieur 23
Crown Prince squash 343
crumble, blueberry 150
cucumber 345
    gazpacho 12
Cumberland sausage 316
cumin 381
cupcakes, red velvet 160
cured meats 314–15
    flavour pairings 495
currants 413
curry: tandoori chicken 84
    Thai beef massaman curry 202
    Thai green chicken curry 88
curry leaves 382
custard 437
    banana cream pie 153
custard apples 403

D
dabs 258
dairy products 425–7
damsons 397
dandelion 358
dates 397, 414
    sticky toffee pudding 234
decorations, pastry 461
deep-frying: chicken 299
    fish 275
demerara sugar 387
dill 376
dill seeds 376
Dover sole 258
    skinning 265
dragon fruit 401
dried fish 262–3
dried fruits 413–15
    flavour pairings 503
    traditional Christmas pudding 133
dried meats 314–15
Dublin Bay prawns see langoustines
duck 290
    cassoulet 58
    crispy roast duck 96
    flavour pairings 494–5
    roasting 70
    seared duck with five-spice and noodles 94
    see also mallard; teal
duck eggs 424
durian 403

E
edamame beans 341
egg noodles 467
eggs 424
    eggs Benedict 20
    freshness 428
    omelette aux fines herbes 22
    omelettes 433
    pasta alla carbonara 112
    poaching 431

scrambling 431
separating yolks and whites 428
smoked haddock timbale with poached
    quail's egg 192
soft- and hard-boiling 430
soufflés 432
whisking whites 429
elderberries 412
elderflowers 412
    raspberry and elderflower jelly 222
elephant garlic 349
endive 356
enoki mushrooms 354
equipment 242–9
    additional equipment 249
    knives 244–5
    pots and pans 246–8
escalopes, breading and frying 301
escarole 356
exploding lemon macaroons 216

F
farfalle 465
Faulkner, Lisa 182, 218
fennel, Florence 339
    fennel remoulade 114
fennel (herb) 377
fennel seeds 377
fenugreek 384
feta cheese 427
field mushrooms 355
figs 404
figs, dried 415
filleting fish 268–9
fish 250–75
    baking in foil 273
    battered and fried 275
    boning 266–7
    bouillabaisse 10
    filleting 268–9
    fisherman's pie 36
    flat fish 258–9
    flavour pairings 492–3
    freshwater fish 260–61
    grilling 274
    gutting 264
    oily sea fish 254–7
    pan-frying 274
    preparing flat fish 270
    round white sea fish 250–53
    scaling and trimming 265
    serving whole fish 272
    skinning 265, 271
    smoked, salted, and dried fish 262–3
    spiced battered fish and chips 198
    steaks 271
    steaming 273
    stock 484
    see also individual types of fish
fishcakes, salmon 33
flageolet beans 442
    rack of lamb with flageolet beans and
    herbs 54
flaked rice 439
flapjacks 168
flat fish 258–9

flavouring sauces and pastes 480–81
fleur de sel sea salt 385
Florence fennel see fennel
flour 441
flowering greens 325
foil, baking fish in 273
Follas, Mat 232
frangipane tart, pear and butterscotch 238
French beans 341
French meringue 435
French trimming rack of lamb 320
freshwater fish 260–61
frogs' legs 279
fruit 394–415
    citrus fruits 406–9
    classic pavlova 148
    currants and berries 410–12
    dried and candied fruits 413–15
    flavour pairings 501–3
    grapes, rhubarb, and figs 404
    melons 405
    orchard fruits 394–5
    preparation 420–23
    stone fruits 396–9
    summer pudding 154
    tropical fruits 400–403
    see also individual types of fruit
fruit vinegar 479
frying see deep-frying; pan-frying
fusilli 465

G
galangal 380
game: birds 292–3
    flavour pairings 495
    larding and barding 92
    roasting 90–93
    trussing 92
    see also pheasant; venison etc
gammon 314
    honey-glazed gammon 69
ganache 392
garlic 348–9
    peeling and chopping 361
    roasting lamb 53
garlic oil 477
garlic salt 385
gâteau, Black Forest 162
Gates, Chris 194, 455, 474
gazpacho 12
gelatine 391
Genoese sponge 462
gherkins 345
Gilmour, Helen 206
ginger 384
    syllabub 212
glazing tarts 461
globe artichokes 338
    preparation 369
gnocchi 473
goat 310
    flavour pairings 494
goat's cheese and red onion tart 182
golden syrup 387
goose 290
    flavour pairings 495

roasting 70
goose eggs 424
gooseberries 410
Gorgonzola cheese 427
grains 440–41
Grana Padano cheese 426
granulated sugar 386
grapefruit 406
grapes 404
grapeseed oil 476
gratin Dauphinois 116
gravy 72–3
green asparagus 338
green beans 341
    salad Niçoise 32
green cabbage 324
green lipped mussels 278
greengages 396
greens: flowering 325
    leafy 326–7
grey mullet 252
grilling: fish 274
    rabbit 312
    steaks 322–3
    veal 312
    venison 312
ground rice 439
groundnut oil 476
grouse 292
    roasting 93
Groves, Steve 322
Gruyère cheese 426
guacamole 128
guava 401
gurnard 252
gutting fish 264

H
haddock 251
    fisherman's pie 36
    smoked haddock timbale 192
hake 250
halibut 259
ham 314
    croque monsieur 23
Hamburg parsley 331
Hamilton, Christine 192
haricot beans: cassoulet 58
harissa paste 481
    roast Moroccan lamb with harissa sauce 206
hazelnut oil 477
hazelnuts 417
    hazelnut and raspberry meringue 22
Helda beans 341
herb oils 477
herb vinegar 479
herbs 376–9
    flavour pairings 499–500
    preparation 389
    see also individual types of herb
herrings 257
hoisin sauce 481
hokey pokey, lavender mousse with 232
Hollandaise 491
    chargrilled asparagus with Hollandaise 120
    eggs Benedict 20

pan-fried chicken breast with a mango Hollandaise 210
honey 386
    honey-glazed gammon 69
horse mackerel 256
horseradish 377
    horseradish sauce 43
hot-smoked fish 262

I
ice cream: pears Belle Hélène 230
icing, glossy 393
icing sugar 386
Indian vermicelli 467
Italian meringue 434

J
jaggery 387
jambon de Paris 315
jamón iberico 315
jamón serrano 315
Japanese rice vinegar 479
jasmine rice 438
jelly, raspberry and elderflower 222
Jerusalem artichokes 335
jicama 335
John Dory 253
    spiced battered fish and chips 198
jointing chicken 294–5
julienne: lemon-zest julienne 390
    vegetable julienne 361, 363
juniper 383

K
kaffir lime leaves 381
kale 327
Kenny, Angela 196
kid 310
kidneys 307
    steak and kidney pie 56
king prawns: paella 106
Kinnaird, Tim 184, 216, 434, 435, 473
Kirsch: Black Forest gâteau 162
    cherries in Kirsch 214
kiwi fruit 400
kneading bread dough 451
knives 244–5
kohl rabi 324
kumquats 407

L
lamb: *boning saddle of* 319
    butterflying leg of 318
    cuts 52, 306–7
    flavour pairings 494
    French trimming rack of 320
    lamb samosas 204
    rack of lamb with flageolet beans and herbs 54
    roast leg of lamb 50
    roast Moroccan lamb with couscous and harissa sauce 206
    roasting 50–53
    shepherd's pie 48
    tunnel boning leg of 321
lamb's lettuce 359

langoustines 276
    paella 106
Lara, Claire 222
larding game birds 92
lasagne 464
    lasagne al forno 100
    open lasagne of roasted squash and wild mushrooms 184
lavender 377
    lavender mousse 232
leafy greens 326–7
leeks 348
    shepherd's pie 48
    vichyssoise 18
    washing and cutting 361
lemon 407
    exploding lemon macaroons 216
    lemon curd 216
    lemon tart 146
    lemon-zest julienne 390
    orange and lemon syllabub 228
    preserved lemons 381
lemon grass 382
lemon sole 259
lentils 445
lettuce 357–8
limes 407
    baked lime cheesecake with rum cream 240
ling 250
linguine alle vongole 102
lining cake tins 463
linseeds 419
liver: chicken liver pâté 79
    pork 309
    poultry 289
lobster 276
    cleaning 280
    extracting meat 282
    lobster bisque 14
    lobster thermidor 29
loganberries 411
lollo rosso 358
loquats 395
lotus root 331
lovage 378
Lumb, Marianne 236
lunette 465
lychees 403

M
macadamia nuts 416
macaroni 464
    macaroni cheese 101
macaroons, exploding lemon 216
mace 383
mackerel 255
    see also smoked mackerel
McLarnon, Liz 200
madeleines 170
Maldon sea salt 385
mallard 293
    roasting 93
malt vinegar 479
mangetout 340
mangoes 400
    dried mangoes 414

pan-fried chicken breast with a mango
    Hollandaise 210
  preparation 423
mangosteen 403
maple syrup 387
  pecan pie 152
marble cake 165
marinating chicken 302
marjoram 378
marrow 342
mascarpone cheese 427
  baked lime cheesecake with rum cream 240
  quick tiramisu 158
  rhubarb tarte tatin served with
    mascarpone 236
mayonnaise 490
  coleslaw 115
  fennel remoulade 114
  rouille 10
  saving curdled mayonnaise 490
meat 304–23
  cooking chart 312–13
  flavour pairings 493–4
  types of 304–17
  see also beef, lamb *etc*
medlars 395
melon 405
meringues: classic pavlova 148
  French meringue 435
  hazelnut and raspberry meringue 22
  Italian meringue 434
  shaping 435
Miles, Hannah 454
milk 425
  crème caramel 140
  rice pudding 141
millet 441
mince pies 169
minestrone 16
minneolas 407
mint 378
  mint sauce 53
mirepoix 366
miso 480
Mistry, Daksha 204
mizuna 359
molasses 387
monkfish 253
morels 355
Moroccan lamb with couscous and harissa
    sauce 206
moules marinières 30
mousses: chocolate mousse 142
  lavender mousse 232
  white chocolate mousse 222
mozzarella 427
muffins: eggs Benedict 20
mulberries 412
mullet *see* grey mullet; red mullet
mung beans 443
Muscat vinegar 478
muscovado sugar 387
mushrooms 354–5
  beef strogonoff 44
  beef Wellington with mash 200
  chicken cacciatore 76

flavour pairings 499
  loin of venison with celeriac purée 208
  open lasagne of roasted squash and wild
    mushrooms 184
mussels 278
  cleaning 284
  moules marinières 30
  paella 106
mustard 380
mustard greens 327
mutton 307

N

nam pla 481
Napa cabbage *see* Chinese leaves
Nathan, James 228, 269, 285, 286
nectarines 398
nigella seeds 383
noodles 466–7
  boiling 468
  pad thai 104
  seared duck with five-spice and noodles 94
North Atlantic prawns 277
nutmeg 383
nuts 416–18

O

oats 441
  flapjacks 168
octopus 277
oils 476–7
oily sea fish 254–7
okra 341
olive oil 476
Oliver, Andy 469
olives 399
  spaghetti puttanesca 110
omelettes 433
  omelette aux fines herbes 22
onions 346–7
  goat's cheese and red onion tart 182
  peeling and dicing 360
  pork belly with onions and potatoes 68
oranges 408–9
  orange and lemon syllabub 228
orchard fruits 394–5
oregano 378
orzo 464
osso bucco 63, 311
oxtail 305
  beef Wellington with mash and an oxtail
    jus 200
oyster mushrooms 355
oyster sauce 481
  pak choi with oyster sauce 123
oysters 279
  opening 286

P

pad thai 104
paella 106
paella rice 439
pak choi 327
  pak choi with oyster sauce 123
palm hearts 339
palm sugar 387

pan-frying: fish 274
  potatoes 373
  rabbit 313
  veal 313
  venison 313
pancakes 449
  Scotch pancakes 174
pancetta 314
  cassoulet 58
  pancetta with scallops 28
  pasta alla carbonara 112
  roast quail 90
panna cotta, almond 218
pans 246–8
papaya 400
pappardelle 464
  pappardelle alla Bolognese 109
paprika 380
Parmesan cheese 426
parsley 379
  tabbouleh 118
parsnips 330
partridge 292
  roasting 93
passion fruit 400
  dark chocolate and almond torte with 224
pasta 464–75
  cooking 468
  cutting dough 473
  lasagne al forno 100
  linguine alle vongole 102
  macaroni cheese 101
  making dough 469
  open lasagne of roasted squash and wild
    mushrooms 184
  pappardelle alla Bolognese 109
  pasta alla carbonara 112
  pasta machines 472
  spaghetti puttanesca 110
  spinach and ricotta ravioli 194
  stretching dough 470–71
  types of 464–5
pastries: lamb samosas 204
  profiteroles 156
  white chocolate mousse 222
pastry: *baking blind* 460
  choux pastry 455
  lining tart tins 458–9
  puff pastry 457
  rough puff pastry 454
  sealing and glazing 461
  shortcrust pastry 454
  sweet shortcrust pastry 455
  trimming and decorating 461
pâtés: chicken liver pâté 79
  smoked mackerel pâté 190
patty pan squashes 344
pavlova, classic 148
peaches 398
  blueberry crumble 150
  dried peaches 414
  peeling 423
peanuts 418
pear palm hearts 339
pears 395
  dried pears 414

pear and butterscotch frangipane tart 238
pears Belle Hélène 230
peas 340
peas, split 444
mushy peas 198
pecan nuts 418
pecan pie 152
Pecorino cheese 426
penne 465
peppercorns 383
crispy squid with green peppercorn and chilli
dressing 188
steak au poivre 57
peppers 352
preparation 370
ratatouille 122
roasting and peeling 370
periwinkles 278
persimmon 401
pesto, walnut 194
Peters, Wendi 234
pheasant 293
roasting 93
physalis 403
pickling vinegar 478
pies: apple pie 130
banana cream pie 153
fisherman's pie 36
mince pies 169
shepherd's pie 48
steak and kidney pie 56
pigeon *see* wood pigeon
pike 261
pilchards 257
pimentos de Padron 352
pine nuts 417
pineapple 401
preparation 421
pinto beans 442
piping bags, filling 436
pistachio nuts 417
pizza, *making bases* 452
plaice 258
plantain 402
plums 396
poaching eggs 431
polenta, *cooking* 448
pollock 251
pomegranate syrup 387
pomegranates 400
pomelo 406
popcorn 440
poppy seeds 383
porcini 355
pork: coarse meat terrine 80
crackling 67
cuts 66, 308–9
flavour pairings 494
pork belly with onions and potatoes 68
roasting 64–7
pork sausages 316
Portabello mushrooms 354
potatoes 333–4
beef Wellington with mash 200
chips 126, 373
crispy roast potatoes 43

fisherman's pie 36
gratin Dauphinois 116
mashing 372
pan frying 373
pork belly with onions and potatoes 68
roasting 372
salmon fishcakes 33
seared tuna with an Asian glaze 196
shepherd's pie 48
spiced battered fish and chips 198
vichyssoise 18
pots and pans 246–8
poultry 288–303
cooking techniques 299–303
flavour pairings 494–5
preparing 294–8
roasting 70–75
stuffing 72
types of 288–91
see also chicken, duck *etc*
poussins 289
roasting 70
spatchcocking 298
prawns 277
fisherman's pie 36
pad thai 104
paella 106
preparing 284
Thai prawn soup with lemongrass 186
profiteroles 156
prosciutto crudo 315
prunes 414
puff pastry 457
rolling out 457
rough puff pastry 454
pulses 442–5
pumpkin 342
pumpkin seed oil 477
pumpkin seeds 419
purple cauliflower 325
purple sprouting broccoli 325
purslane 359
Puy lentils 445

Q
quail 292
roast quail 90
roasting 93
quail eggs 424
smoked haddock timbale with poached
quail's egg 192
quiche Lorraine 26
quinces 395
quinoa 440

R
rabbit 310
cooking chart 312–13
radicchio 356
radishes 332
rainbow chard 326
rainbow trout 261
raisins 413
rambutan 403
ramen noodles 467
ramsons 349

rapeseed oil 476
raspberries 411
dark chocolate and almond torte with 224
hazelnut and raspberry meringue 22
raspberry and elderflower jelly 222
raspberry coulis 136
ratatouille 122
ravioli 465, 474
spinach and ricotta ravioli 194
ray 258
razor clams 278
red cabbage 324
loin of venison with celeriac purée, braised
cabbage 208
red gurnard 252
red kidney beans 444
red mullet 252
red onion squash 342
red rice 438
red velvet cupcakes 160
redcurrants 410
loin of venison with recurrant jus 208
rhubarb 404
rhubarb crumble tart with syllabub 212
rhubarb tarte tatin 236
rice 438–9
cooking 446
paella 106
rice pudding 141
risotto 447
risotto alla Milanese 108
smoked haddock risotto 98
Thai beef massaman curry with jasmine
rice 202
rice crispie cake 214
rice flour 439
rice noodles 466
rice vermicelli 466
rice vinegar 479
ricotta cheese 427
baked lime cheesecake 240
spinach and ricotta ravioli 194
rigatone 465
risotto 447
risotto alla Milanese 108
smoked haddock risotto 98
roasting: beef 38–42
game birds 90–93
lamb 50–53
pork 64–7
potatoes 372
poultry 70–75
rabbit 313
veal 313
venison 313
rock salt 385
rocket 358
romanesco 325
root vegetables 328–32
see also individual types of root vegetable
rosemary 379
rough puff pastry 454
rouille 10
roulades: chocolate and walnut roulade 136
rolling 463
round green cabbage 324

round squashes 344
rowan berries 411
rum cream, baked lime cheesecake with 240
runner beans 341
Rushmer, Alex 208, 447
Russell, Dennice 240
rye 441

S

sablé biscuits 228
saffron 382
sage 378
  sage butter 184
salad cress 359
salads: coleslaw 115
  fennel remoulade 114
  preparing leaves 367
  salad leaves 356–9
  salad Niçoise 32
  tabbouleh 118
salame di Genoa 317
salmon 256
  salmon fishcakes 33
  smoked salmon 262, 263
salmon trout 257
salsify 330
salt 385
  sea bass in a salt crust 34
salt cod 263
salted fish 262–3
sambal oelek 481
samosas, lamb 204
sardines 257
satsumas 409
saucepans 248
sauces: apple sauce 67
  béchamel sauce 489
  caramel sauce 392
  crème pâtissière 437
  custard 437
  flavouring 480–81
  gravy 72–3
  Hollandaise 491
  horseradish sauce 43
  mint sauce 53
  velouté sauce 486
sausages 316–17
  cassoulet 58
  flavour pairings 495
sauté pans 247
sautéing vegetables 375
Savoy cabbage 324
Sawalha, Nadia 226
scad 256
scaling fish 265
scallops 279
  pancetta with scallops 28
  preparing 285
scones 172
scorzonera 330
Scotch pancakes 174
scrambling eggs 431
sea bass 252
  sea bass in a salt crust 34
sea bream 251
sea fish: flat fish 258–9

oily sea fish 254–7
round white sea fish 250–53
sea trout 257
sea urchins 279
seafood 276–87
seeds 419
sesame oil 477
sesame seeds 419
  pan-fried chicken breast with sesame
    seeds 210
shallots 346–8
shellfish 276–87
  bouillabaisse 10
  flavour pairings 493
  preparing 280–87
  see also individual types of shellfish
shepherd's pie 48
sherry vinegar 478
shiitake mushrooms 355
shortbread 175
shortcrust pastry 454
  sweet shortcrust pastry 455
shrimp 277
Sichuan pepper 384
skate 258
skillets 246
skinning fish 265, 271
skipjack tuna 254
sloes 397
smoked fish 262–3
smoked haddock 263
  fisherman's pie 36
  smoked haddock risotto 98
  smoked haddock timbale 192
smoked mackerel 262
  smoked mackerel pâté 190
smoked salmon 262, 263
smoked trout 262
snails 279
soba noodles 467
sole 258–9
  skinning 265
somen noodles 467
sorbet, cherry 214
sorrel 379
soufflés 432
  banana soufflé with blueberry coulis 220
  cheese soufflé 24
soups: bouillabaisse 10
  chicken consommé 483
  gazpacho 12
  lobster bisque 14
  minestrone 16
  roast tomato soup 17
  Thai prawn soup with lemongrass 186
  vichyssoise 18
soured cream 425
southern fried chicken 87
soy sauce 481
  seared tuna with an Asian glaze 196
soya beans 443
spaghetti 464
  spaghetti puttanesca 110
spaghetti marrow 342
spatchcocking poussins 298
spelt 441

spices 380–84
  flavour pairings 500–501
  preparation 388
  see also individual types of spice
spinach 326
  spinach and ricotta ravioli 194
sponge fingers: quick tiramisu 158
sponges: Genoese sponge 462
  rolling roulades 463
  Victoria sponge cake 178
sprats 256
spring greens 327
spring onions 347
squashes 342–4
  open lasagne of roasted squash and wild
    mushrooms 184
squid 277
  cleaning 287
  crispy squid with green peppercorn and chilli
    dressing 188
  paella 106
star anise 382
star fruit 402
steak 304–5
  cooking 322–3
steak and kidney pie 56
steak au poivre 57
steamed puddings: traditional Christmas
    pudding 133
steamers 247
steaming: fish 273
  vegetables 375
Stewart, Stacie 372, 430
stews and casseroles:
  blanquette de veau 62
  boeuf bourguignon 46
  cassoulet 58
  coq au vin 82
  rabbit 313
  veal 313
  venison 313
sticky rice 438–9
sticky toffee pudding 234
Stilton cheese 427
stir-frying vegetables 374
stock: beef 485
  chicken 482
  fish 484
  vegetable 484
stone fruits 396–9
strawberries 411
  strawberries with sablé biscuits 228
Strawbridge, Dick 212
stuffings: *stuffing poultry* 72
  watercress and apricot stuffing 72
sturgeon 261
sugar 386–7
sugar snap peas 340
sugar syrup 391
sultanas 413
  scones 172
sumac 383
summer pudding 154
summer savory 379
sunflower oil 477
sunflower seeds 419

swede 329
sweet chilli sauce 481
sweet potatoes 334
sweet shortcrust pastry 455
sweetcorn 340
    removing kernels 365
Swiss chard 326
swordfish 254
syllabub: orange and lemon syllabub 228
    rhubarb crumble tart with syllabub 212
syrup, sugar 391
syrups 387

T
tabasco sauce 480
tabbouleh 118
table salt 385
tagliatelle 464
tahini paste 480
tamari sauce 481
tamarillos 403
    almond panna cotta with poached
        tamarillos 218
tamarind 384
tandoori chicken 84
tangerines 409
taro 334
tarragon 377
tarts: *glazing* 461
    goat's cheese and red onion tart 182
    lemon tart 146
    lining tins 458–9
    pear and butterscotch frangipane tart 238
    pecan pie 152
    quiche Lorraine 26
    rhubarb crumble tart 212
    rhubarb tarte tatin 236
    tarte Tatin 145
teal 293
    roasting 93
terrine, coarse meat 80
Thai beef massaman curry 202
Thai green chicken curry 88
Thai jasmine rice 438
Thai prawn soup with lemongrass 186
Thomas, Iwan 186
thyme 379
tiger prawns 277
    pad thai 104
    Thai prawn soup with lemongrass 186
tilapia 260
tins, preparing and lining 458–9, 463
tiramisu, quick 158
toffee: sticky toffee pudding 234
tomato purée 480
tomatoes 350
    cassoulet 58
    chicken cacciatore 76
    gazpacho 12
    linguine alle vongole 102
    ratatouille 122
    roast tomato soup 17
    skinning and deseeding 362
    spaghetti puttanesca 110
tortelloni 475
torte, dark chocolate and almond 224

Toulouse sausage 316
treacle 387
tree onions 349
trofie 465
trout 261
    see also sea trout; smoked trout
truffle oil 477
truffles 355
trussing game birds 92
tubers 333–5
tuile biscuits 176
tuna 254
    salad Niçoise 32
    seared tuna with an Asian glaze 196
tunnel boning leg of lamb 321
turbot 259
turkey 291
    flavour pairings 494, 495
    roast turkey 74
    roasting times 70
Turk's turban 343
turmeric 382
turning vegetables 366
turnips 329

U
udon noodles 466
ugli fruit 407

V
vanilla pods 384
    extracting seeds 390
veal 311
    blanquette de veau 62
    coarse meat terrine 80
    cooking chart 312–13
    flavour pairings 493–4
    osso bucco 63, 311
    veal Milanese 60
vegetables: *buying* 336
    cabbages 324
    cooking chart 337
    cooking techniques 372–5
    cutting into julienne 361, 363
    flavour pairings 496–9
    flowering greens 325
    leafy greens 326–7
    minestrone 16
    mirepoix 356
    onions, shallots, leeks, and garlic 346–9
    peas, beans, and other pods 340–41
    preparation 360–71
    ratatouille 122
    roasted vegetables 124
    root vegetables 328–32
    salad leaves 356–9
    squashes, cucumbers, and chayote 342–5
    stems, shoots, and flowers 338–9
    stock 484
    storing 336
    tubers 333–5
    turning 366
    vegetable fruits 350–53
    see also individual types of vegetable
velouté sauce 486
venison 311

    cooking chart 312–13
    loin of venison with celeriac purée 208
vermicelli 464, 466, 467
vichyssoise 18
Victoria sponge cake 178
vinaigrette 487
vinegars 478–9

W
Wakelin, Jaye 210
Wallis, Steven 190, 230
walnut oil 477
walnuts 418
    chocolate and walnut roulade 136
    chocolate brownies 164
water chestnuts 330
watercress 359
    watercress and apricot stuffing 72
watermelon 405
wheat flours 441
wheat noodles 466
whelks 278
whisking egg whites 429
white asparagus 338
white cabbage 324
white chocolate mousse 222
white pudding 317
white sticky rice 439
white Swiss chard 326
whitecurrants 410
whiting 251
wild rice 439
wine: boeuf bourguignon 46
    coq au vin 82
wine vinegar 478
woks 248
wood blewit 355
wood pigeon 93, 293
woodcock 93, 292
Worcestershire sauce 480

Y
yams 335
yellow wax beans 341
yellowfin tuna 254
yogurt 425
Yorkshire puddings 42

London, New York, Munich, Melbourne, and Delhi

First published in Great Britain in 2011
by Dorling Kindersley Limited
80 Strand, London WC2R 0RL

Penguin Group (UK)

MasterChef
www.masterchef.com

2 4 6 8 10 9 7 5 3 1
001 – 180671 – Sept/2011

A CIP catalogue record for this book is available from the
British Library.

ISBN 978 1 4053 7388 3

Discover more at **www.dk.com**

Cookery Editor Carolyn Humphries
Designer Miranda Harvey
Editor Claire Tennant-Scull

Project Editor Cressida Tuson
Project Art Editor Tessa Bindloss
Editorial Assistant David Fentiman
Design Assistant Danaya Bunnag
Managing Editor Dawn Henderson
Managing Art Editor Christine Keilty
Senior Jacket Creative Nicola Powling
Senior Production Editor Jennifer Murray
Senior Production Controller Alice Sykes
Creative Technical Support Sonia Charbonnier
Art Director Peter Luff
Publisher Mary-Clare Jerram

DK India
Editor Kokila Manchanda
Art Editor Shruti Soharia Singh
Managing Editor Glenda Fernandes
Managing Art Editor Navidita Thapa
Production Manager Pankaj Sharma
DTP Manager Sunil Sharma
Assistant DTP Designer Sourabh Challariya

Recipe and cover photography William Reavell
Photography art direction Miranda Harvey, Kat Mead
Food stylists Fergal Connolly, Jane Lawrie
Prop stylists Jessica Georgiades, Caroline de Souza

Images of John Torode and Gregg Wallace on pages 6–7
© John Wright

Printed and bound by Leo Paper Group, China

Acknowledgements

Shine would like to thank
Frances Adams, Cassie Allen, David Ambler, Michele Bennett, Jessica Boydell, Ange Braid, Martin Buckett, Jo
Carlton, Bev Comboy, Simone Foots, John Gilbert, Jessica Hannan, Lori Heiss, Victoria Howarth, Matt Jarvis,
Ozen Kazim, Digby Lewis, Alex Mahon, Maya Maraj, Jamie Munro, Elisabeth Murdoch, Lou Plank, Lyndsey
Posner, Scott Richardson, Franc Roddam, Karen Ross, Rosemary Scoular, Caroline Stott, John Torode, Gregg
Wallace, Heidi Wallace, David Wilson-Nunn, and Gordon Wise.

MasterChef alumni whose recipes and quotes are reproduced in this book:
Dhruv Baker, Natalie Brenner, Susie Carter, Alex Carwood, David Coulson, Lisa Faulkner, Mat Follas, Chris
Gates, Helen Gilmour, Daniel Graham, Steve Groves, Christine Hamilton, Angela Kenney, Tim Kinnaird, Claire
Lara, Marianne Lumb, Liz McClarnon, Hannah Miles, Daksha Mistry, James Nathan, Andy Oliver, Wendi Peters,
Alex Rushmer, Dennice Russell, Nadia Sawalha, Stacie Stewart, Dick Strawbridge, Iwan Thomas, Jake Wakelin,
and Steven Wallis.

Quotes on pages 268, 269, 275, 284, 285, 286, 320, 322, 372, 423, 430, 434, 435, 447, 454, 455, 469,
473, 474, 490, and 491 are derived from the MasterChef Academy iPhone and iPad application, available from
iTunes now.

Dorling Kindersley would like to thank
Kajal Mistry, Laura Nickoll, and Tia Sarkar for editorial help; Dave Almond, Adam Brackenbury, and Jennifer Murray
for help with retouching; Hilary Bird for indexing.

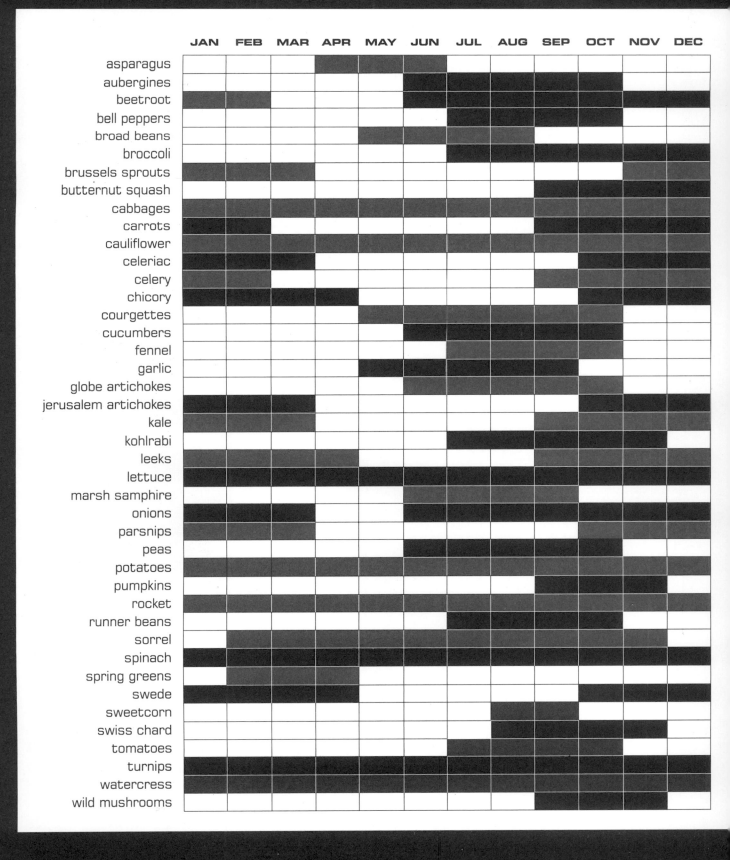